MAO

3

Story and Art by
Rumiko Takahashi

CONTENTS

Story thus far...

When Nanoka Kiba was seven years old, she was orphaned in a violent accident. Now she is a third-year student in middle school. One day she passes the spot where the accident occurred and is miraculously transported to the Taisho era. There she meets an exorcist named Mao who informs her that she is not a human but an ayakashi, possibly cursed by Byoki, the same cat demon that cursed him. Determined to find Byoki, Mao enlists Nanoka's help. She warns him and his shikigami Otomo to flee the area because the Great Kanto Earthquake is about to strike, but he refuses. In the wake of the tremors, a huge cat eye appears in the smoke-filled skies, and Mao's eyes turn into cat eyes as well!

Chapter 1: Byoki

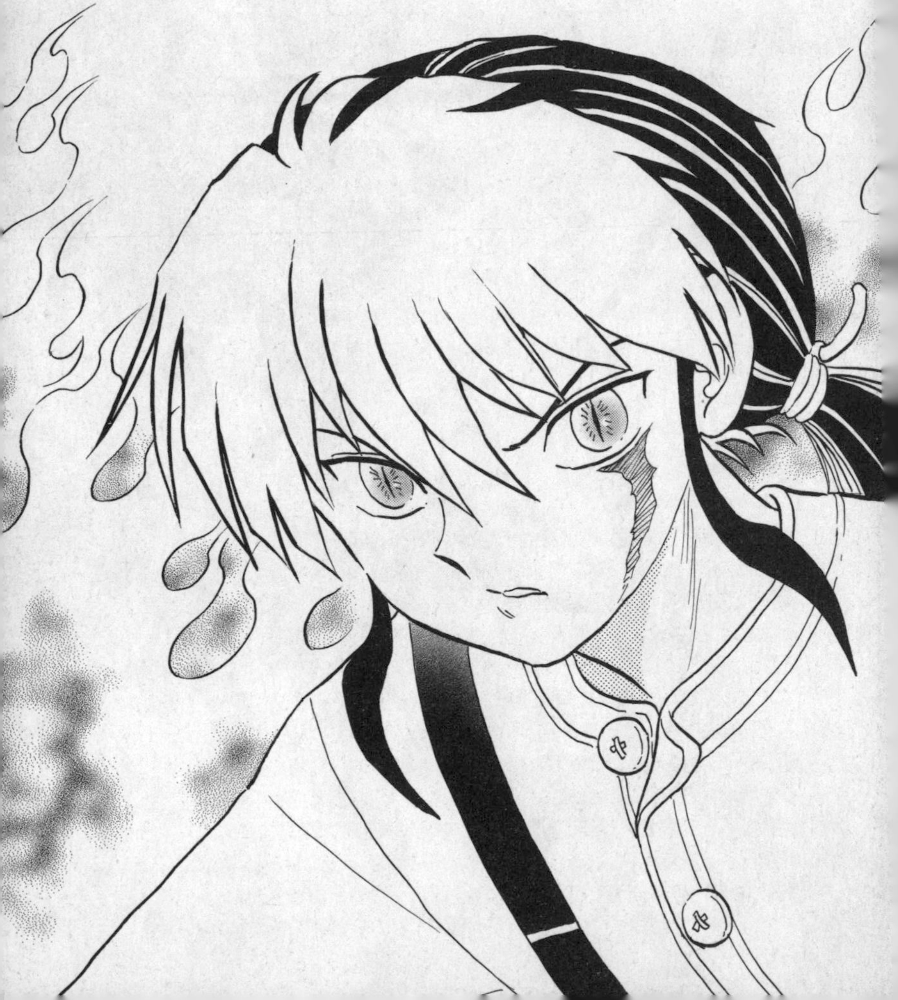

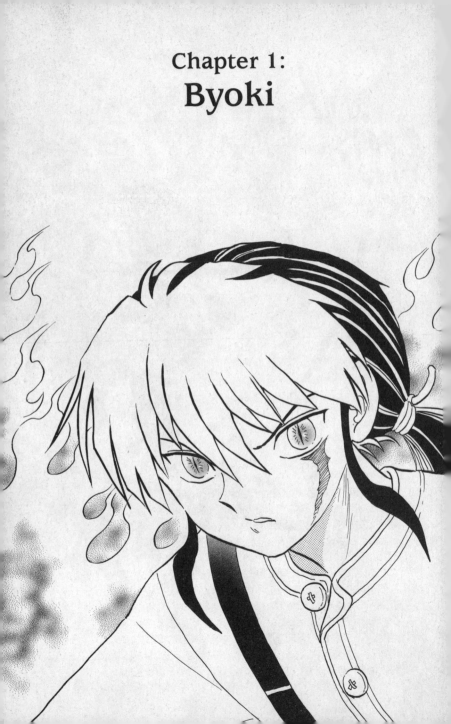

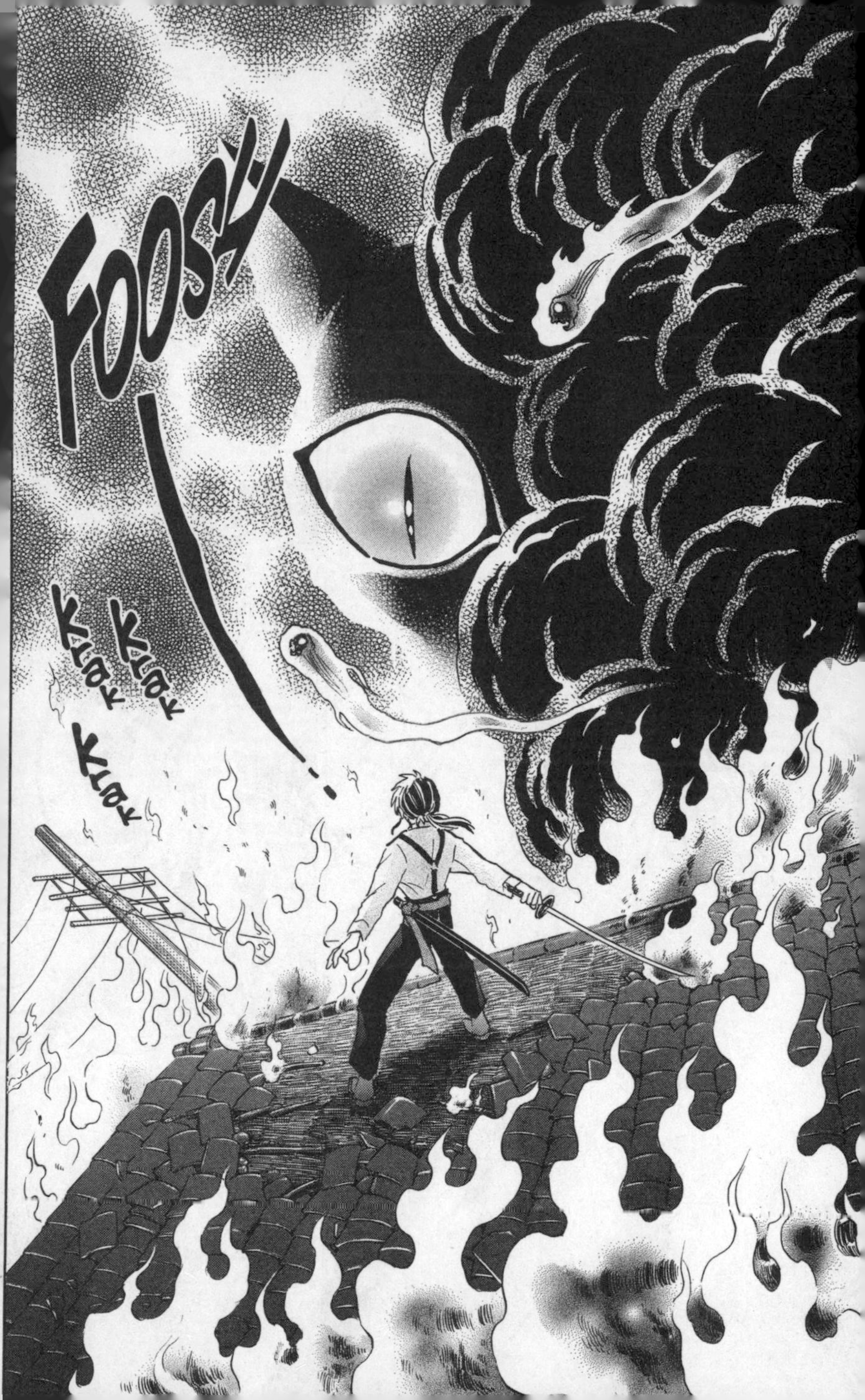
FOOSH
KRAK KRAK
KRAK

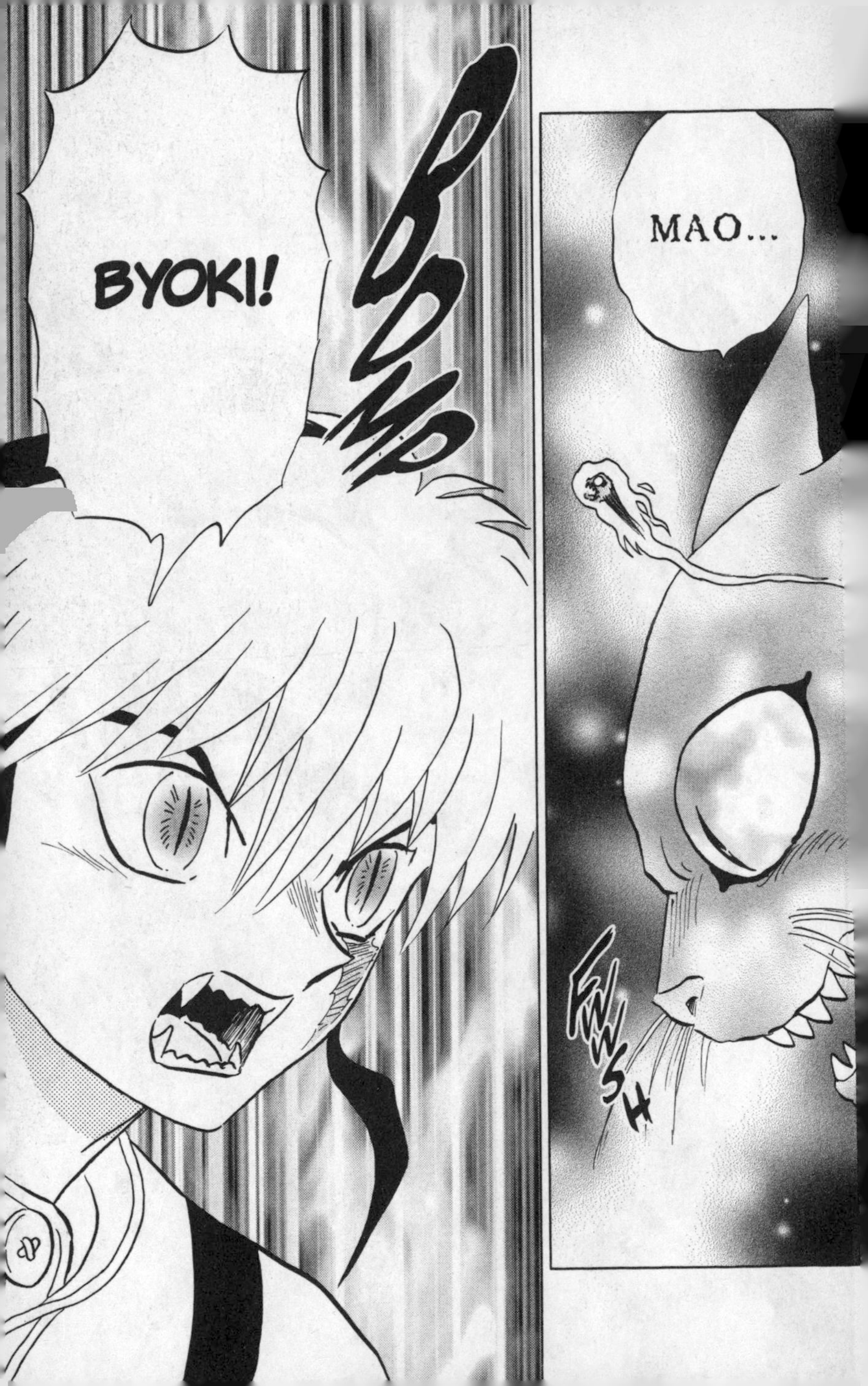
MAO...
FWWSH
BYOKI!
BDUMP

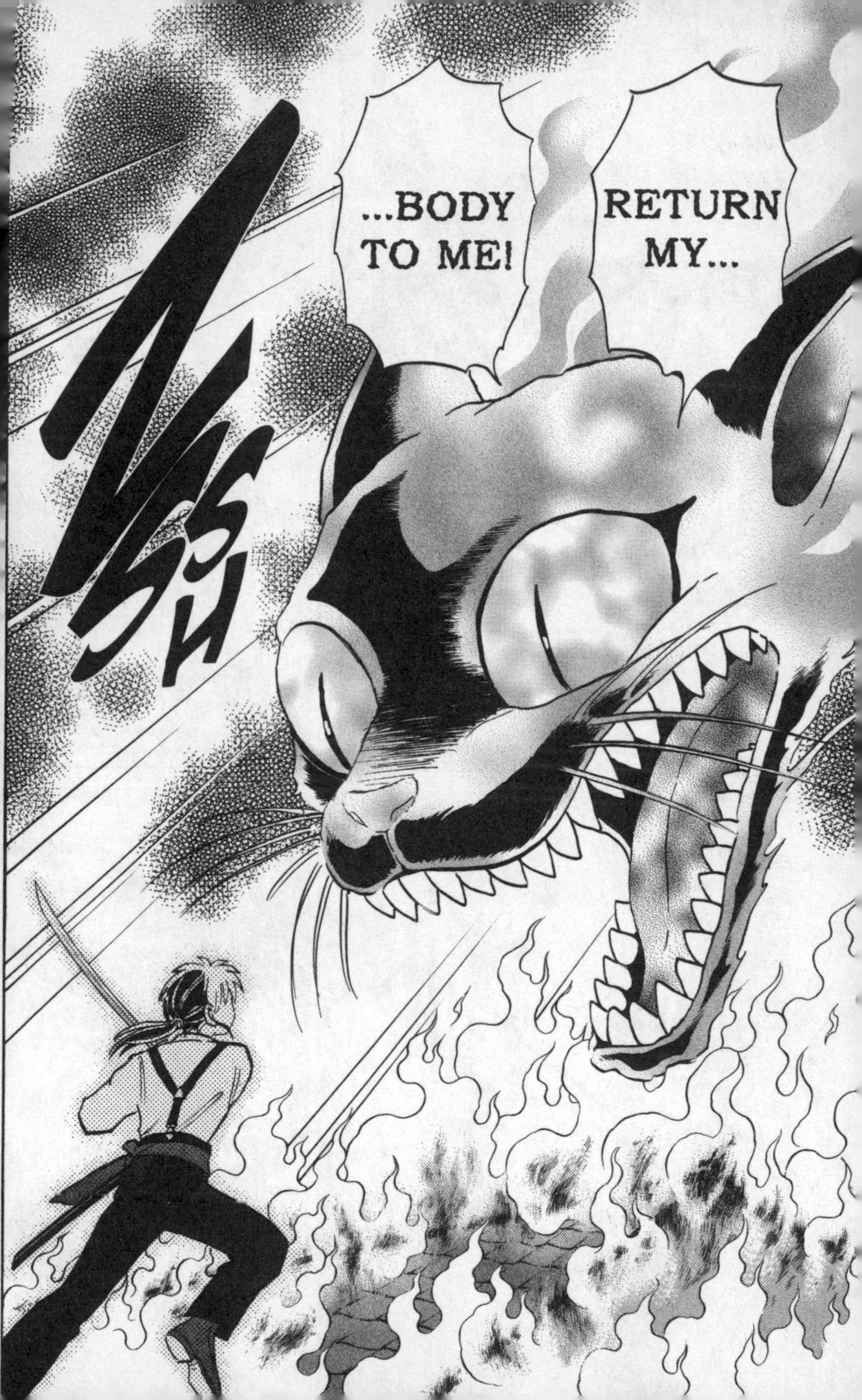
RETURN MY...
...BODY TO ME!

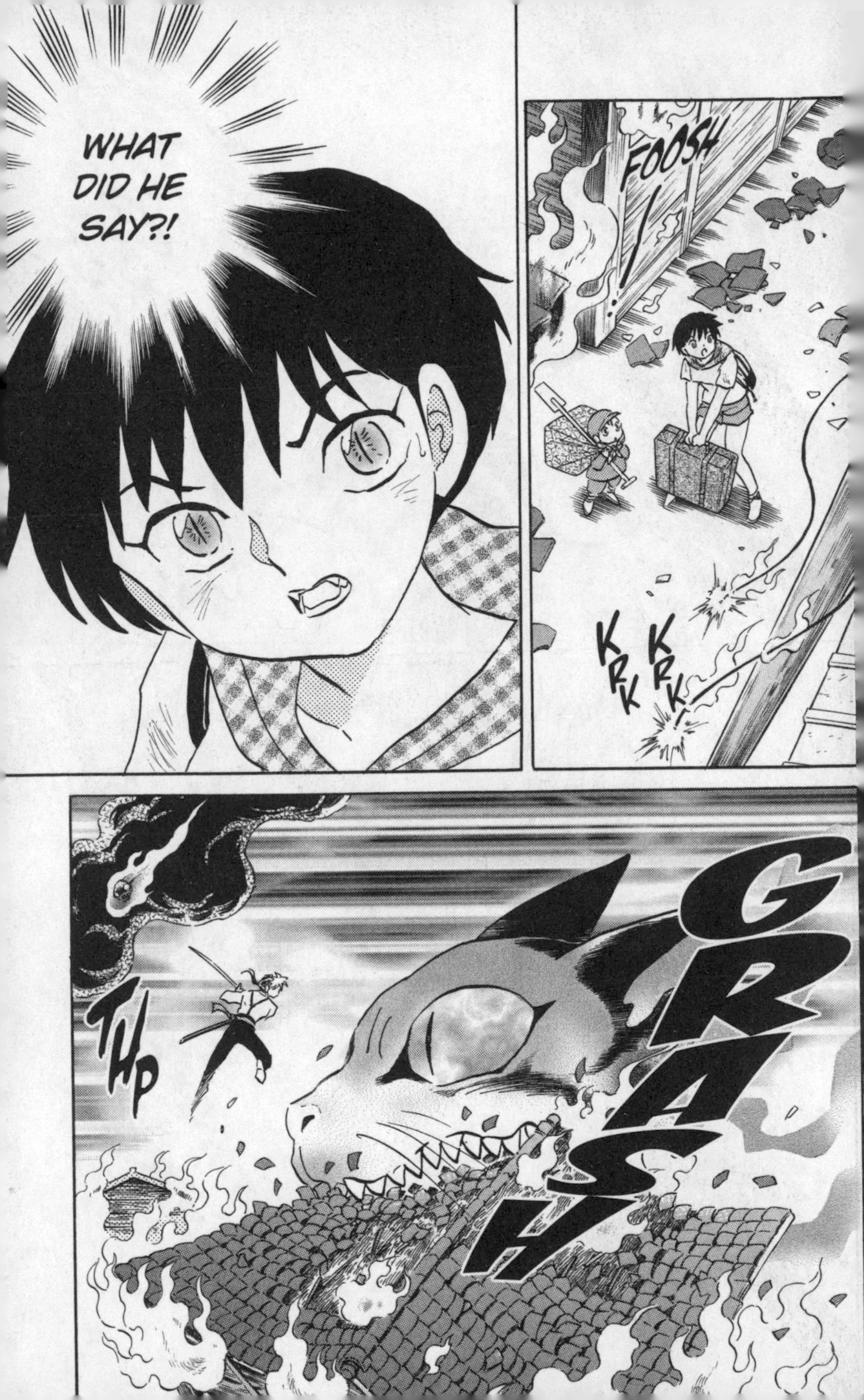
FOOSH
KRK KRK
WHAT DID HE SAY?!
GRASH
THP

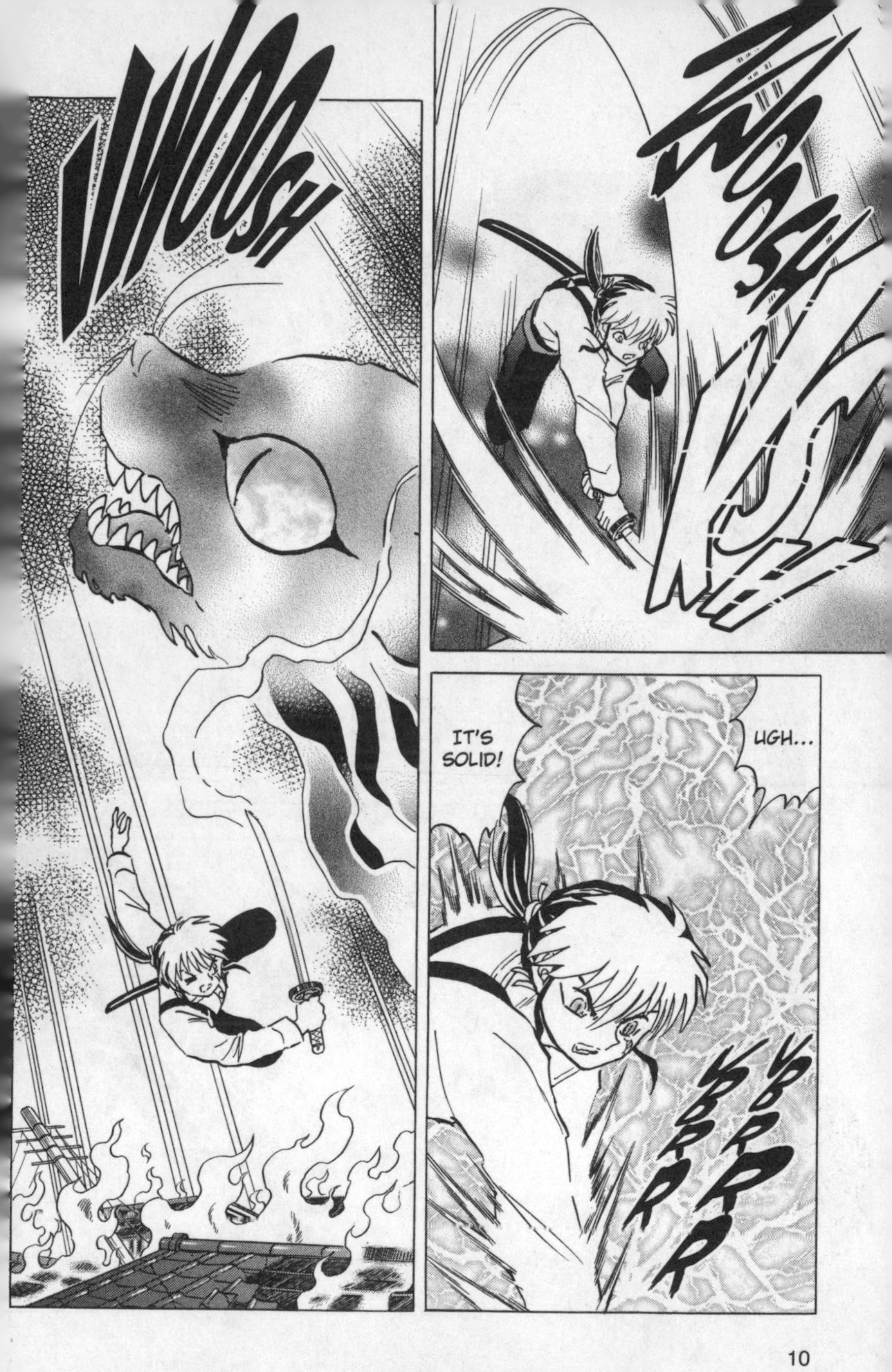
WHOOSH
UGH...
IT'S SOLID!
VBRRR
VBRR
WHOOSH

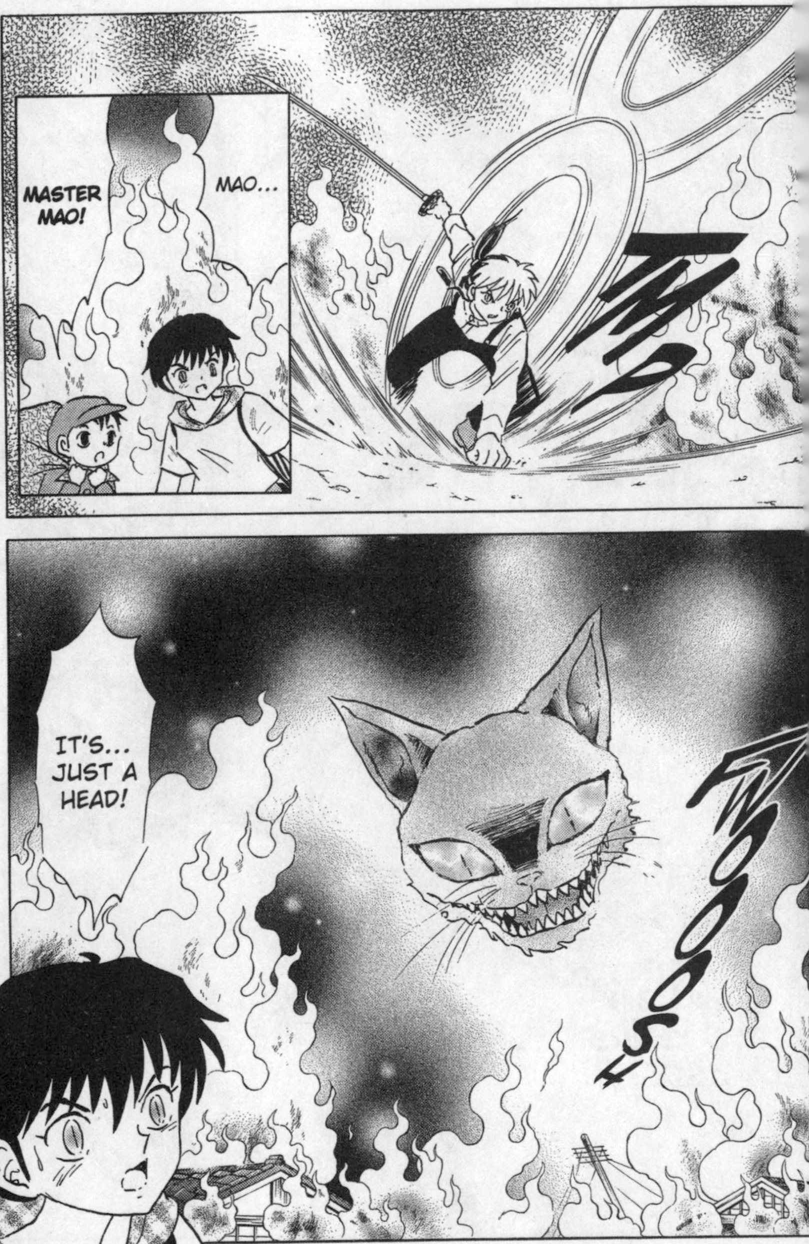
TMP
MAO...
MASTER MAO!
IT'S... JUST A HEAD!
WHOOOSH

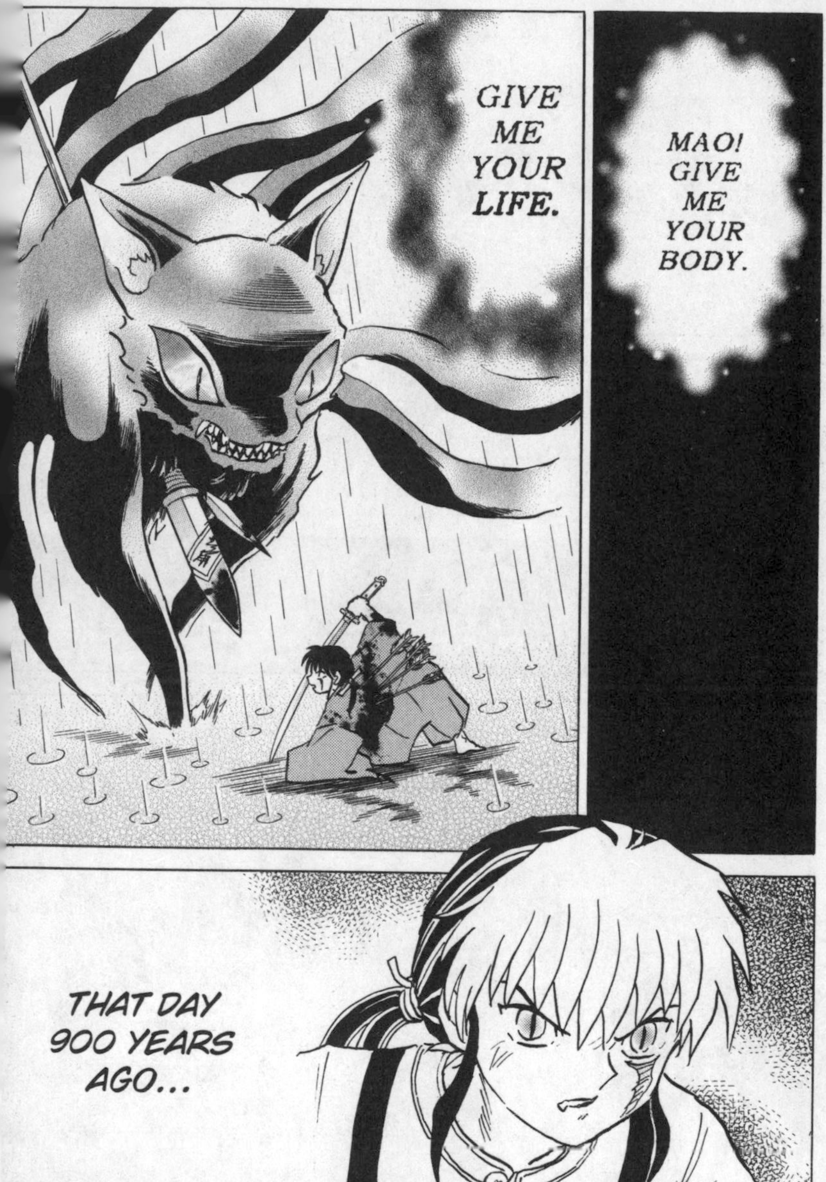
MAO! GIVE ME YOUR BODY.
GIVE ME YOUR LIFE.
THAT DAY 900 YEARS AGO...

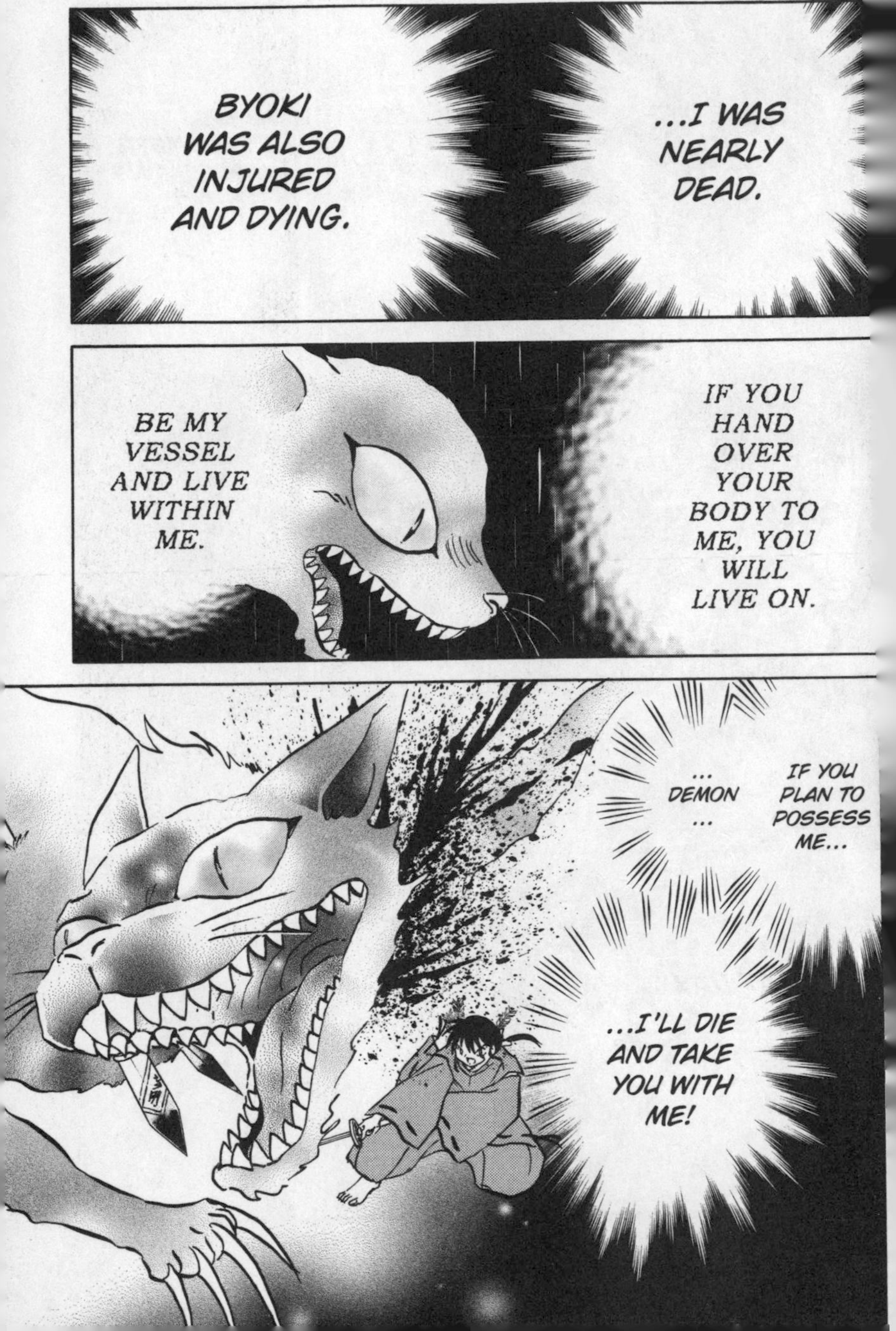
...I WAS NEARLY DEAD.
BYOKI WAS ALSO INJURED AND DYING.
IF YOU HAND OVER YOUR BODY TO ME, YOU WILL LIVE ON.
BE MY VESSEL AND LIVE WITHIN ME.
IF YOU PLAN TO POSSESS ME...
... DEMON ...
...I'LL DIE AND TAKE YOU WITH ME!

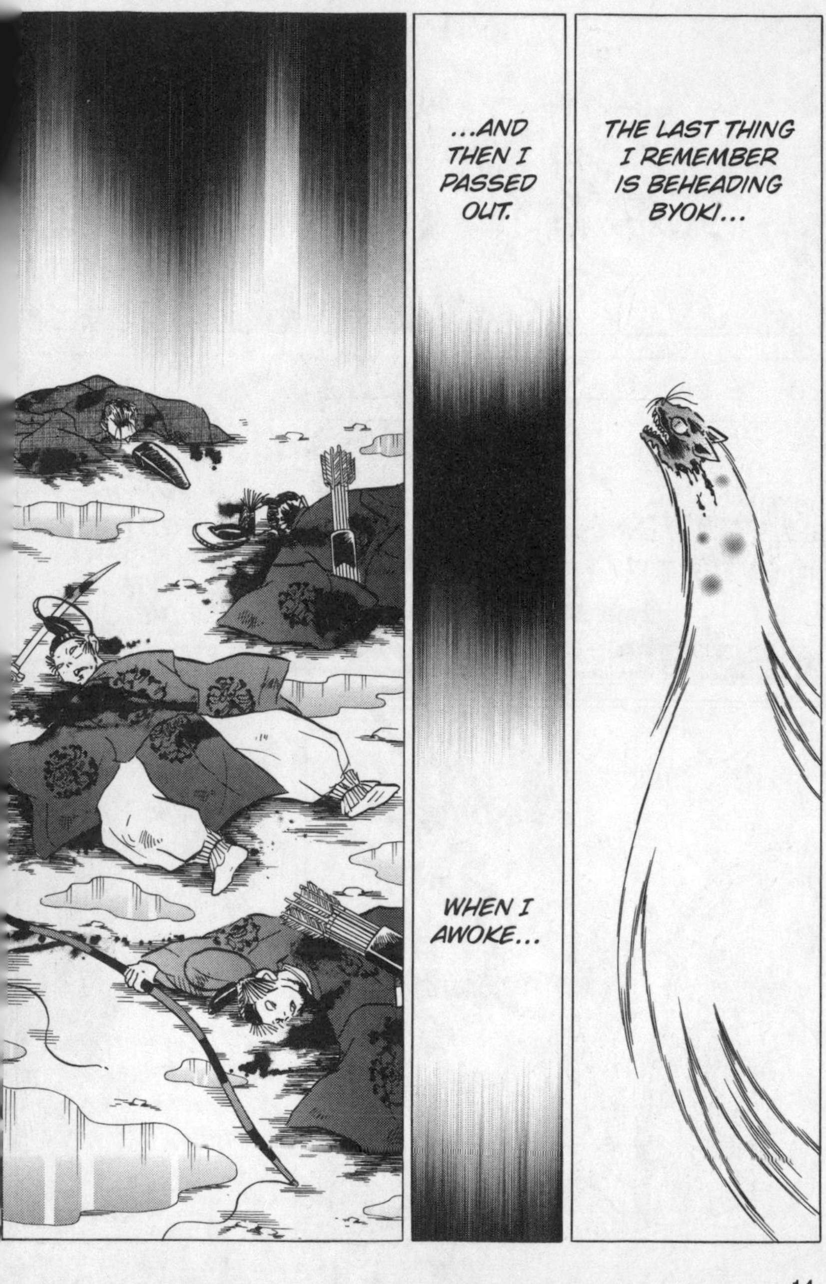
THE LAST THING I REMEMBER IS BEHEADING BYOKI...
...AND THEN I PASSED OUT.
WHEN I AWOKE...

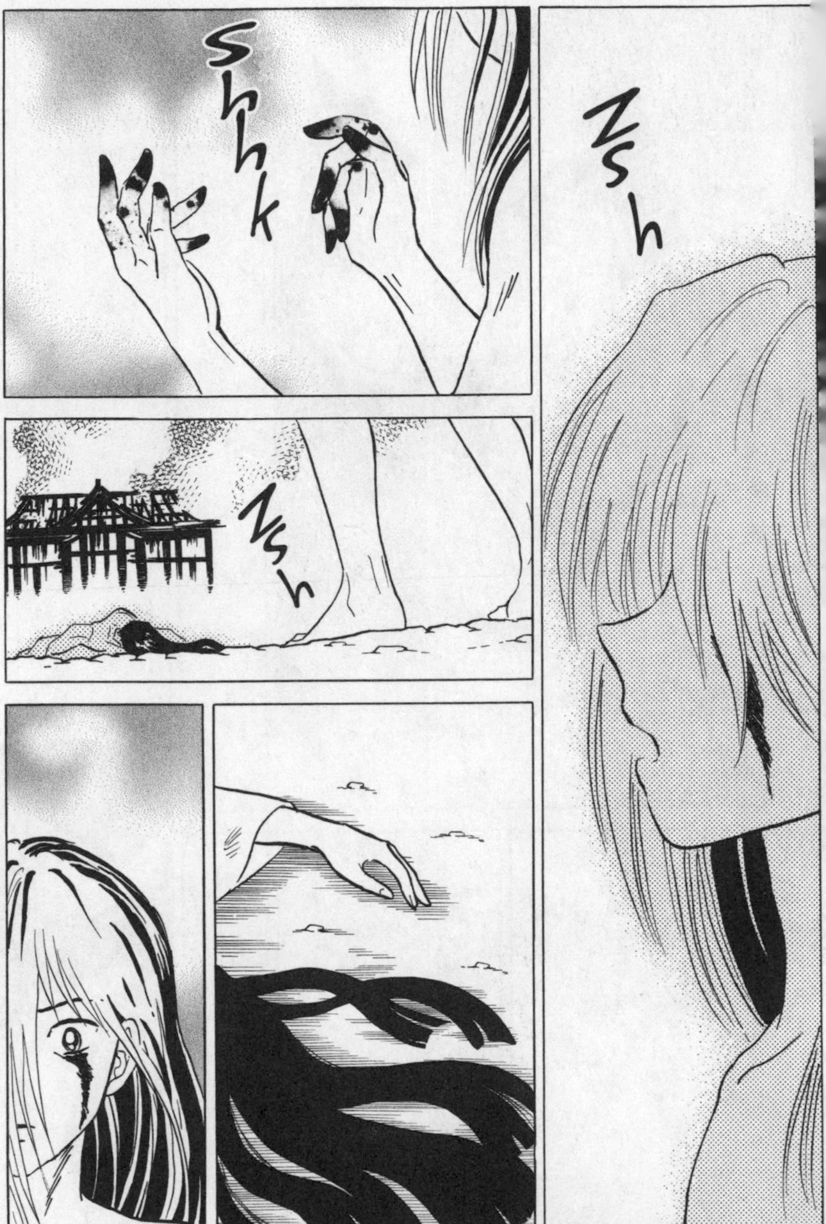
Zsh
Shhk
Zsh

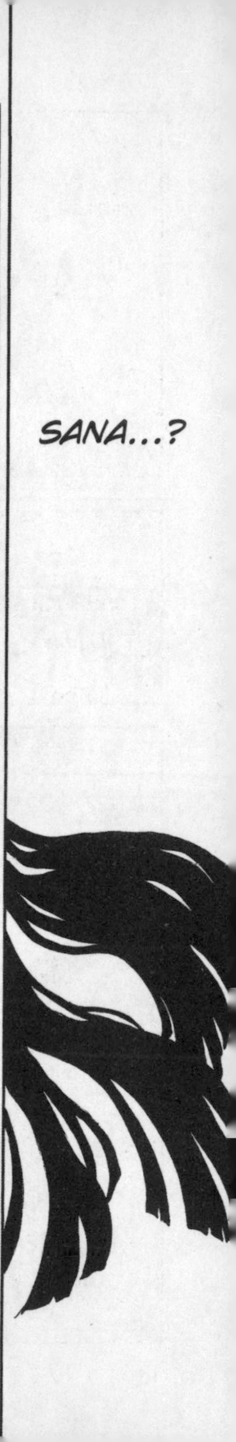
SANA...?

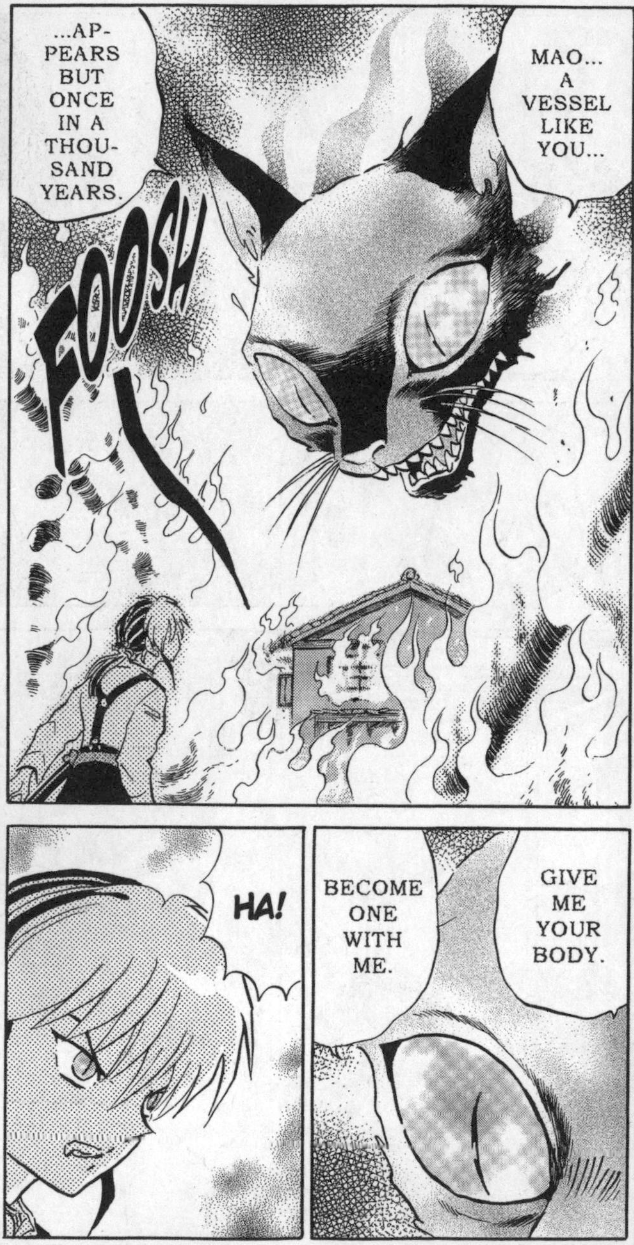
MAO... A VESSEL LIKE YOU...
...AP-PEARS BUT ONCE IN A THOU-SAND YEARS.
FOOSH
GIVE ME YOUR BODY.
BECOME ONE WITH ME.
HA!

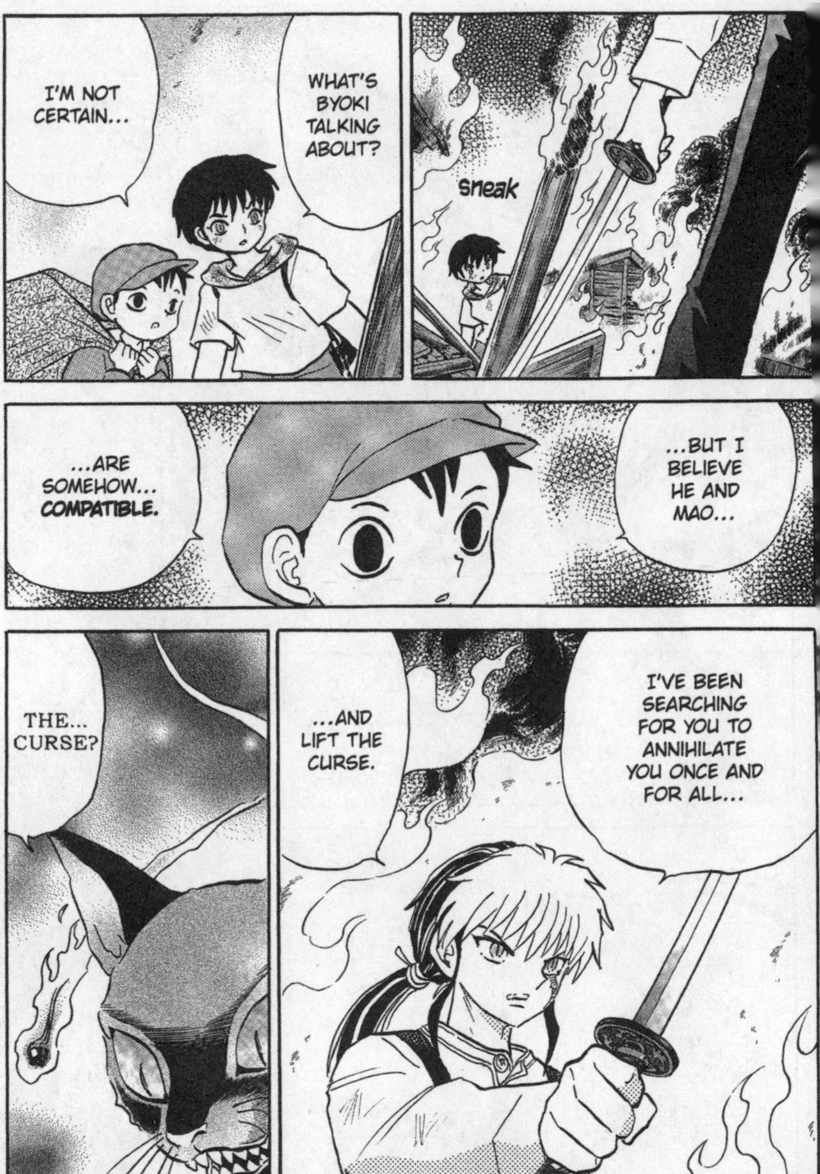
sneak
WHAT'S BYOKI TALKING ABOUT?
I'M NOT CERTAIN...
...BUT I BELIEVE HE AND MAO...
...ARE SOMEHOW... **COMPATIBLE.**
I'VE BEEN SEARCHING FOR YOU TO ANNIHILATE YOU ONCE AND FOR ALL...
...AND LIFT THE CURSE.
THE... CURSE?

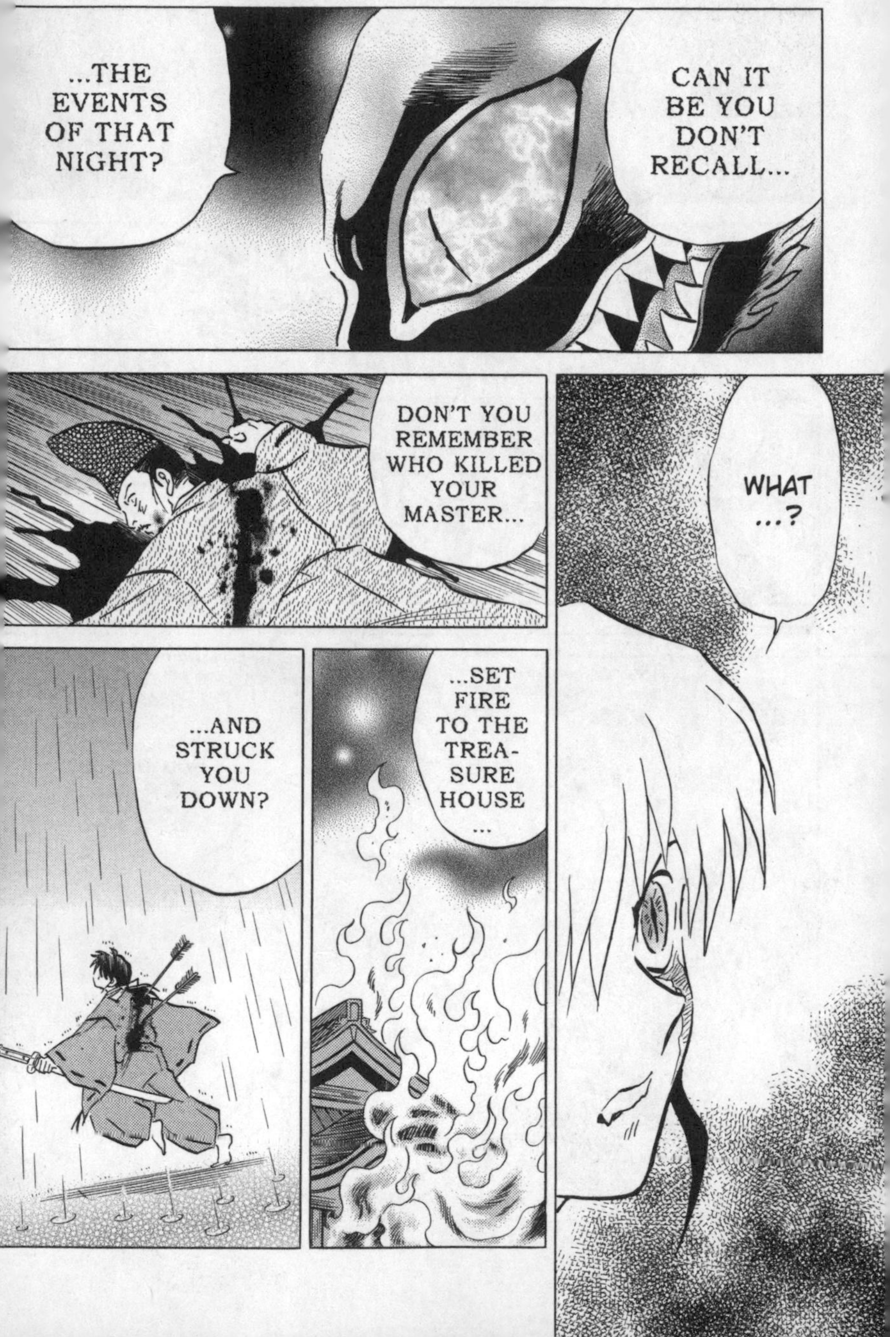
CAN IT BE YOU DON'T RECALL...
...THE EVENTS OF THAT NIGHT?
WHAT ...?
DON'T YOU REMEMBER WHO KILLED YOUR MASTER...
...SET FIRE TO THE TREA-SURE HOUSE ...
...AND STRUCK YOU DOWN?

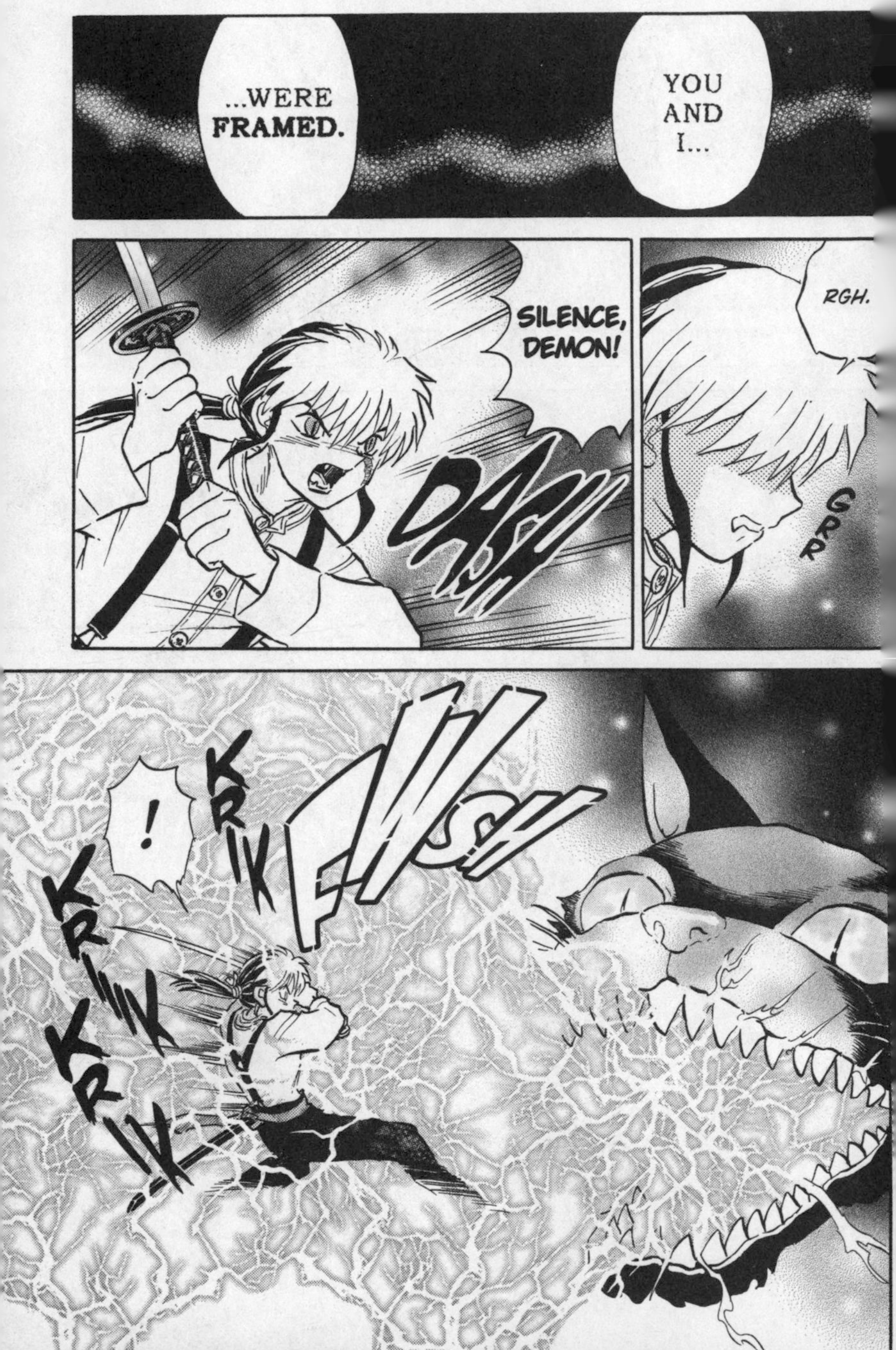
YOU AND I...
...WERE FRAMED.
RGH.
GRR
SILENCE, DEMON!
DASH
FWSH
KRIK
!
KRIIIK KRIIK

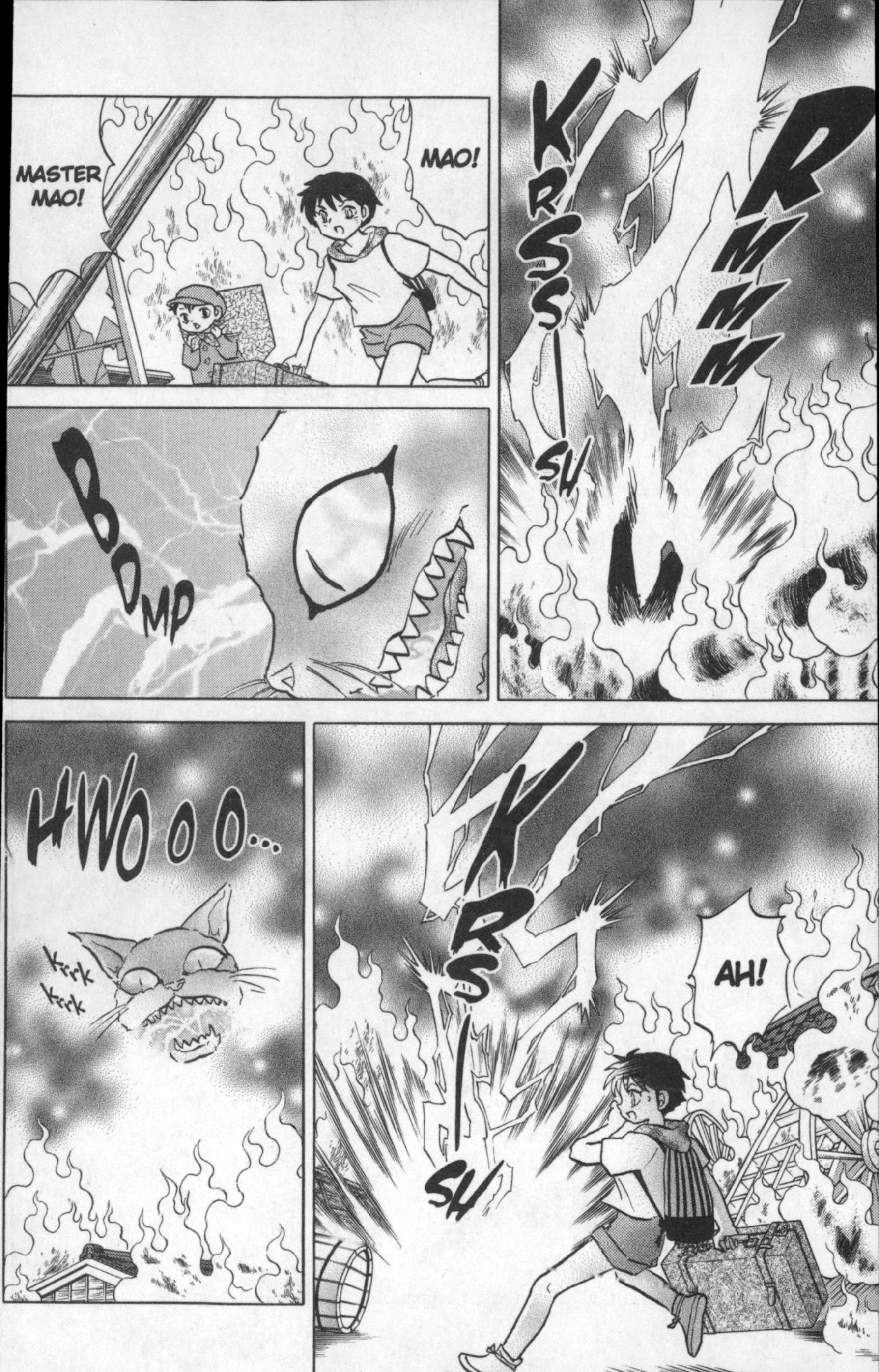
RMMMMU
KRSS—SH
MAO!
MASTER MAO!
BOOMP
AH!
KRSS—SH
HWO O O...
Krrk Krrk

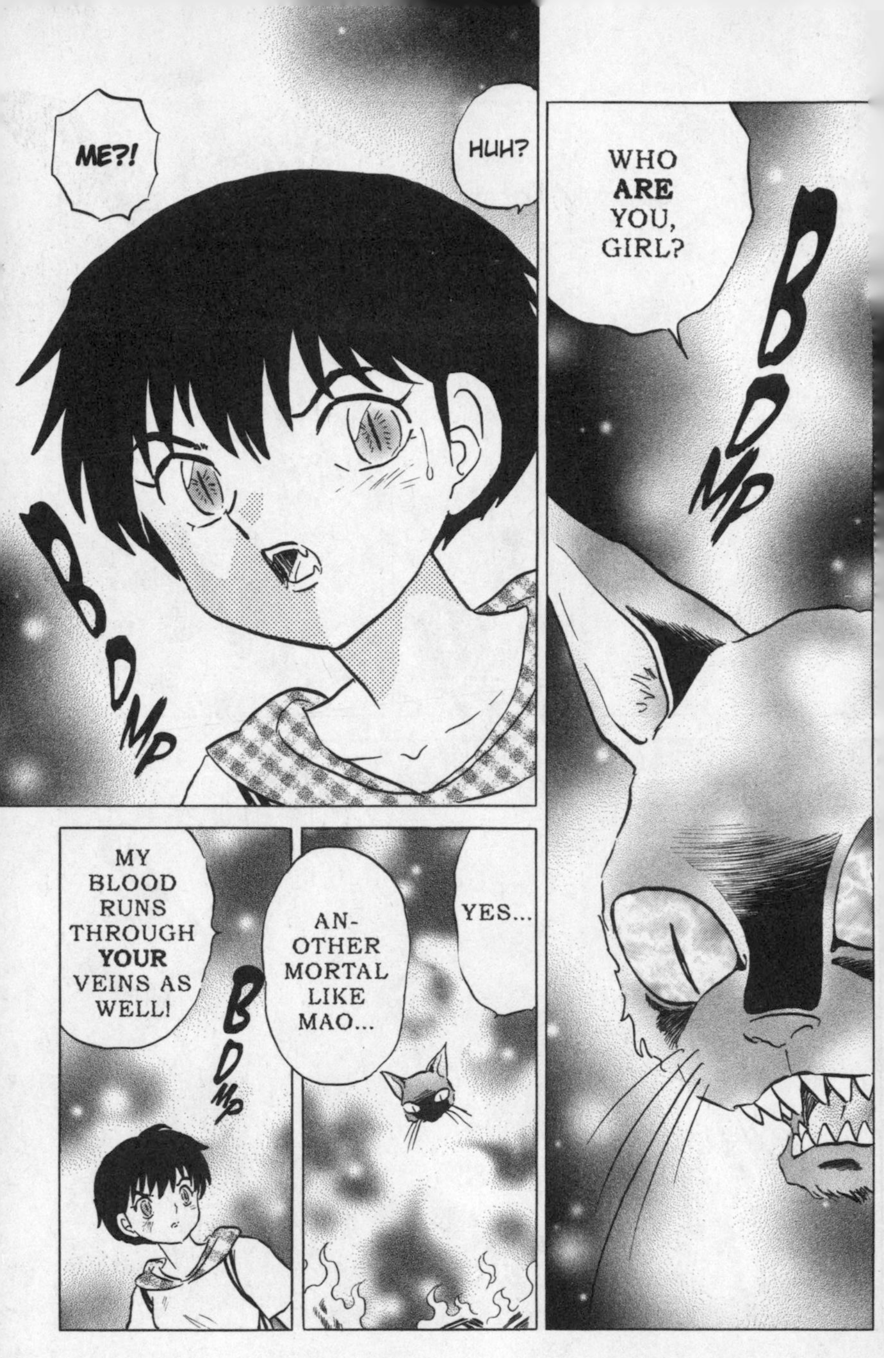
WHO ARE YOU, GIRL?
BDOMP
HUH?
ME?!
BDOMP
YES...
AN-OTHER MORTAL LIKE MAO...
MY BLOOD RUNS THROUGH YOUR VEINS AS WELL!
BDOMP

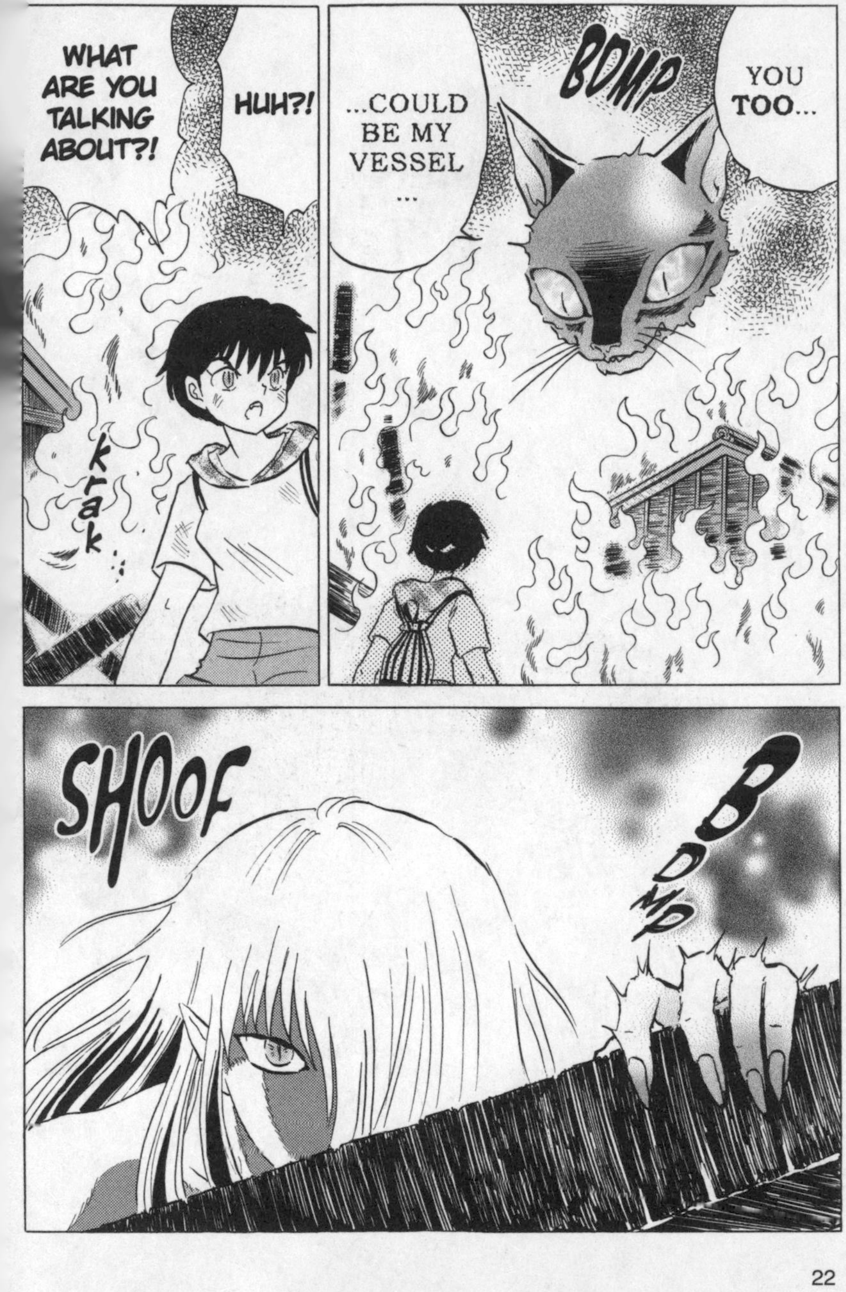
YOU TOO...
BDMP
...COULD BE MY VESSEL ...
HUH?!
WHAT ARE YOU TALKING ABOUT?!
krak
BDMP
SHOOF

Chapter 2:
Seven Tails

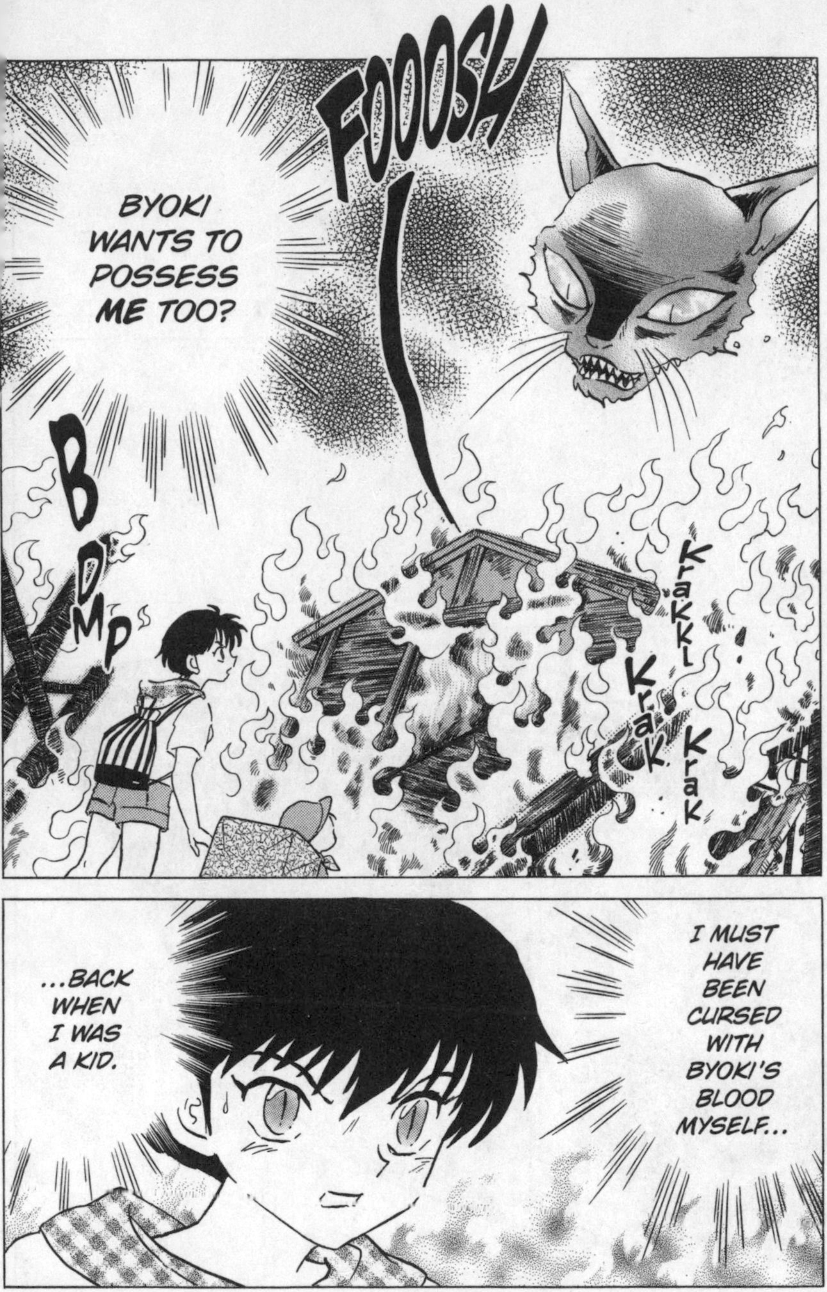
FOOSH
BYOKI WANTS TO POSSESS ME TOO?
Krakkl
Krak
Krak
BDMP
I MUST HAVE BEEN CURSED WITH BYOKI'S BLOOD MYSELF...
...BACK WHEN I WAS A KID.

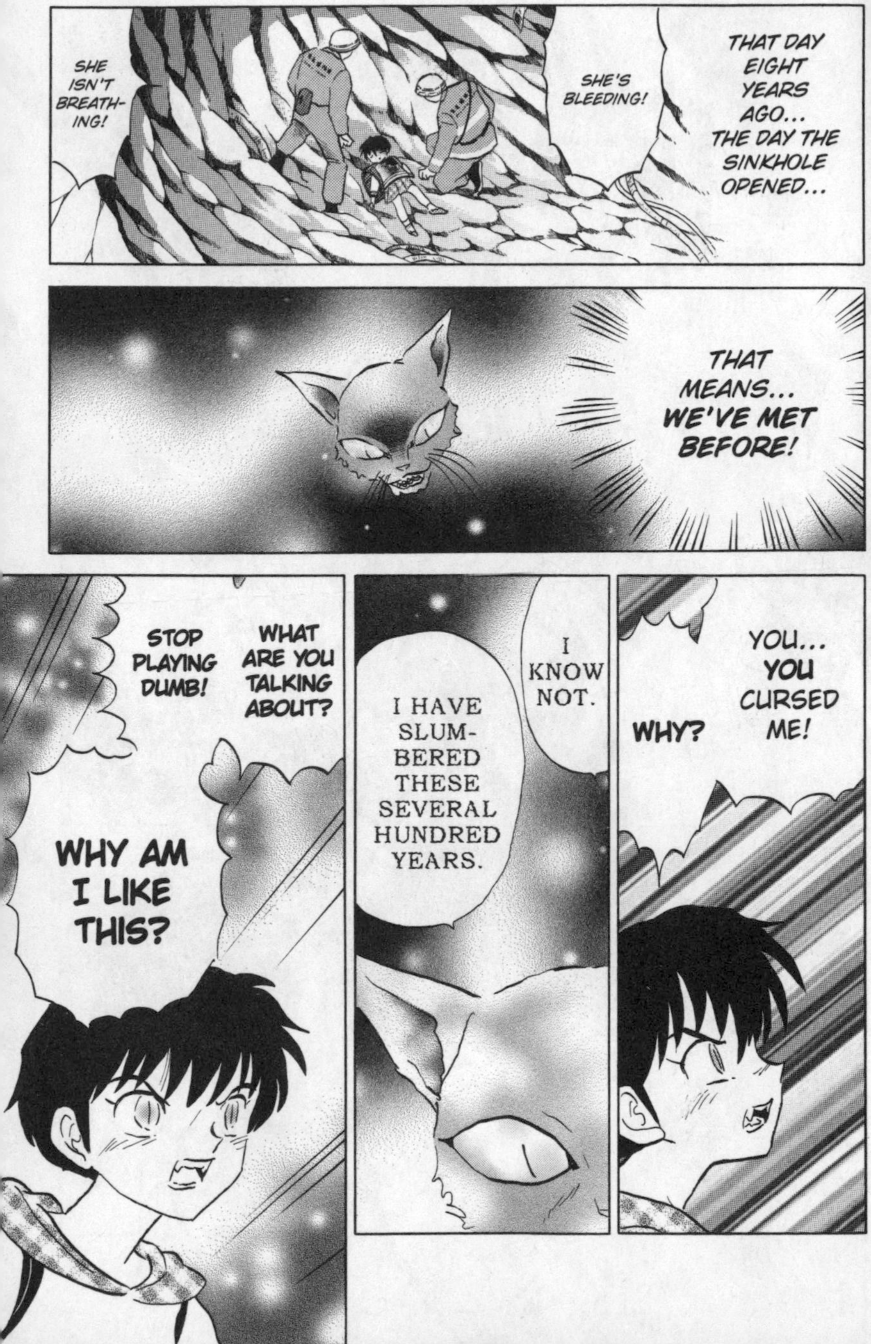
THAT DAY EIGHT YEARS AGO... THE DAY THE SINKHOLE OPENED...
SHE'S BLEEDING!
SHE ISN'T BREATHING!
THAT MEANS... WE'VE MET BEFORE!
YOU... YOU CURSED ME!
WHY?
I KNOW NOT.
I HAVE SLUMBERED THESE SEVERAL HUNDRED YEARS.
WHAT ARE YOU TALKING ABOUT?
STOP PLAYING DUMB!
WHY AM I LIKE THIS?

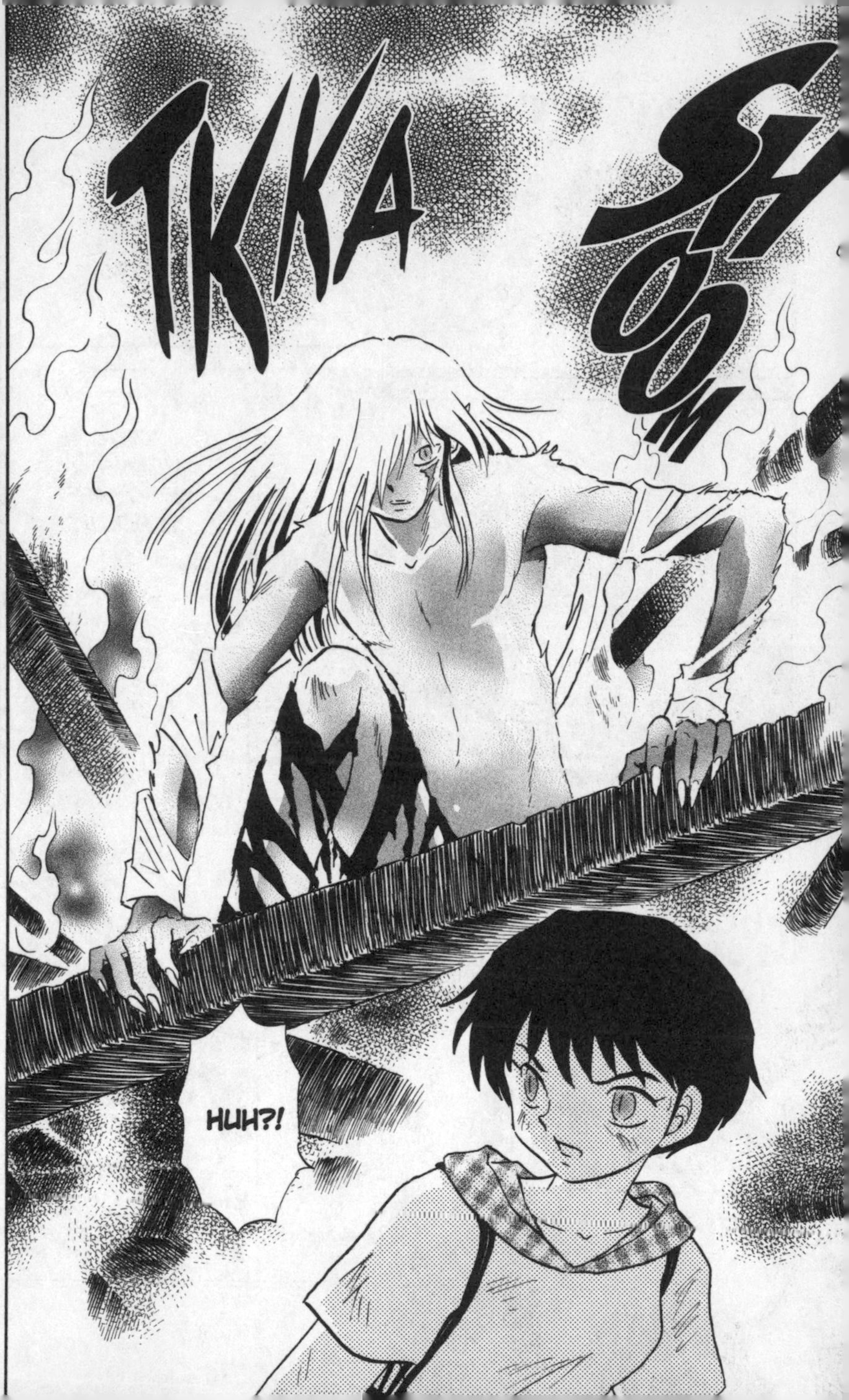
SHOOM
TKKA
HUH?!

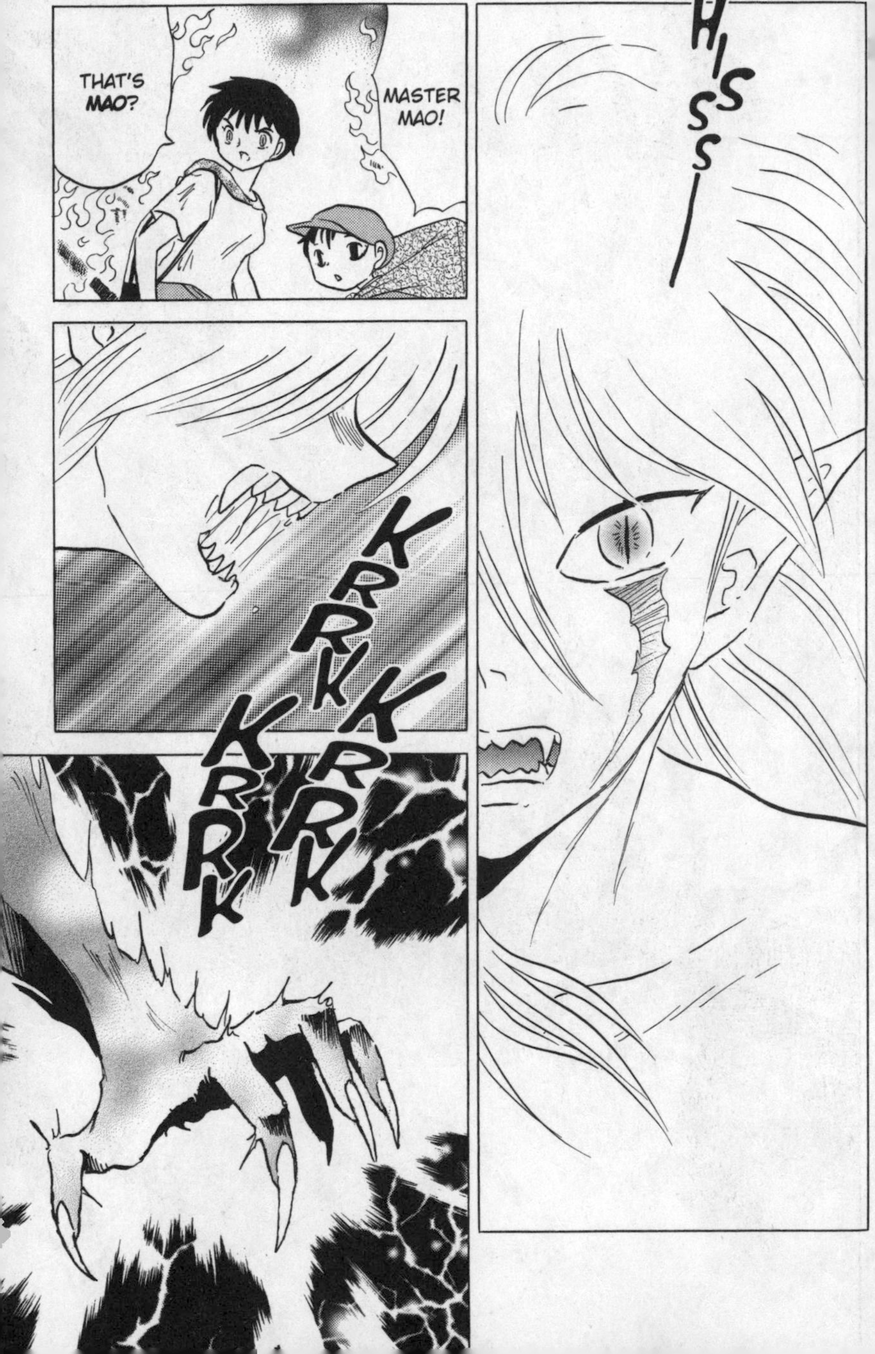
HISS
MASTER MAO!
THAT'S MAO?
KRRK KRRK
KRRK

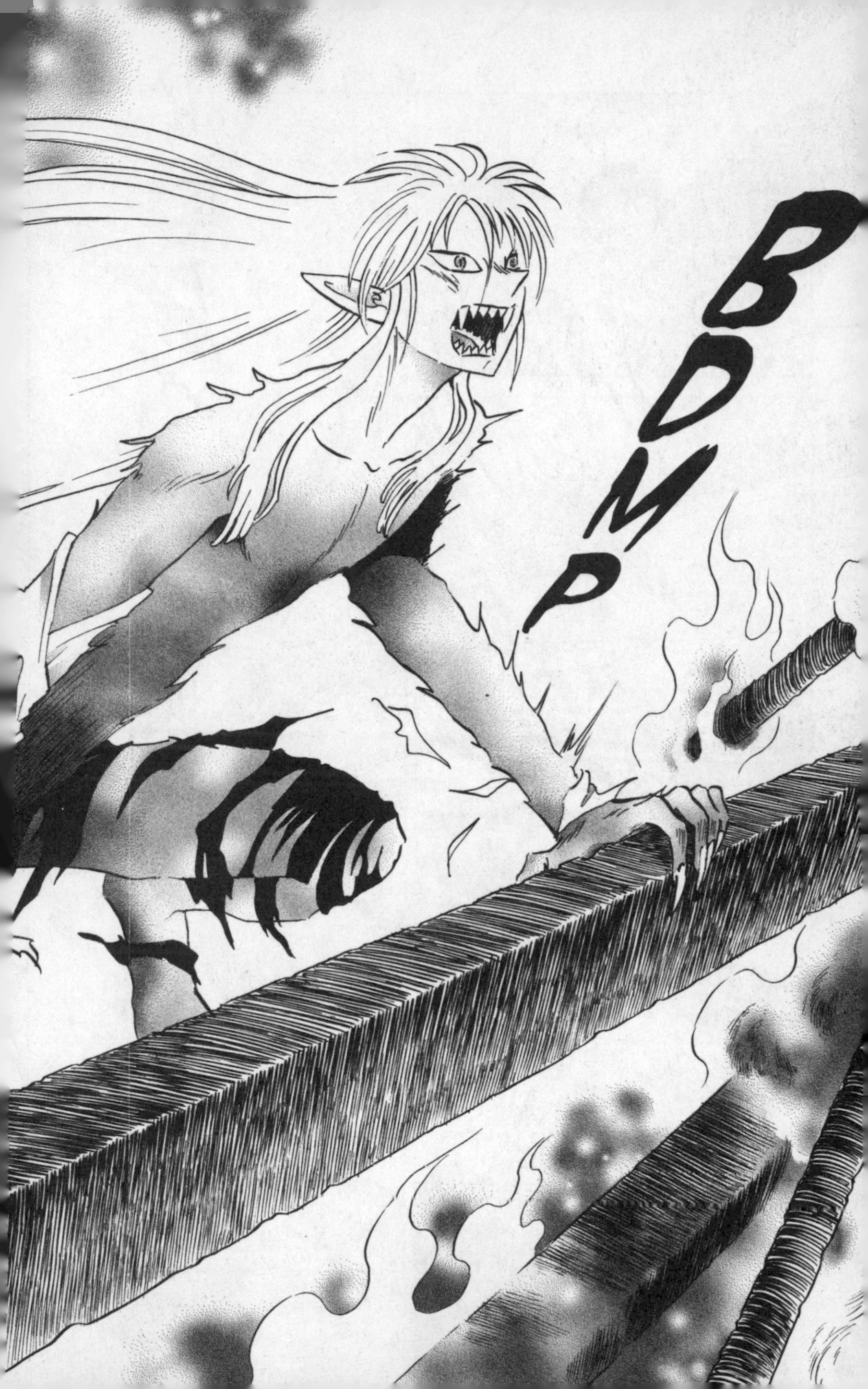
BDMP

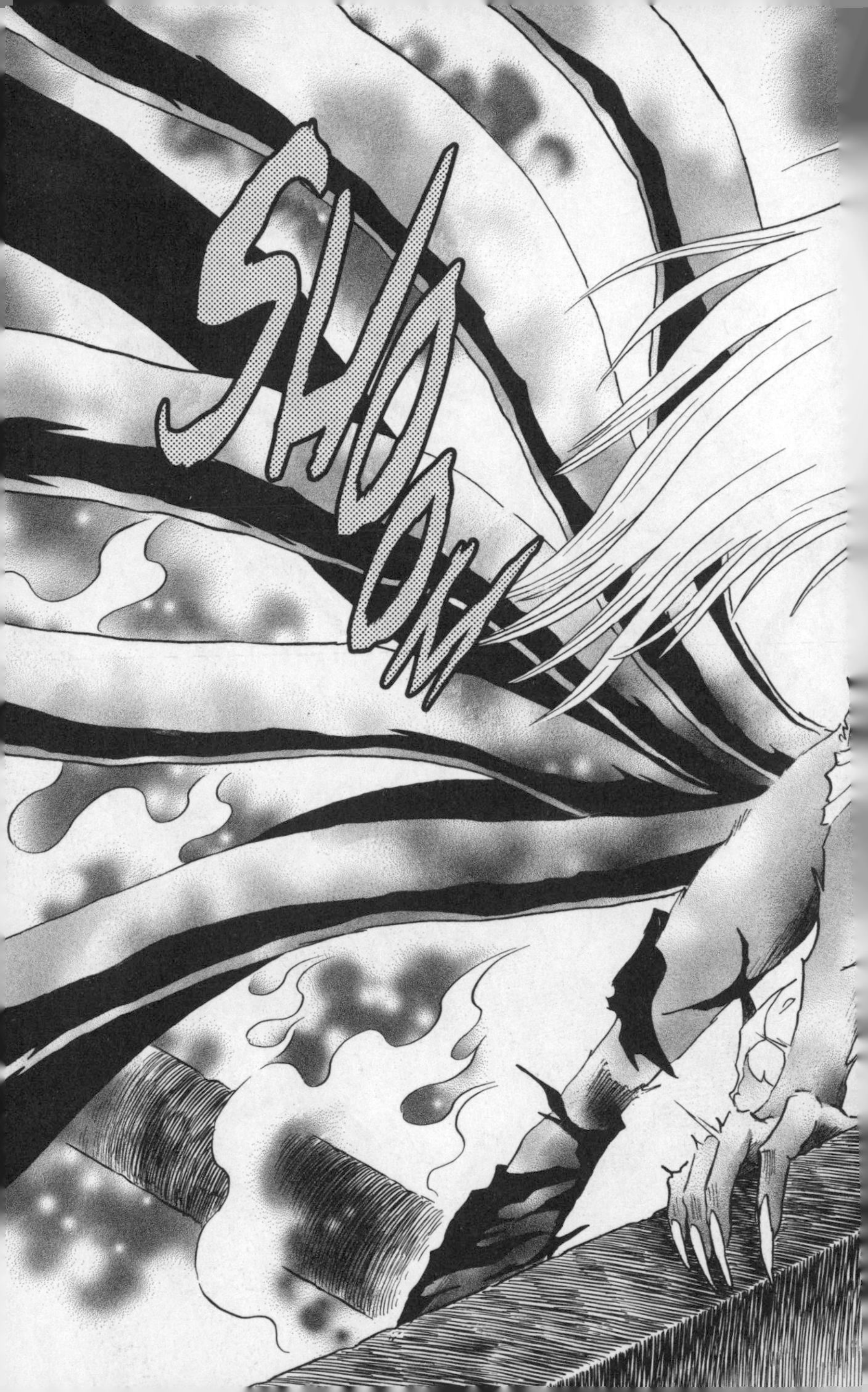
SHOOM

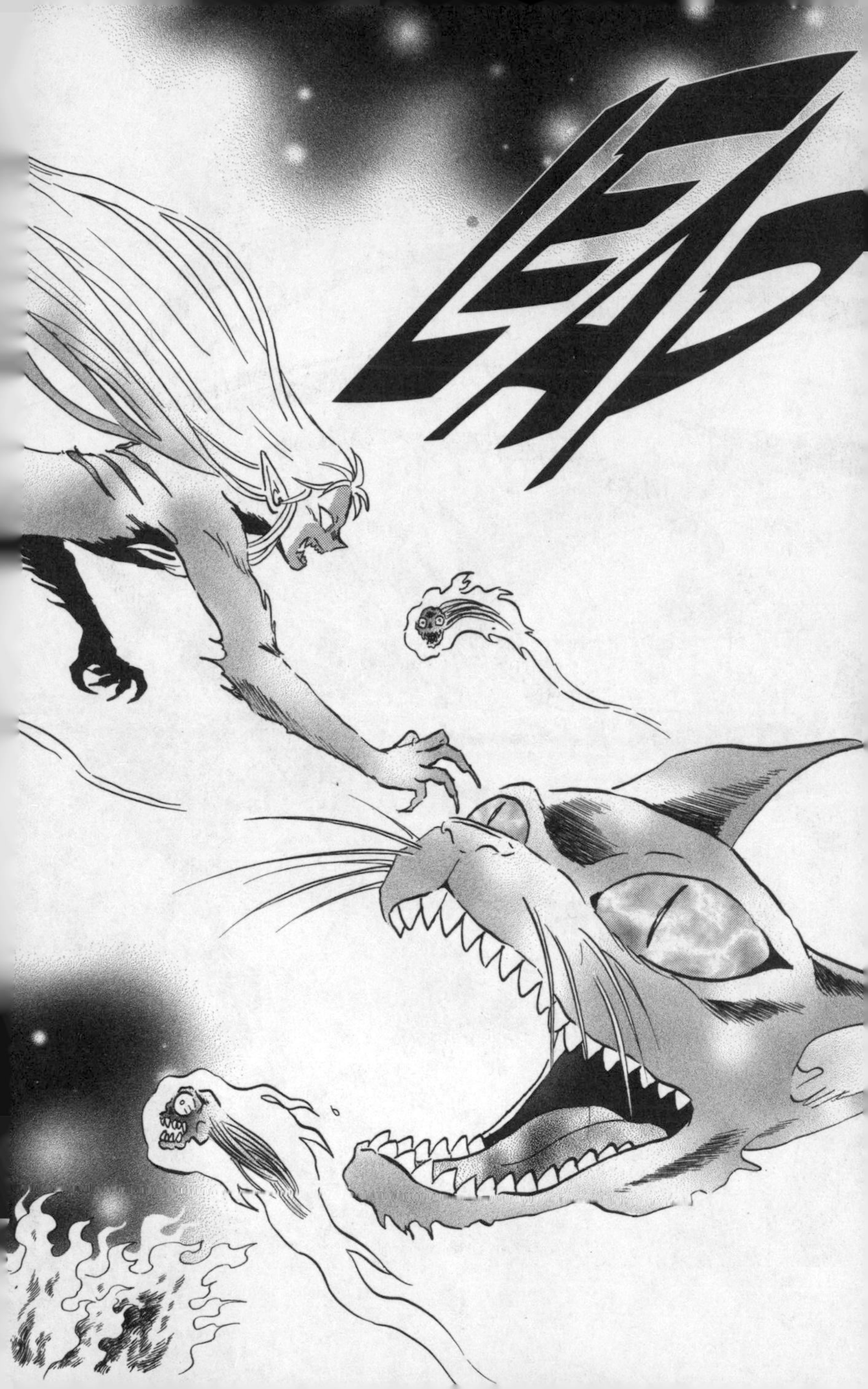

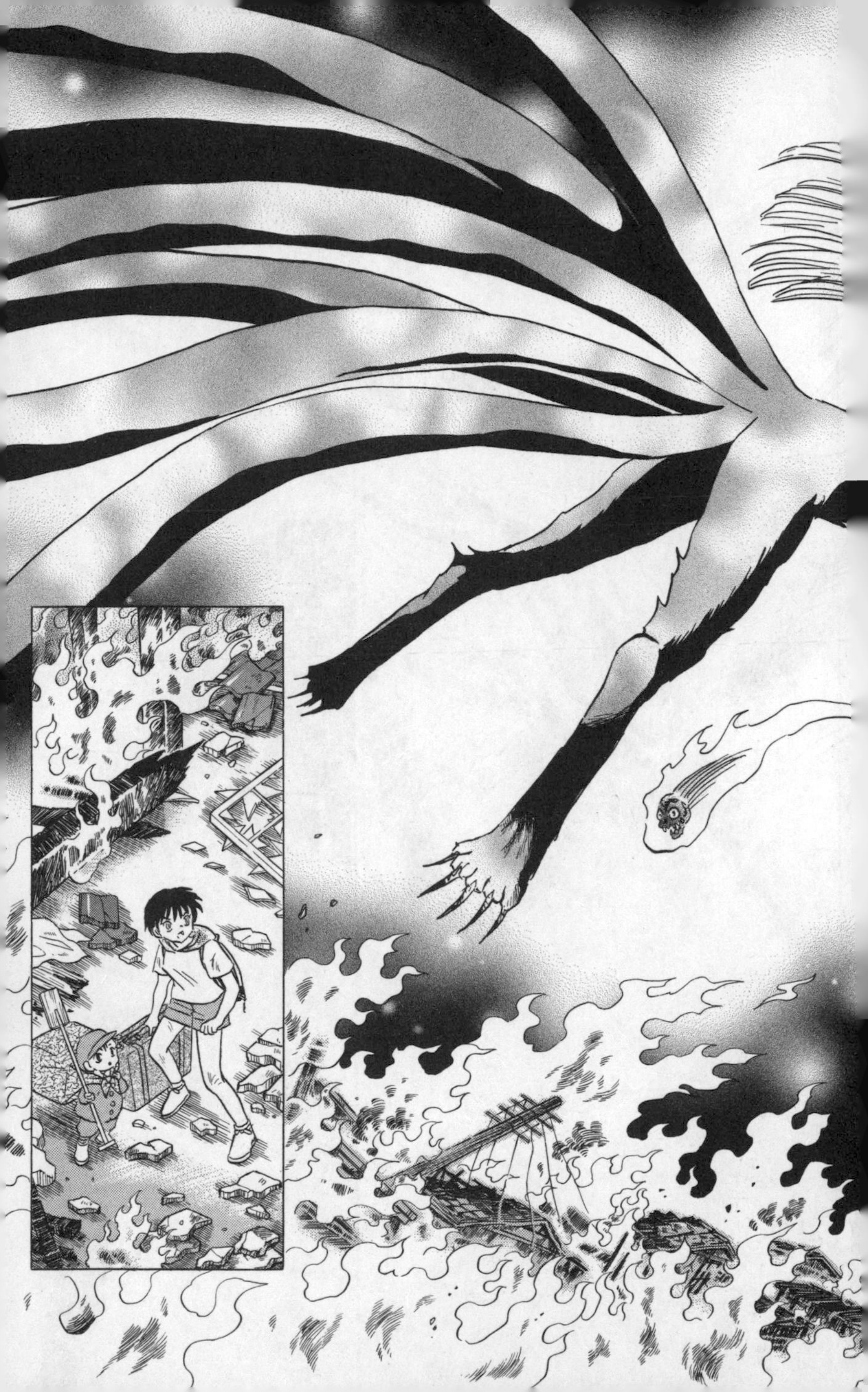

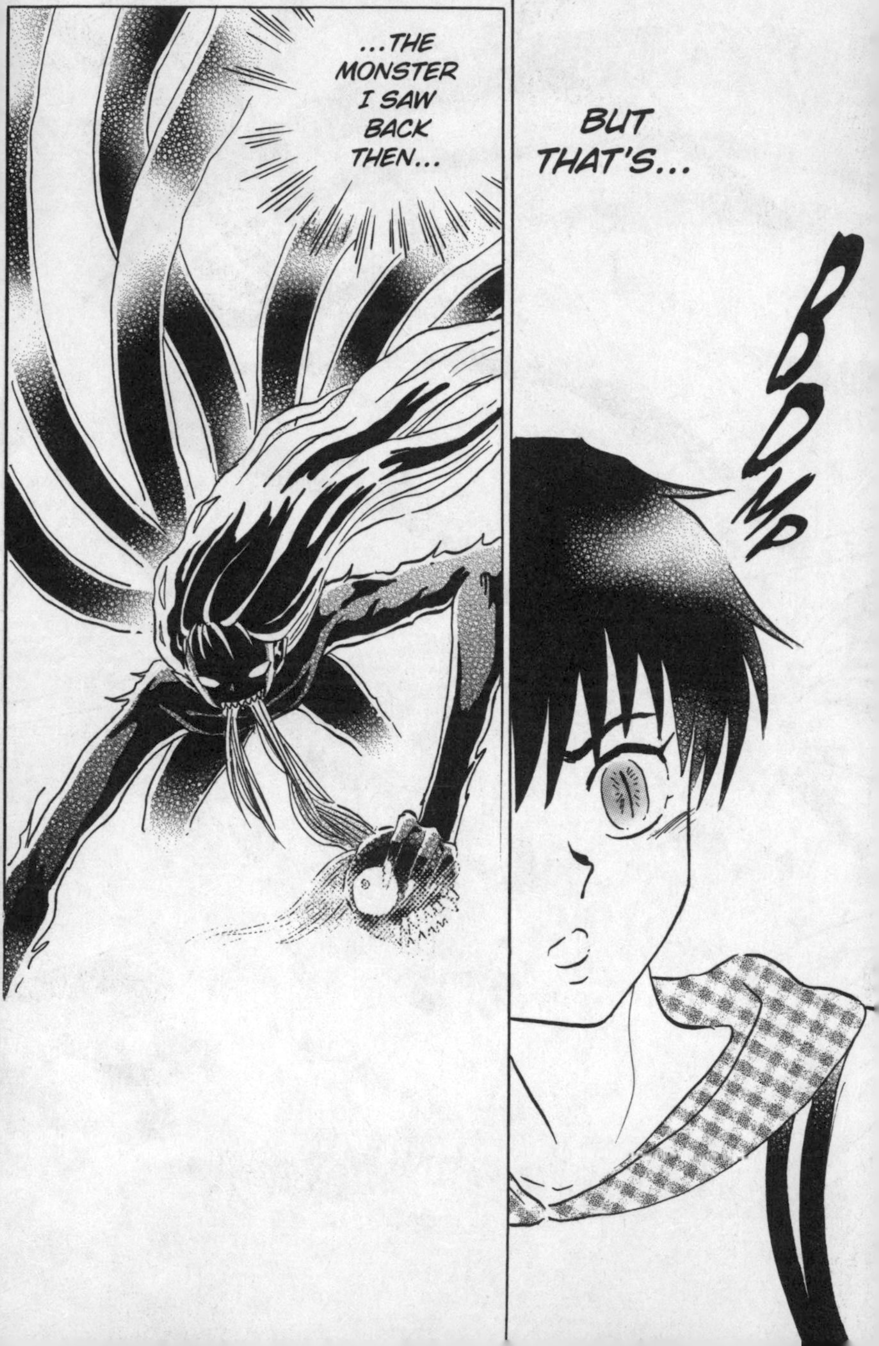
BUT THAT'S...
BDMP
...THE MONSTER I SAW BACK THEN...

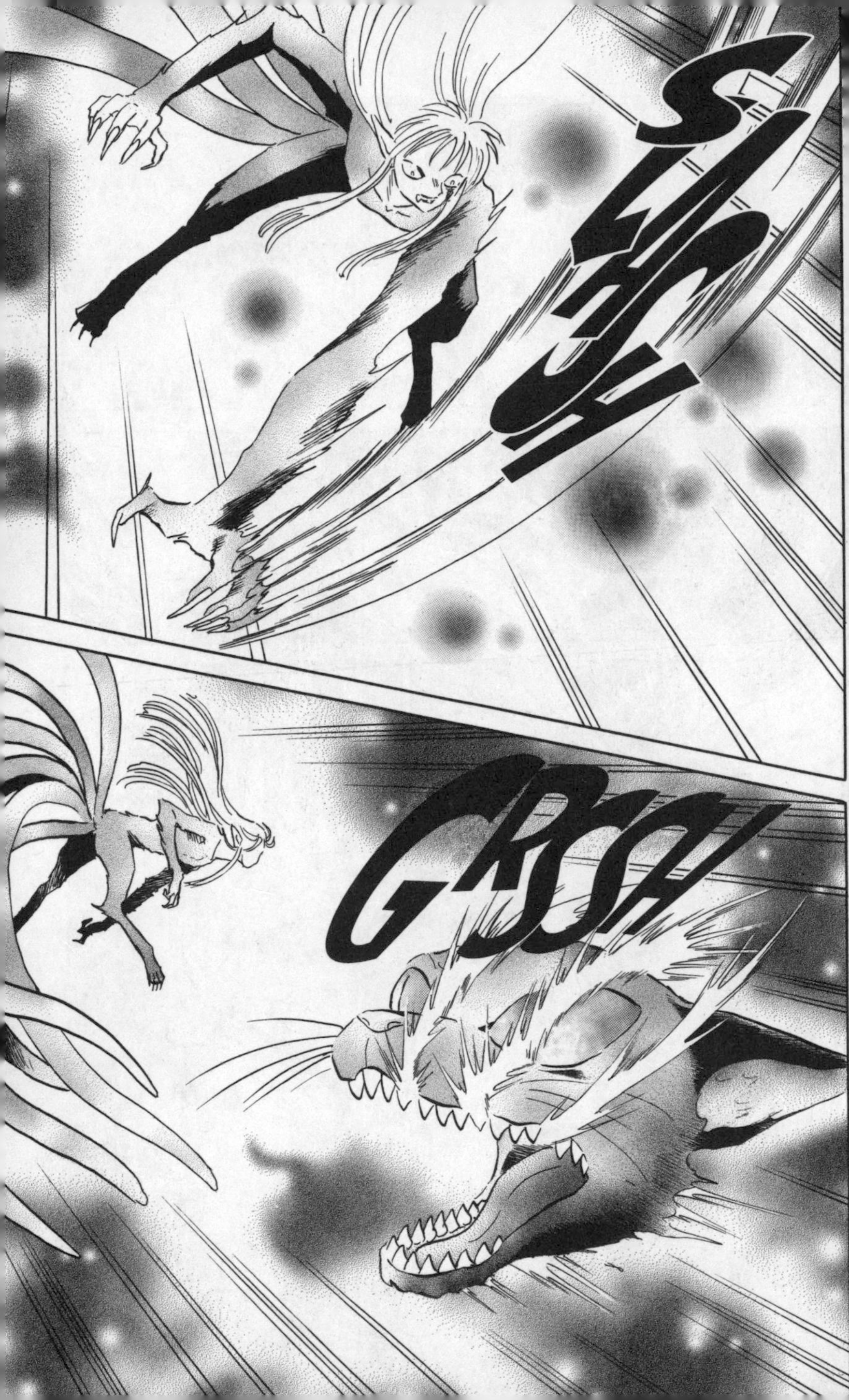
SHOOM
GASH

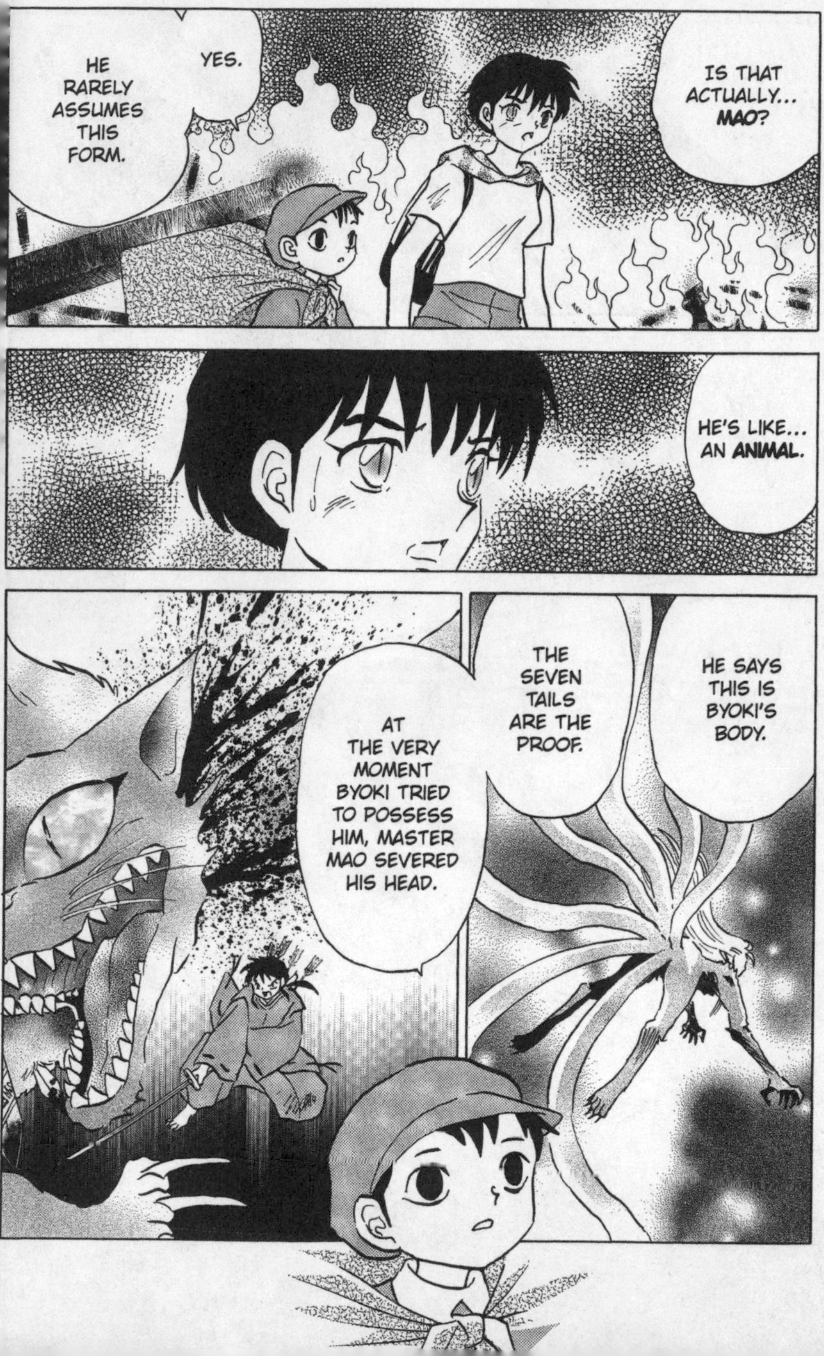
IS THAT ACTUALLY... **MAO?**
YES.
HE RARELY ASSUMES THIS FORM.
HE'S LIKE... AN **ANIMAL.**
HE SAYS THIS IS BYOKI'S BODY.
THE SEVEN TAILS ARE THE PROOF.
AT THE VERY MOMENT BYOKI TRIED TO POSSESS HIM, MASTER MAO SEVERED HIS HEAD.

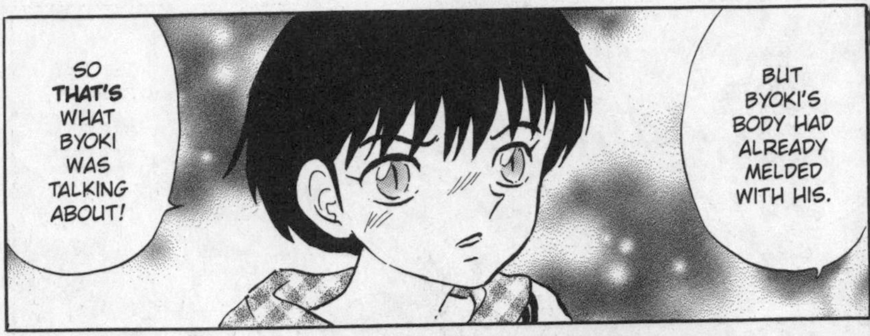
BUT BYOKI'S BODY HAD ALREADY MELDED WITH HIS.
SO **THAT'S** WHAT BYOKI WAS TALKING ABOUT!

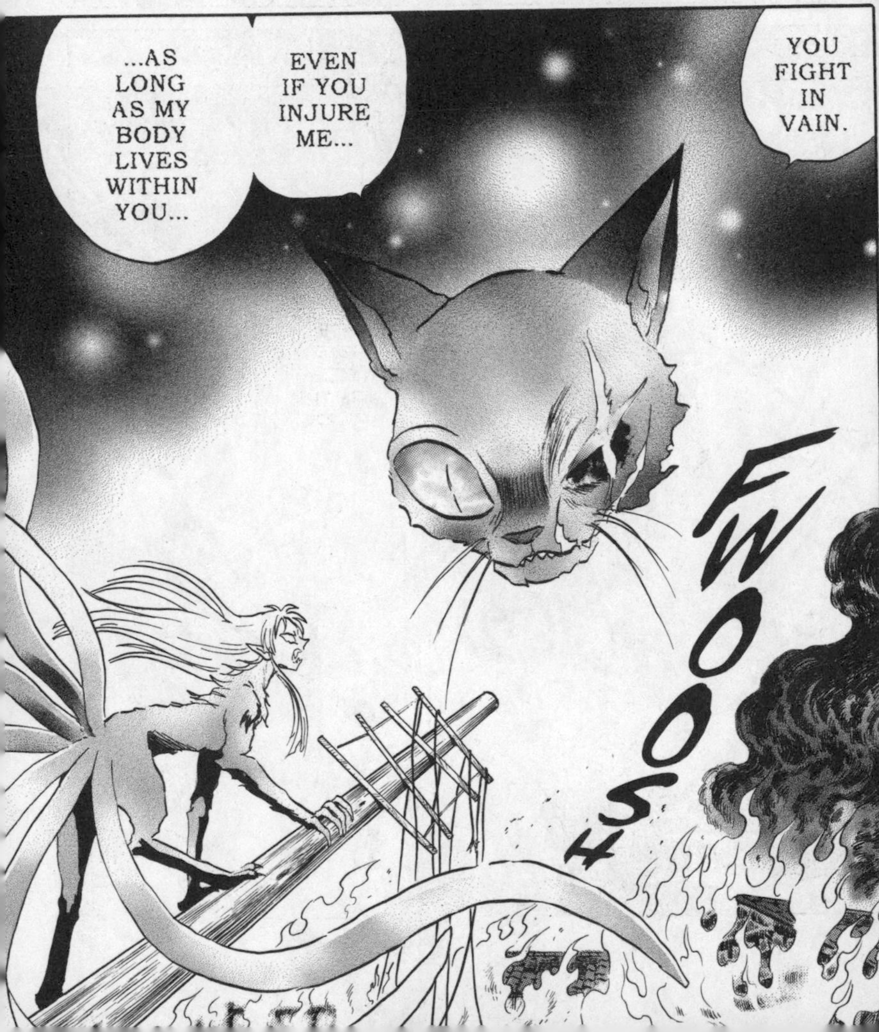
YOU FIGHT IN VAIN.
EVEN IF YOU INJURE ME...
...AS LONG AS MY BODY LIVES WITHIN YOU...
FWOOOSH

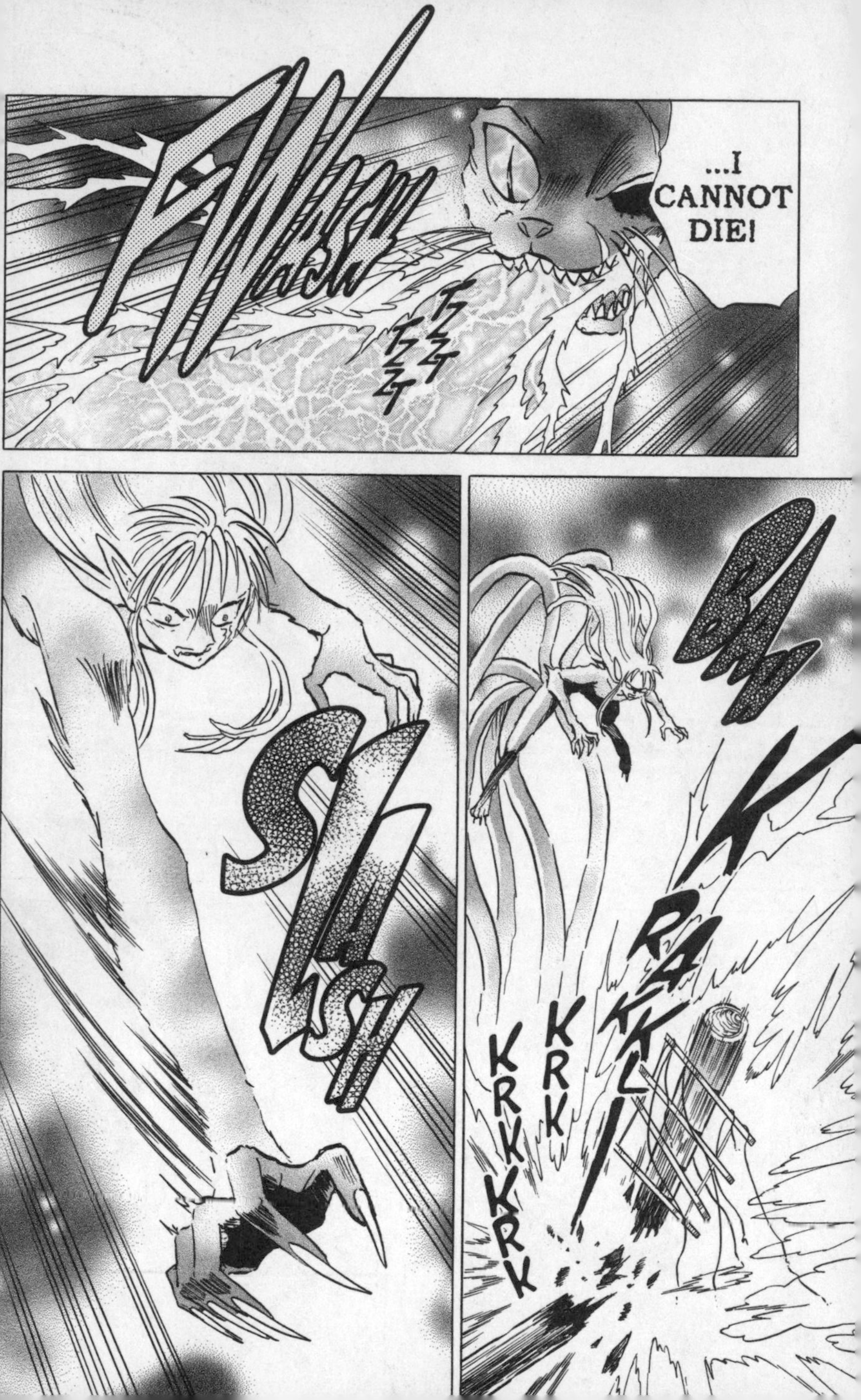
...I CANNOT DIE!
BAM
KRAKKL
KRK KRK
KRKKRKKRK
SLASH

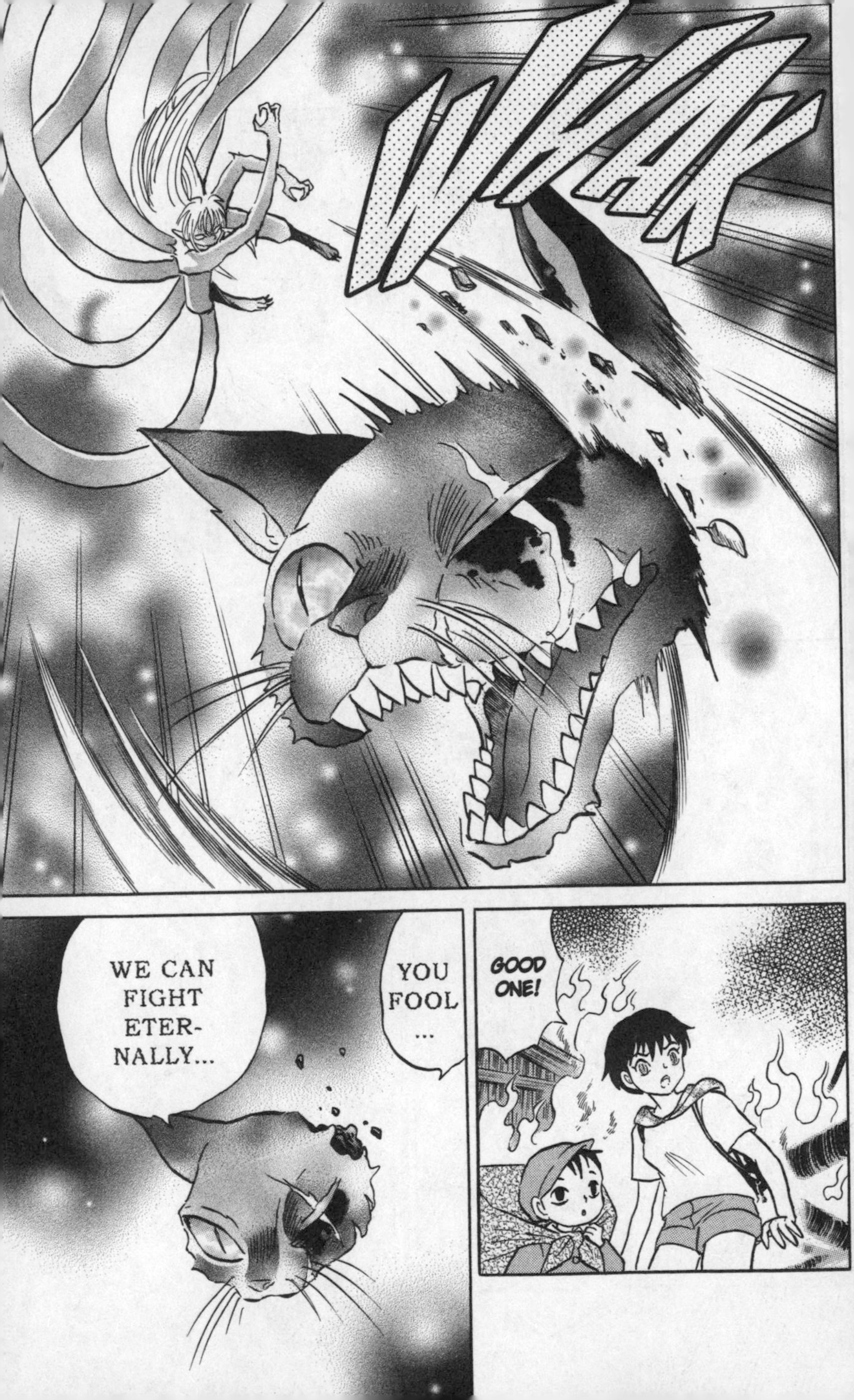
WHAK
GOOD ONE!
YOU FOOL ...
WE CAN FIGHT ETERNALLY...

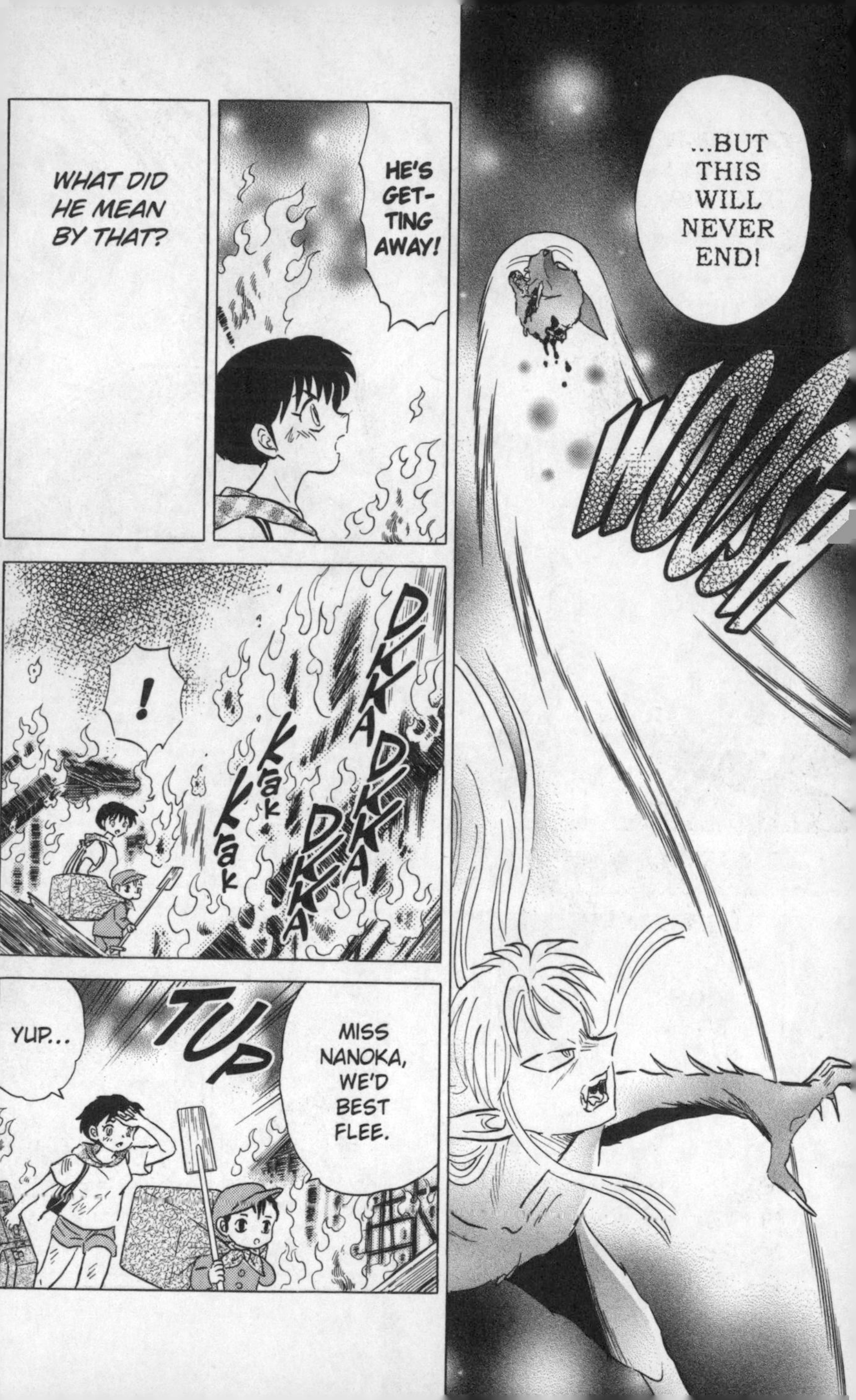
...BUT THIS WILL NEVER END!
WOOSH
HE'S GET-TING AWAY!
WHAT DID HE MEAN BY THAT?
!
DKADKA
DKKA
krak
krak
MISS NANOKA, WE'D BEST FLEE.
TUP
YUP...

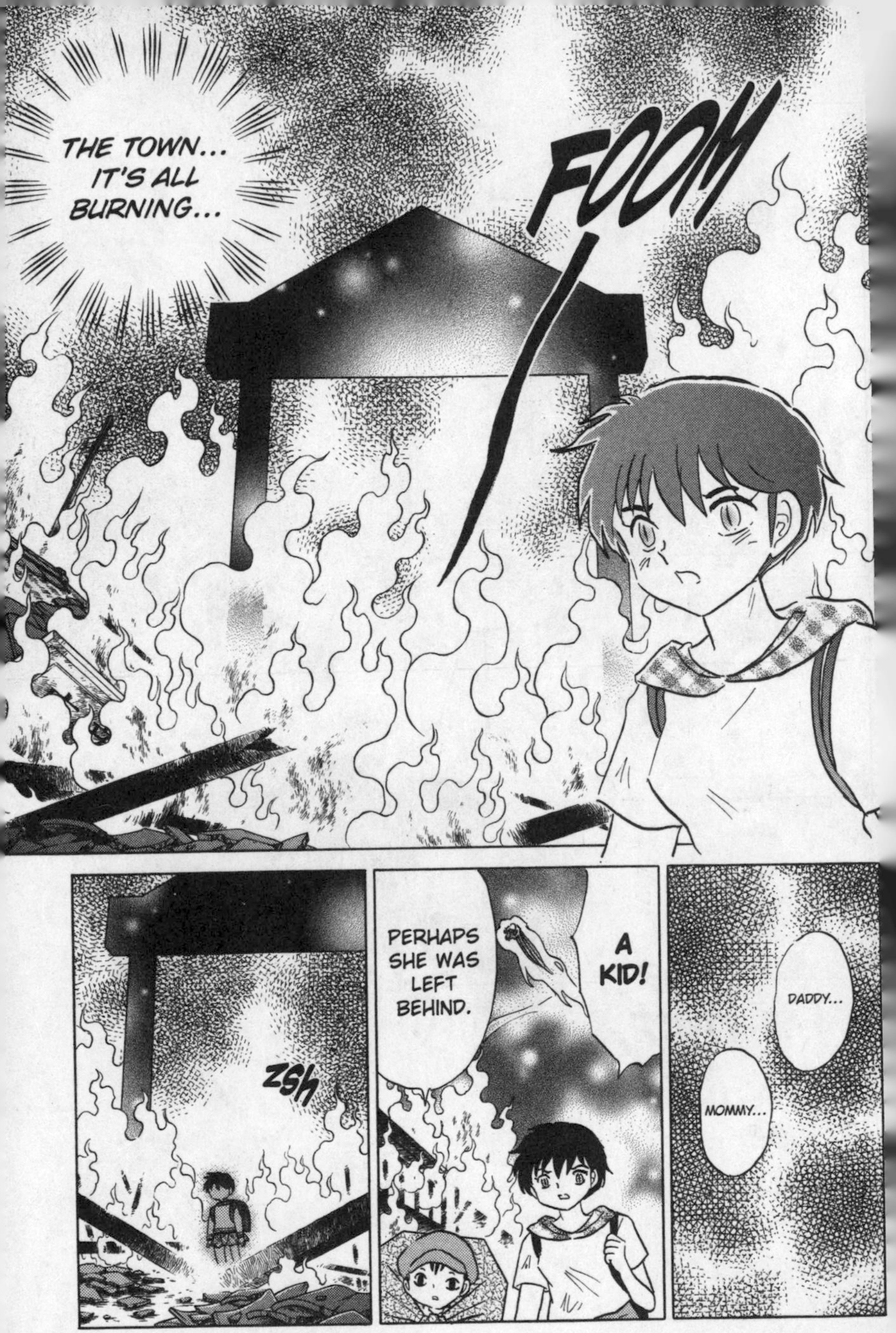
THE TOWN... IT'S ALL BURNING...
FOOM
DADDY...
MOMMY...
A KID!
PERHAPS SHE WAS LEFT BEHIND.
ZSH

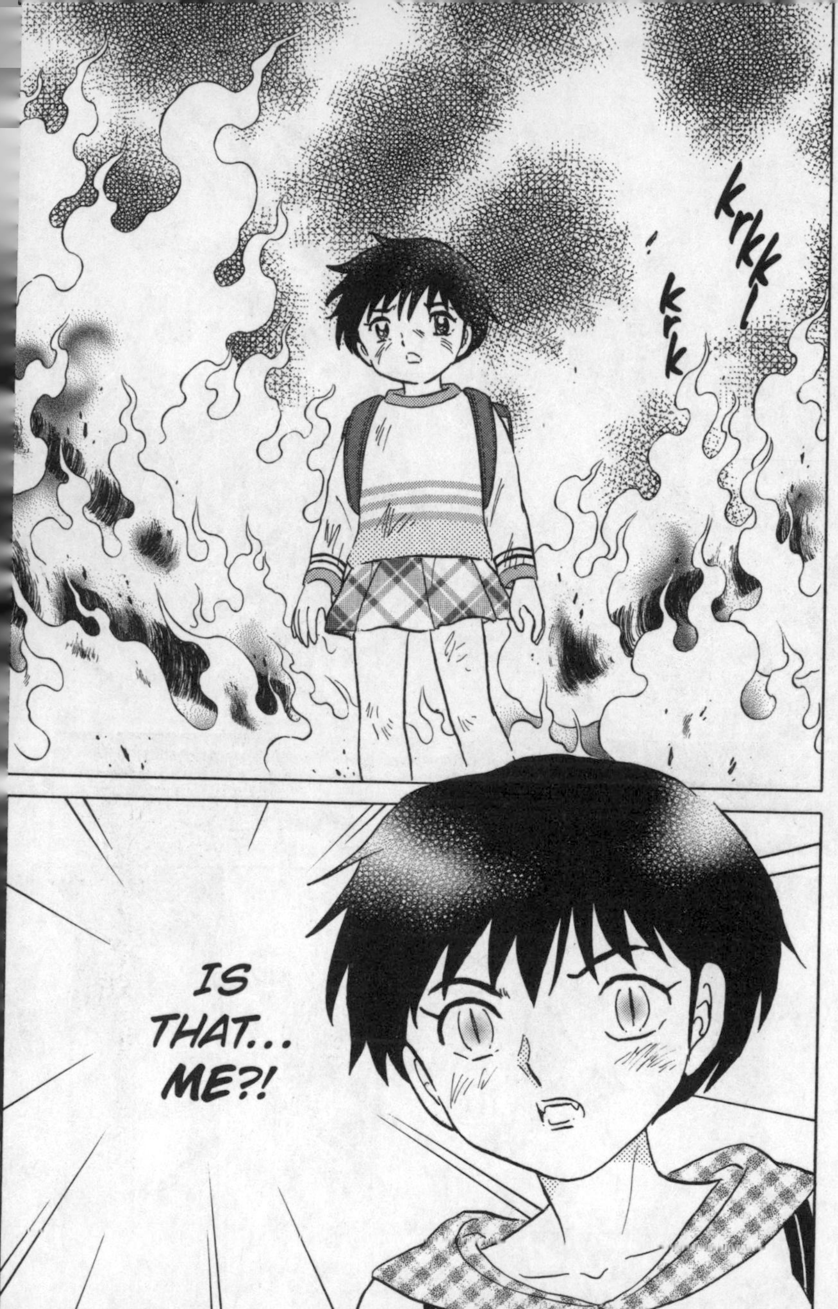
krkk
krk
IS THAT... ME?!

Chapter 3:
The New Vessel

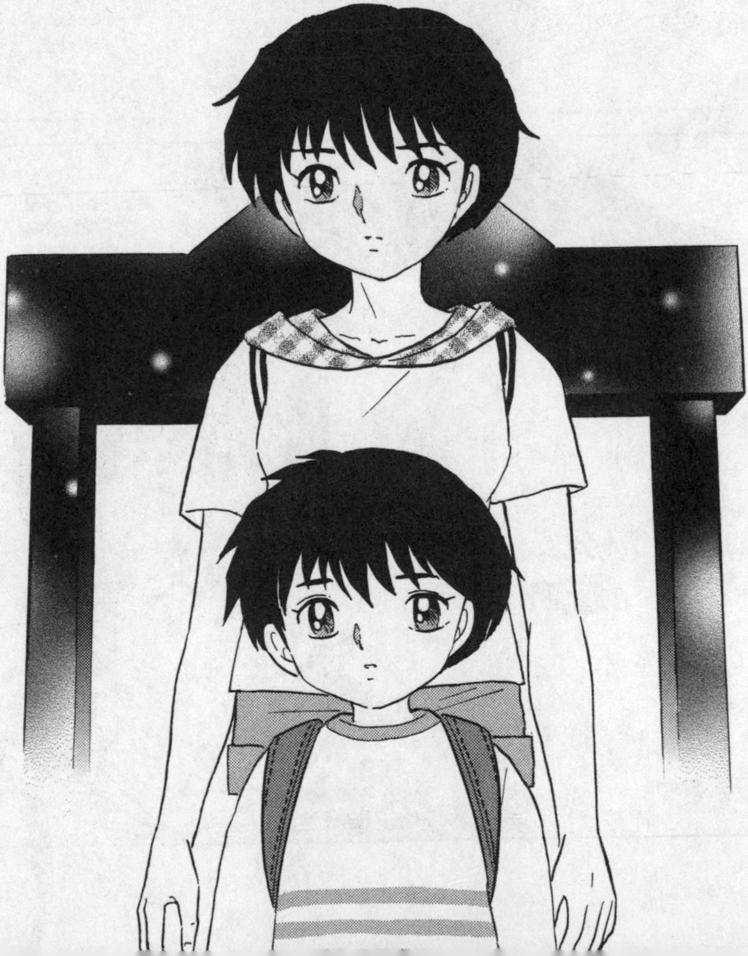

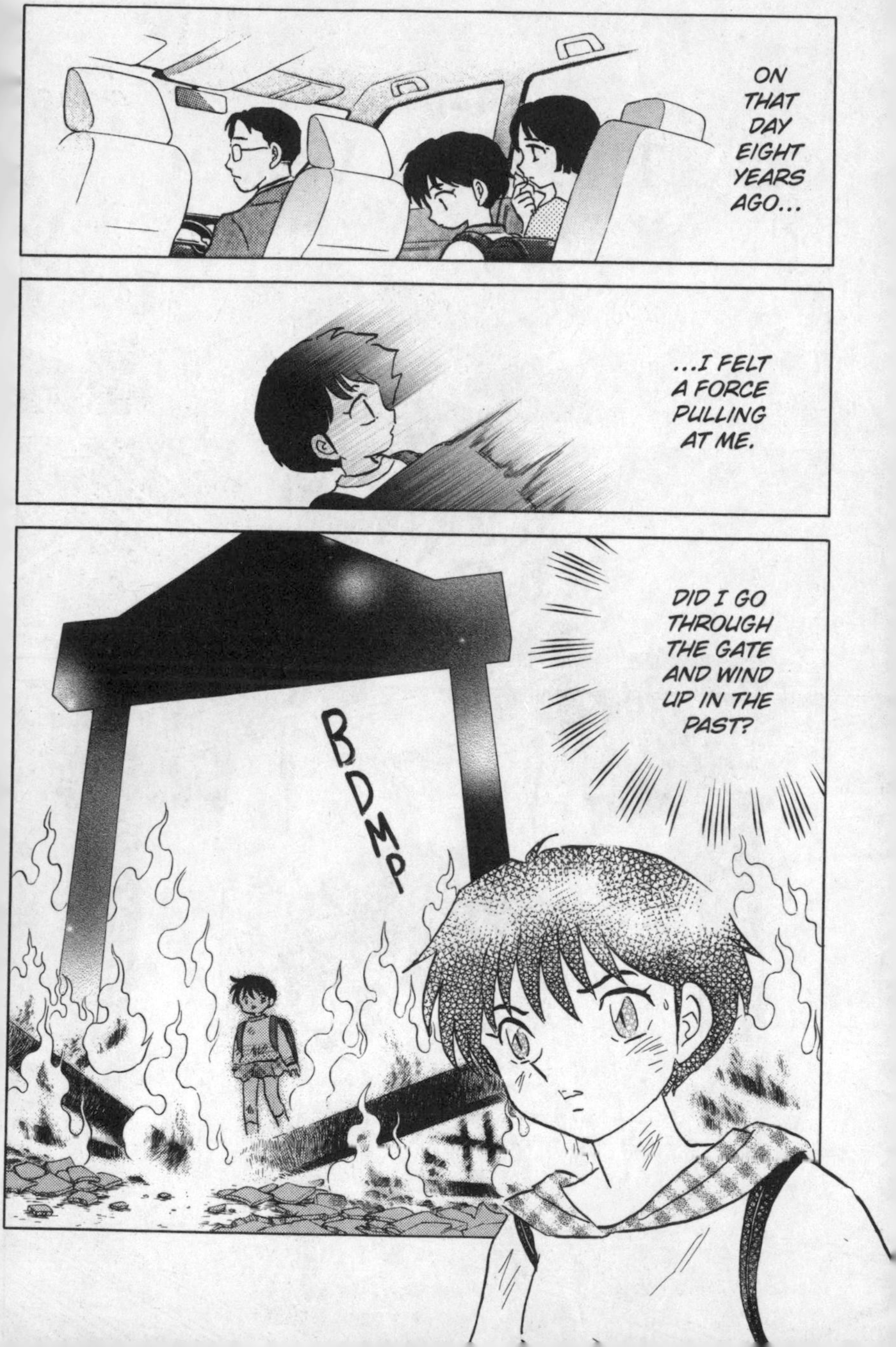
ON THAT DAY EIGHT YEARS AGO...
...I FELT A FORCE PULLING AT ME.
DID I GO THROUGH THE GATE AND WIND UP IN THE PAST?
BDMP

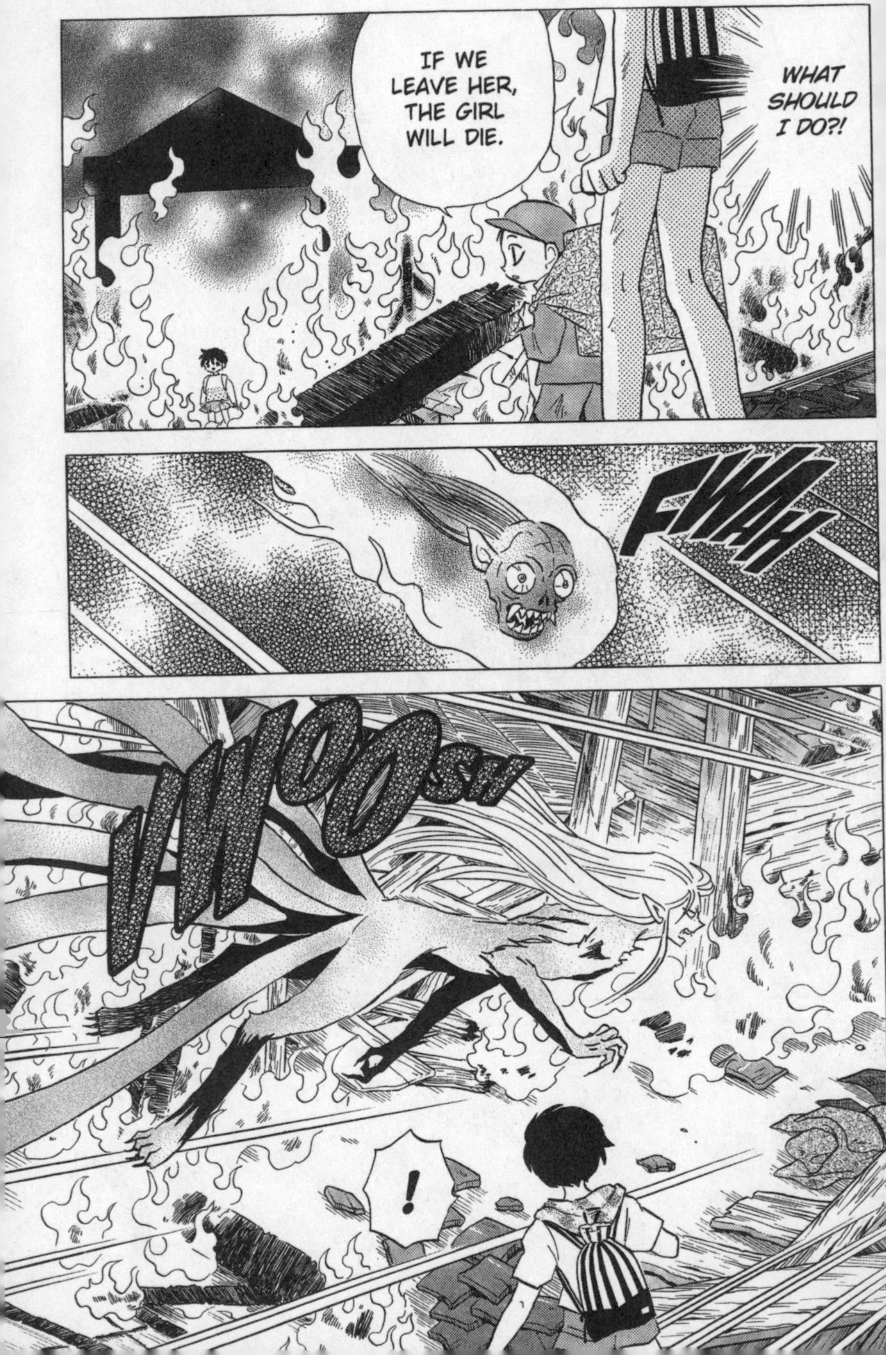
WHAT SHOULD I DO?!
IF WE LEAVE HER, THE GIRL WILL DIE.
FWAH
WHOOSH
!

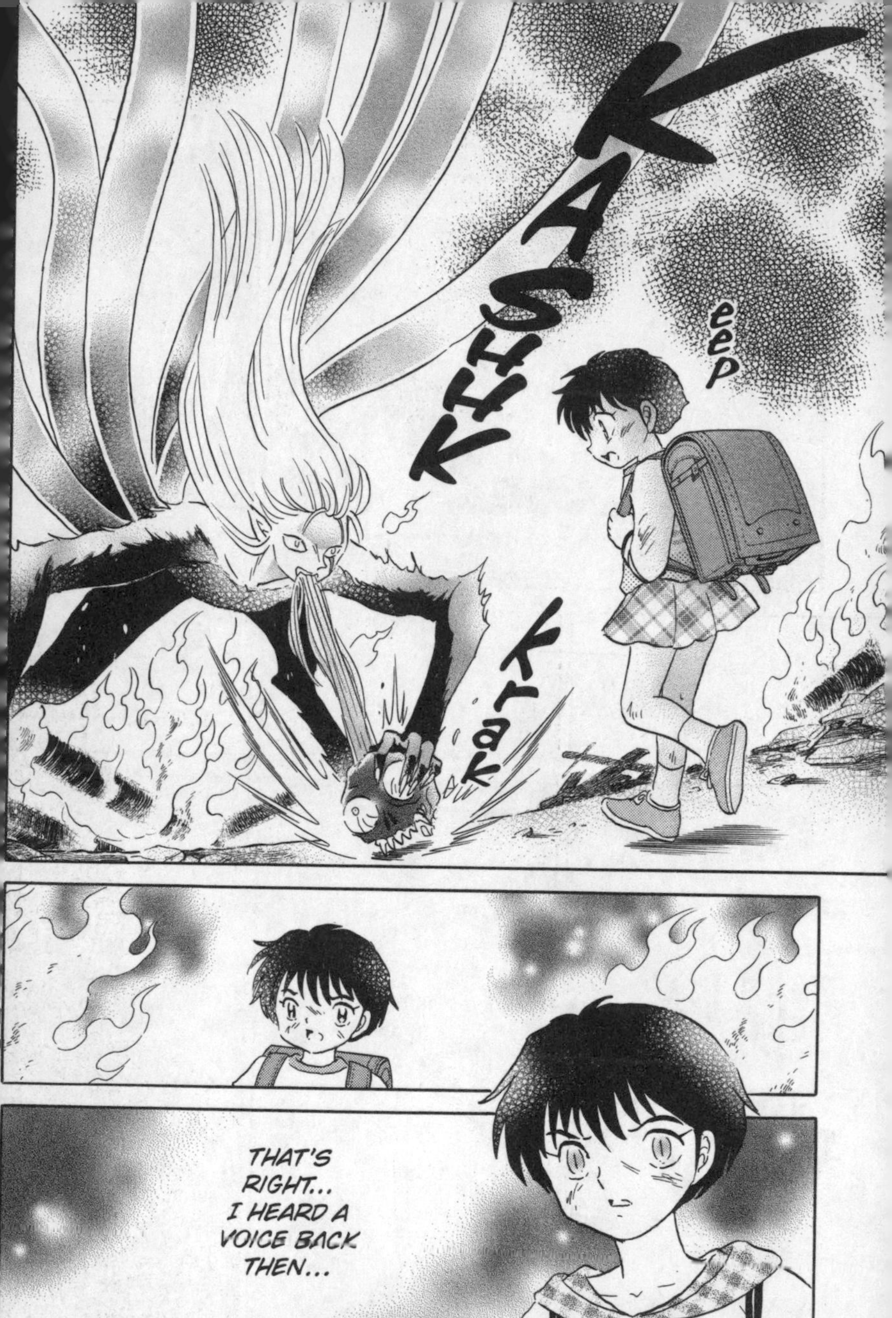
KASHHK
eep
krak
THAT'S RIGHT... I HEARD A VOICE BACK THEN...

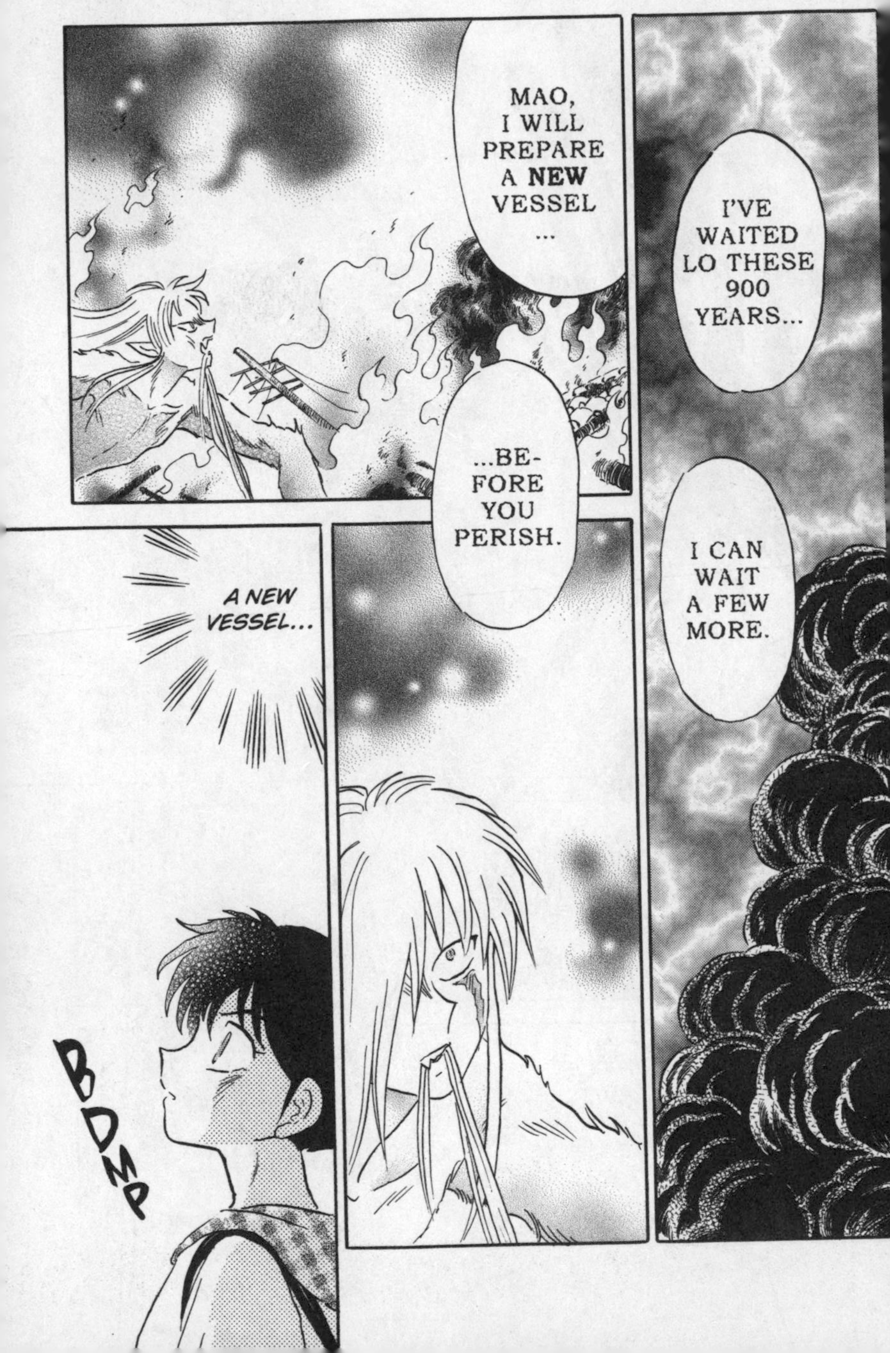
I'VE WAITED LO THESE 900 YEARS...
I CAN WAIT A FEW MORE.
MAO, I WILL PREPARE A **NEW** VESSEL ...
...BE-FORE YOU PERISH.
A NEW VESSEL...
BDMP

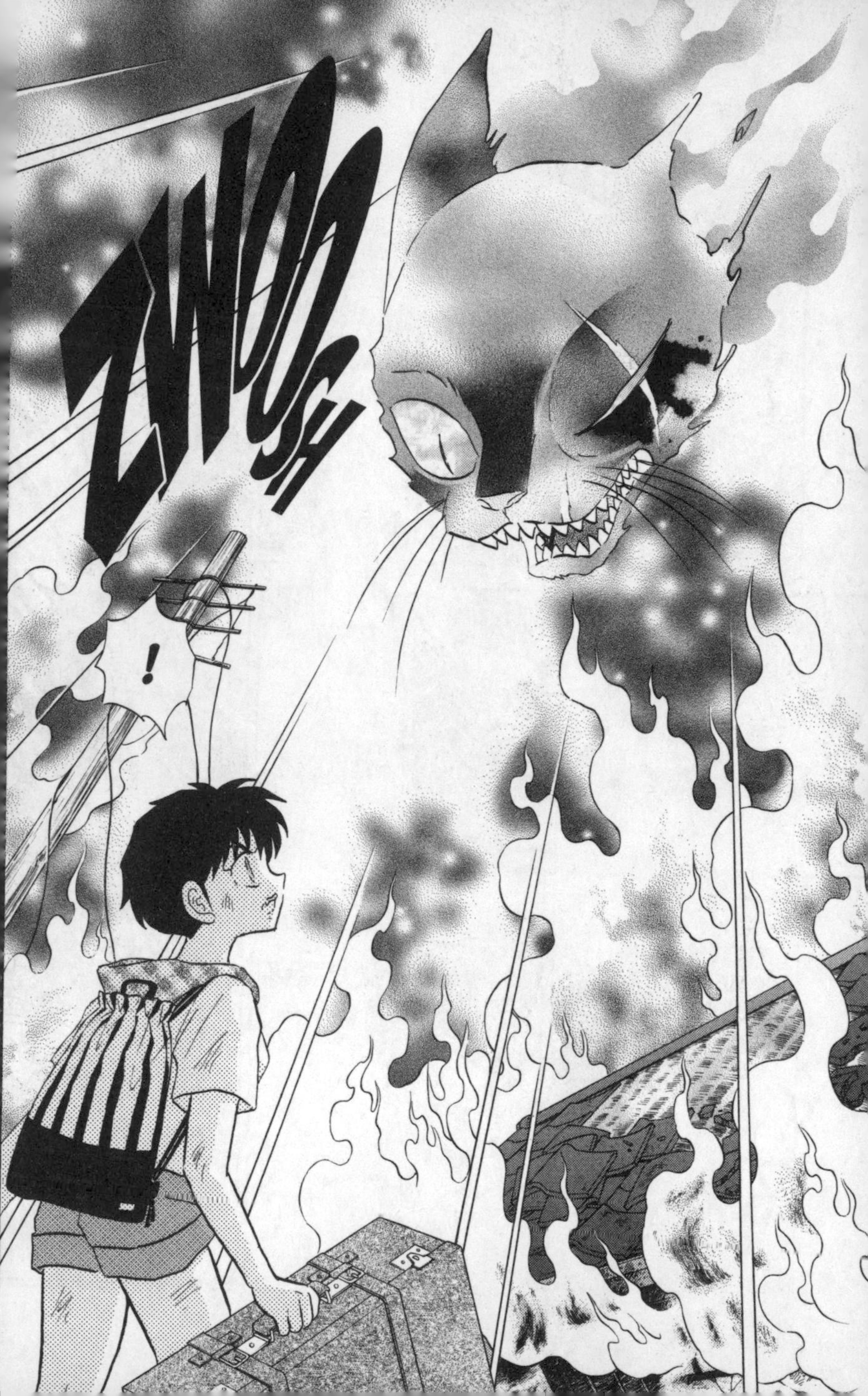
ZWOOSH
!

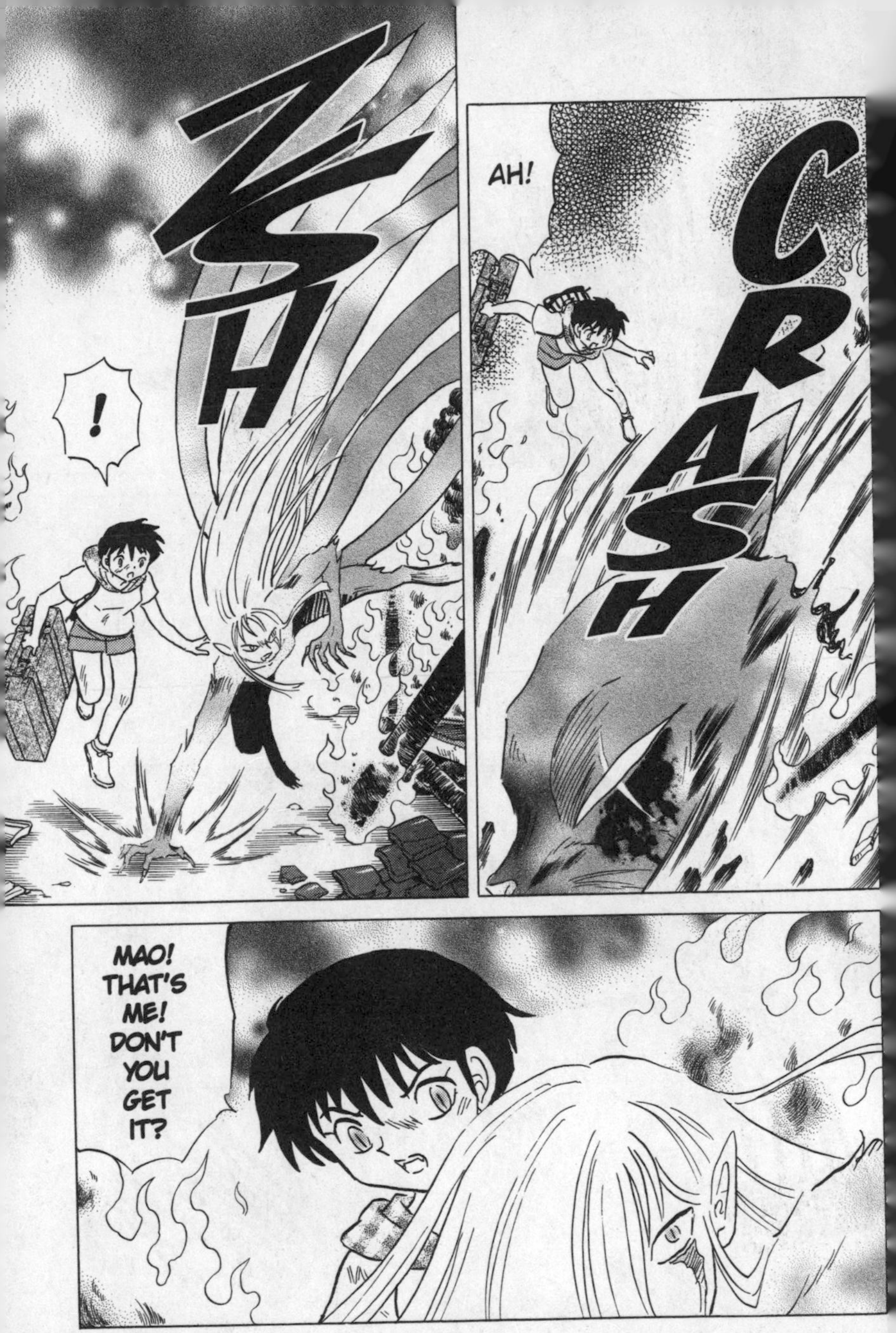
AH!
CRASH
ZSH
!
MAO! THAT'S ME! DON'T YOU GET IT?

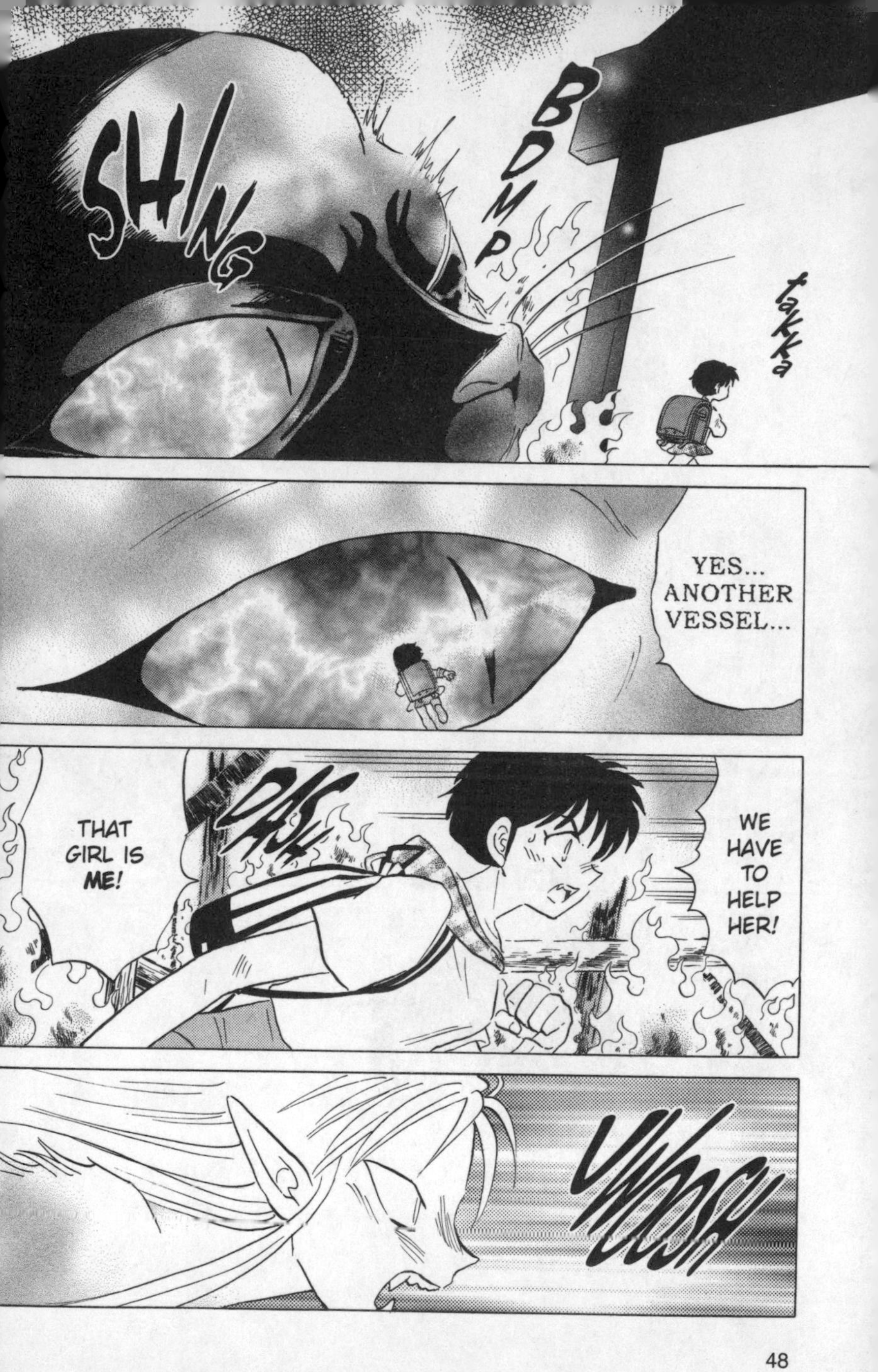
takka
BOMP
SHING
YES... ANOTHER VESSEL...
WE HAVE TO HELP HER!
DASH
THAT GIRL IS ME!
VWOSH

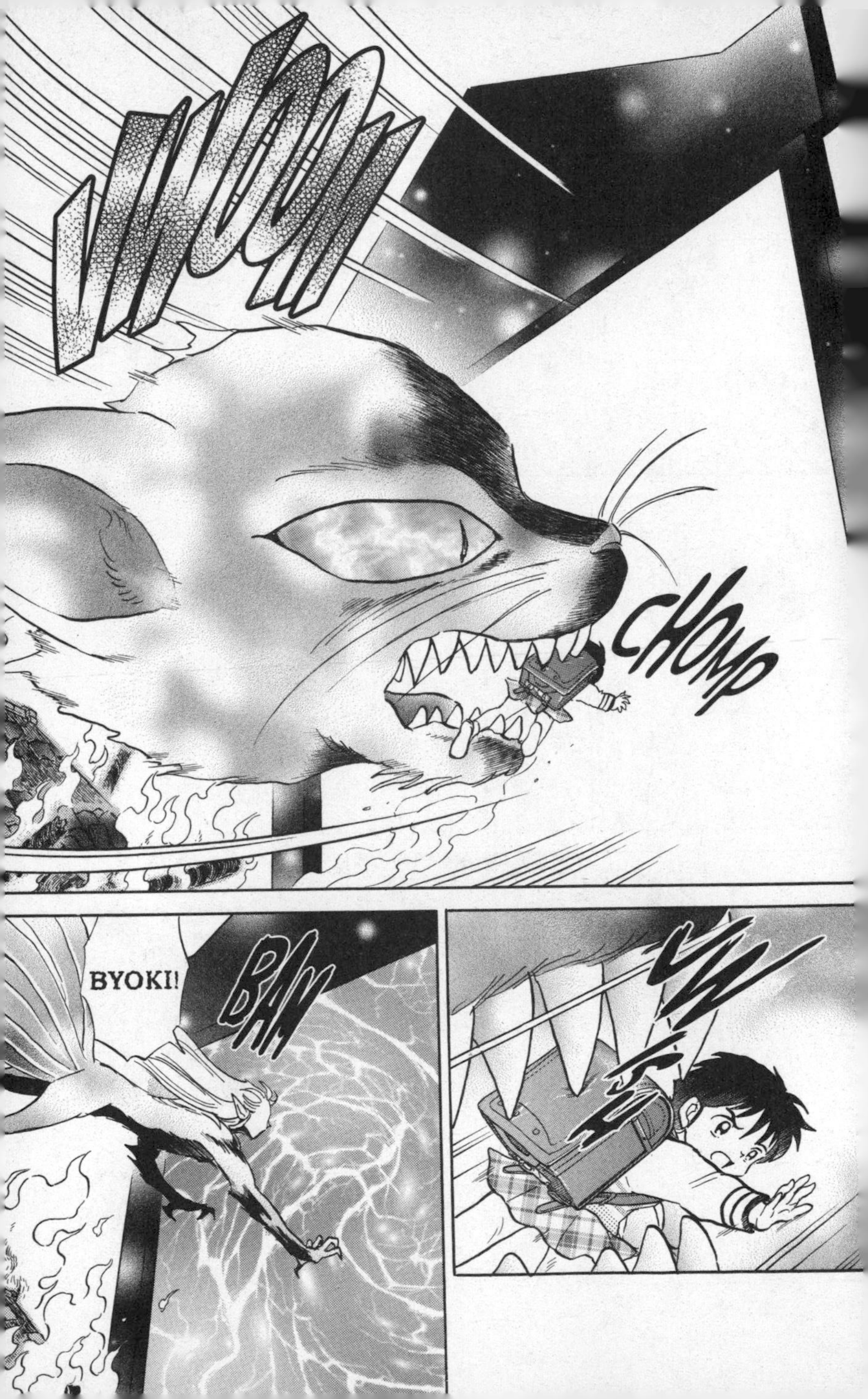
CHOMP
BYOKI!
BAM

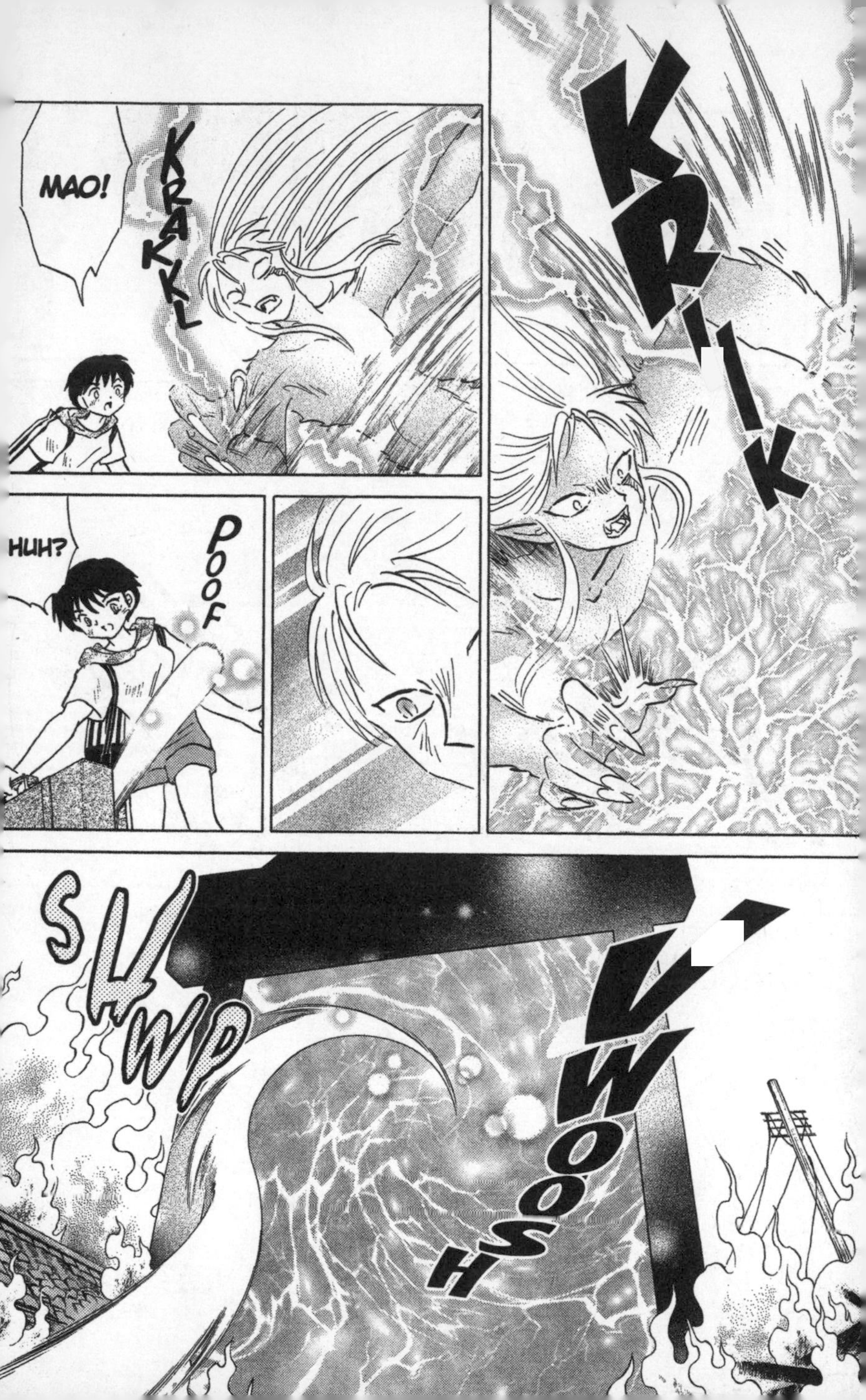
KRIIK
MAO!
KRAKKL
HUH?
POOF
VWOOSH
SHWP

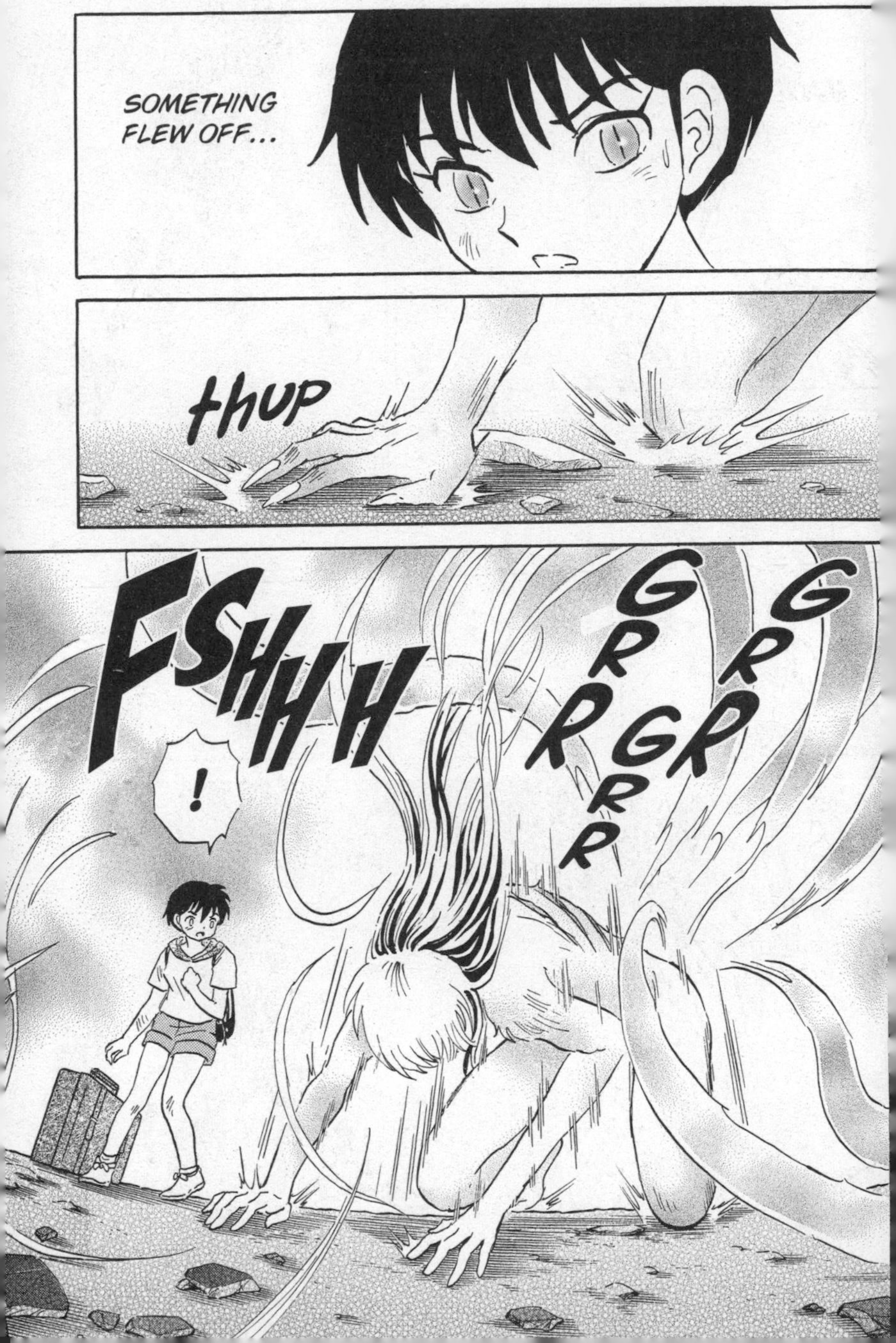
SOMETHING FLEW OFF...
thup
GRGRR
GRGRRR
FSHHH
!

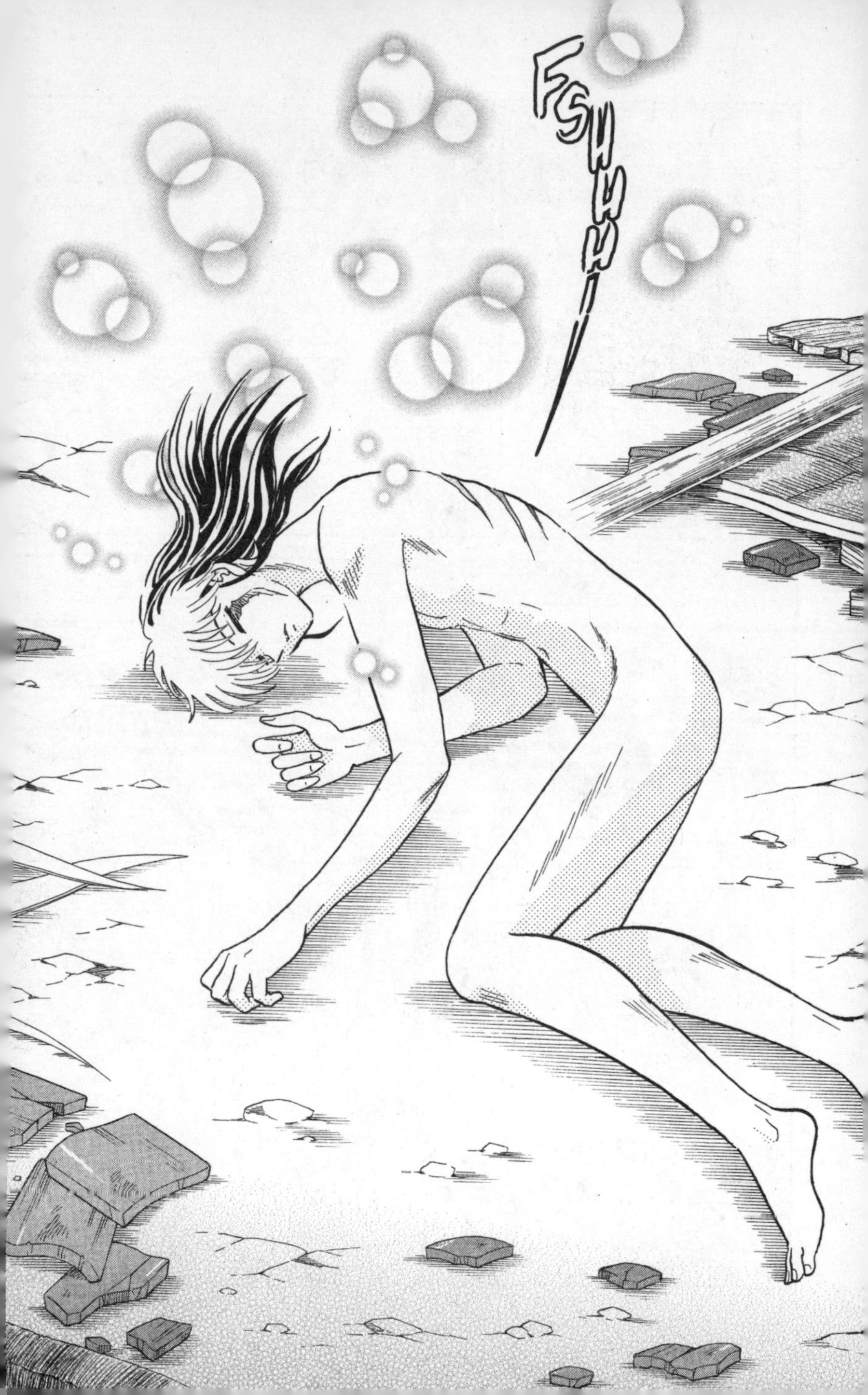
FSHHH

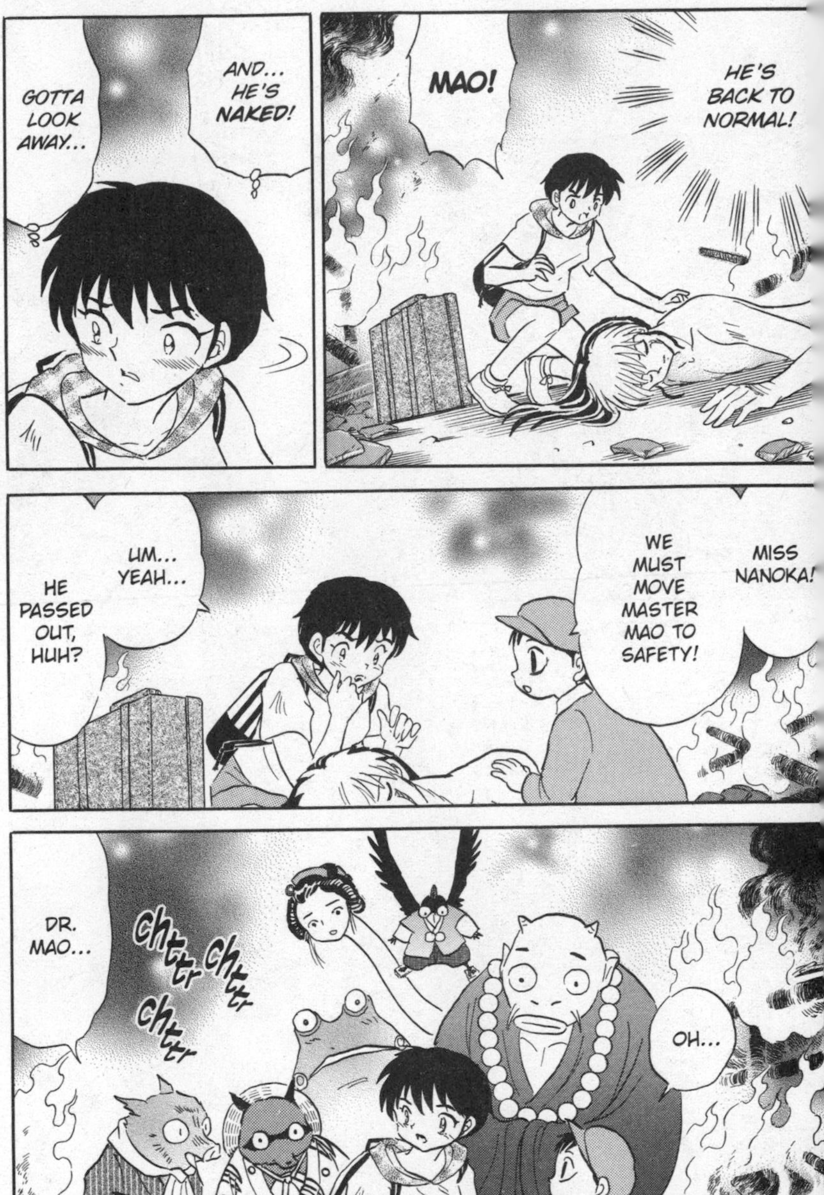
HE'S BACK TO NORMAL!
MAO!
AND... HE'S NAKED!
GOTTA LOOK AWAY...
MISS NANOKA!
WE MUST MOVE MASTER MAO TO SAFETY!
UM... YEAH...
HE PASSED OUT, HUH?
OH...
chttr chttr
chttr
DR. MAO...

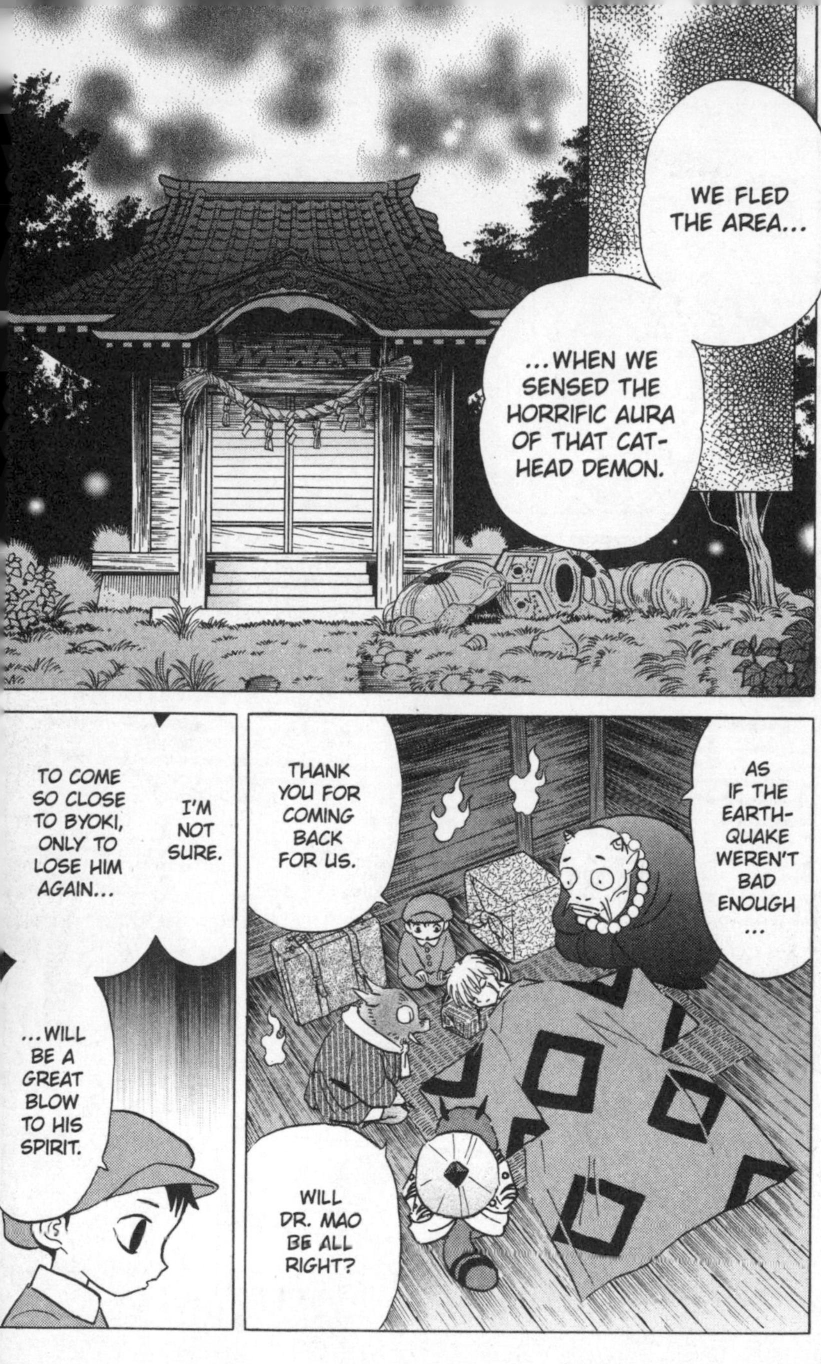
WE FLED THE AREA...
...WHEN WE SENSED THE HORRIFIC AURA OF THAT CAT-HEAD DEMON.
AS IF THE EARTH-QUAKE WEREN'T BAD ENOUGH...
THANK YOU FOR COMING BACK FOR US.
WILL DR. MAO BE ALL RIGHT?
I'M NOT SURE.
TO COME SO CLOSE TO BYOKI, ONLY TO LOSE HIM AGAIN...
...WILL BE A GREAT BLOW TO HIS SPIRIT.

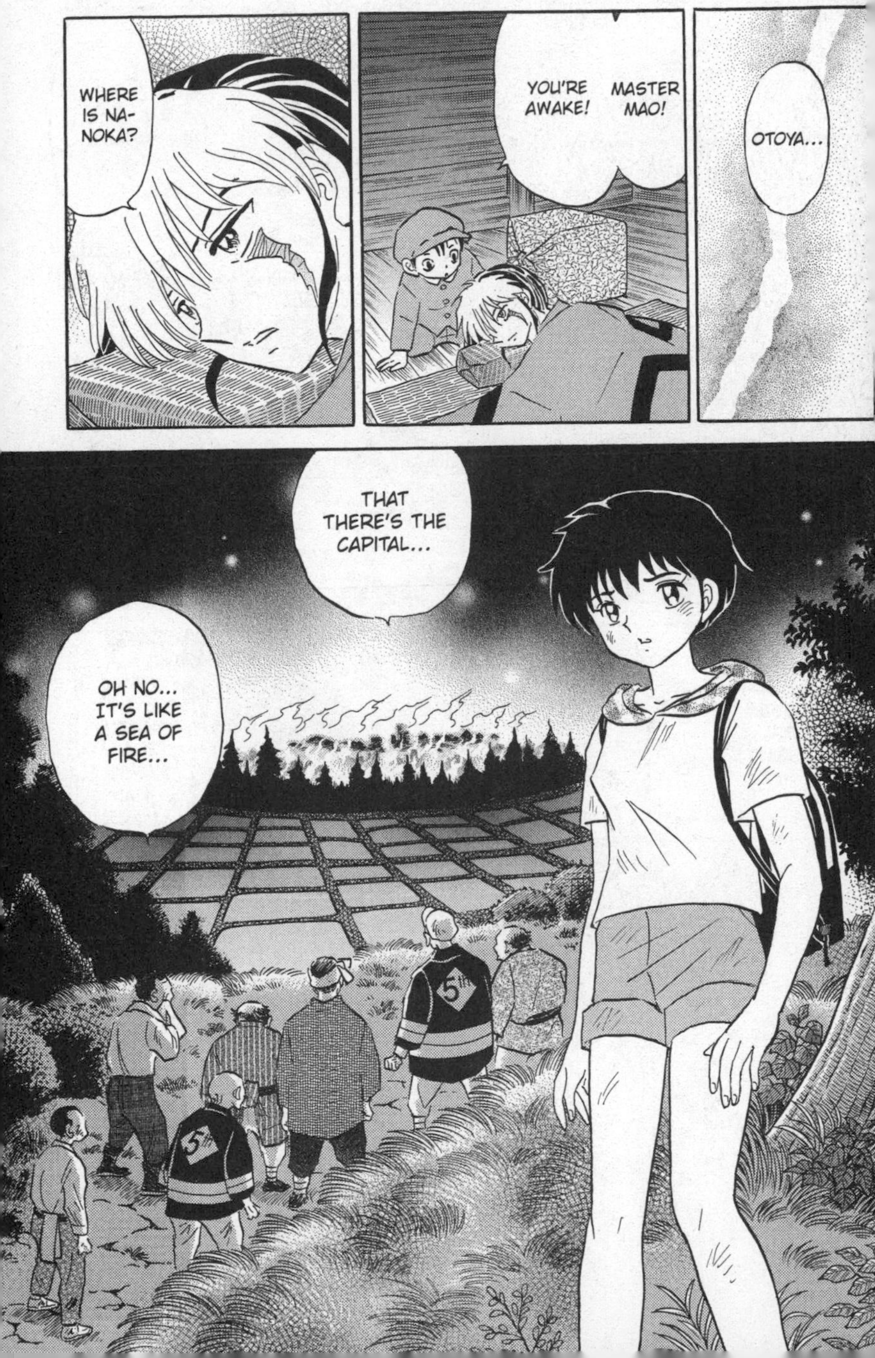
OTOYA...
MASTER MAO!
YOU'RE AWAKE!
WHERE IS NA-NOKA?
THAT THERE'S THE CAPITAL...
OH NO... IT'S LIKE A SEA OF FIRE...

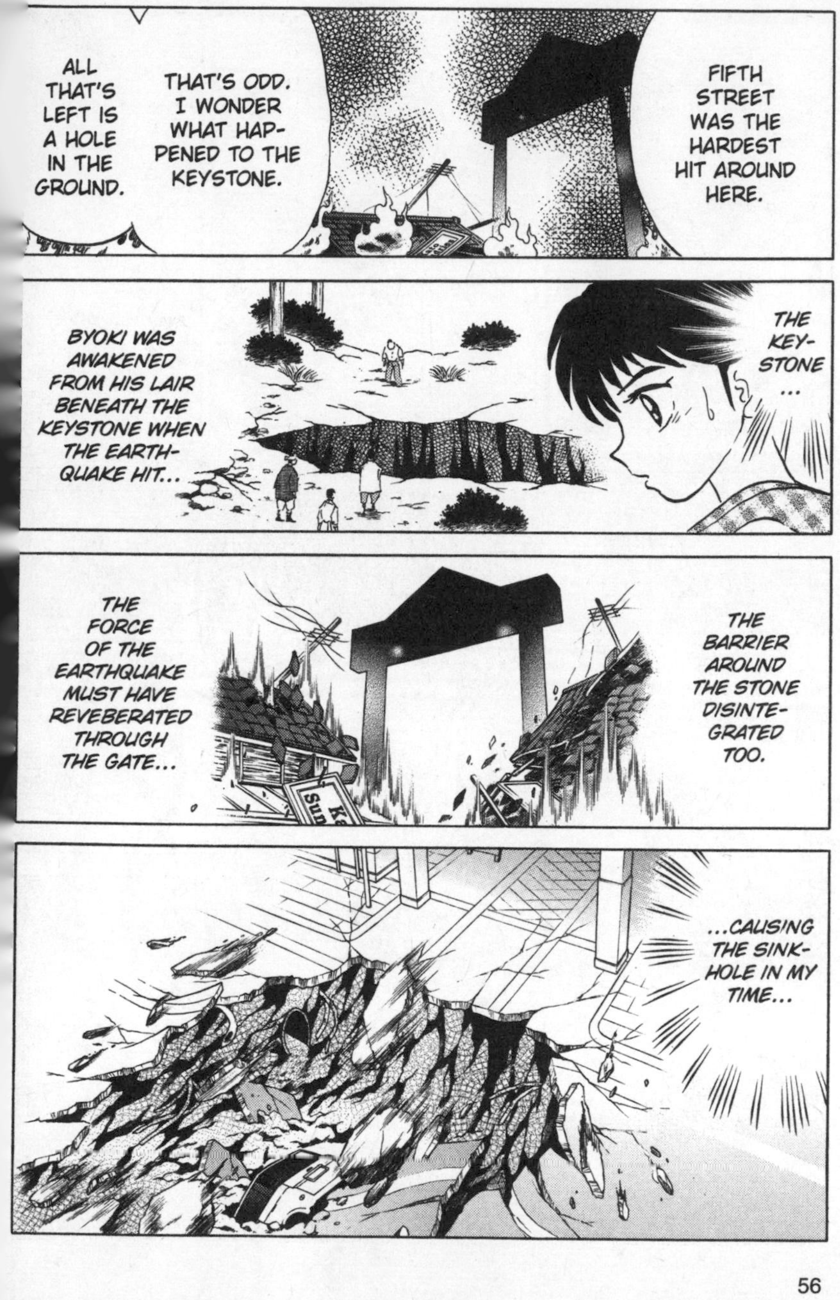
FIFTH STREET WAS THE HARDEST HIT AROUND HERE.
THAT'S ODD. I WONDER WHAT HAPPENED TO THE KEYSTONE.
ALL THAT'S LEFT IS A HOLE IN THE GROUND.
THE KEYSTONE...
BYOKI WAS AWAKENED FROM HIS LAIR BENEATH THE KEYSTONE WHEN THE EARTHQUAKE HIT...
THE BARRIER AROUND THE STONE DISINTEGRATED TOO.
THE FORCE OF THE EARTHQUAKE MUST HAVE REVEBERATED THROUGH THE GATE...
...CAUSING THE SINKHOLE IN MY TIME...

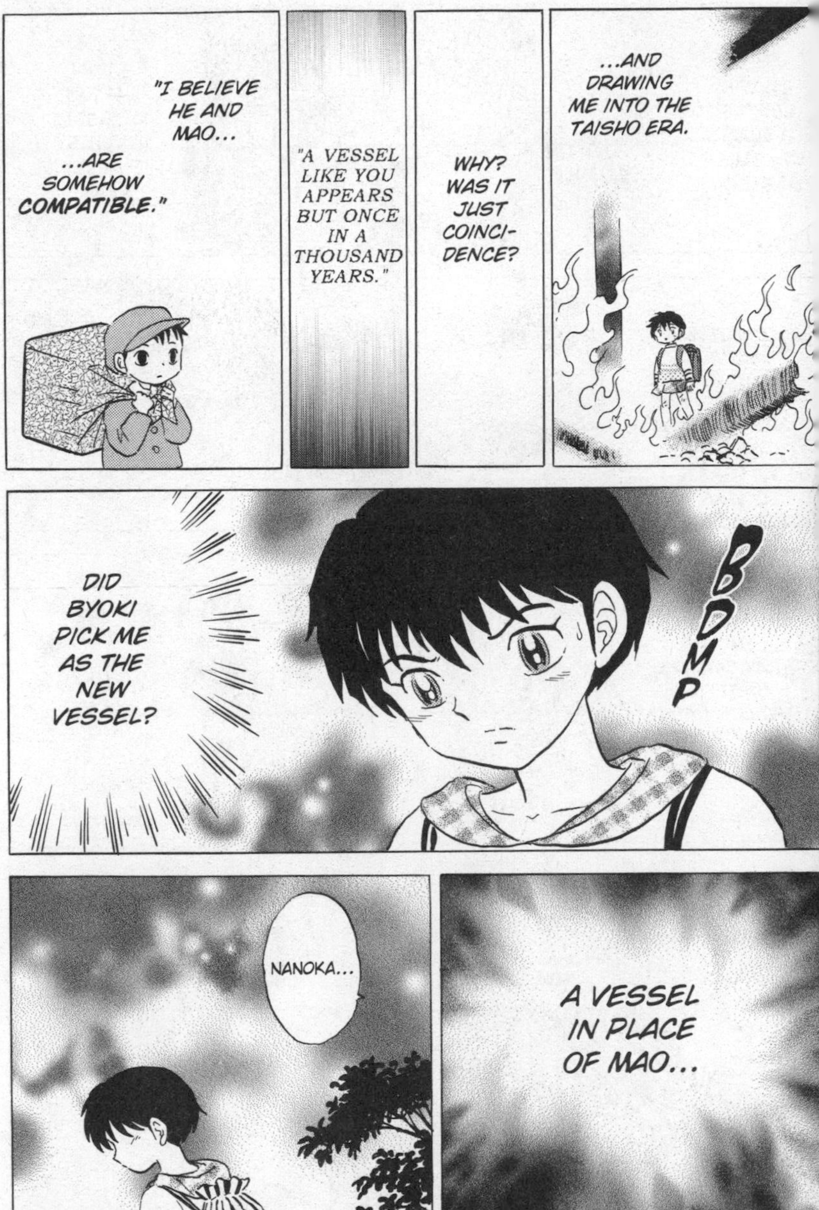
...AND DRAWING ME INTO THE TAISHO ERA.
WHY? WAS IT JUST COINCIDENCE?
"A VESSEL LIKE YOU APPEARS BUT ONCE IN A THOUSAND YEARS."
"I BELIEVE HE AND MAO...
...ARE SOMEHOW COMPATIBLE."
BDMP
DID BYOKI PICK ME AS THE NEW VESSEL?
A VESSEL IN PLACE OF MAO...
NANOKA...

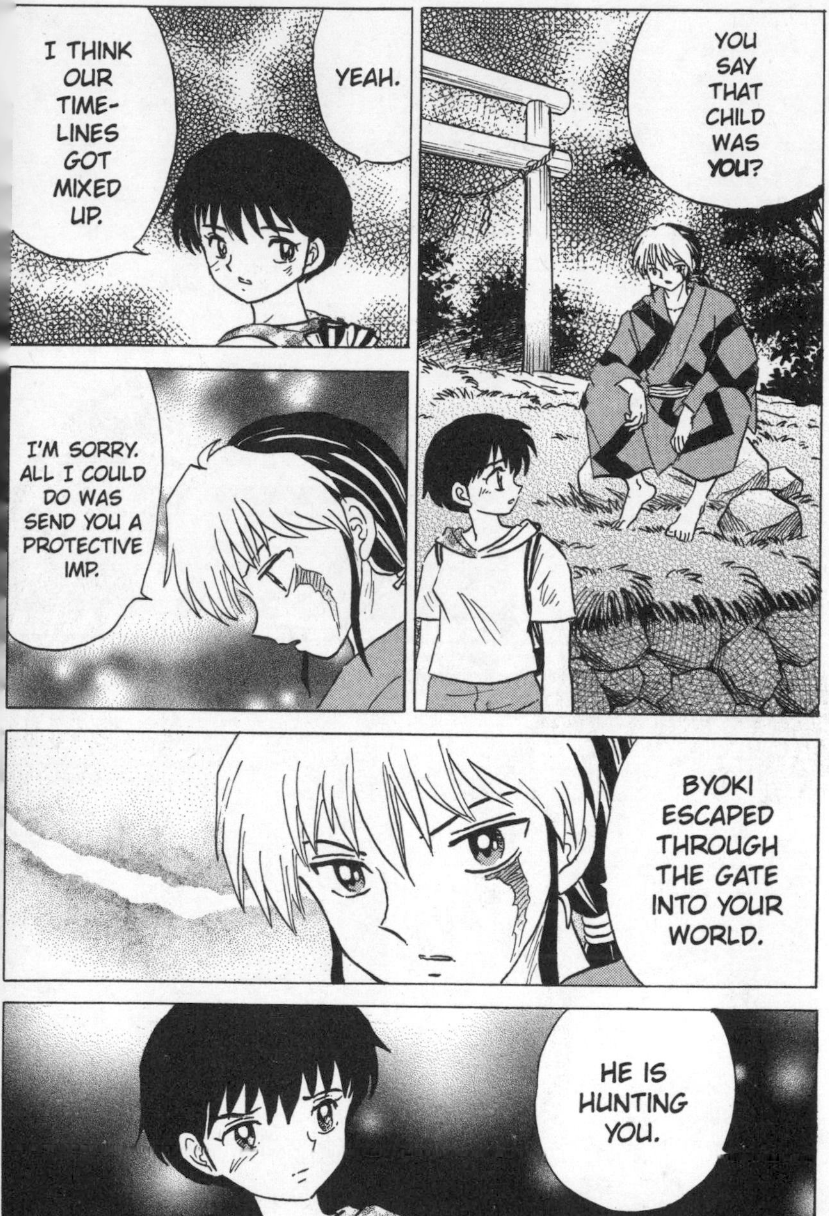
YOU SAY THAT CHILD WAS YOU?
YEAH.
I THINK OUR TIME-LINES GOT MIXED UP.
I'M SORRY. ALL I COULD DO WAS SEND YOU A PROTECTIVE IMP.
BYOKI ESCAPED THROUGH THE GATE INTO YOUR WORLD.
HE IS HUNTING YOU.

Chapter 4:
The Shikigami

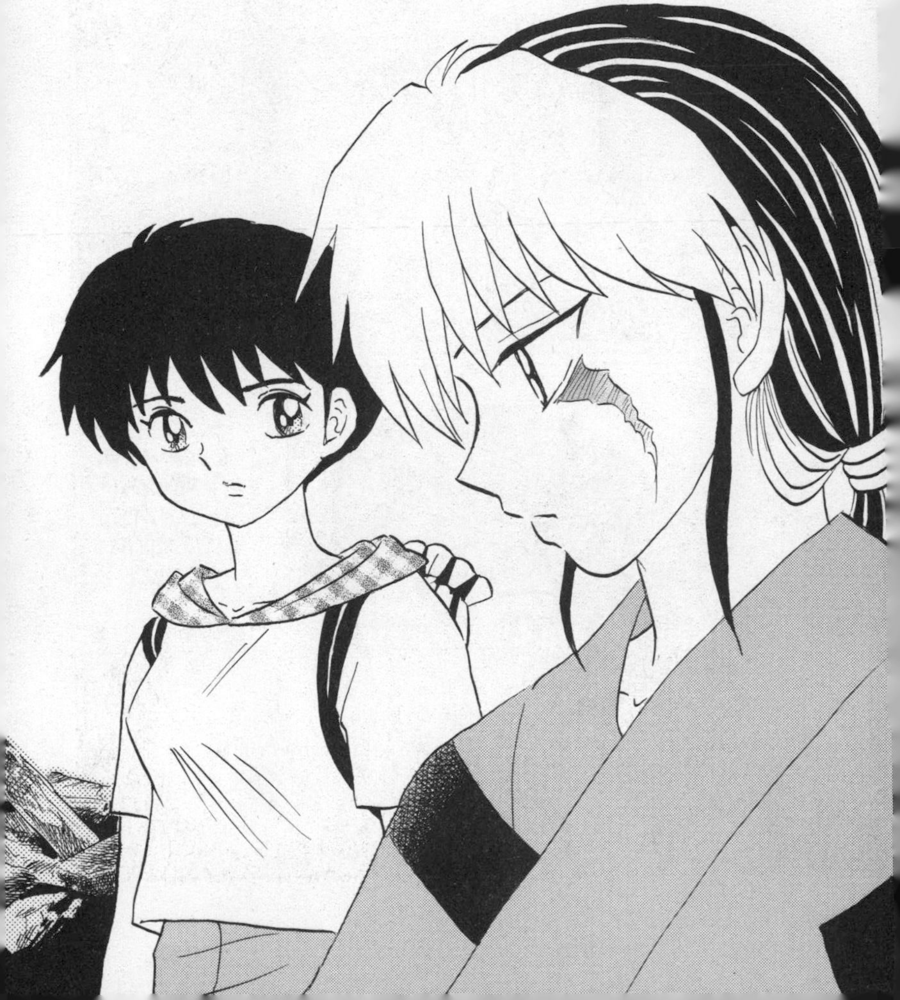

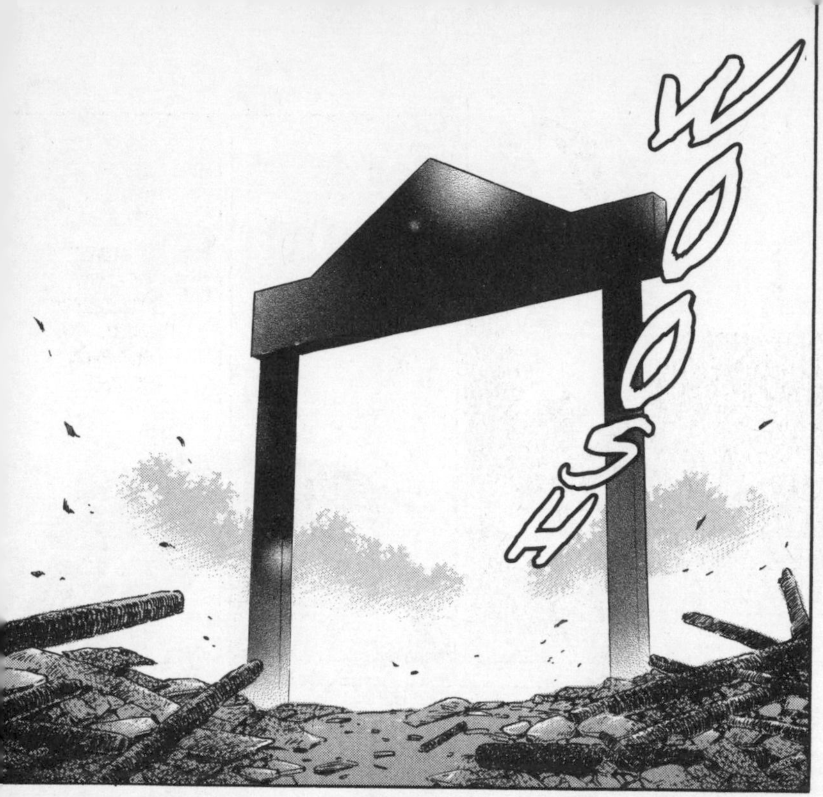
WOOOSH

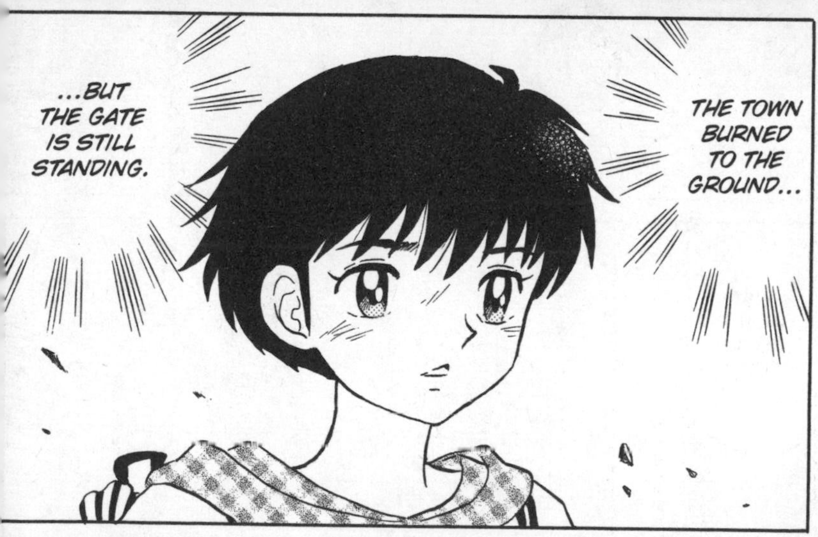
THE TOWN BURNED TO THE GROUND...
...BUT THE GATE IS STILL STANDING.

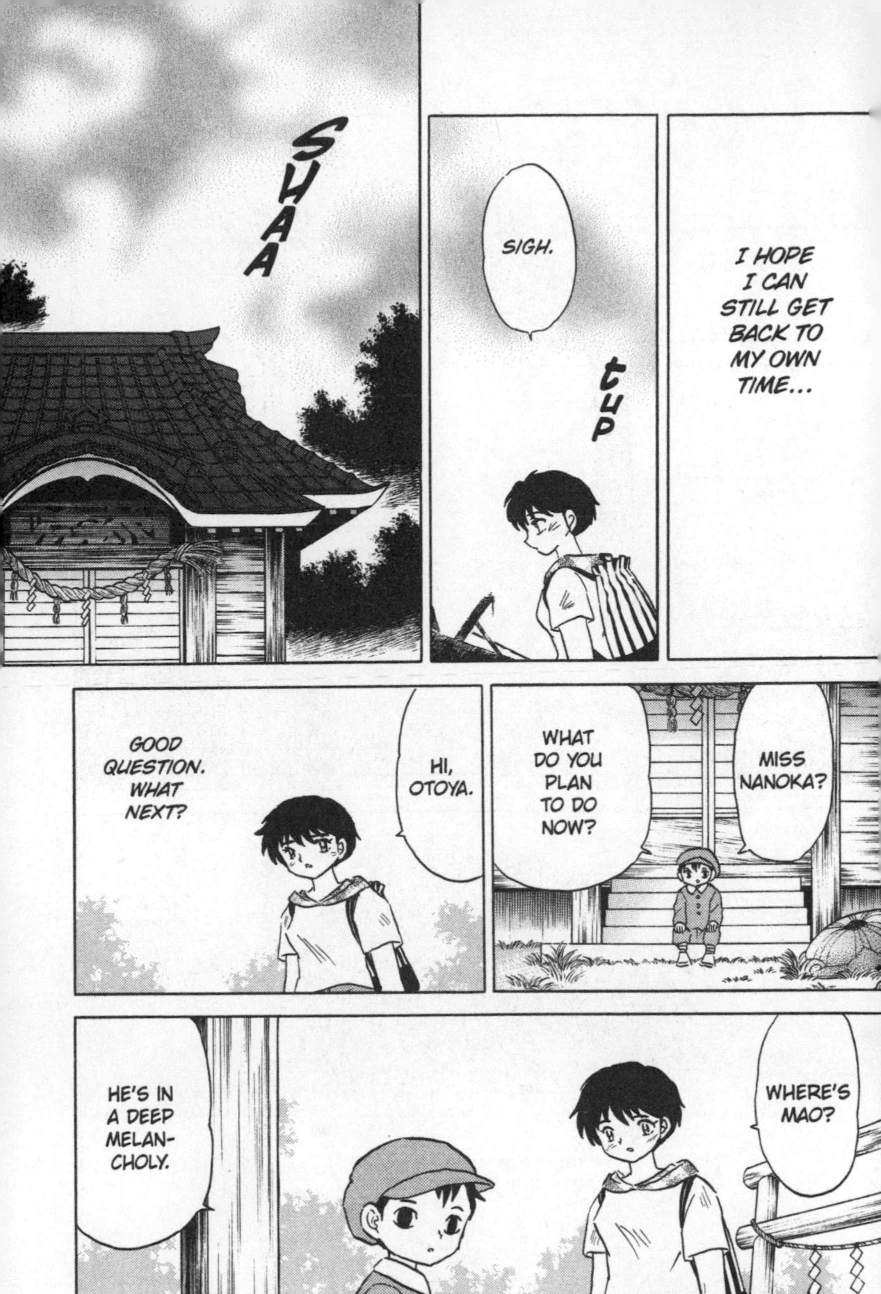
I HOPE I CAN STILL GET BACK TO MY OWN TIME...
SIGH.
tup
SHAA
MISS NANOKA?
WHAT DO YOU PLAN TO DO NOW?
HI, OTOYA.
GOOD QUESTION. WHAT NEXT?
WHERE'S MAO?
HE'S IN A DEEP MELAN-CHOLY.

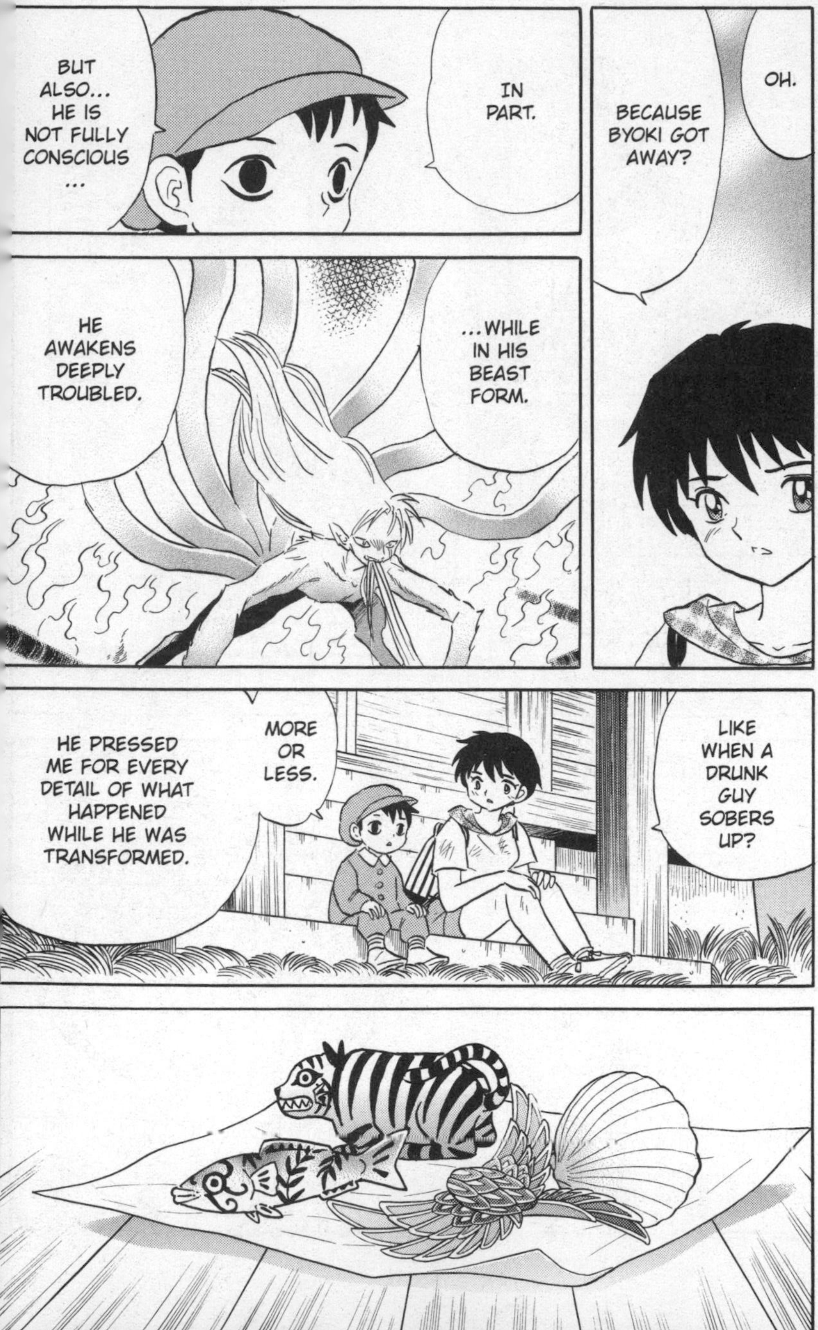
OH.
BECAUSE BYOKI GOT AWAY?
IN PART.
BUT ALSO... HE IS NOT FULLY CONSCIOUS ...
...WHILE IN HIS BEAST FORM.
HE AWAKENS DEEPLY TROUBLED.
LIKE WHEN A DRUNK GUY SOBERS UP?
MORE OR LESS.
HE PRESSED ME FOR EVERY DETAIL OF WHAT HAPPENED WHILE HE WAS TRANSFORMED.

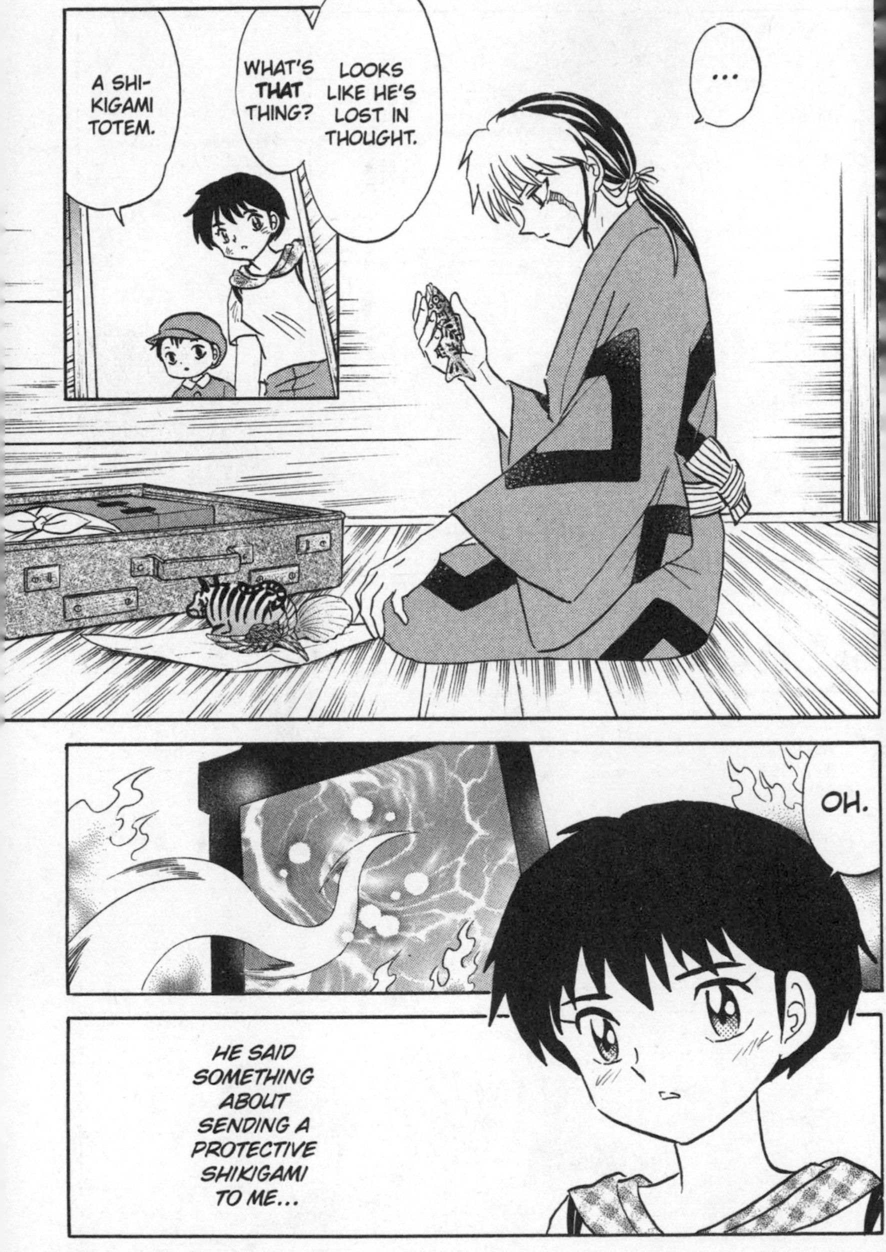
...
LOOKS LIKE HE'S LOST IN THOUGHT.
WHAT'S THAT THING?
A SHI-KIGAMI TOTEM.
OH.
HE SAID SOMETHING ABOUT SENDING A PROTECTIVE SHIKIGAMI TO ME...

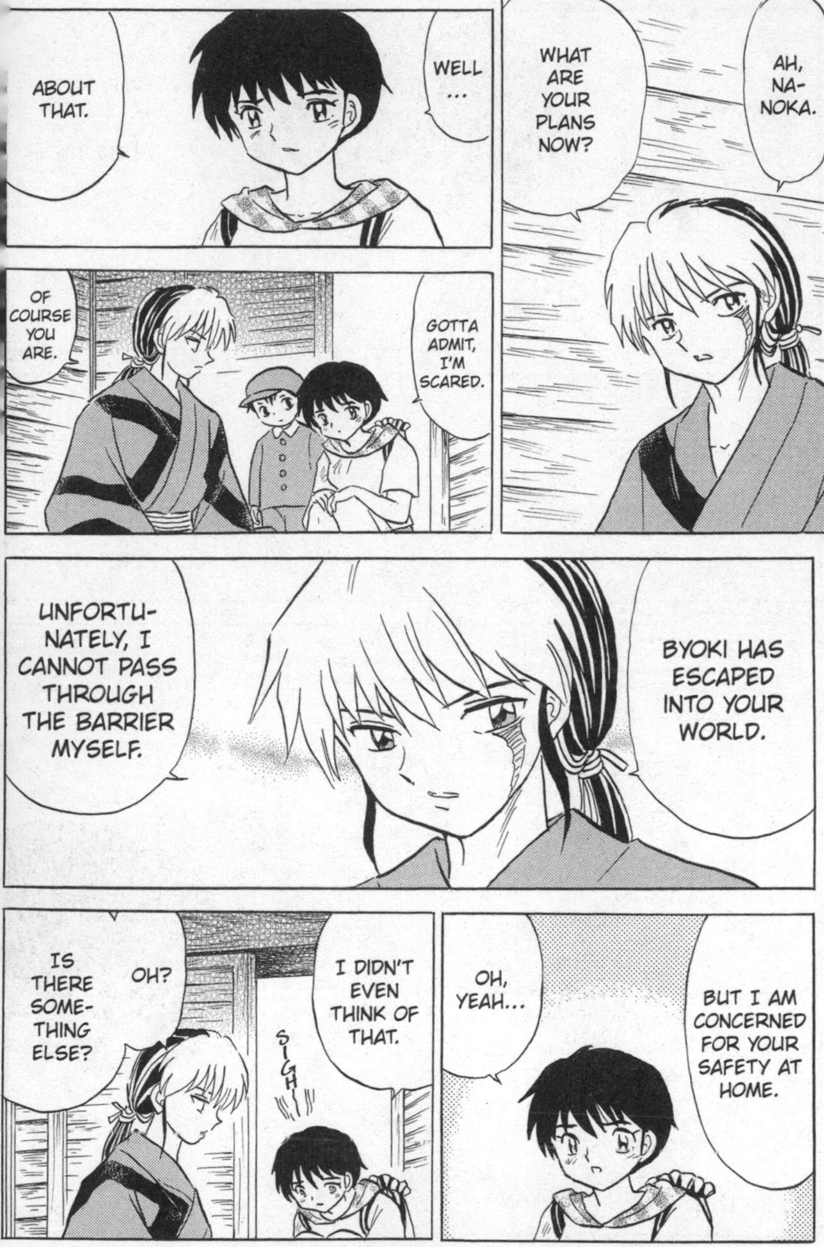
AH, NA-NOKA.
WHAT ARE YOUR PLANS NOW?
WELL...
ABOUT THAT.
GOTTA ADMIT, I'M SCARED.
OF COURSE YOU ARE.
BYOKI HAS ESCAPED INTO YOUR WORLD.
UNFORTUNATELY, I CANNOT PASS THROUGH THE BARRIER MYSELF.
BUT I AM CONCERNED FOR YOUR SAFETY AT HOME.
OH, YEAH...
I DIDN'T EVEN THINK OF THAT.
SIGH
OH?
IS THERE SOMETHING ELSE?

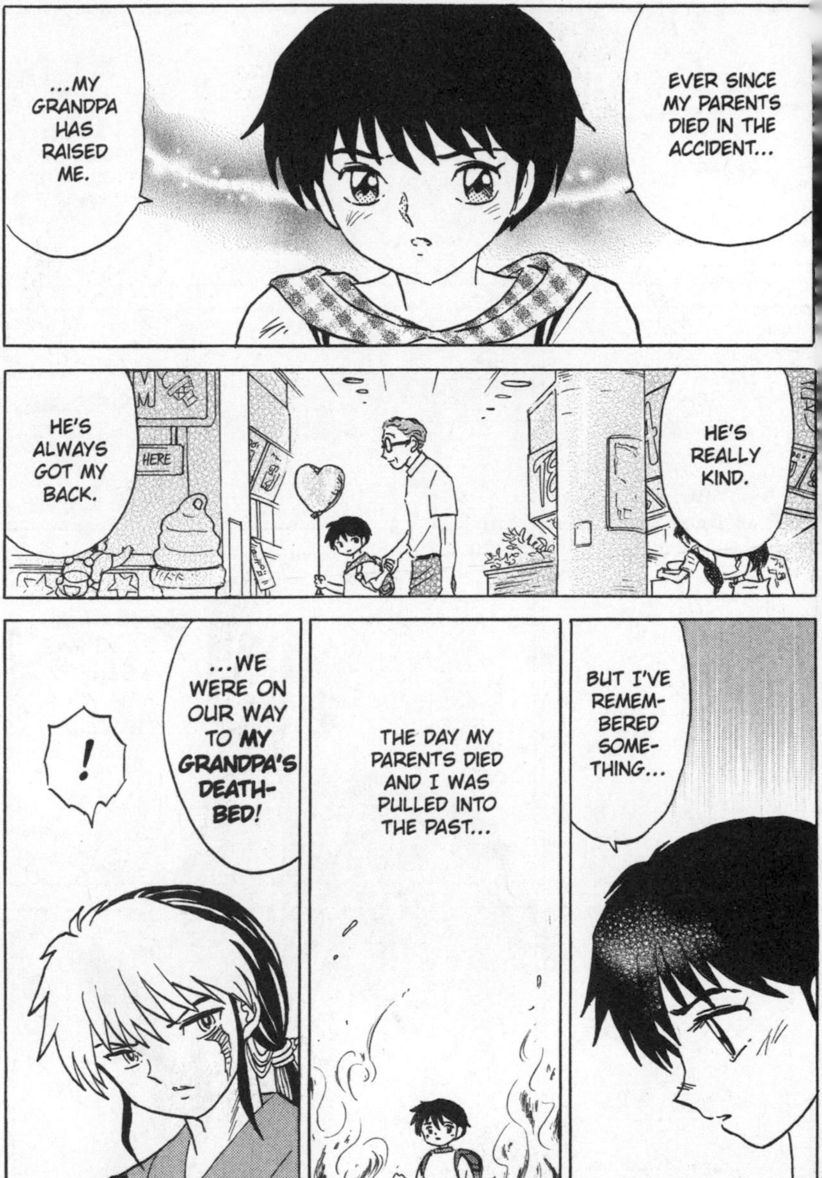
EVER SINCE MY PARENTS DIED IN THE ACCIDENT...
...MY GRANDPA HAS RAISED ME.
HE'S REALLY KIND.
HE'S ALWAYS GOT MY BACK.
HERE
BUT I'VE REMEM-BERED SOME-THING...
THE DAY MY PARENTS DIED AND I WAS PULLED INTO THE PAST...
...WE WERE ON OUR WAY TO **MY GRANDPA'S DEATH-BED!**
!

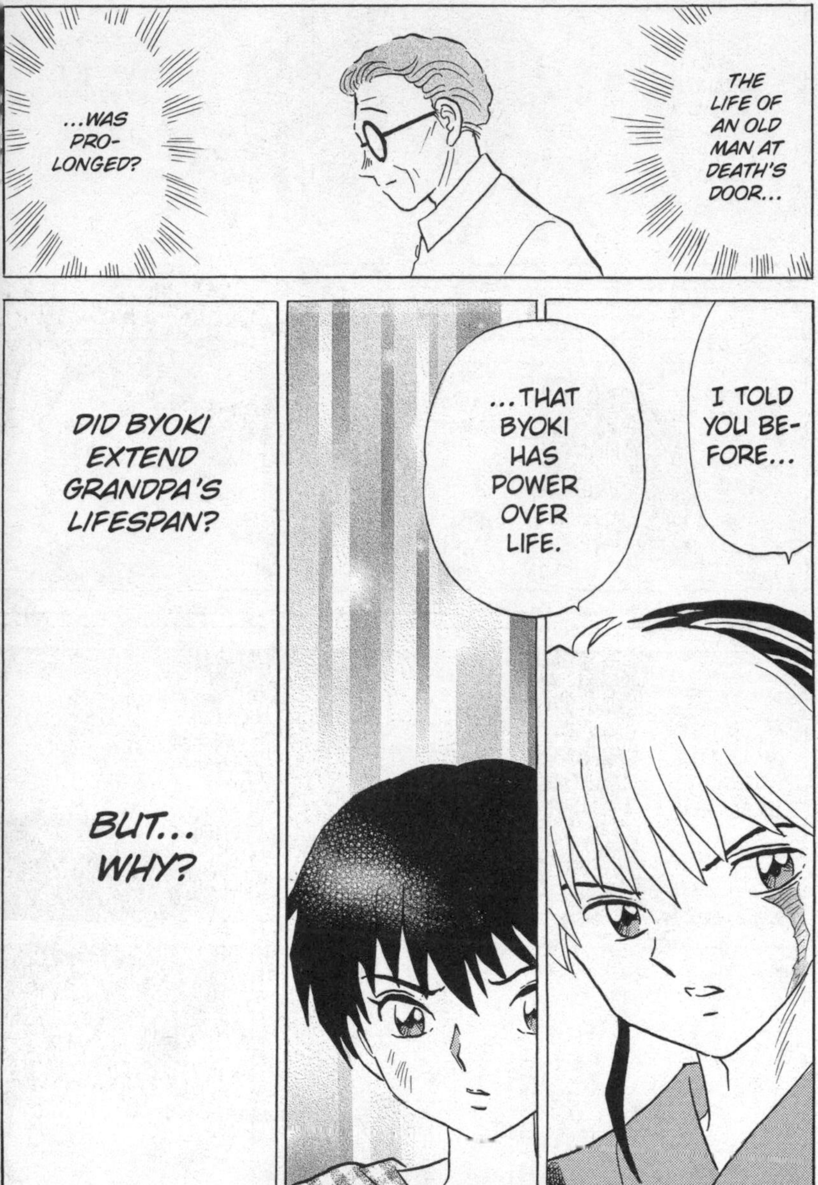
THE LIFE OF AN OLD MAN AT DEATH'S DOOR...
...WAS PRO-LONGED?
I TOLD YOU BE-FORE...
...THAT BYOKI HAS POWER OVER LIFE.
DID BYOKI EXTEND GRANDPA'S LIFESPAN?
BUT... WHY?

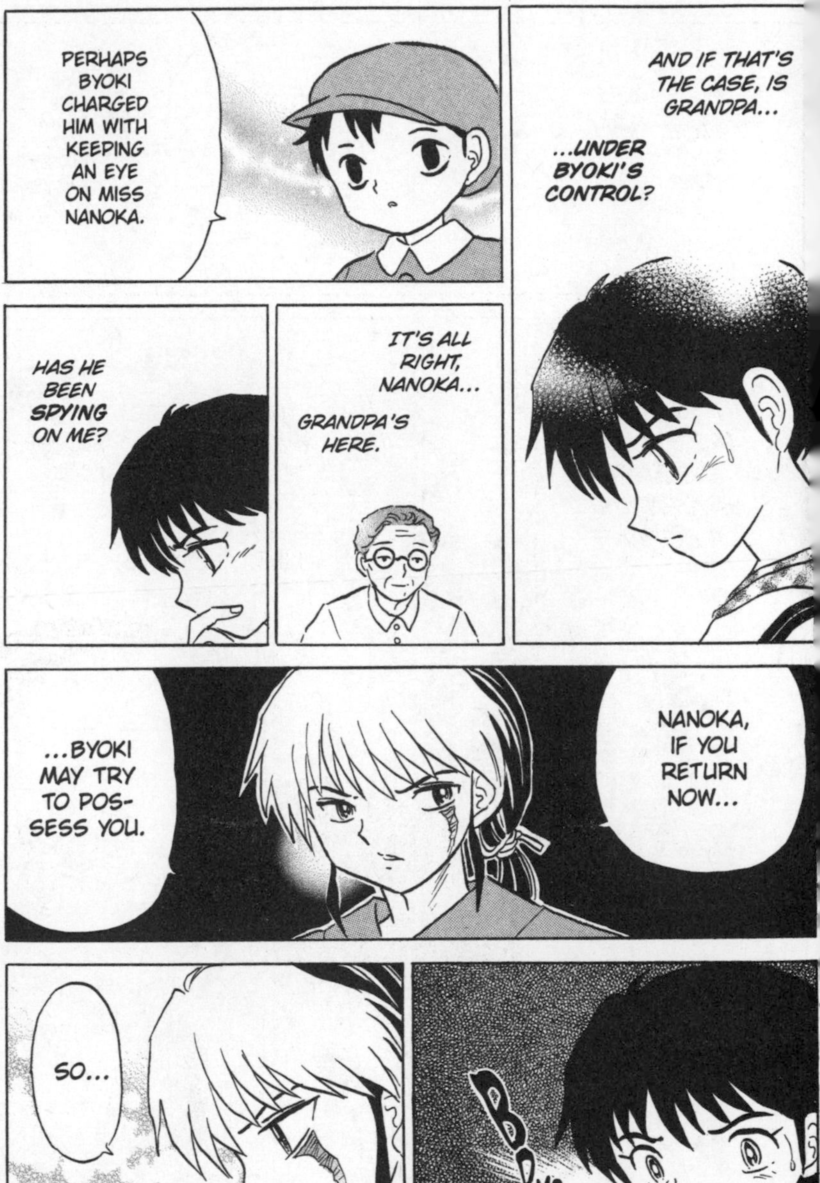
AND IF THAT'S THE CASE, IS GRANDPA...
...UNDER BYOKI'S CONTROL?
PERHAPS BYOKI CHARGED HIM WITH KEEPING AN EYE ON MISS NANOKA.
IT'S ALL RIGHT, NANOKA...
GRANDPA'S HERE.
HAS HE BEEN SPYING ON ME?
NANOKA, IF YOU RETURN NOW...
...BYOKI MAY TRY TO POS-SESS YOU.
BADOMP
SO...

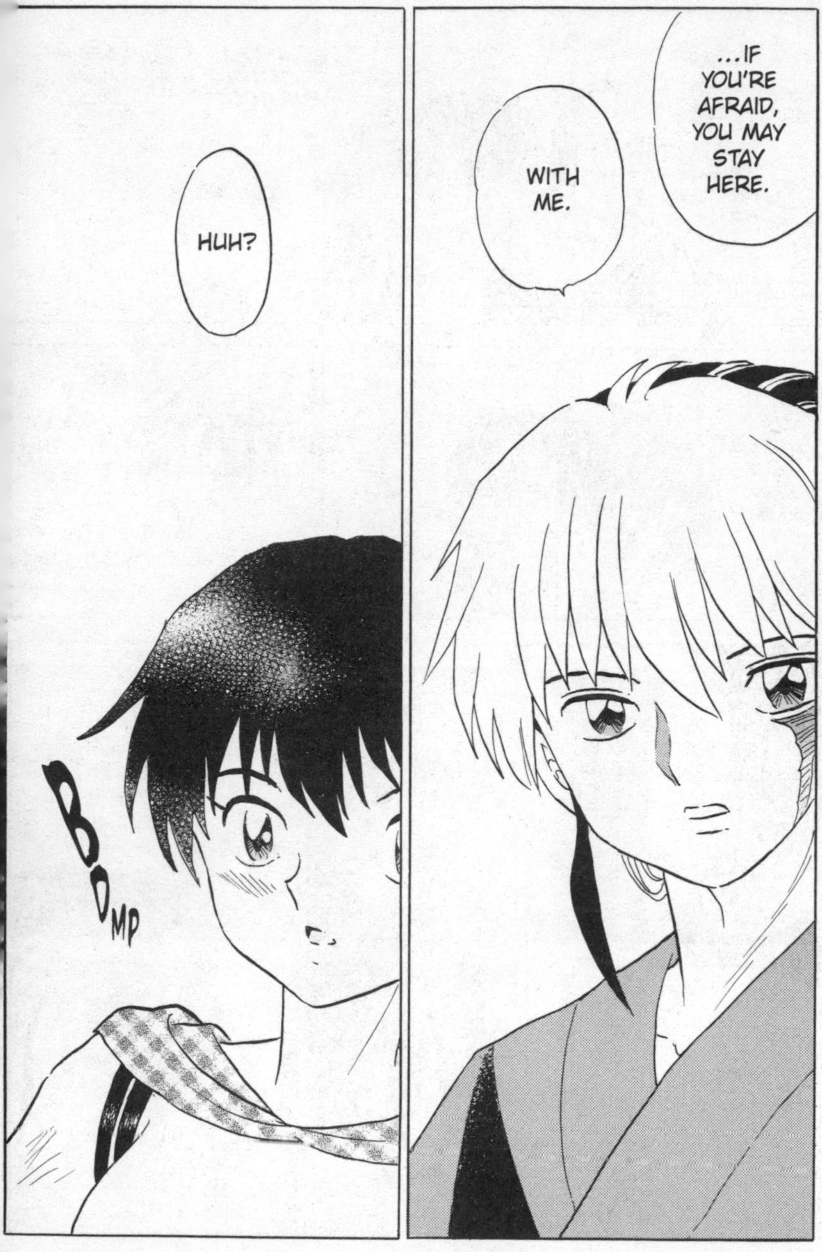
...IF YOU'RE AFRAID, YOU MAY STAY HERE.
WITH ME.
HUH?
BOOMP

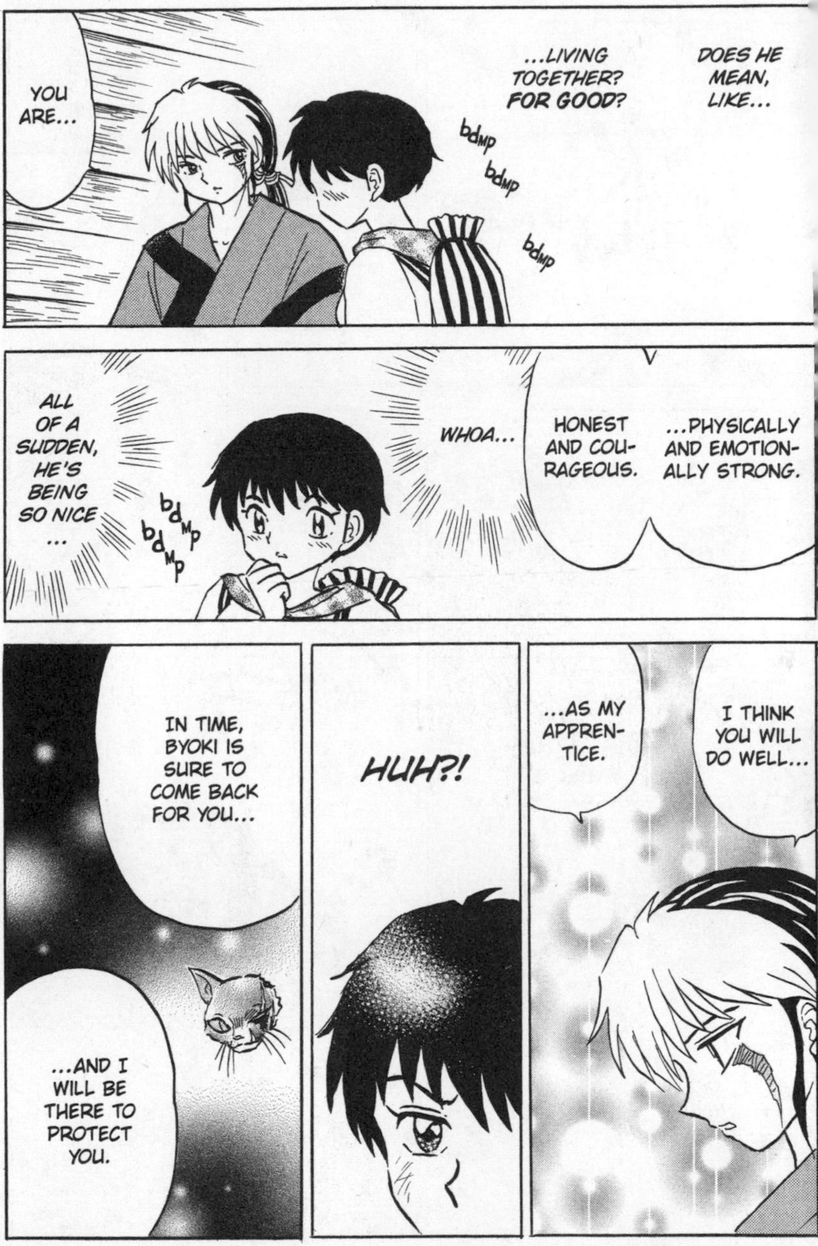
DOES HE MEAN, LIKE...
...LIVING TOGETHER? FOR GOOD?
bdmp
bdmp
bdmp
YOU ARE...
...PHYSICALLY AND EMOTIONALLY STRONG.
HONEST AND COURAGEOUS.
WHOA...
bdmp
bdmp
ALL OF A SUDDEN, HE'S BEING SO NICE...
I THINK YOU WILL DO WELL...
...AS MY APPRENTICE.
HUH?!
IN TIME, BYOKI IS SURE TO COME BACK FOR YOU...
...AND I WILL BE THERE TO PROTECT YOU.

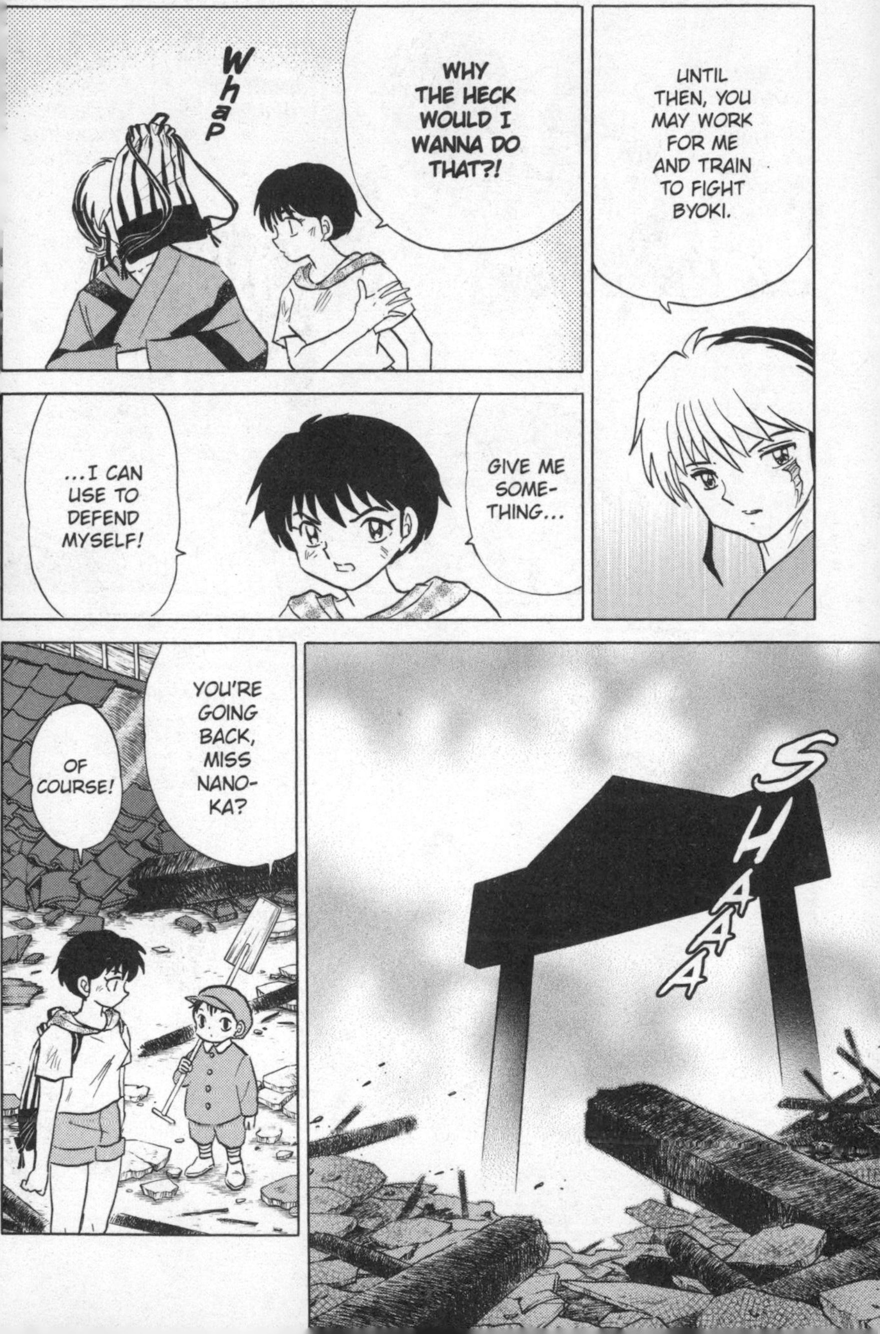
UNTIL THEN, YOU MAY WORK FOR ME AND TRAIN TO FIGHT BYOKI.
WHY THE HECK WOULD I WANNA DO THAT?!
Whap
GIVE ME SOME-THING...
...I CAN USE TO DEFEND MYSELF!
SHAAAA
YOU'RE GOING BACK, MISS NANO-KA?
OF COURSE!

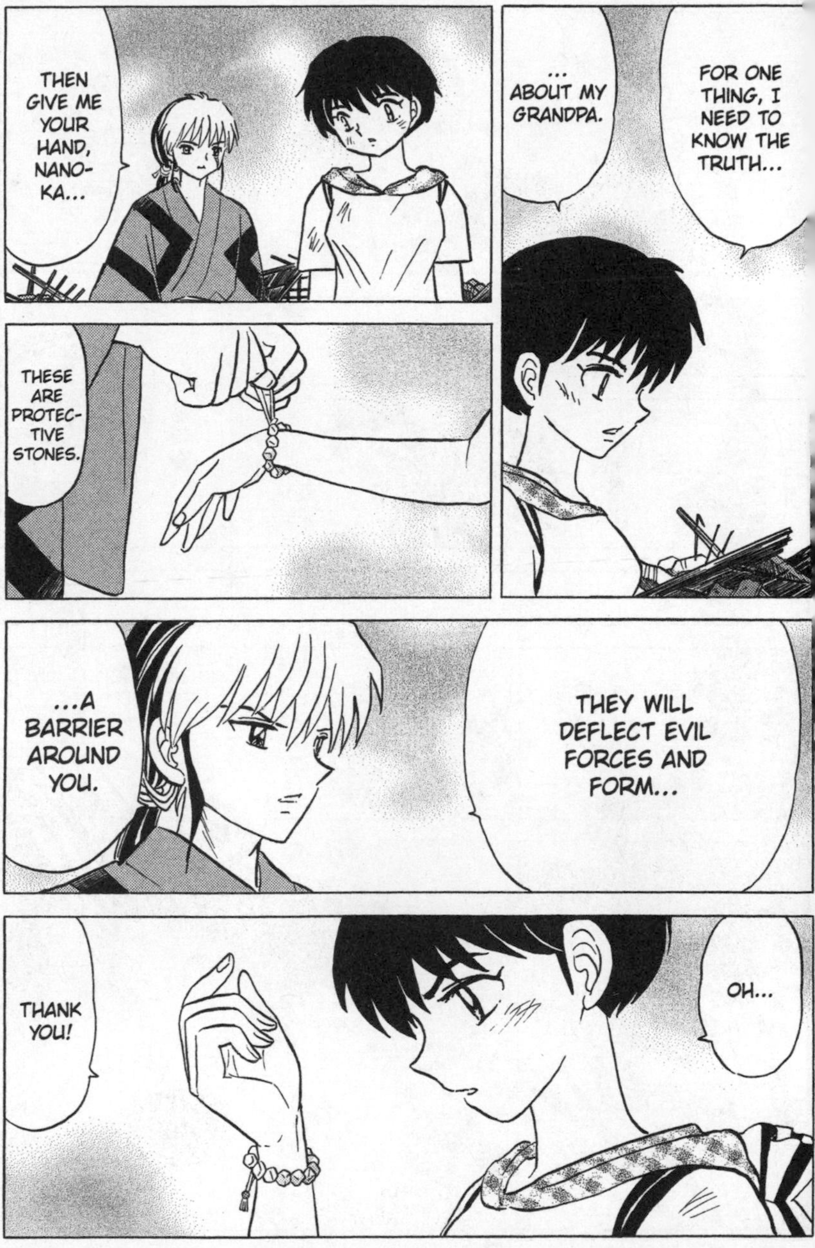
FOR ONE THING, I NEED TO KNOW THE TRUTH...
... ABOUT MY GRANDPA.
THEN GIVE ME YOUR HAND, NANO-KA...
THESE ARE PROTEC-TIVE STONES.
THEY WILL DEFLECT EVIL FORCES AND FORM...
...A BARRIER AROUND YOU.
OH...
THANK YOU!

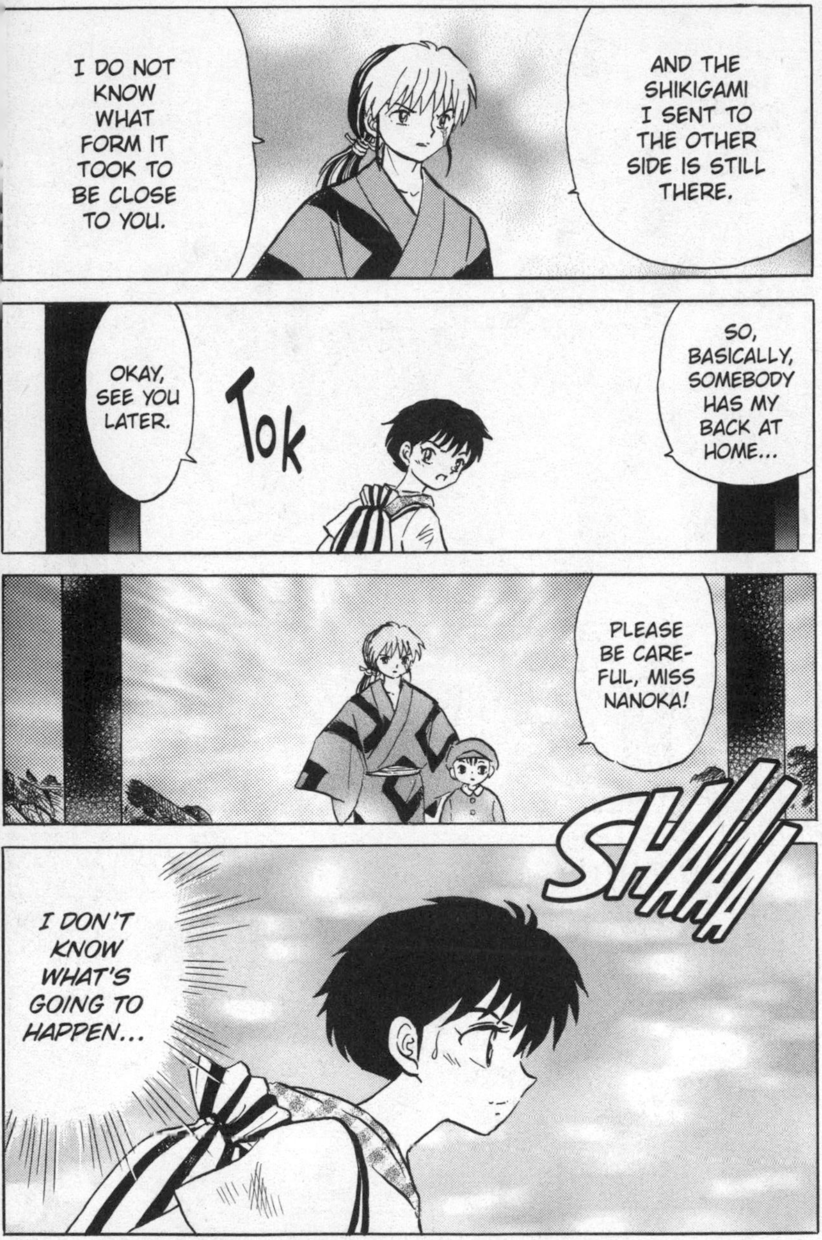
AND THE SHIKIGAMI I SENT TO THE OTHER SIDE IS STILL THERE.
I DO NOT KNOW WHAT FORM IT TOOK TO BE CLOSE TO YOU.
SO, BASICALLY, SOMEBODY HAS MY BACK AT HOME...
TOK
OKAY, SEE YOU LATER.
PLEASE BE CARE-FUL, MISS NANOKA!
SHAAA
I DON'T KNOW WHAT'S GOING TO HAPPEN...

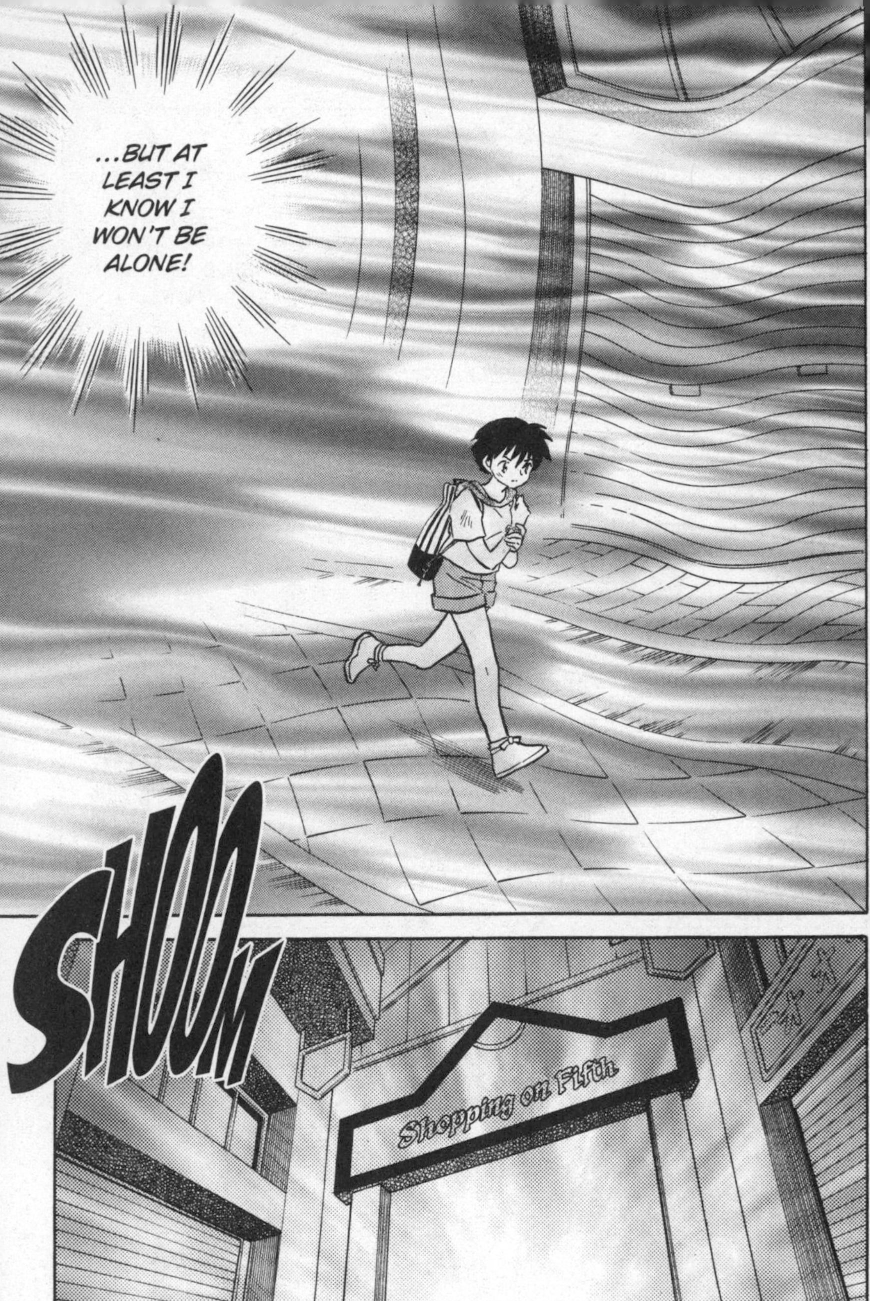
...BUT AT LEAST I KNOW I WON'T BE ALONE!
SHOOM
Shopping on Fifth

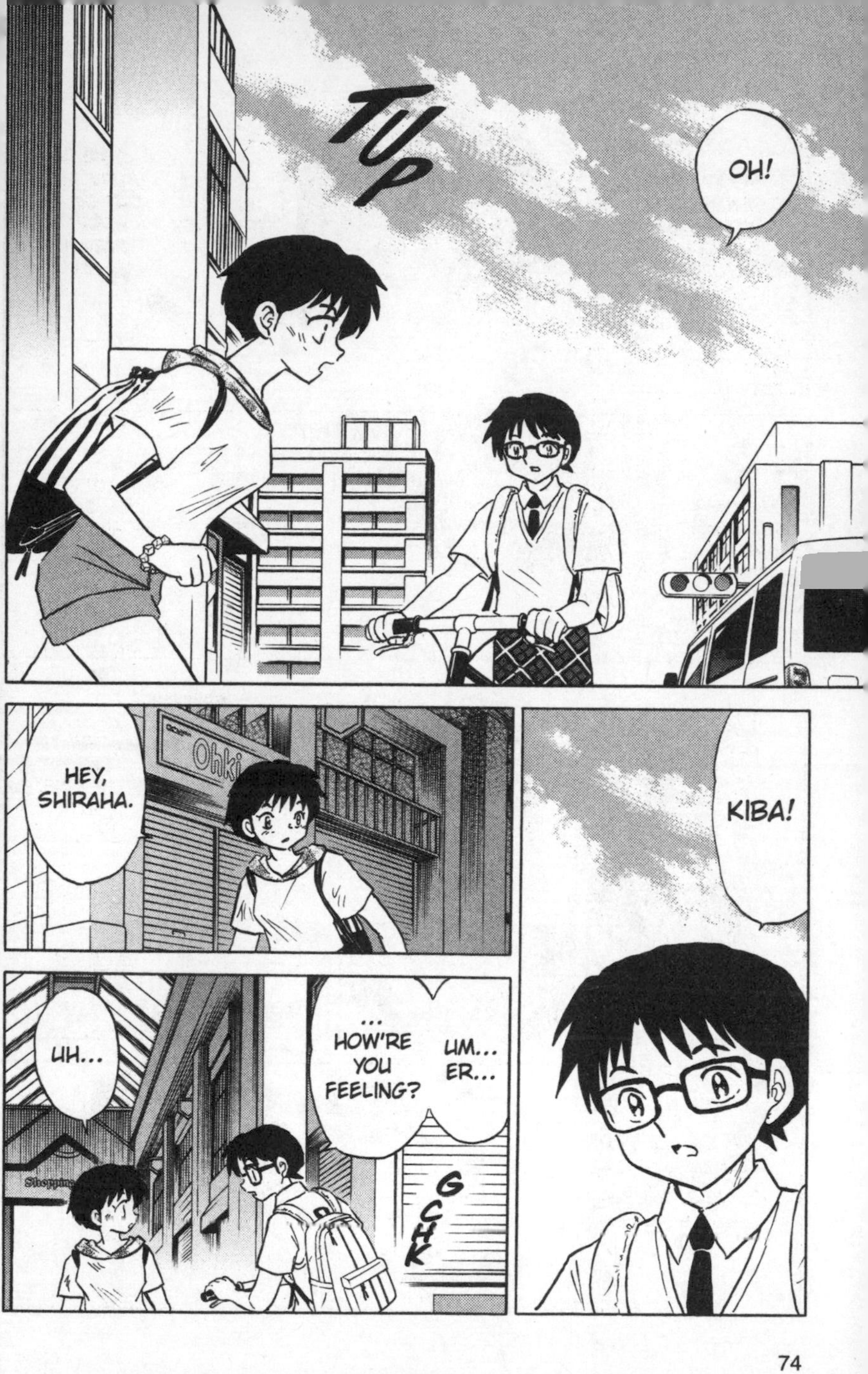
OH!
TUP
KIBA!
Ohki
HEY, SHIRAHA.
UM... ER...
... HOW'RE YOU FEELING?
UH...
GCHK

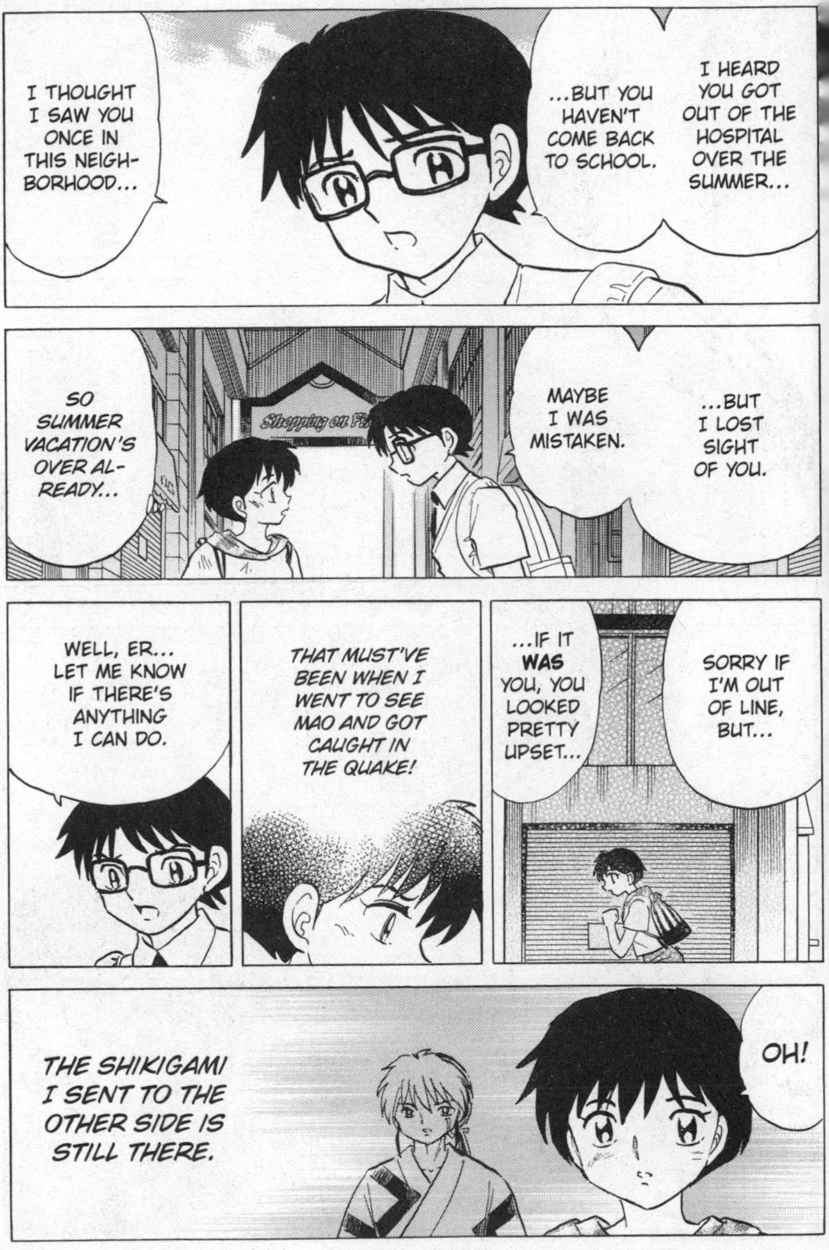
I HEARD YOU GOT OUT OF THE HOSPITAL OVER THE SUMMER...
...BUT YOU HAVEN'T COME BACK TO SCHOOL.
I THOUGHT I SAW YOU ONCE IN THIS NEIGHBORHOOD...
...BUT I LOST SIGHT OF YOU.
MAYBE I WAS MISTAKEN.
SO SUMMER VACATION'S OVER ALREADY...
SORRY IF I'M OUT OF LINE, BUT...
...IF IT **WAS** YOU, YOU LOOKED PRETTY UPSET...
THAT MUST'VE BEEN WHEN I WENT TO SEE MAO AND GOT CAUGHT IN THE QUAKE!
WELL, ER... LET ME KNOW IF THERE'S ANYTHING I CAN DO.
OH!
THE SHIKIGAMI I SENT TO THE OTHER SIDE IS STILL THERE.

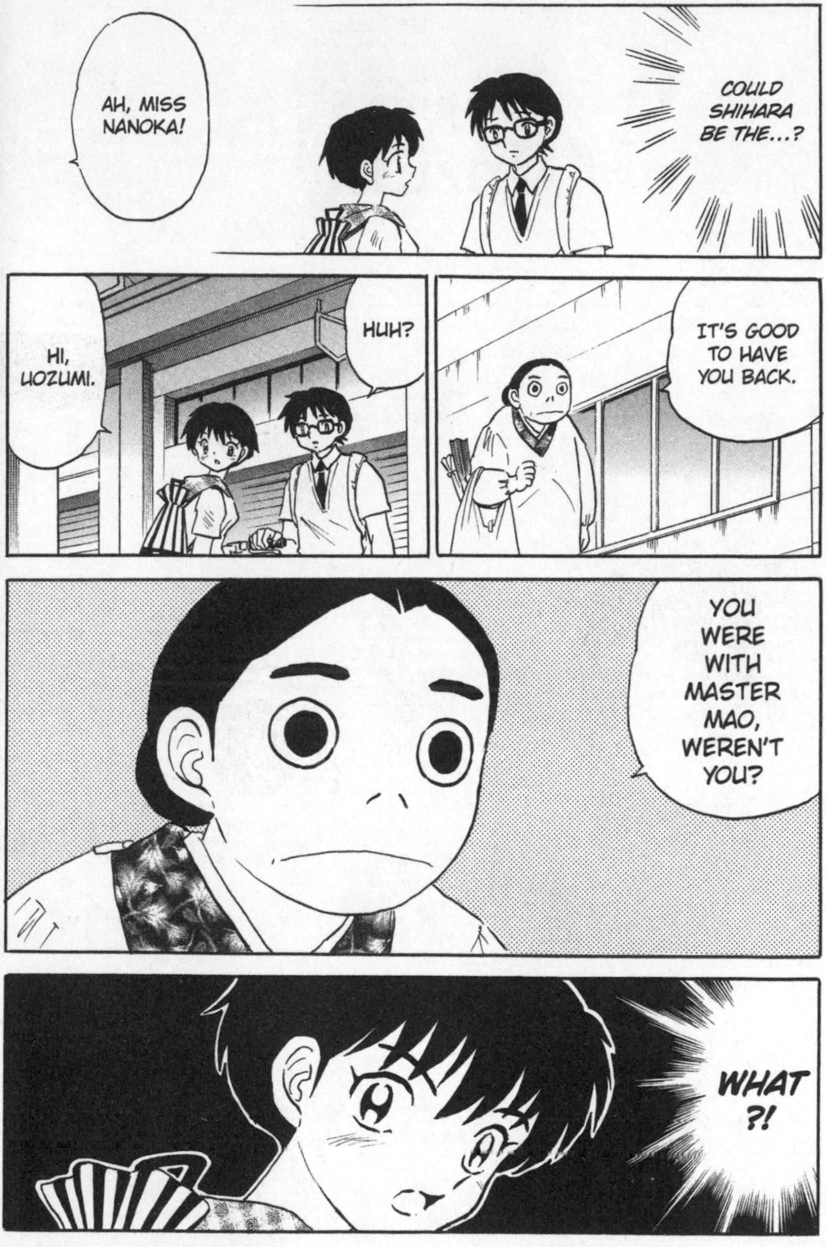
COULD SHIHARA BE THE...?
AH, MISS NANOKA!
IT'S GOOD TO HAVE YOU BACK.
HUH?
HI, UOZUMI.
YOU WERE WITH MASTER MAO, WEREN'T YOU?
WHAT?!

Chapter 5: Uozumi

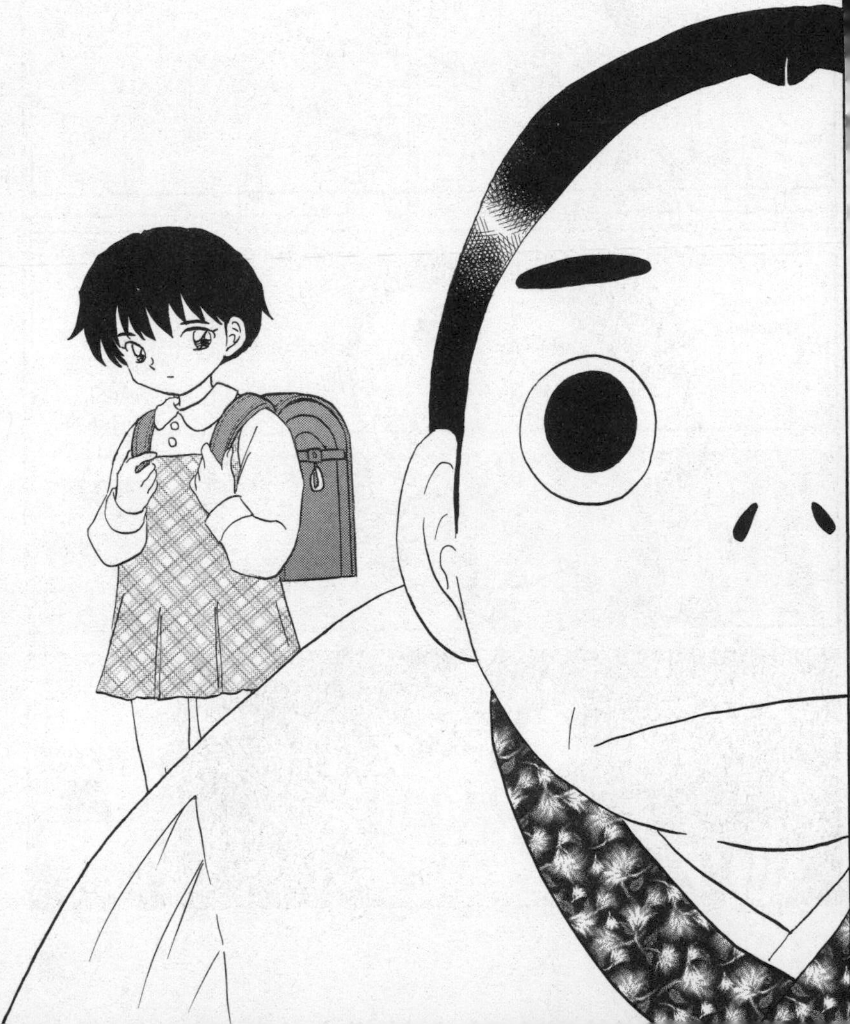

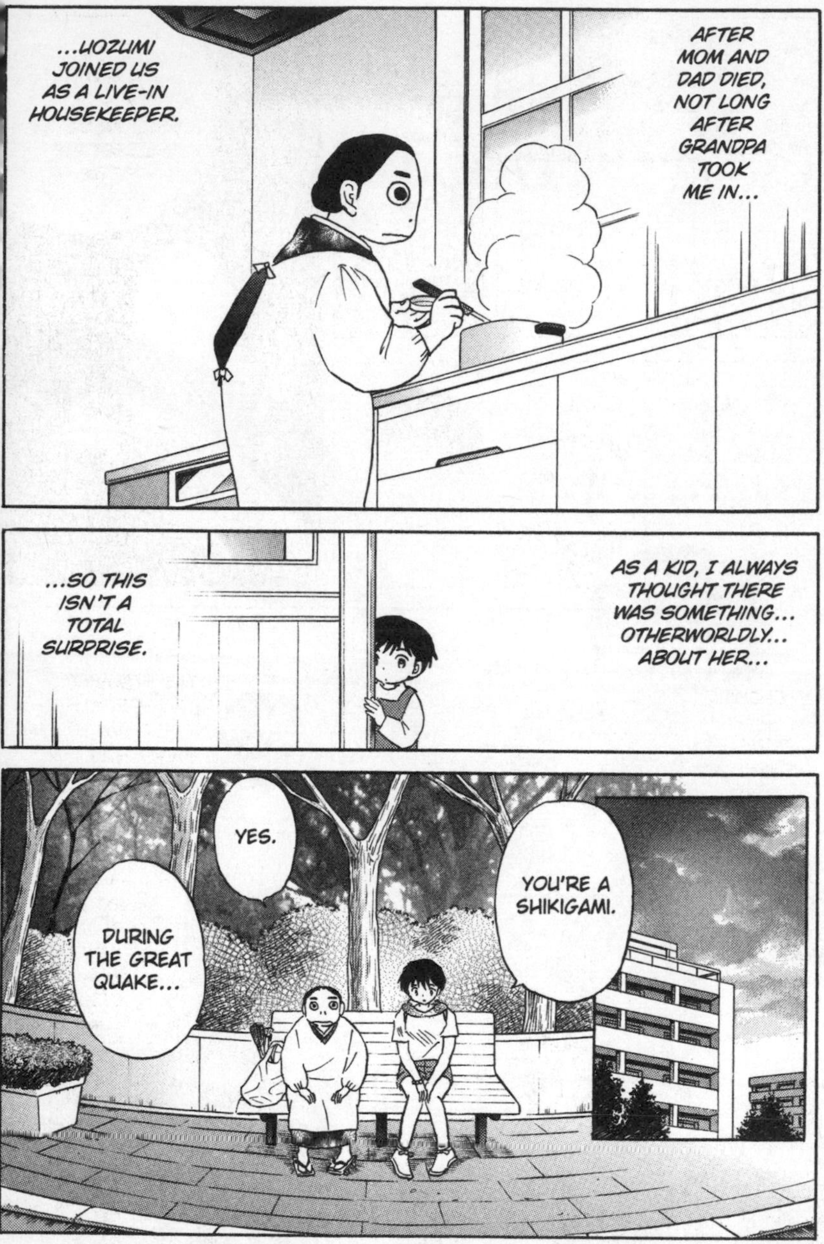
AFTER MOM AND DAD DIED, NOT LONG AFTER GRANDPA TOOK ME IN...
...UOZUMI JOINED US AS A LIVE-IN HOUSEKEEPER.
AS A KID, I ALWAYS THOUGHT THERE WAS SOMETHING... OTHERWORLDLY... ABOUT HER...
...SO THIS ISN'T A TOTAL SURPRISE.
YOU'RE A SHIKIGAMI.
YES.
DURING THE GREAT QUAKE...

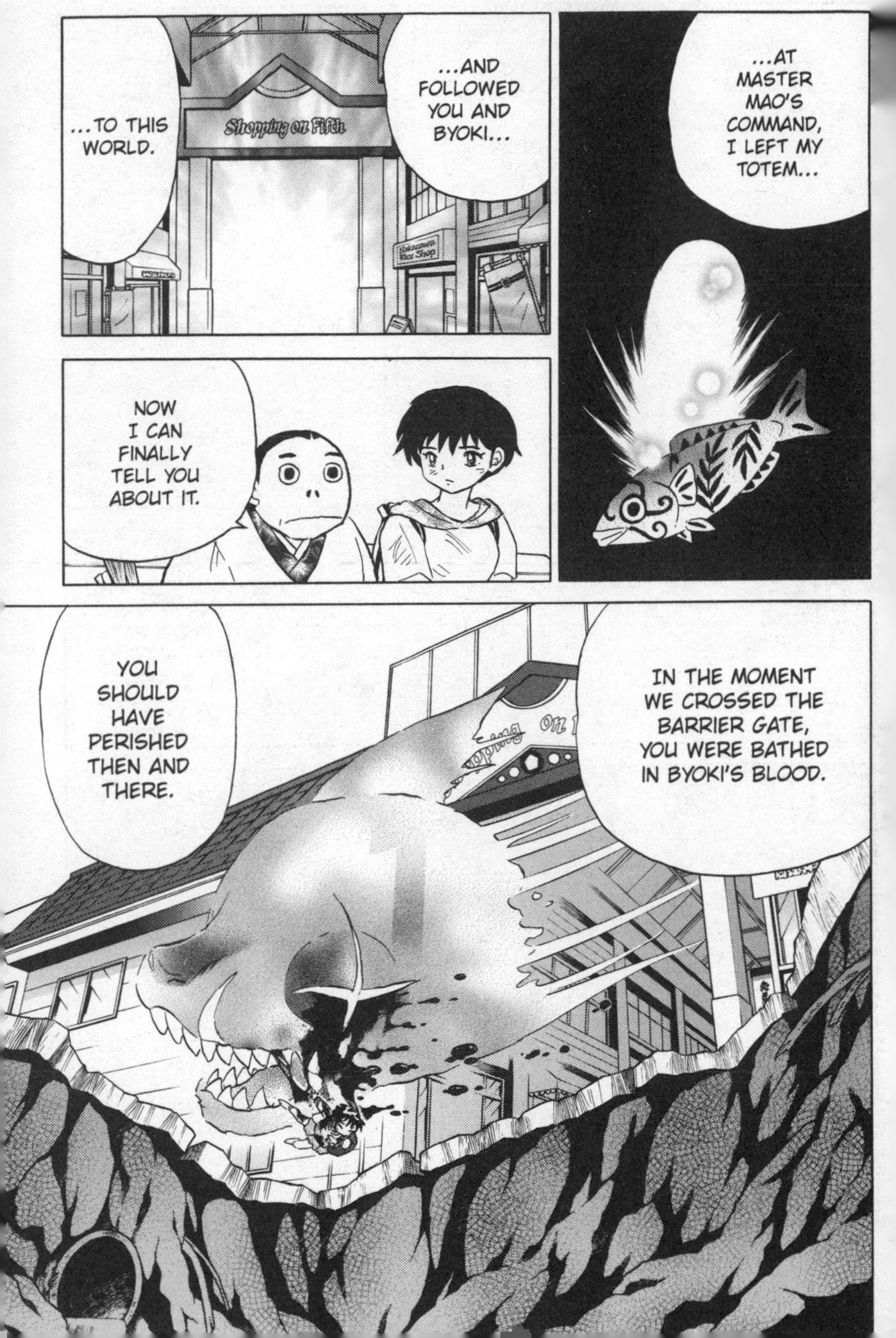
...AT MASTER MAO'S COMMAND, I LEFT MY TOTEM...
...AND FOLLOWED YOU AND BYOKI...
Shopping on Fifth
...TO THIS WORLD.
NOW I CAN FINALLY TELL YOU ABOUT IT.
IN THE MOMENT WE CROSSED THE BARRIER GATE, YOU WERE BATHED IN BYOKI'S BLOOD.
YOU SHOULD HAVE PERISHED THEN AND THERE.

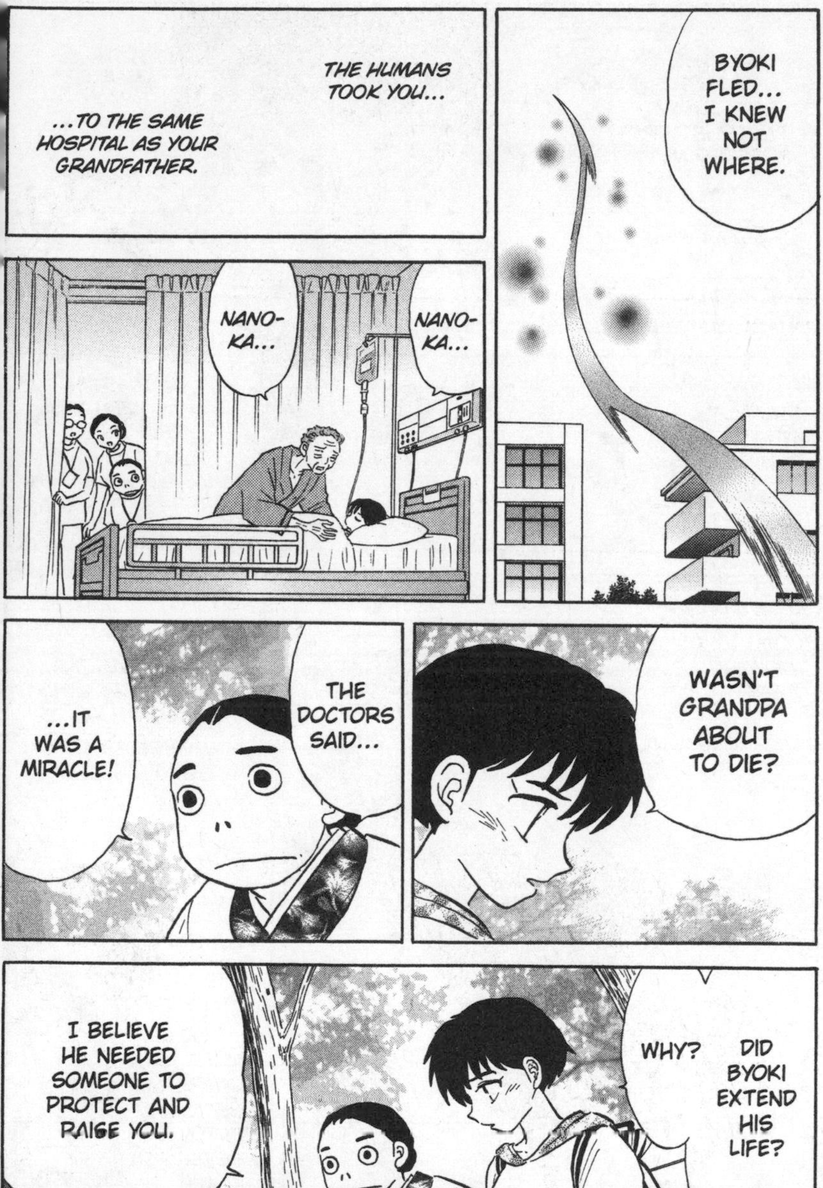
BYOKI FLED... I KNEW NOT WHERE.
THE HUMANS TOOK YOU...
...TO THE SAME HOSPITAL AS YOUR GRANDFATHER.
NANO-KA...
NANO-KA...
WASN'T GRANDPA ABOUT TO DIE?
THE DOCTORS SAID...
...IT WAS A MIRACLE!
WHY?
DID BYOKI EXTEND HIS LIFE?
I BELIEVE HE NEEDED SOMEONE TO PROTECT AND RAISE YOU.

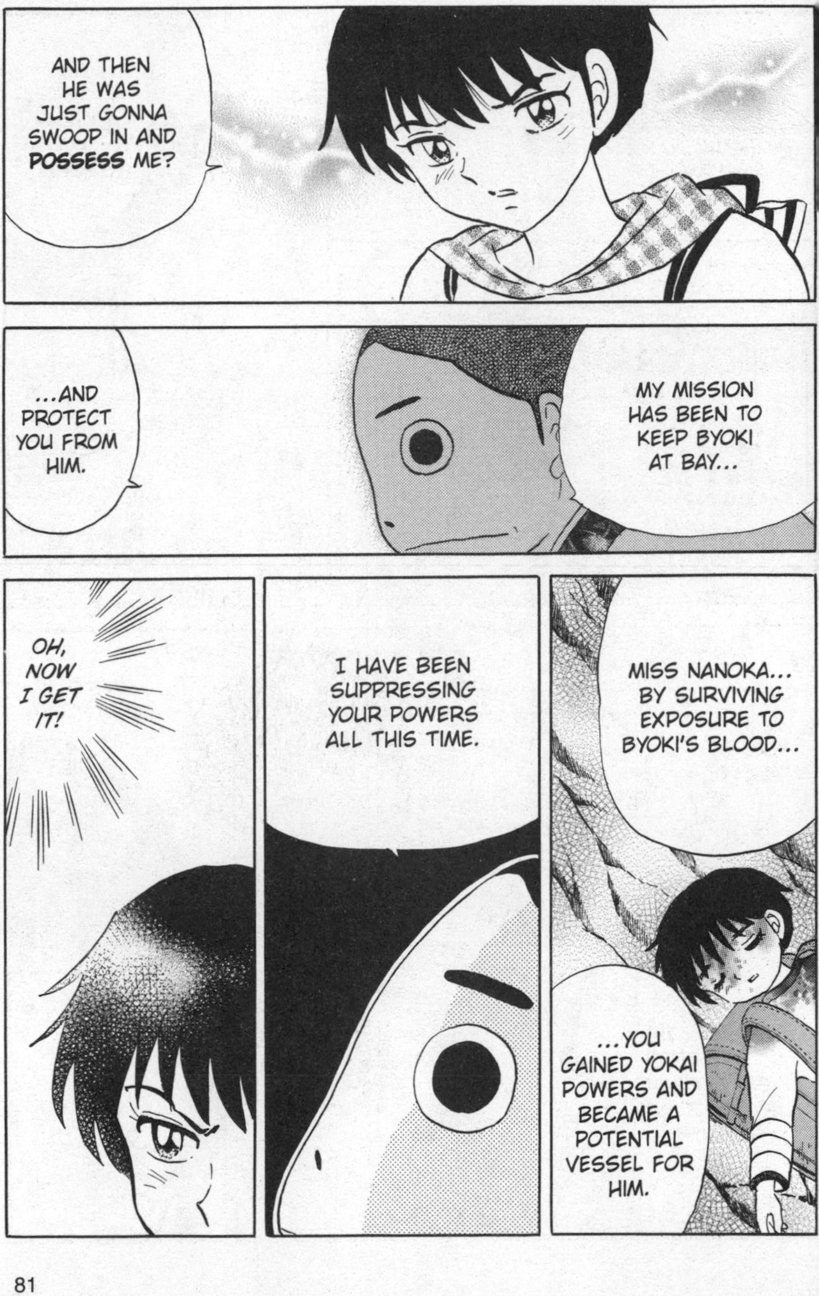
AND THEN HE WAS JUST GONNA SWOOP IN AND **POSSESS** ME?
MY MISSION HAS BEEN TO KEEP BYOKI AT BAY...
...AND PROTECT YOU FROM HIM.
MISS NANOKA... BY SURVIVING EXPOSURE TO BYOKI'S BLOOD...
...YOU GAINED YOKAI POWERS AND BECAME A POTENTIAL VESSEL FOR HIM.
I HAVE BEEN SUPPRESSING YOUR POWERS ALL THIS TIME.
OH, NOW I GET IT!

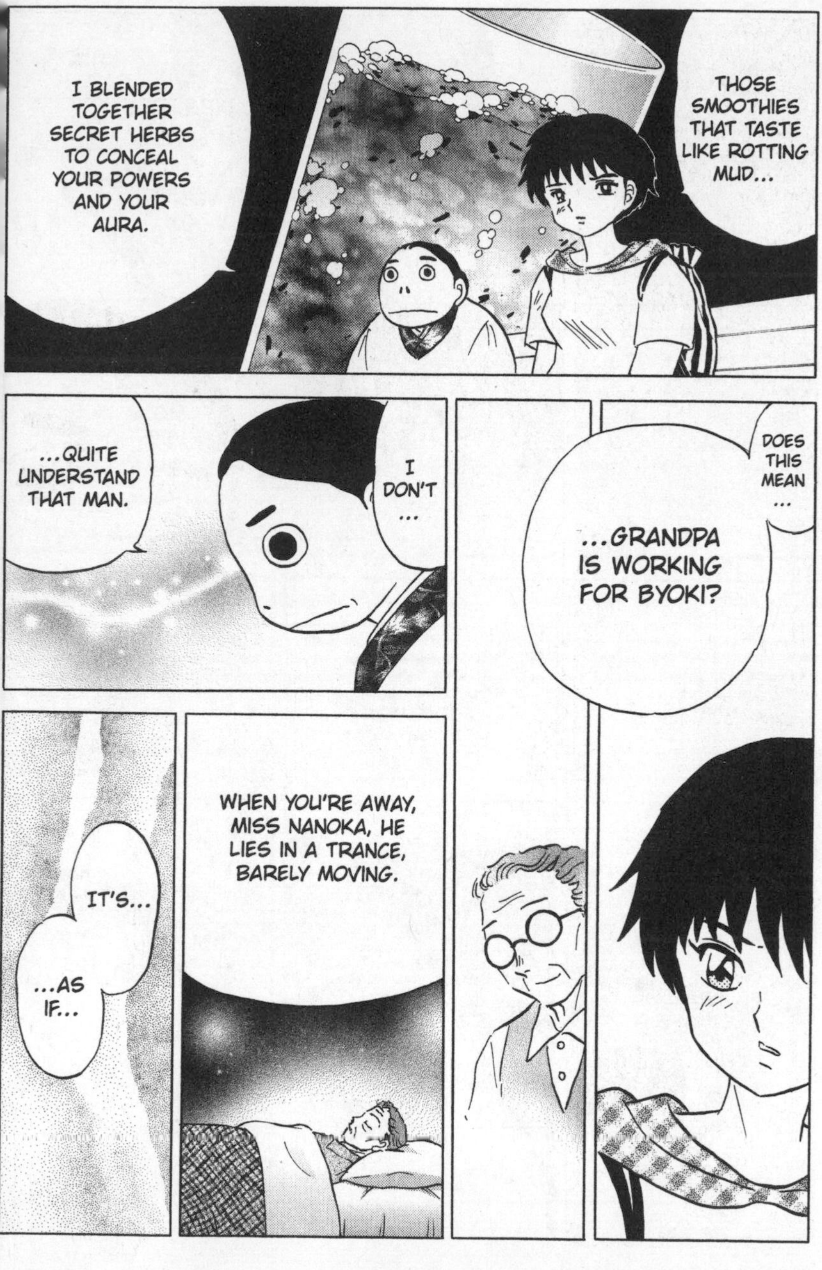
THOSE SMOOTHIES THAT TASTE LIKE ROTTING MUD...
I BLENDED TOGETHER SECRET HERBS TO CONCEAL YOUR POWERS AND YOUR AURA.
DOES THIS MEAN...
...GRANDPA IS WORKING FOR BYOKI?
I DON'T...
...QUITE UNDERSTAND THAT MAN.
WHEN YOU'RE AWAY, MISS NANOKA, HE LIES IN A TRANCE, BARELY MOVING.
IT'S...
...AS IF...

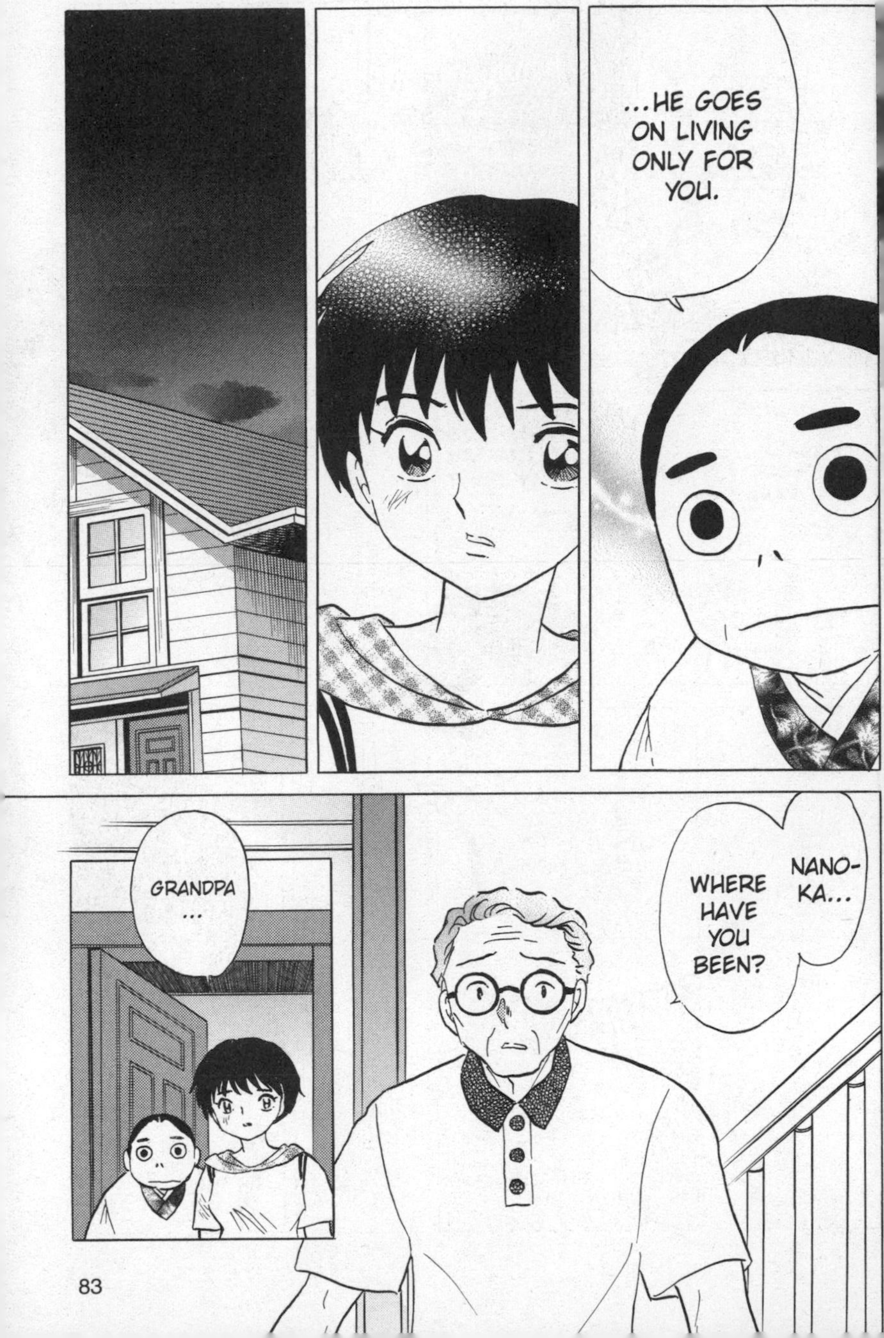
...HE GOES ON LIVING ONLY FOR YOU.
NANO-KA... WHERE HAVE YOU BEEN?
GRANDPA ...

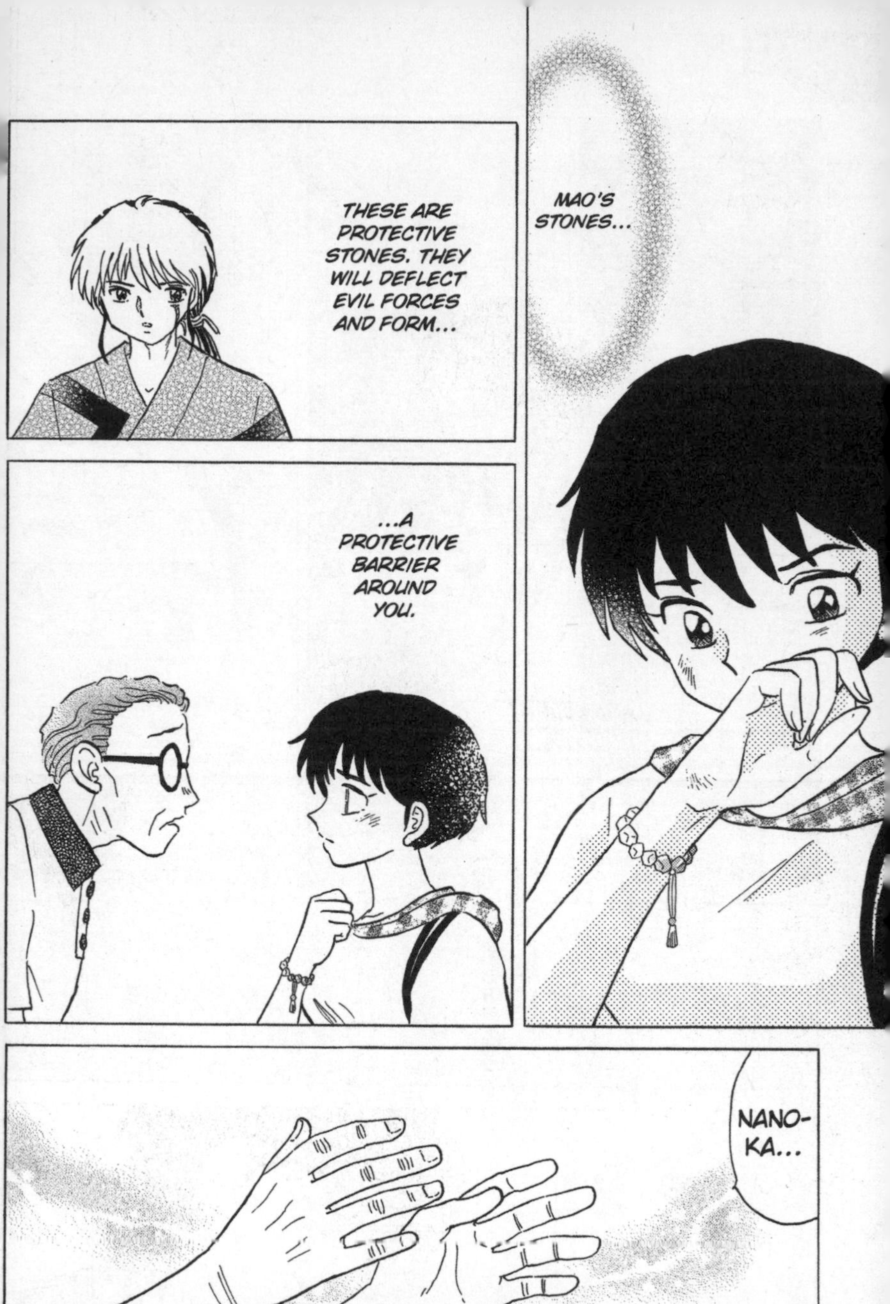
MAO'S STONES...
THESE ARE PROTECTIVE STONES. THEY WILL DEFLECT EVIL FORCES AND FORM...
...A PROTECTIVE BARRIER AROUND YOU.
NANO-KA...

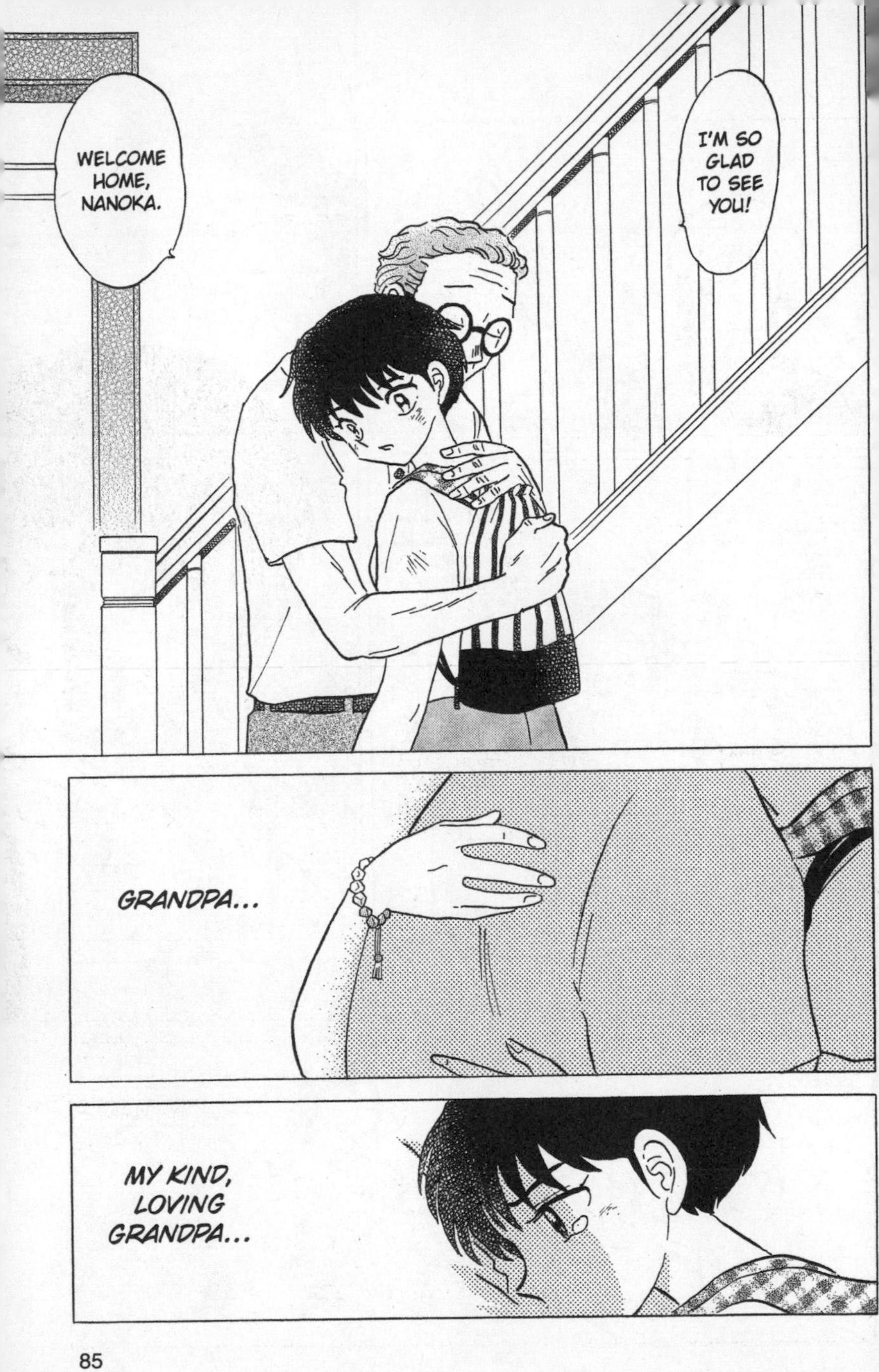
I'M SO GLAD TO SEE YOU!
WELCOME HOME, NANOKA.
GRANDPA...
MY KIND, LOVING GRANDPA...

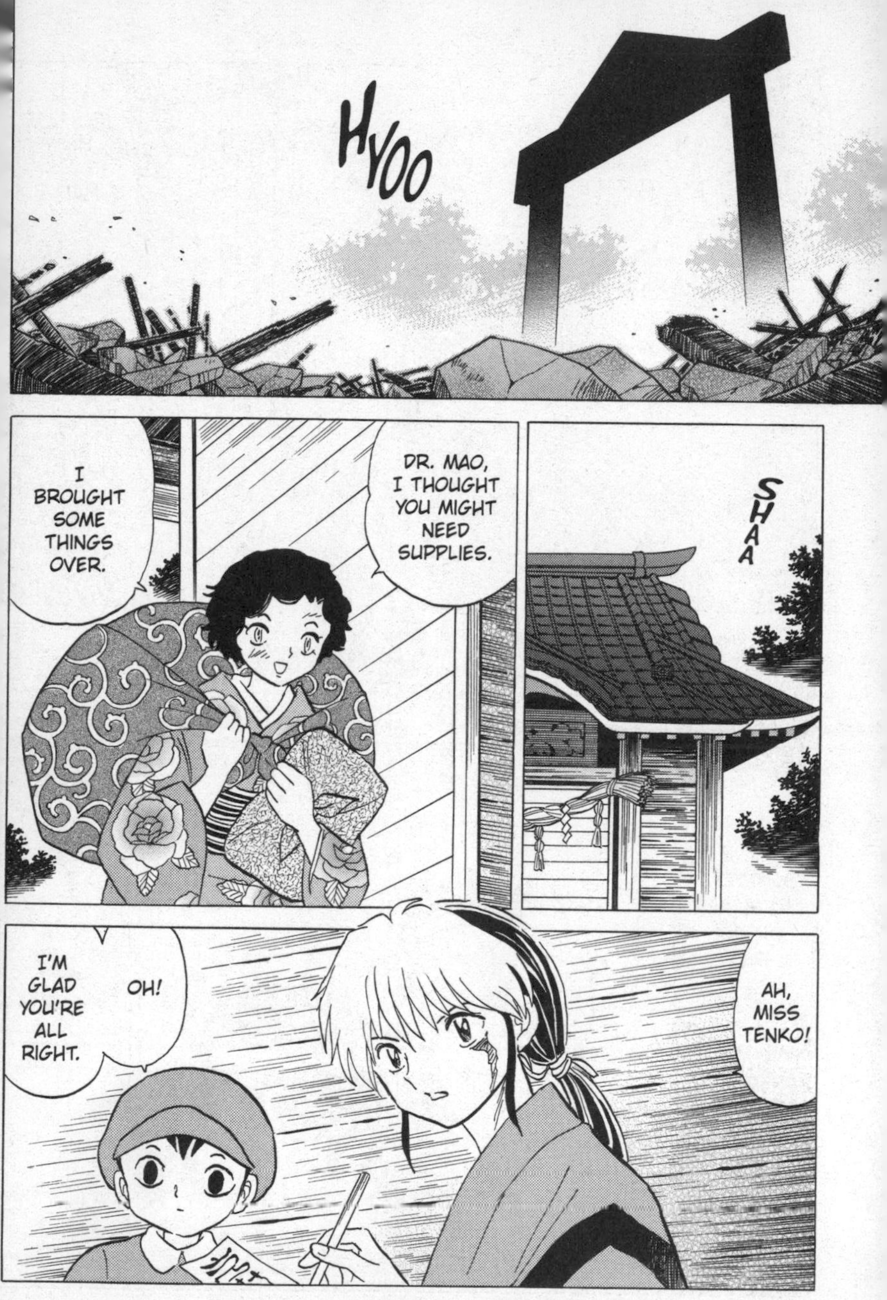
HYOO
SHAA
DR. MAO, I THOUGHT YOU MIGHT NEED SUPPLIES.
I BROUGHT SOME THINGS OVER.
AH, MISS TENKO!
OH!
I'M GLAD YOU'RE ALL RIGHT.

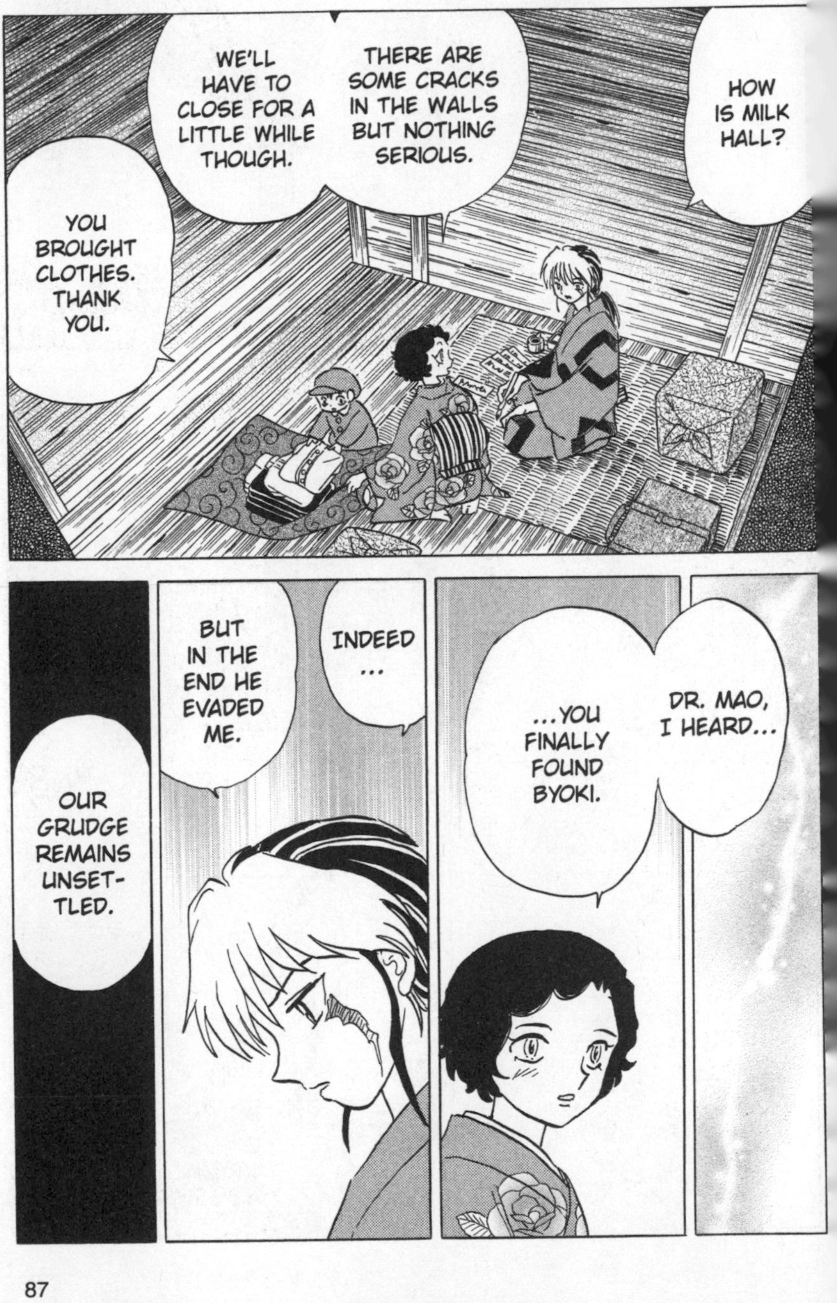
HOW IS MILK HALL?
THERE ARE SOME CRACKS IN THE WALLS BUT NOTHING SERIOUS.
WE'LL HAVE TO CLOSE FOR A LITTLE WHILE THOUGH.
YOU BROUGHT CLOTHES. THANK YOU.
DR. MAO, I HEARD...
...YOU FINALLY FOUND BYOKI.
INDEED...
BUT IN THE END HE EVADED ME.
OUR GRUDGE REMAINS UNSET-TLED.

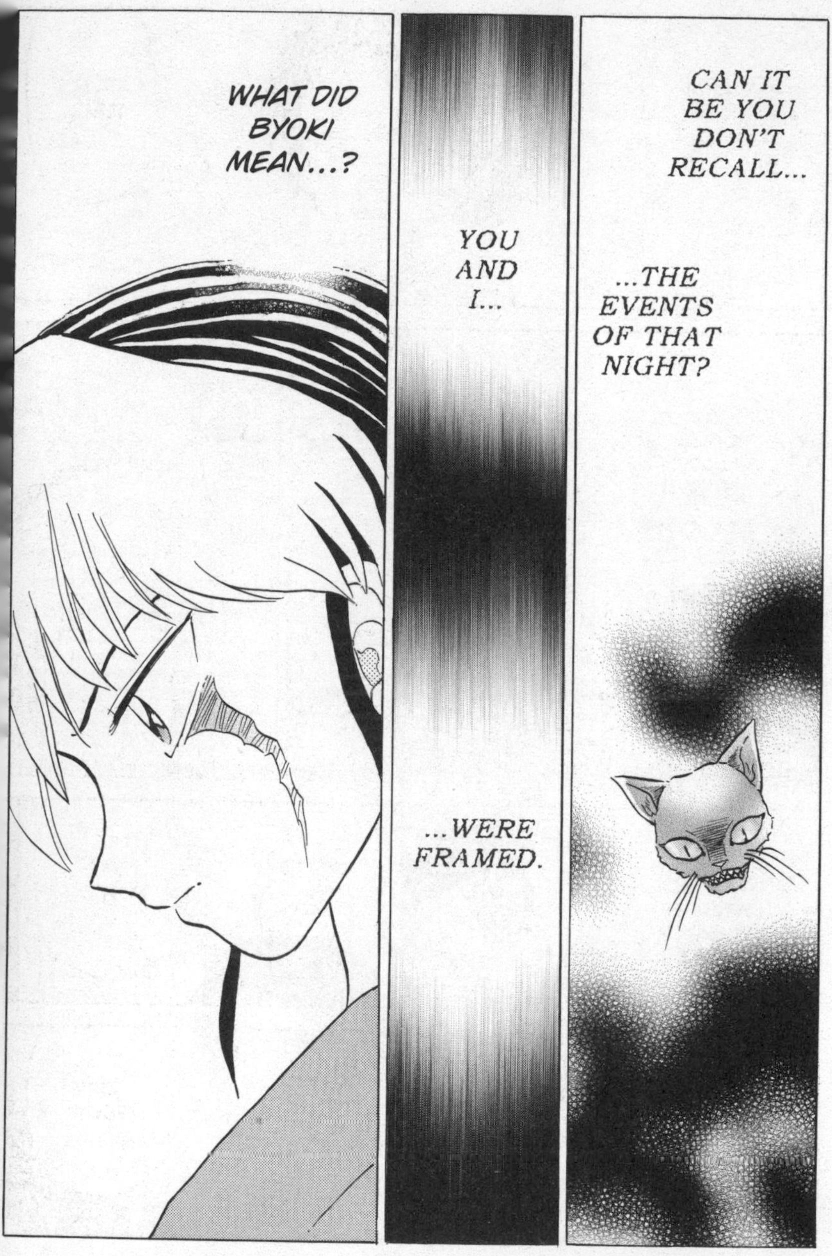
CAN IT BE YOU DON'T RECALL...
...THE EVENTS OF THAT NIGHT?
YOU AND I...
...WERE FRAMED.
WHAT DID BYOKI MEAN...?

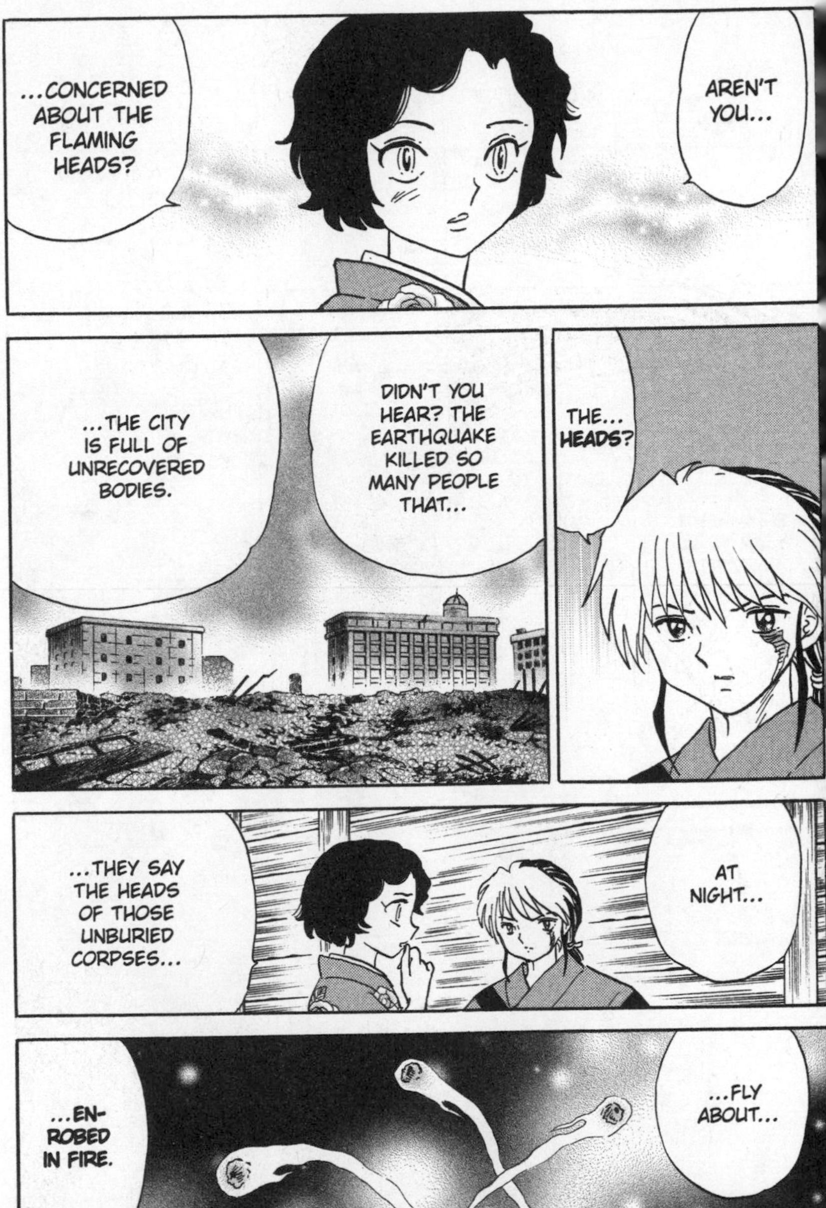
AREN'T YOU...
...CONCERNED ABOUT THE FLAMING HEADS?
THE... HEADS?
DIDN'T YOU HEAR? THE EARTHQUAKE KILLED SO MANY PEOPLE THAT...
...THE CITY IS FULL OF UNRECOVERED BODIES.
AT NIGHT...
...THEY SAY THE HEADS OF THOSE UNBURIED CORPSES...
...FLY ABOUT...
...EN-ROBED IN FIRE.

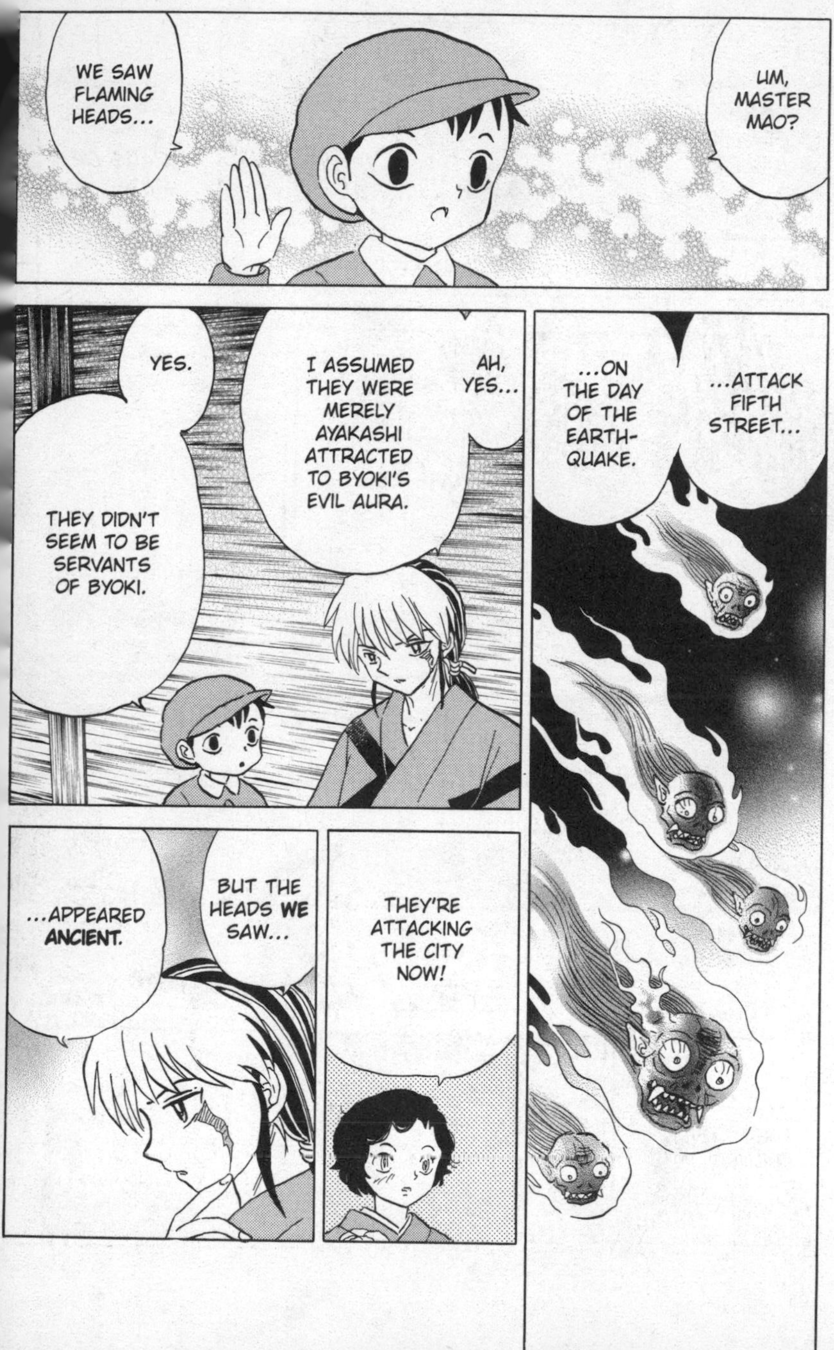
UM, MASTER MAO?
WE SAW FLAMING HEADS...
...ATTACK FIFTH STREET...
...ON THE DAY OF THE EARTHQUAKE.
AH, YES...
I ASSUMED THEY WERE MERELY AYAKASHI ATTRACTED TO BYOKI'S EVIL AURA.
YES.
THEY DIDN'T SEEM TO BE SERVANTS OF BYOKI.
THEY'RE ATTACKING THE CITY NOW!
BUT THE HEADS WE SAW...
...APPEARED ANCIENT.

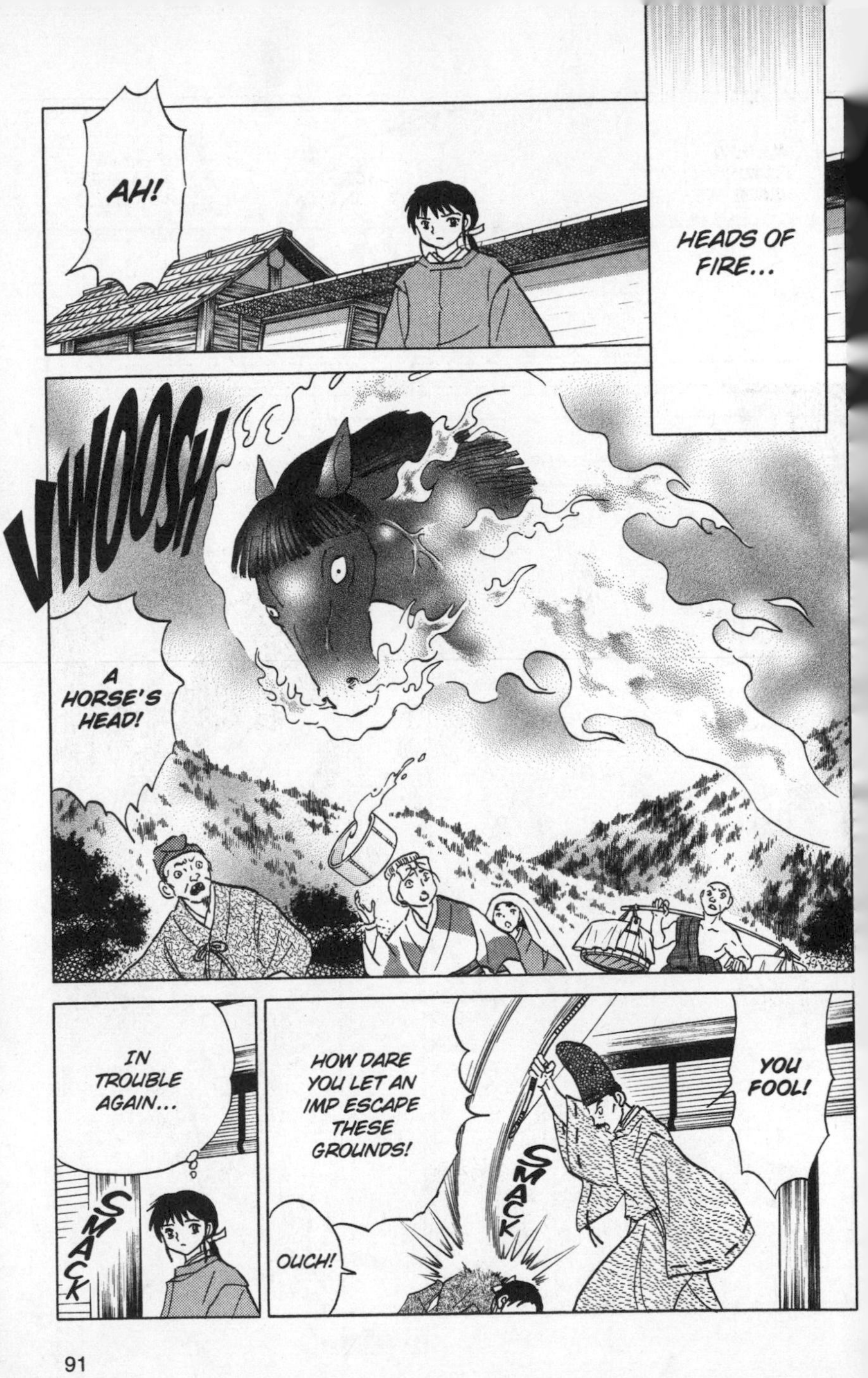
HEADS OF FIRE...
AH!
VWOOSH
A HORSE'S HEAD!
YOU FOOL!
HOW DARE YOU LET AN IMP ESCAPE THESE GROUNDS!
SMACK
OUCH!
IN TROUBLE AGAIN...
SMACK

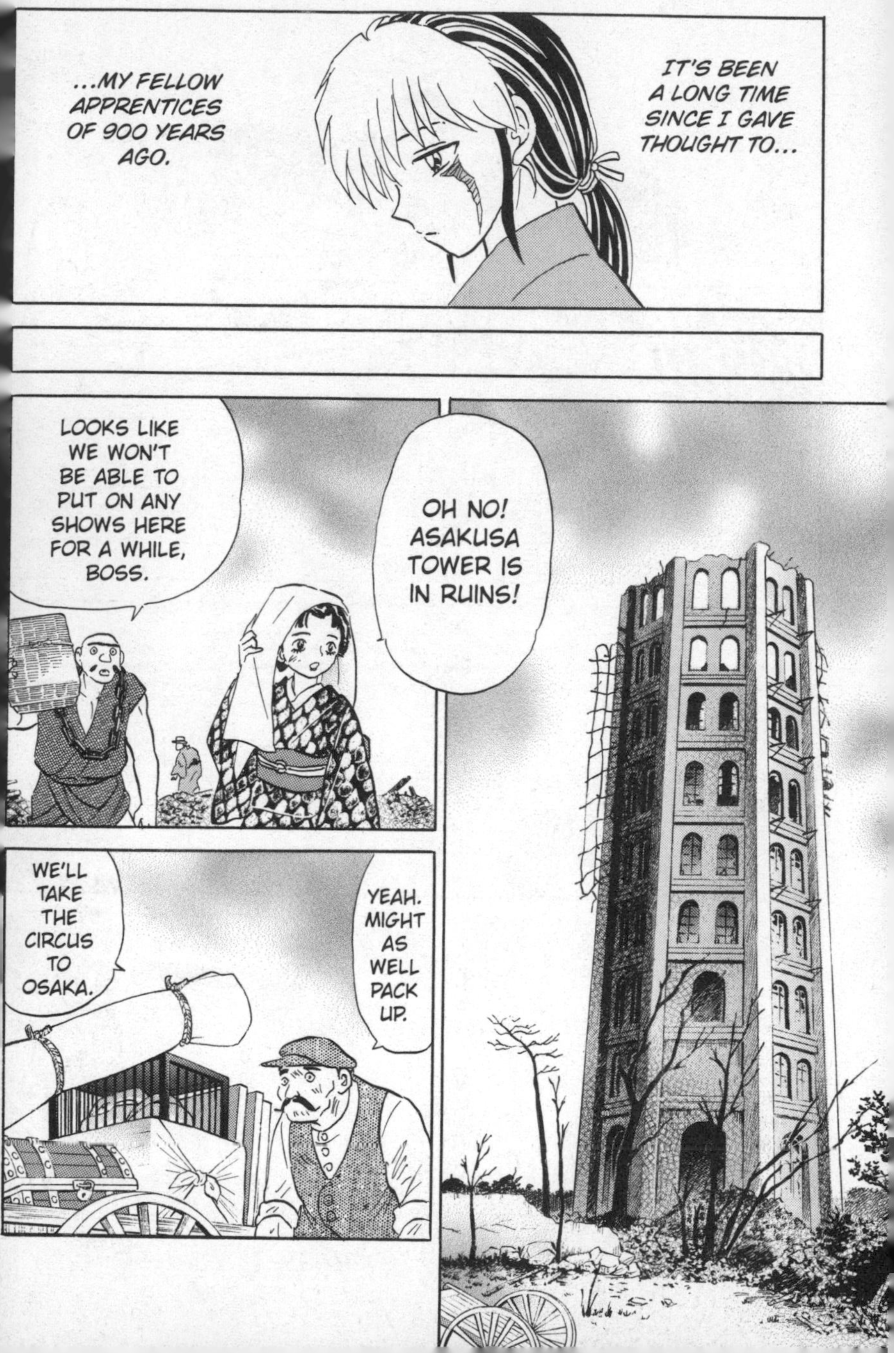
IT'S BEEN A LONG TIME SINCE I GAVE THOUGHT TO...
...MY FELLOW APPRENTICES OF 900 YEARS AGO.
OH NO! ASAKUSA TOWER IS IN RUINS!
LOOKS LIKE WE WON'T BE ABLE TO PUT ON ANY SHOWS HERE FOR A WHILE, BOSS.
YEAH. MIGHT AS WELL PACK UP.
WE'LL TAKE THE CIRCUS TO OSAKA.

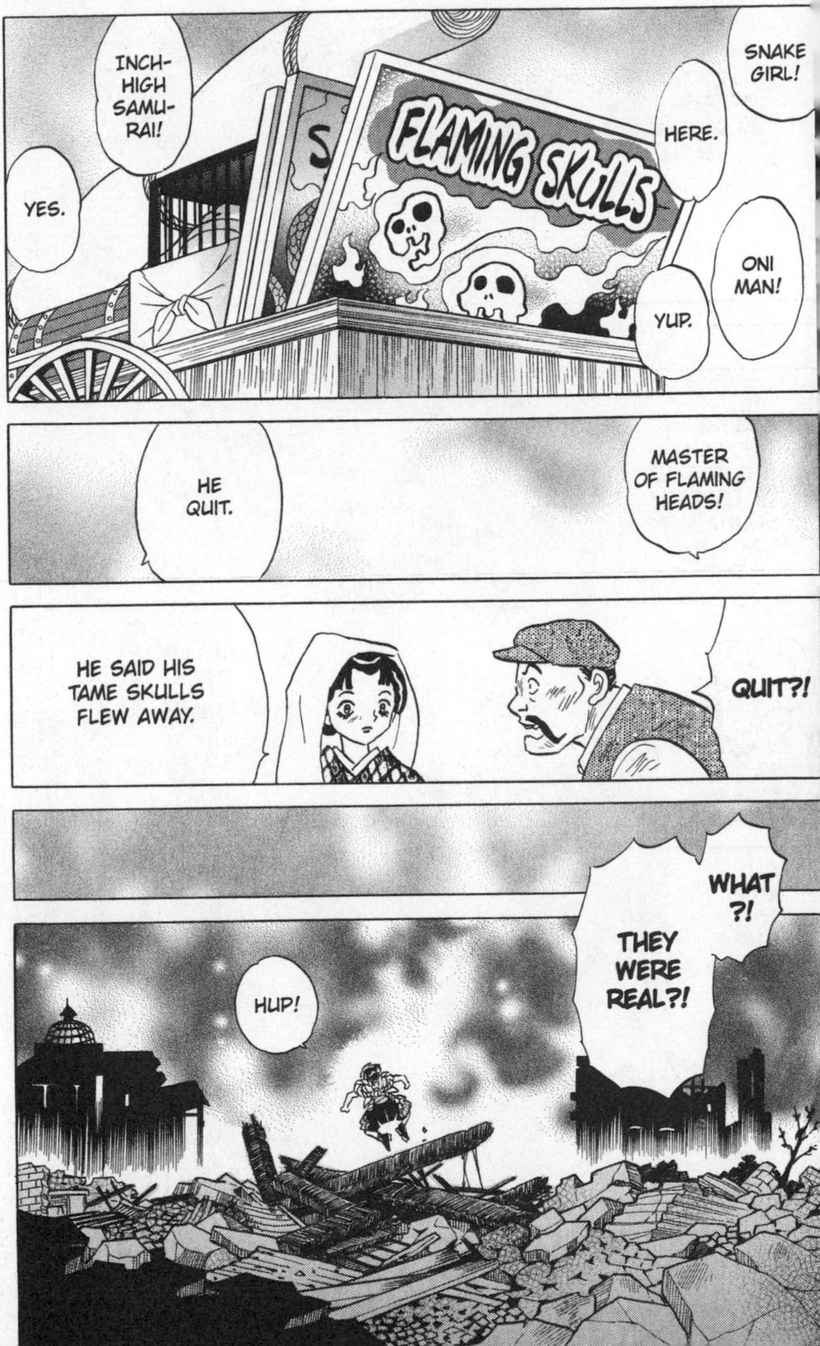
SNAKE GIRL!
HERE.
FLAMING SKULLS
ONI MAN!
YUP.
INCH-HIGH SAMURAI!
YES.
MASTER OF FLAMING HEADS!
HE QUIT.
QUIT?!
HE SAID HIS TAME SKULLS FLEW AWAY.
WHAT?!
THEY WERE REAL?!
HUP!

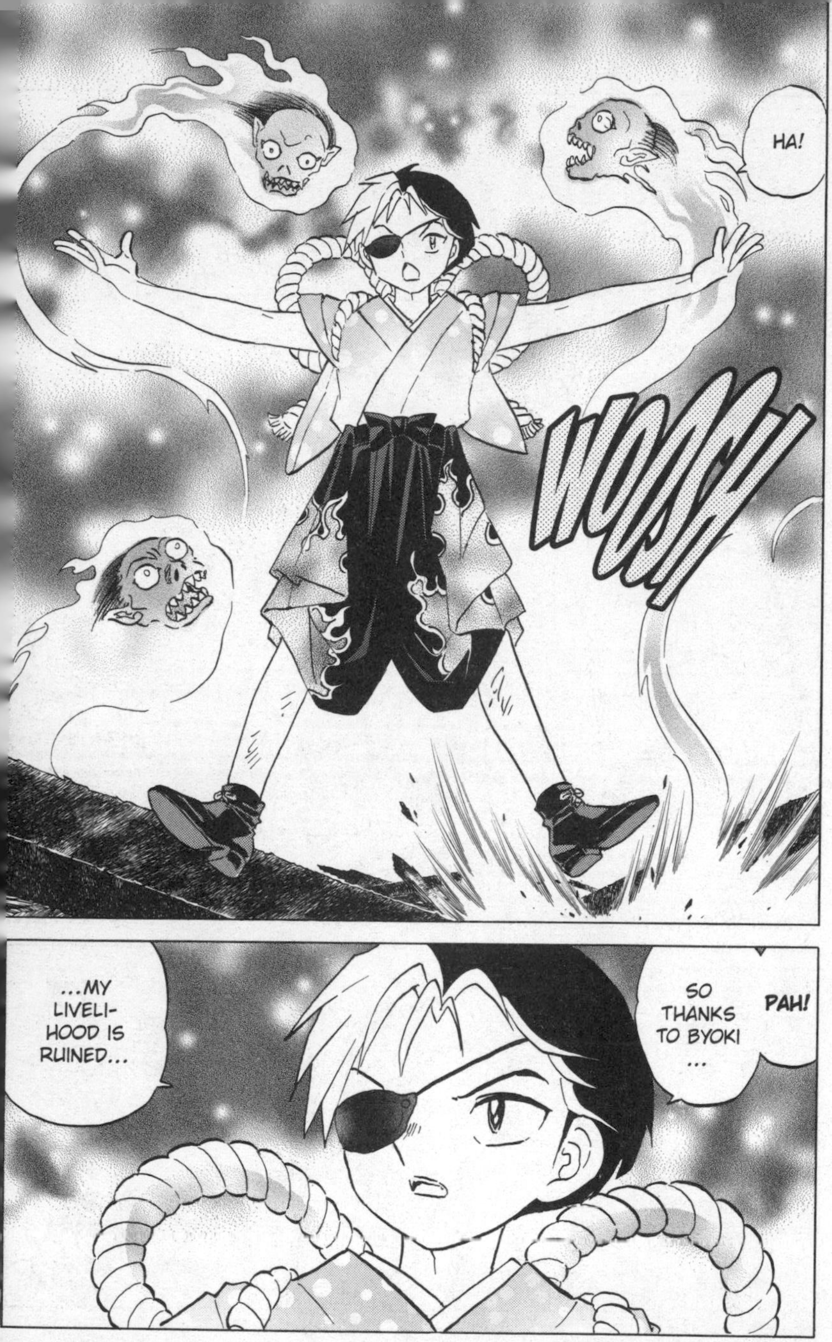
HA!
WOOSH
PAH!
SO THANKS TO BYOKI ...
...MY LIVELI-HOOD IS RUINED...

Chapter 6: Asakusa Tower

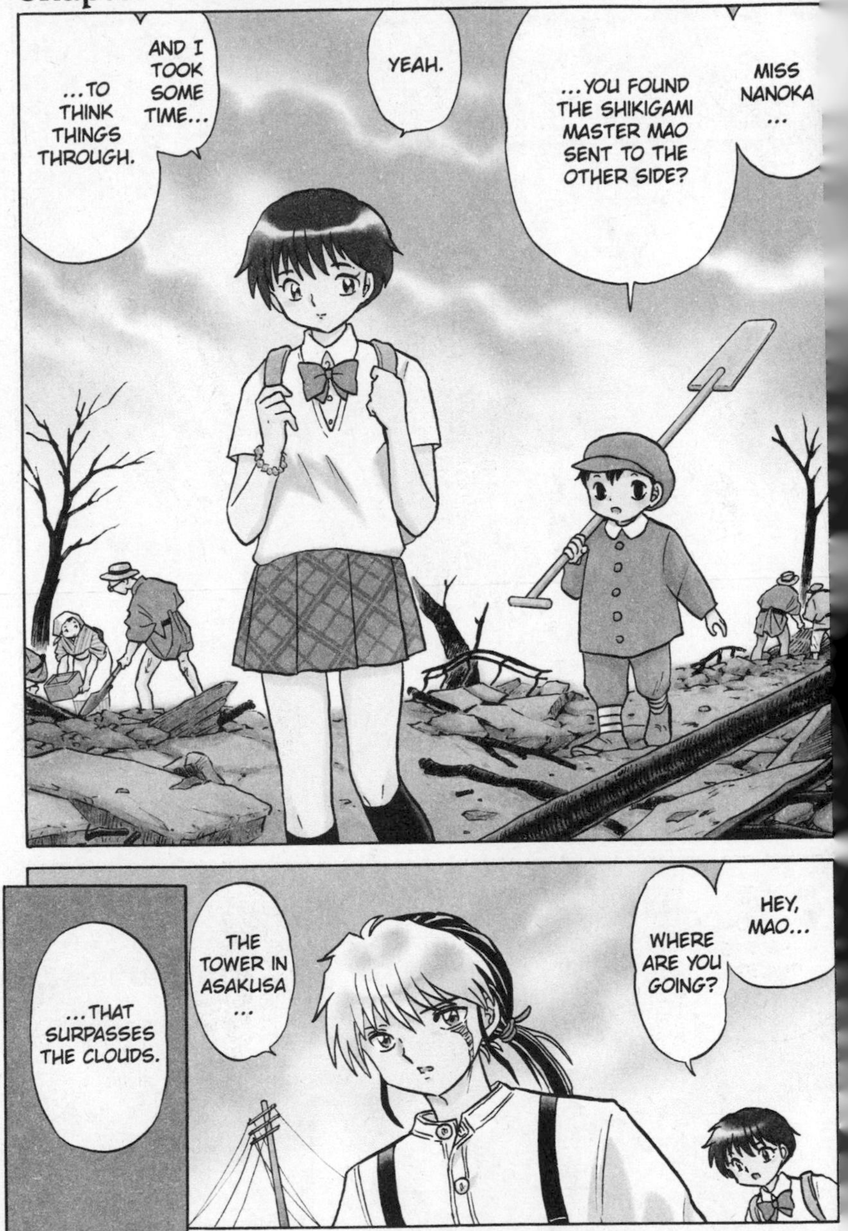
MISS NANOKA...
...YOU FOUND THE SHIKIGAMI MASTER MAO SENT TO THE OTHER SIDE?
YEAH.
AND I TOOK SOME TIME...
...TO THINK THINGS THROUGH.
HEY, MAO...
WHERE ARE YOU GOING?
THE TOWER IN ASAKUSA...
...THAT SURPASSES THE CLOUDS.

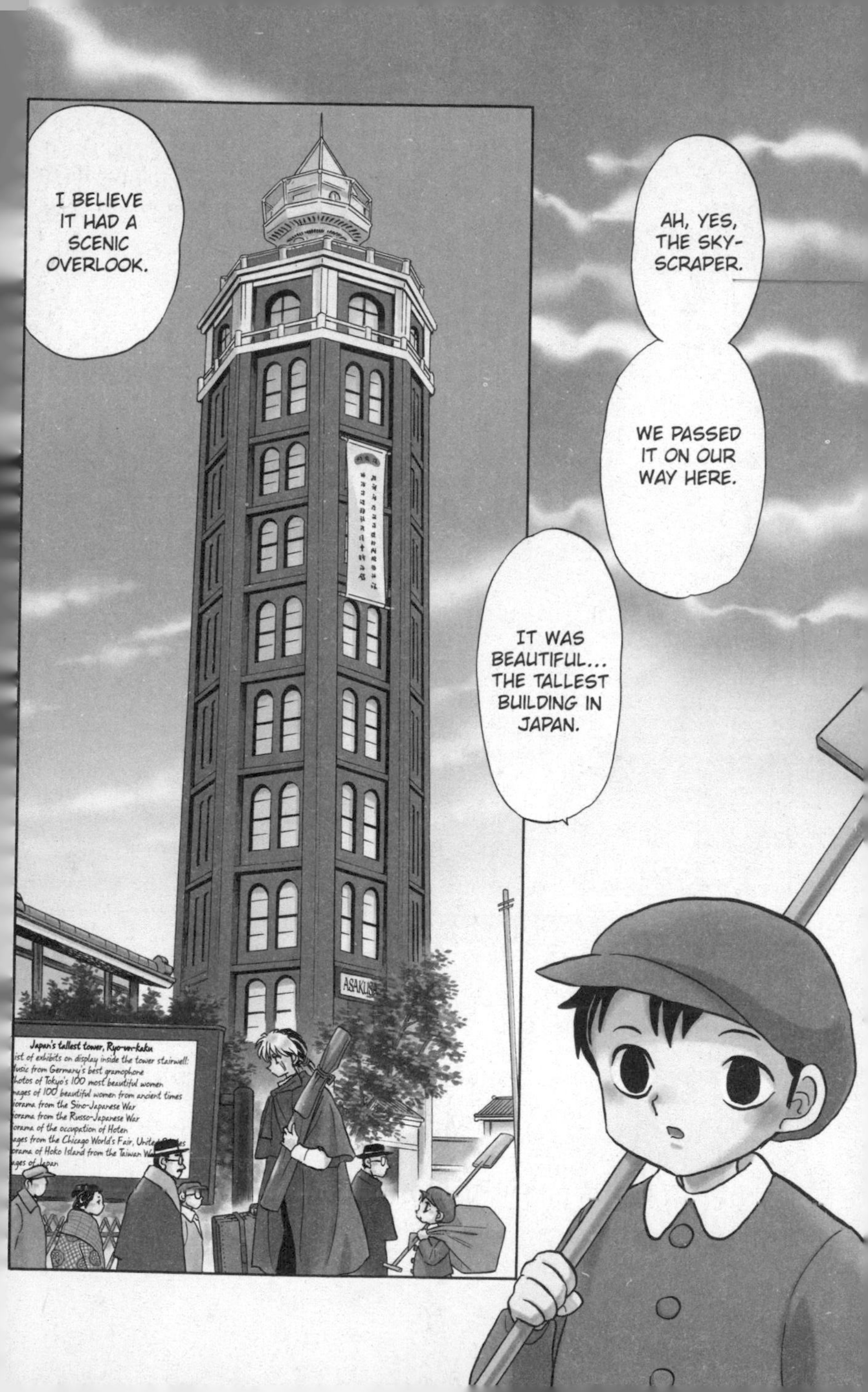

AH, YES, THE SKY-SCRAPER.
WE PASSED IT ON OUR WAY HERE.
IT WAS BEAUTIFUL... THE TALLEST BUILDING IN JAPAN.
I BELIEVE IT HAD A SCENIC OVERLOOK.
ASAKUSA
Japan's tallest tower, Ryo-un-kaku
ist of exhibits on display inside the tower stairwell:
usic from Germany's best gramophone
hotos of Tokyo's 100 most beautiful women
nages of 100 beautiful women from ancient times
iorama from the Sino-Japanese War
iorama from the Russo-Japanese War
iorama of the occupation of Hoten
ages from the Chicago World's Fair, Unite
orama of Hoko Island from the Taiwan W
ages of Japan

Chapter 6:
Asakusa Tower

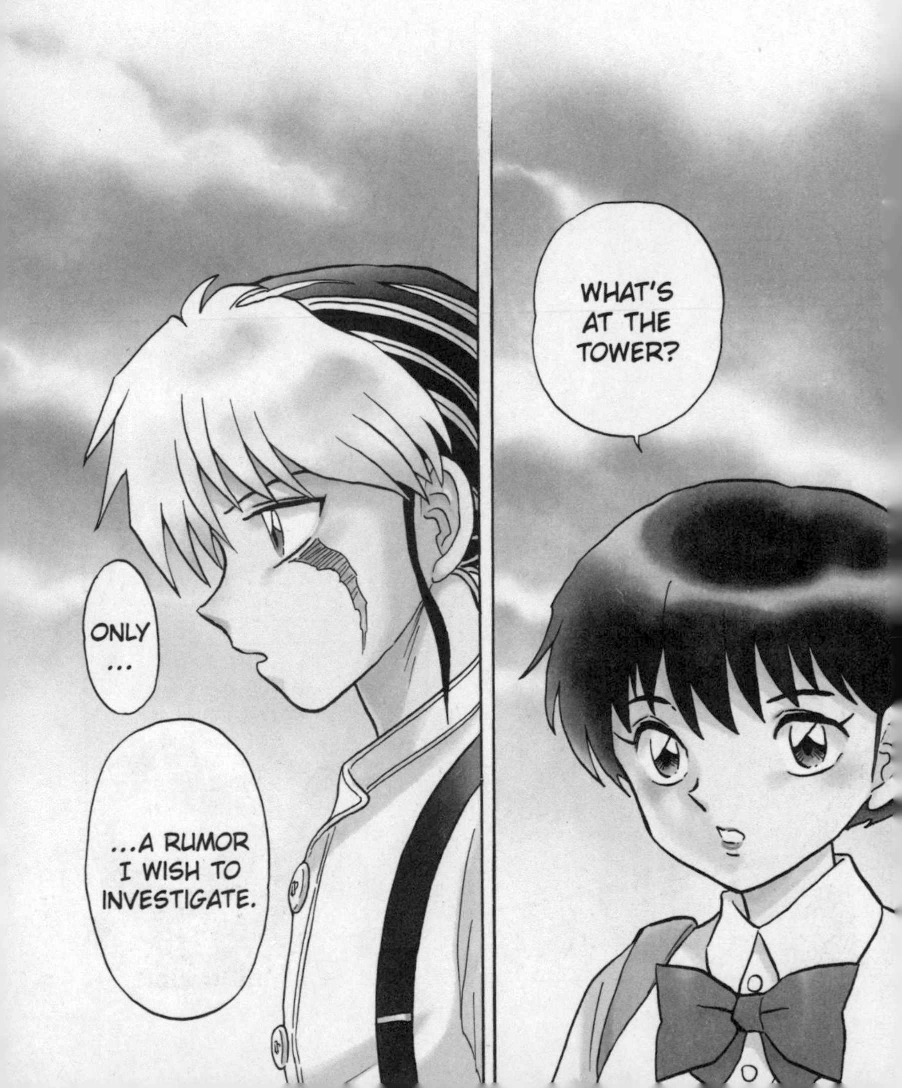
WHAT'S AT THE TOWER?
ONLY...
...A RUMOR I WISH TO INVESTIGATE.

MAO

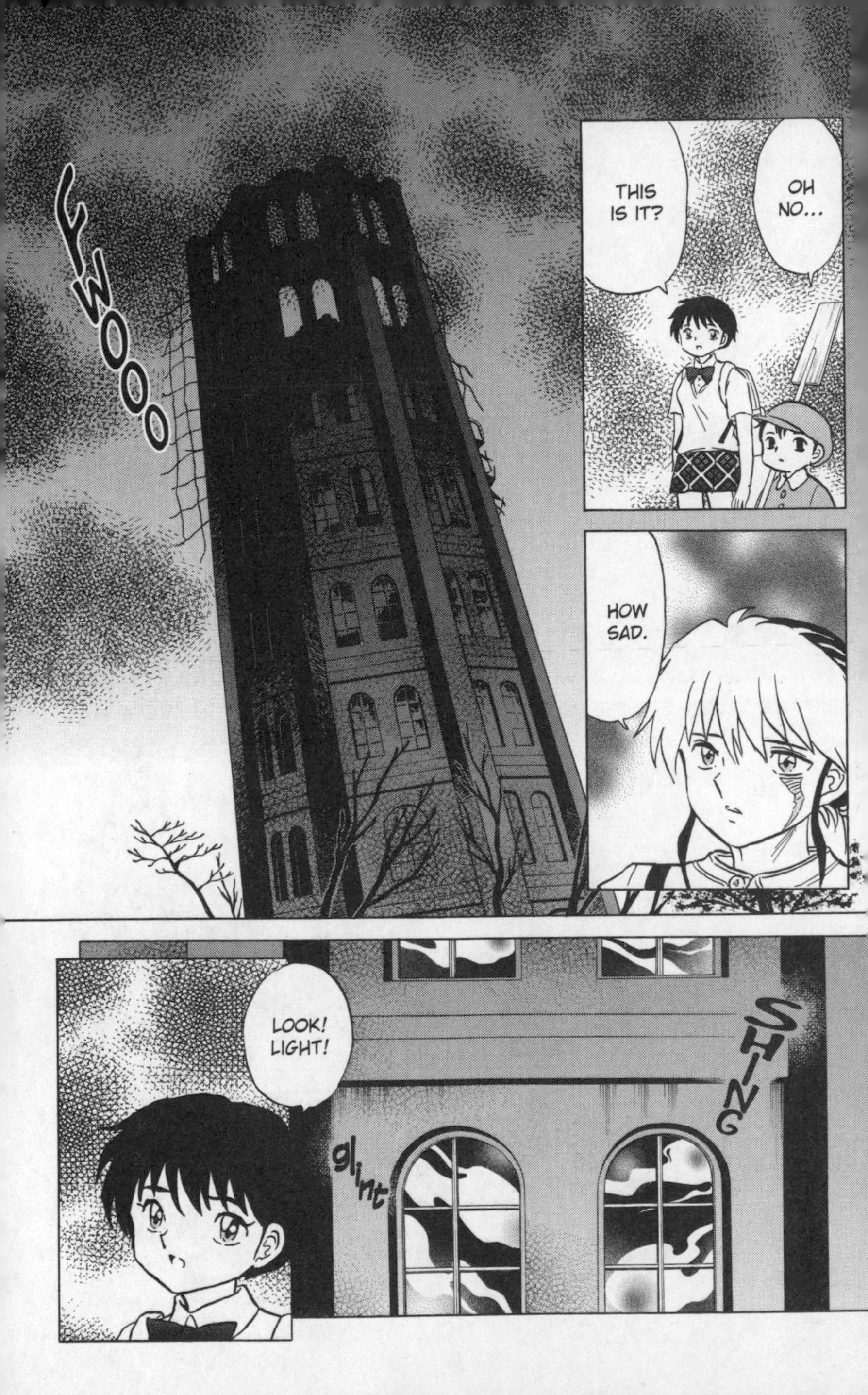
OH NO...
THIS IS IT?
HOW SAD.
FWOOO
SHING
glint
LOOK! LIGHT!

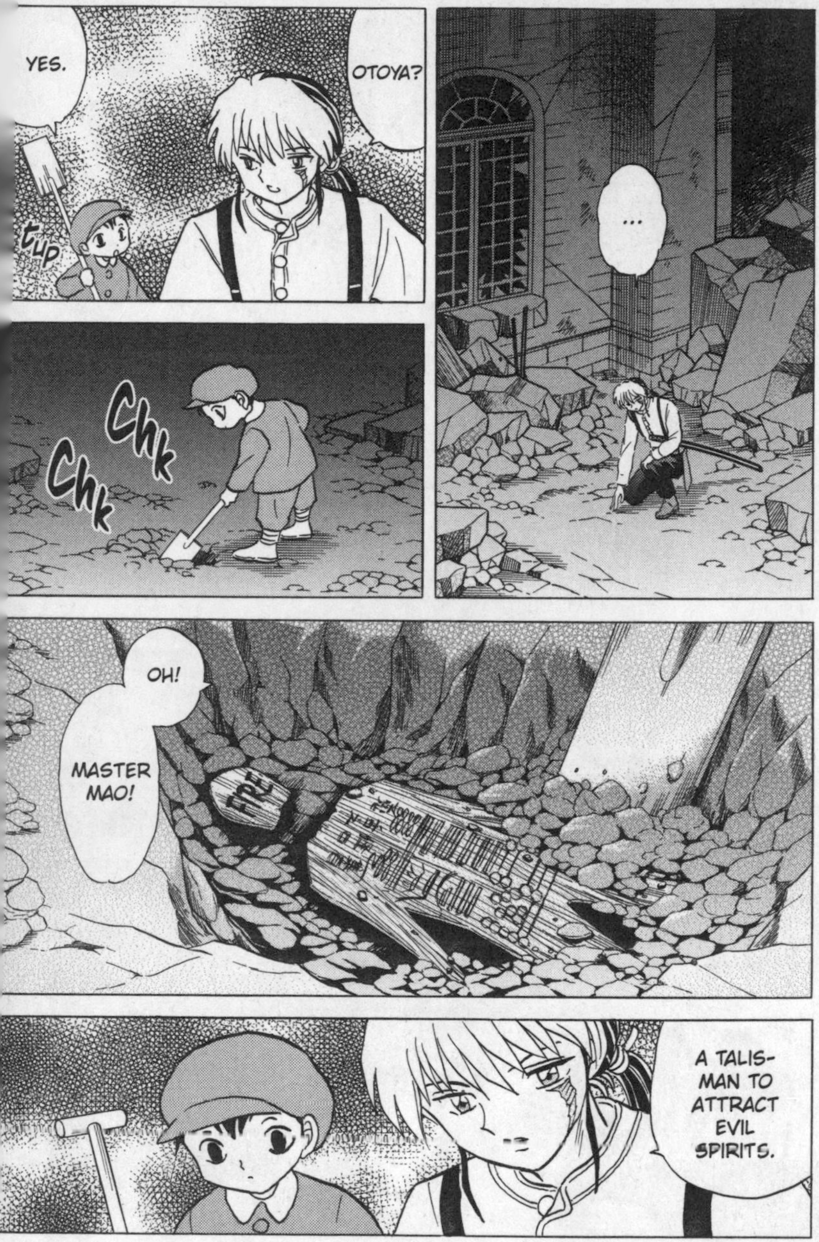
...
OTOYA?
YES.
tup
Chk
Chk
OH!
MASTER MAO!
A TALIS-MAN TO ATTRACT EVIL SPIRITS.

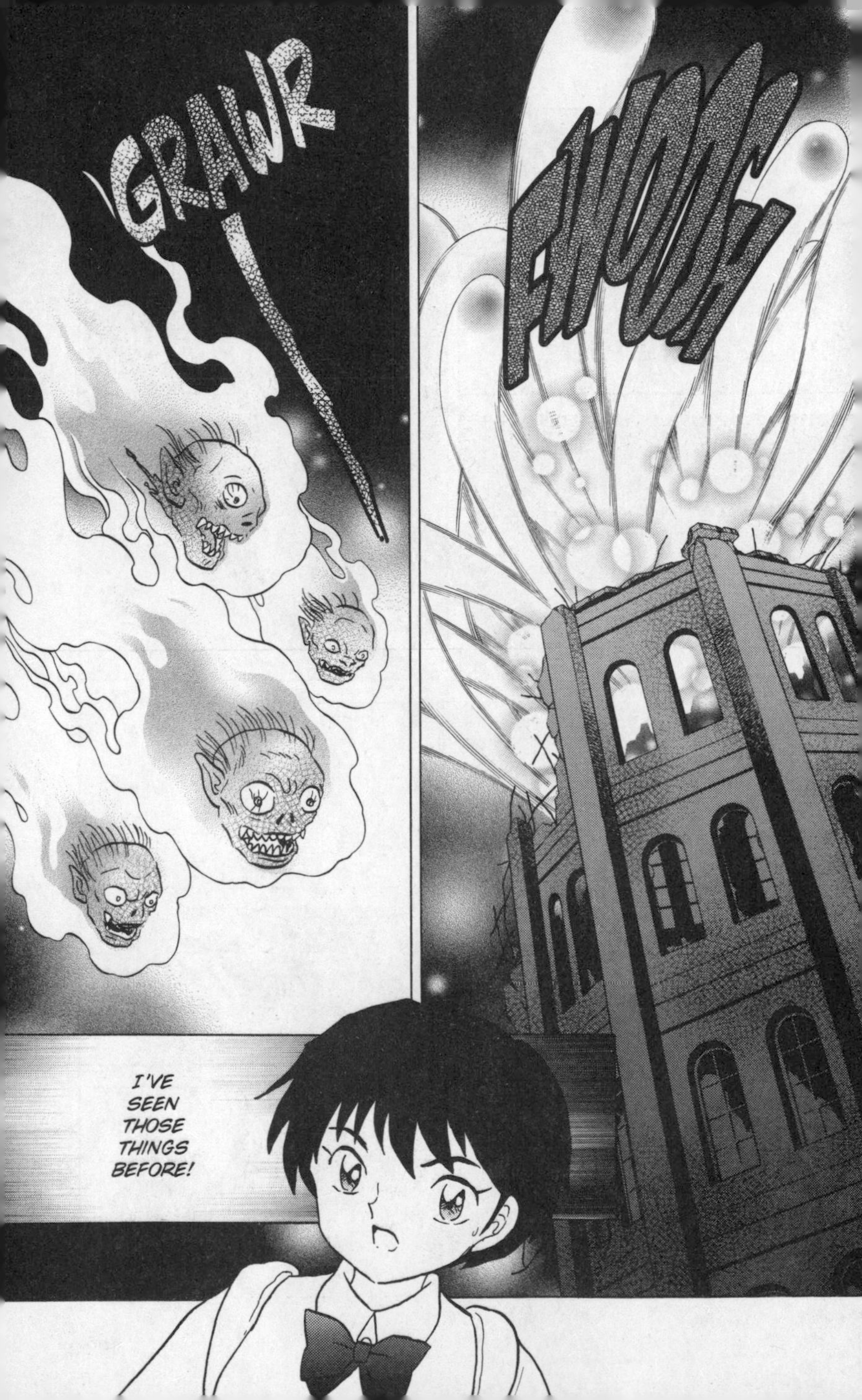
FWOOM
GRAWR
I'VE SEEN THOSE THINGS BEFORE!

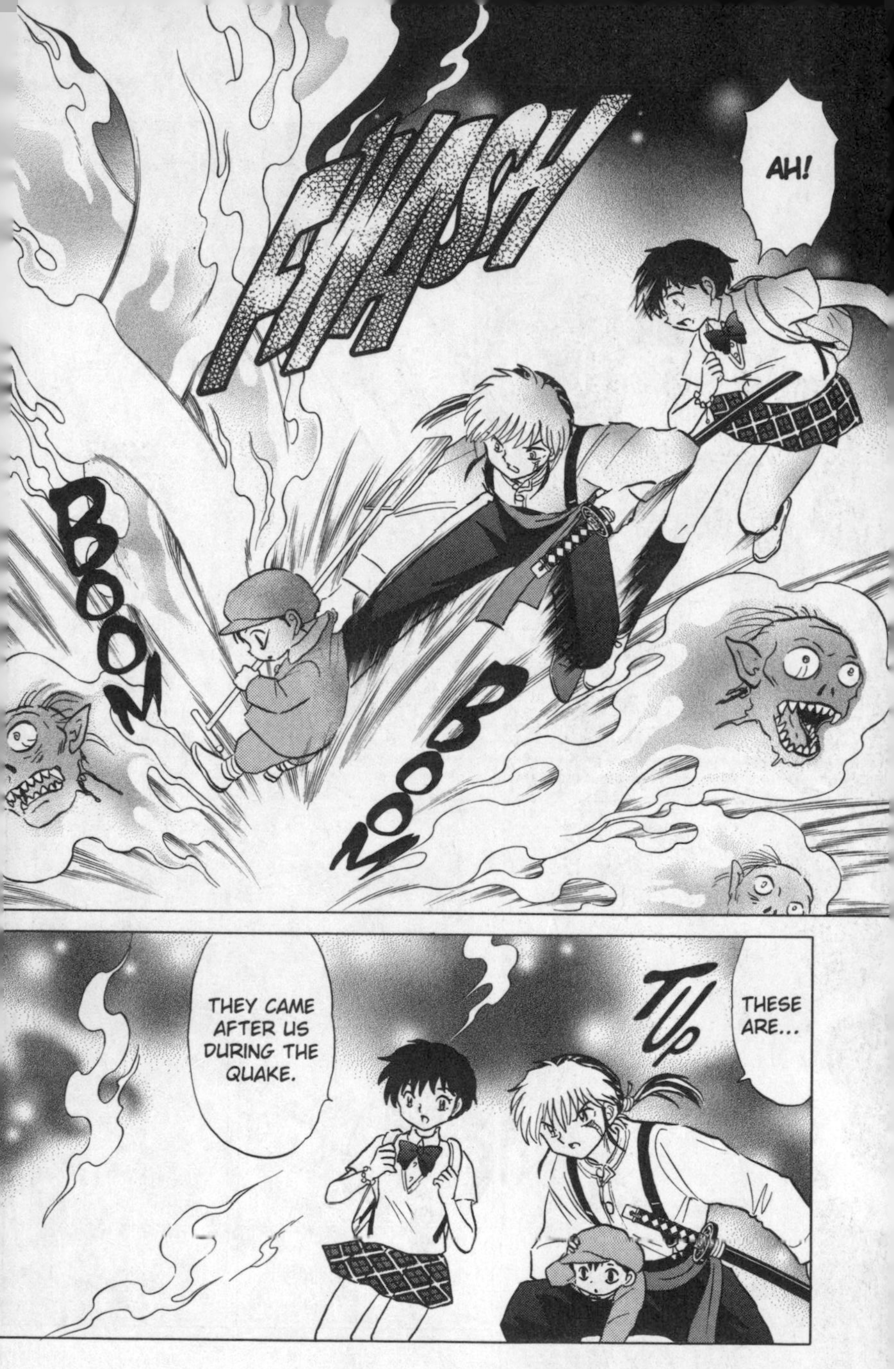
AH!
BOOM
BOOM
THESE ARE...
TUP
THEY CAME AFTER US DURING THE QUAKE.

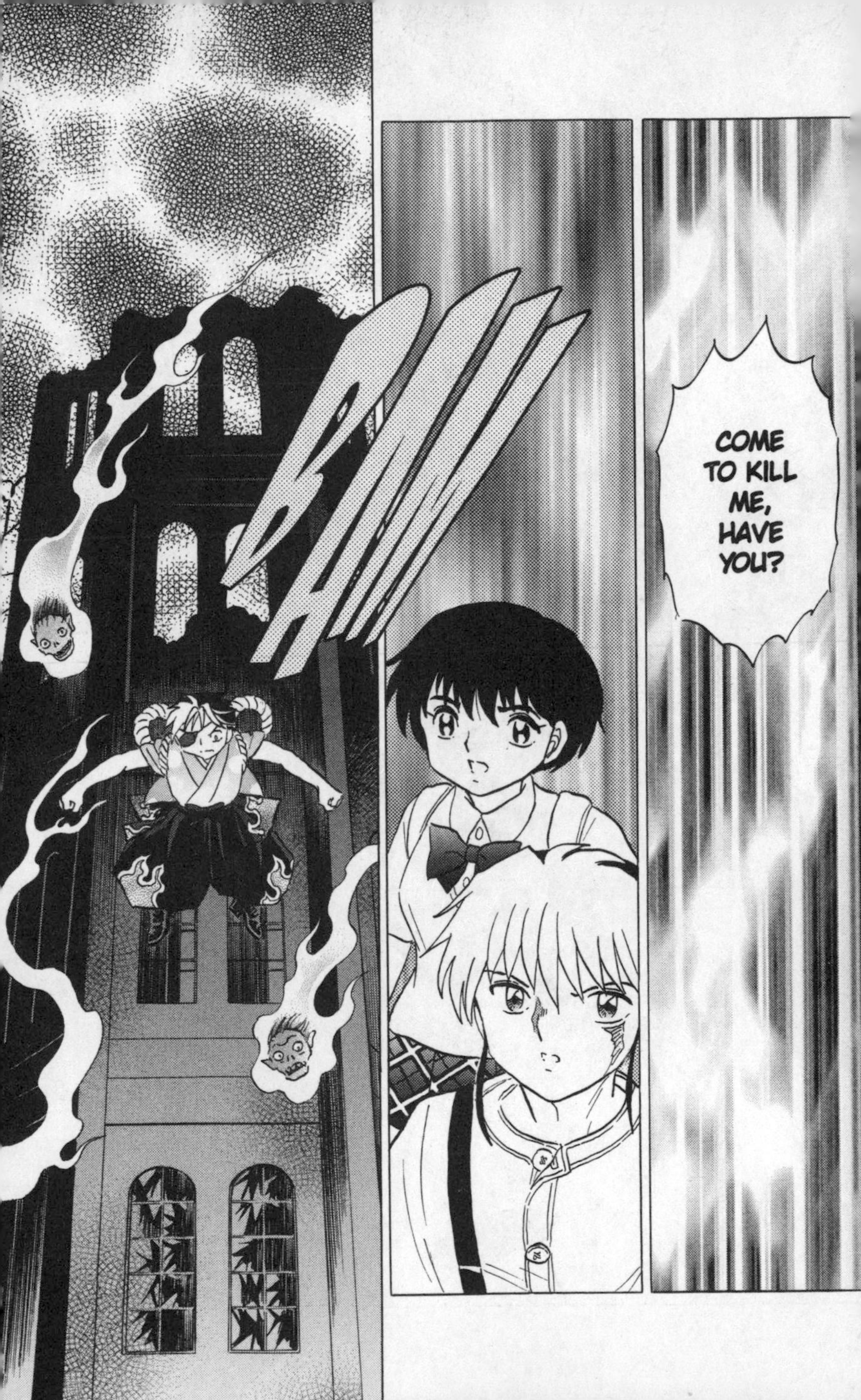
COME TO KILL ME, HAVE YOU?

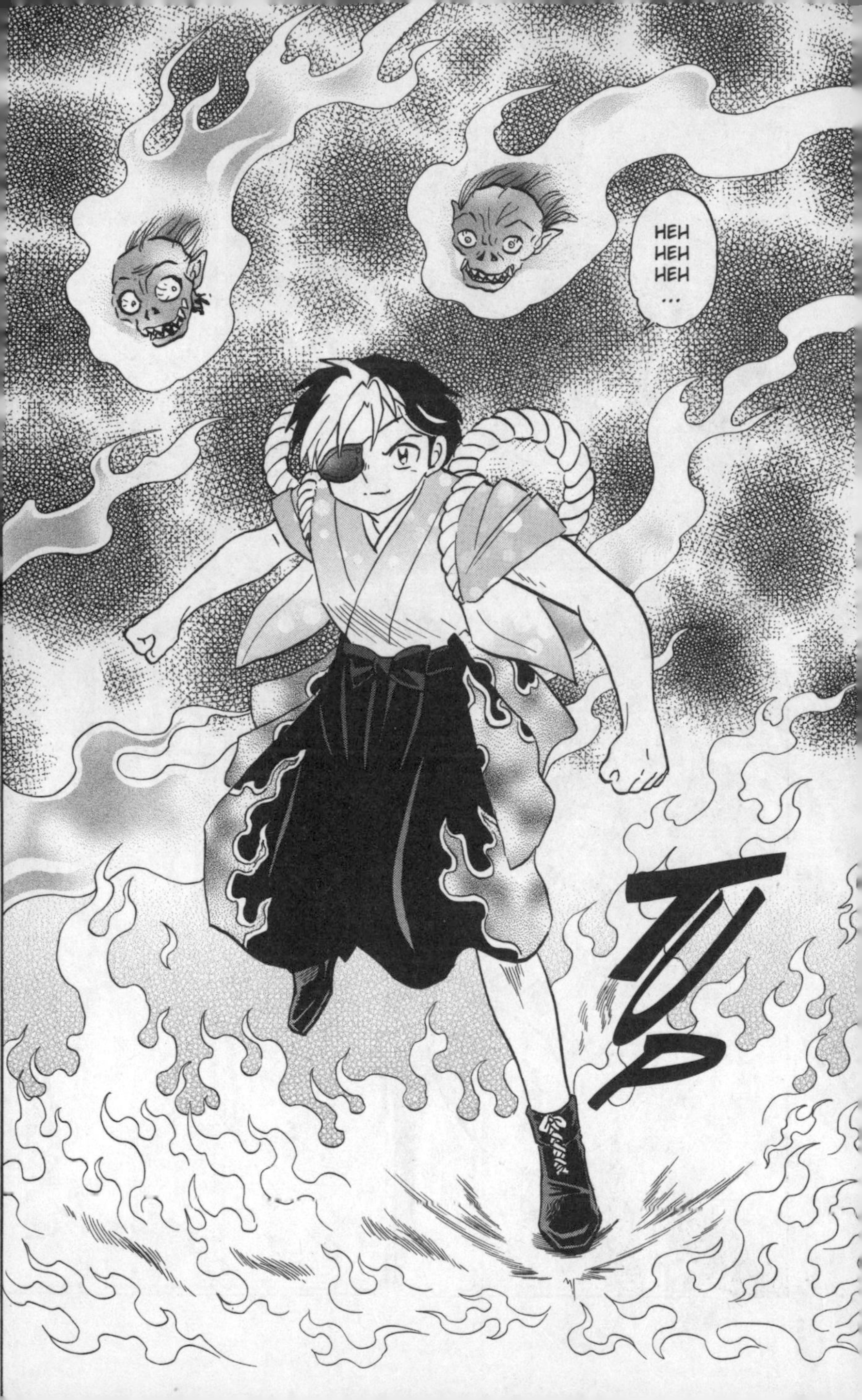
HEH HEH HEH ...
TUP

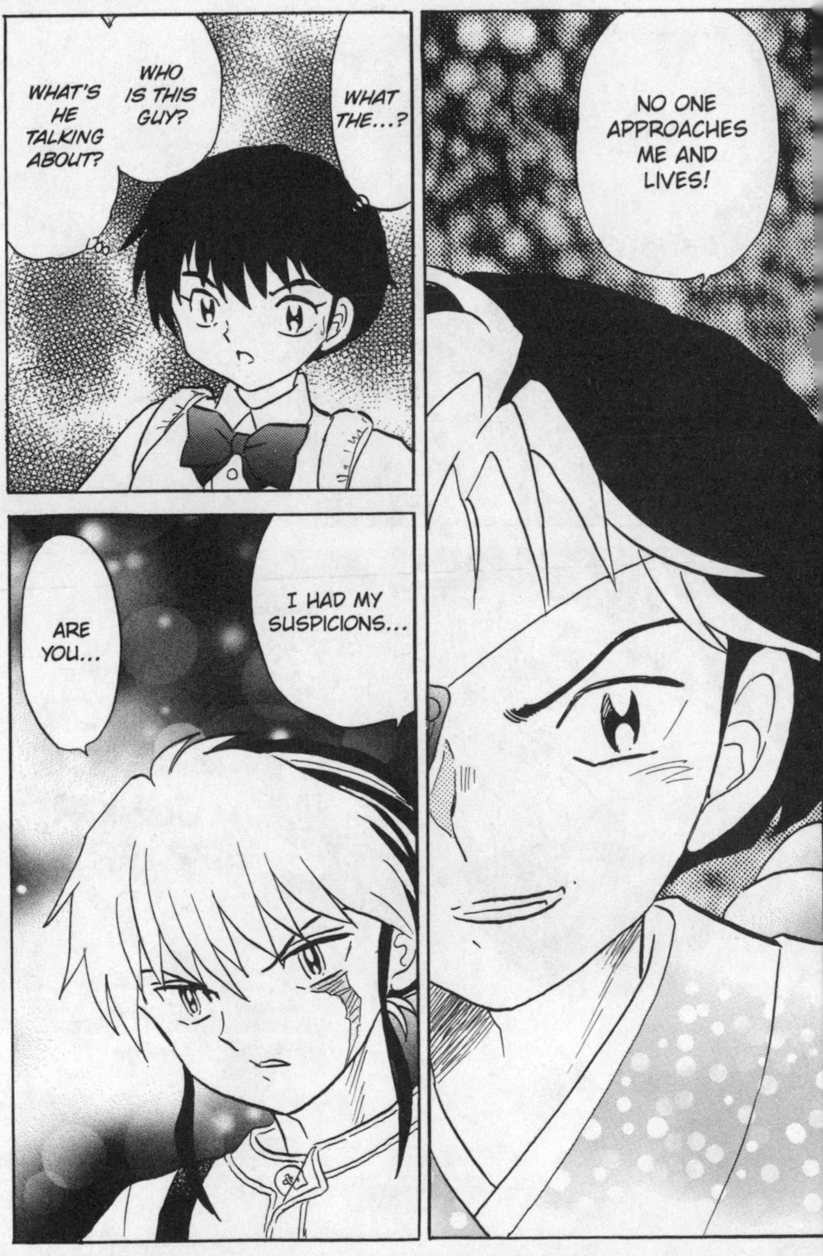
NO ONE APPROACHES ME AND LIVES!
WHAT THE...?
WHO IS THIS GUY?
WHAT'S HE TALKING ABOUT?
I HAD MY SUSPICIONS...
ARE YOU...

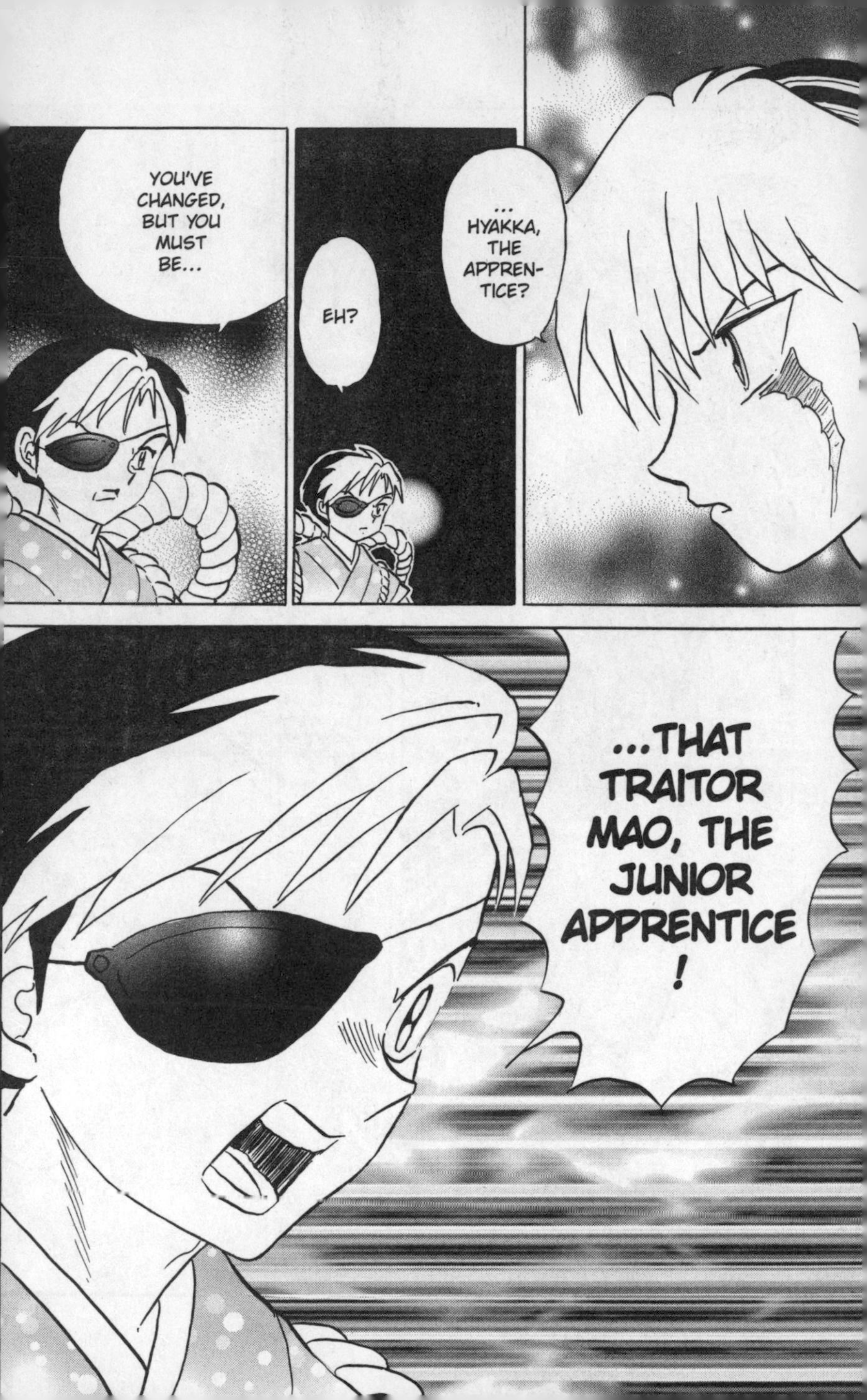
...HYAKKA, THE APPRENTICE?
EH?
YOU'VE CHANGED, BUT YOU MUST BE...
...THAT TRAITOR MAO, THE JUNIOR APPRENTICE!

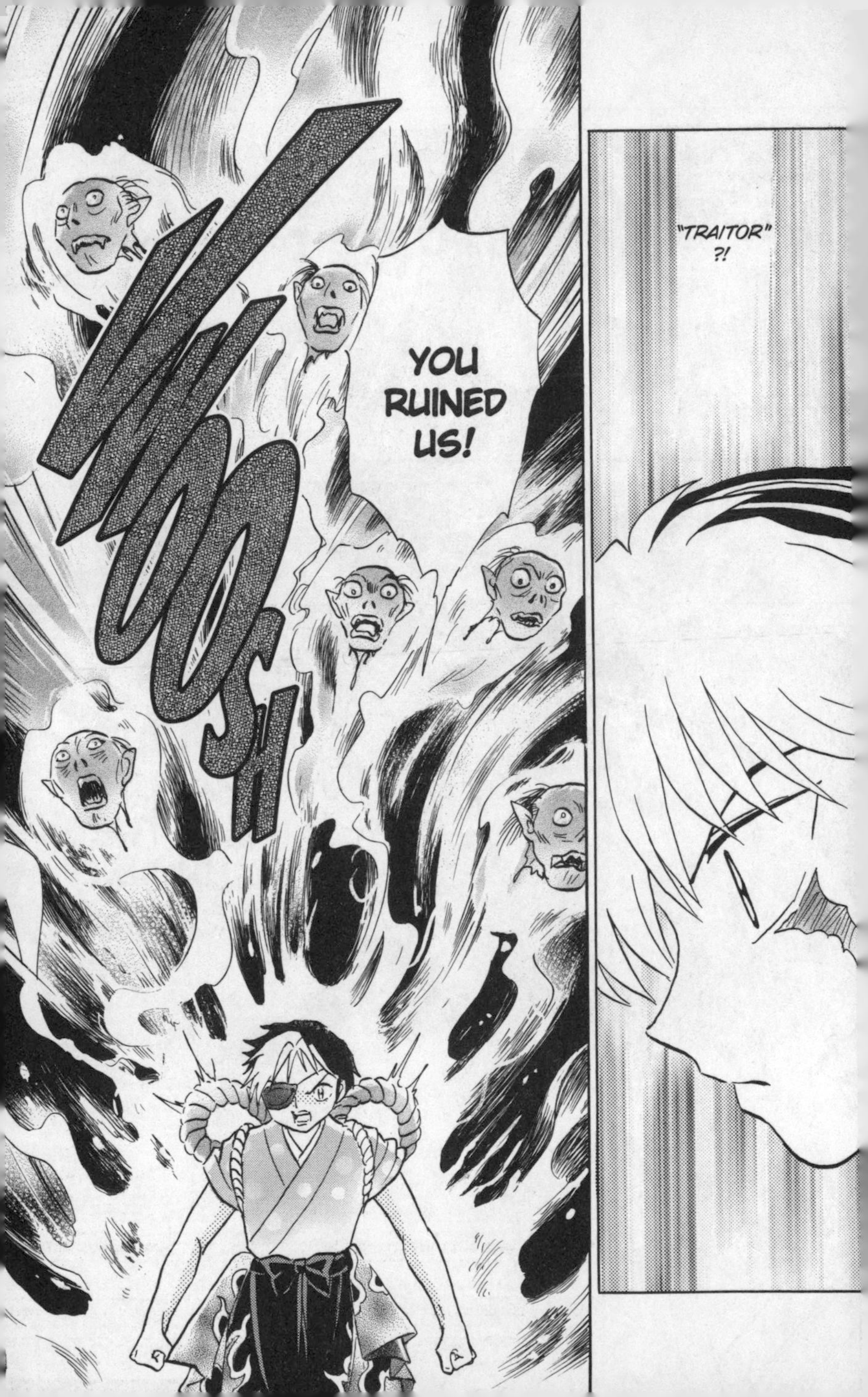
"TRAITOR"
?!
WHOOSH
YOU RUINED US!

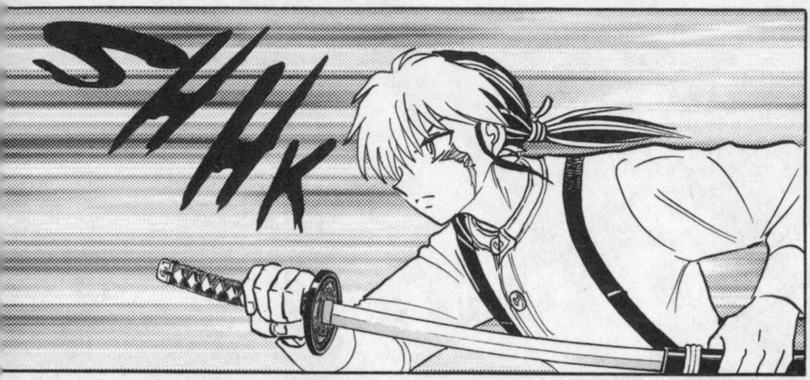
SHHK
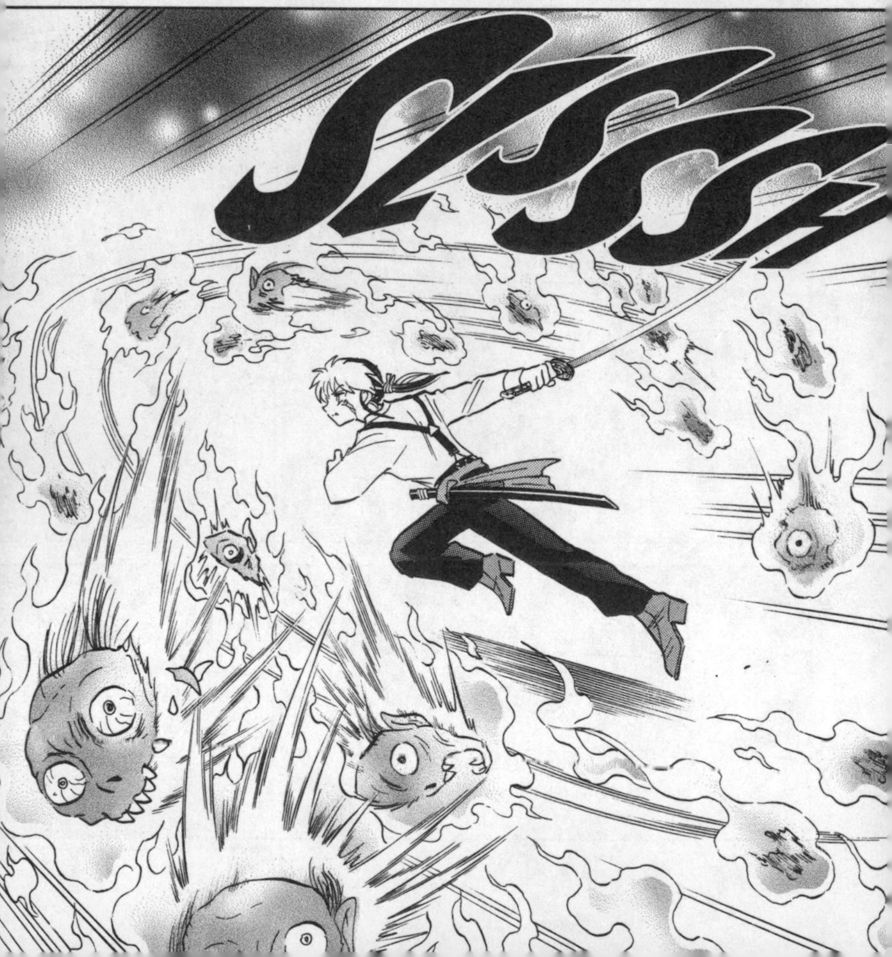
SLISSH

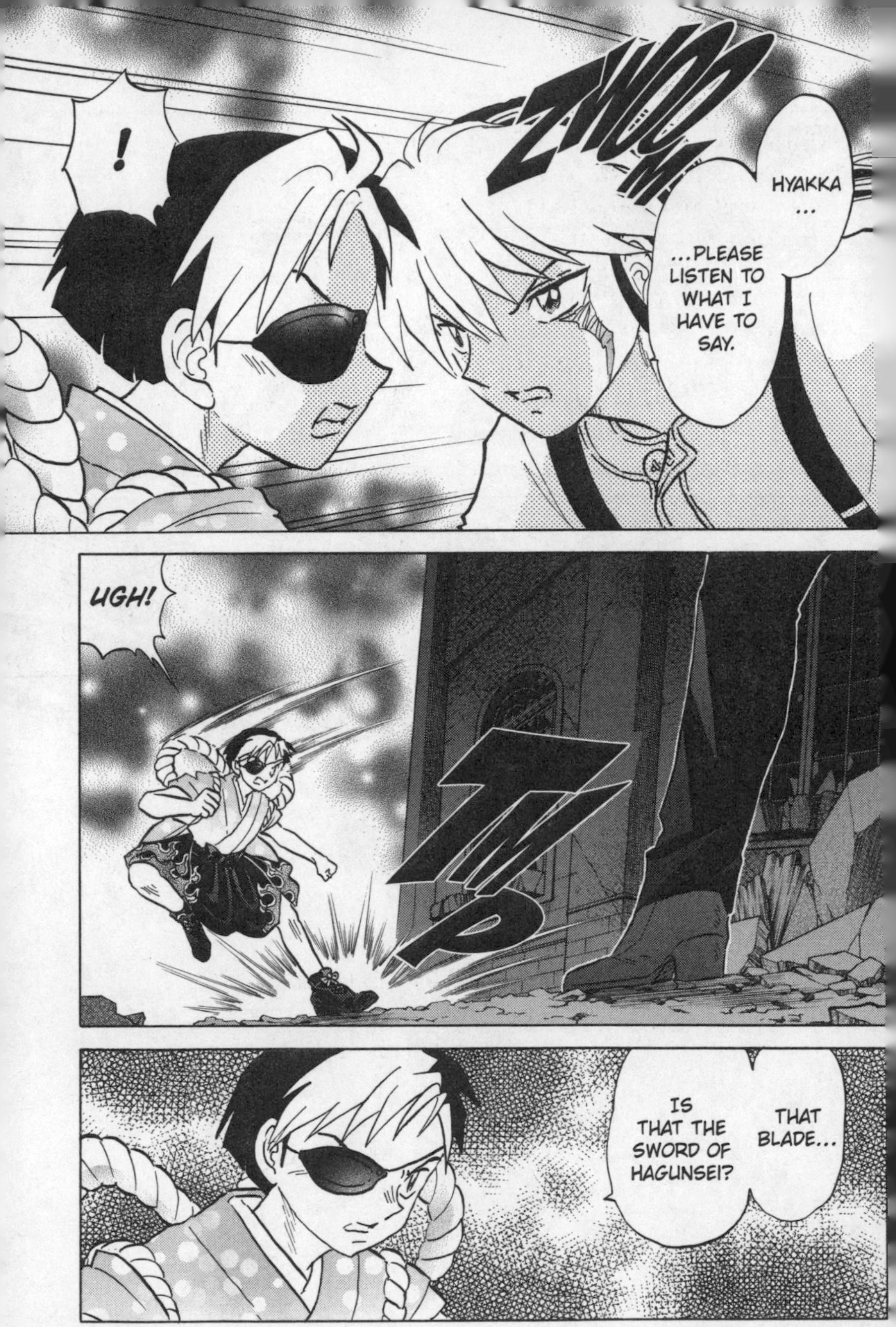
ZWOOM
HYAKKA ...
...PLEASE LISTEN TO WHAT I HAVE TO SAY.
!
TMP
UGH!
THAT BLADE...
IS THAT THE SWORD OF HAGUNSEI?

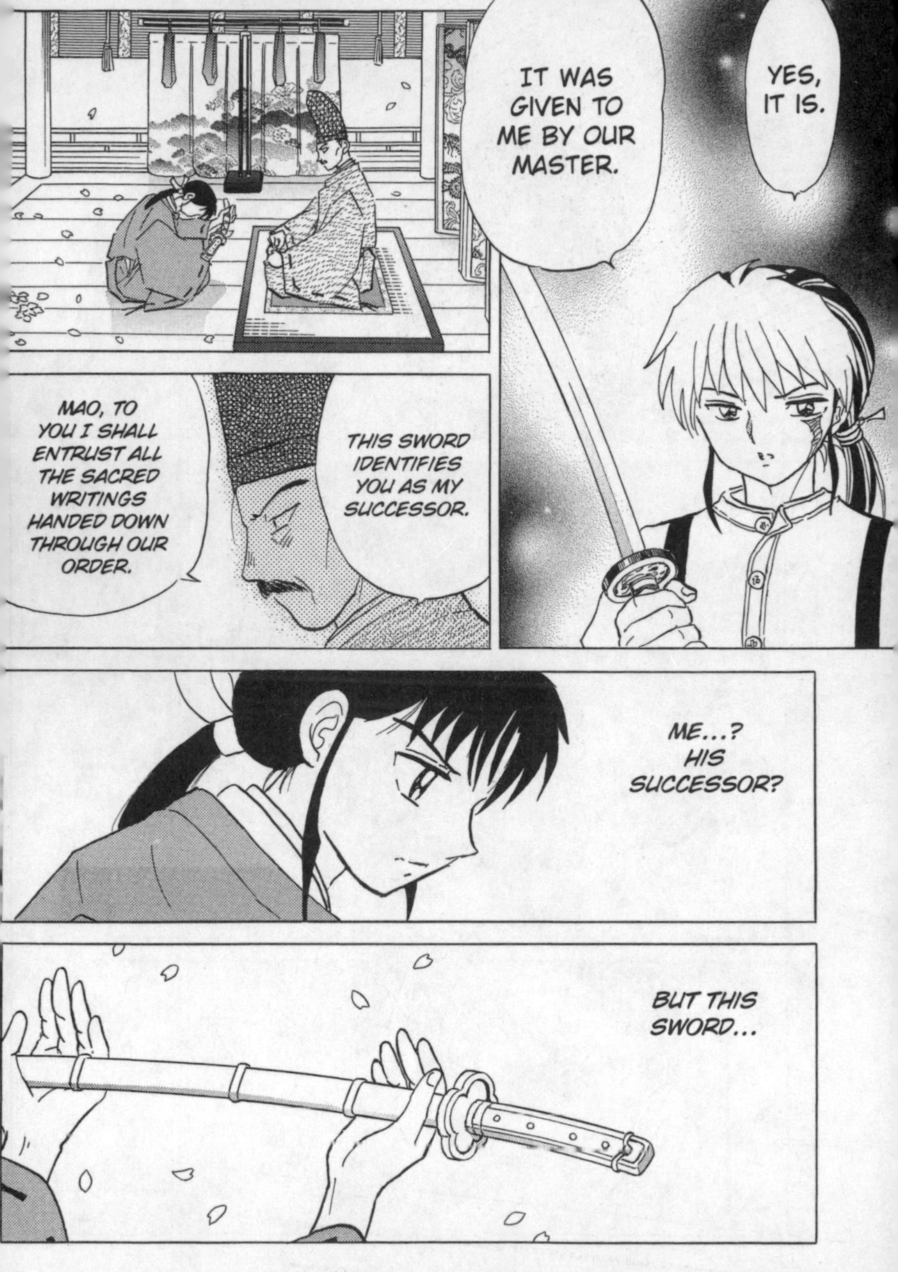
YES, IT IS.
IT WAS GIVEN TO ME BY OUR MASTER.
MAO, TO YOU I SHALL ENTRUST ALL THE SACRED WRITINGS HANDED DOWN THROUGH OUR ORDER.
THIS SWORD IDENTIFIES YOU AS MY SUCCESSOR.
ME...? HIS SUCCESSOR?
BUT THIS SWORD...

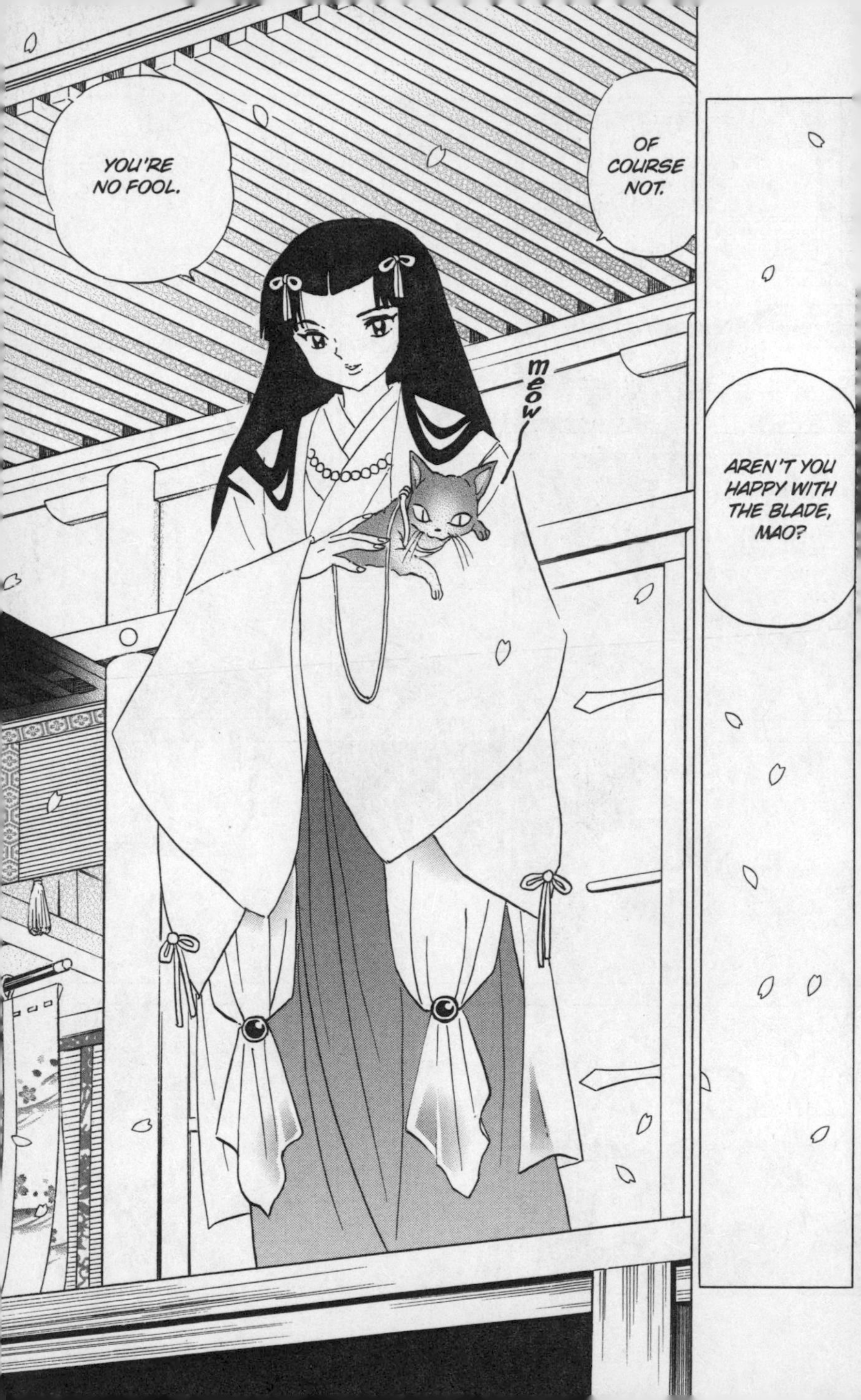
AREN'T YOU HAPPY WITH THE BLADE, MAO?
OF COURSE NOT.
YOU'RE NO FOOL.
meow

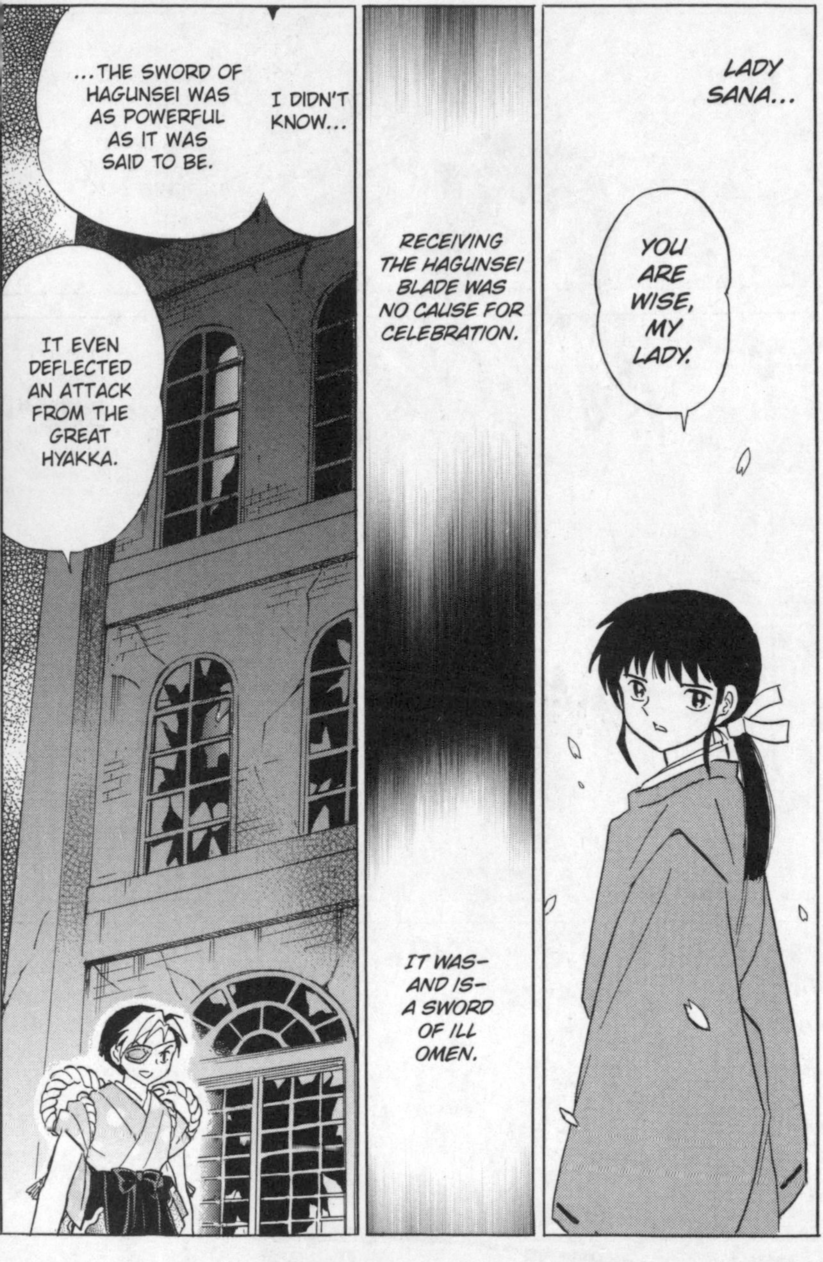
LADY SANA...
YOU ARE WISE, MY LADY.
RECEIVING THE HAGUNSEI BLADE WAS NO CAUSE FOR CELEBRATION.
IT WAS—AND IS—A SWORD OF ILL OMEN.
I DIDN'T KNOW...
...THE SWORD OF HAGUNSEI WAS AS POWERFUL AS IT WAS SAID TO BE.
IT EVEN DEFLECTED AN ATTACK FROM THE GREAT HYAKKA.

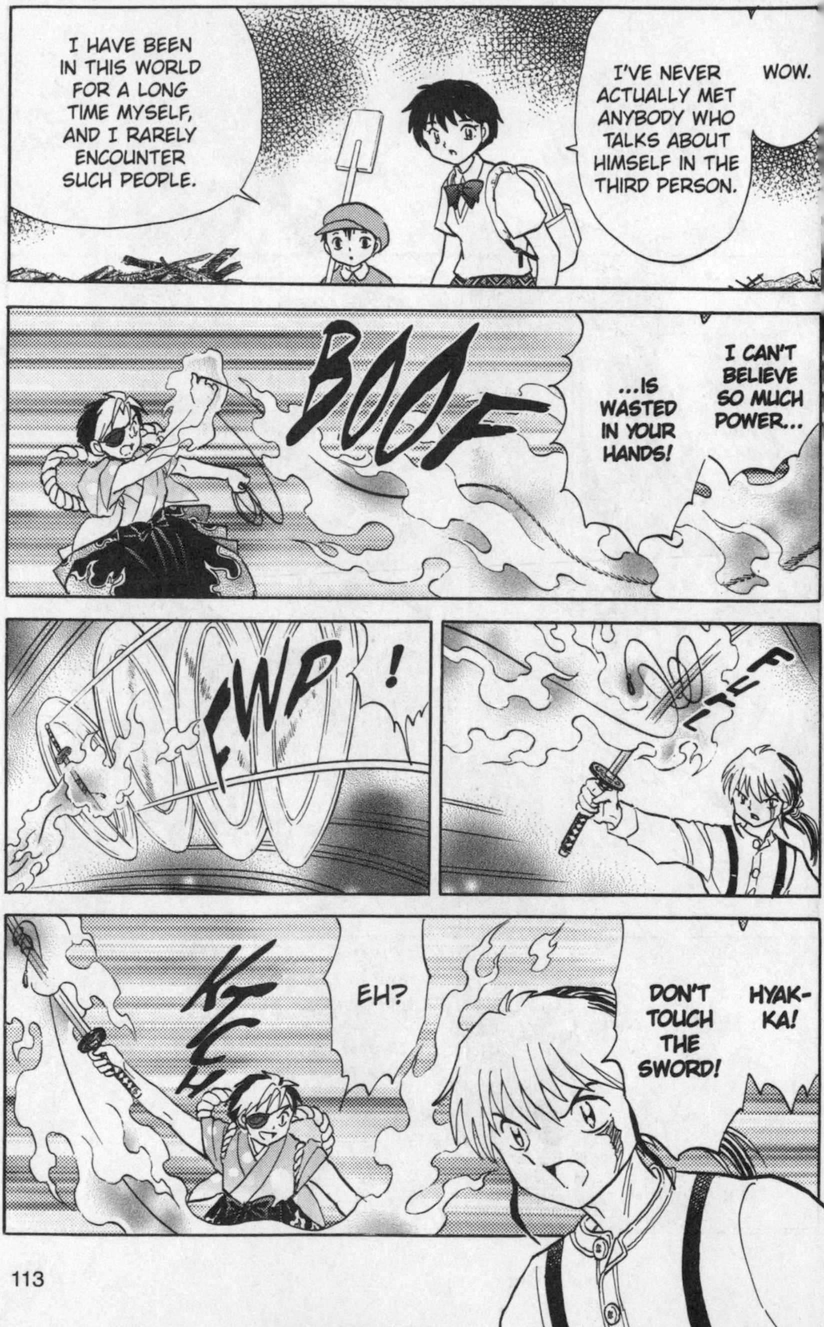

WOW.
I'VE NEVER ACTUALLY MET ANYBODY WHO TALKS ABOUT HIMSELF IN THE THIRD PERSON.
I HAVE BEEN IN THIS WORLD FOR A LONG TIME MYSELF, AND I RARELY ENCOUNTER SUCH PEOPLE.
I CAN'T BELIEVE SO MUCH POWER...
...IS WASTED IN YOUR HANDS!
BOOF
FWP !
HYAK-KA!
DON'T TOUCH THE SWORD!
EH?

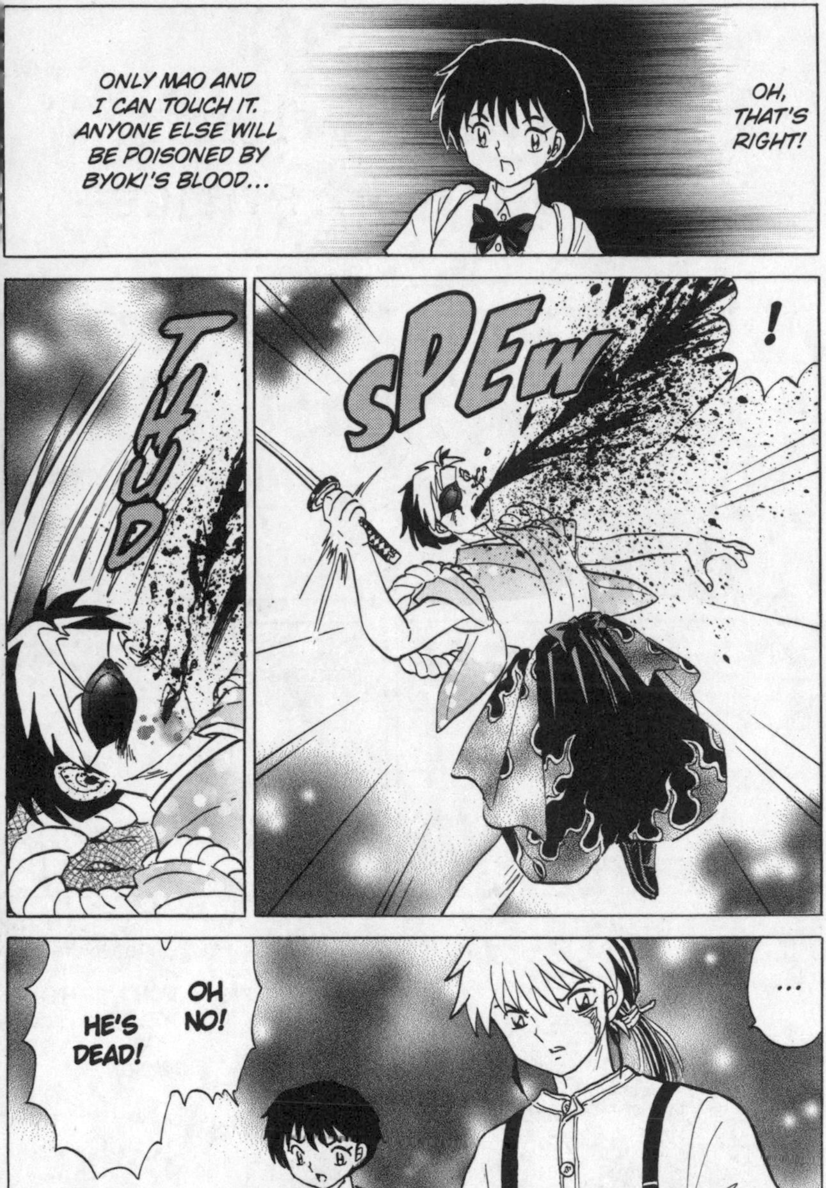
OH, THAT'S RIGHT!
ONLY MAO AND I CAN TOUCH IT. ANYONE ELSE WILL BE POISONED BY BYOKI'S BLOOD...
SPEW
!
THUD
...
OH NO!
HE'S DEAD!

Chapter 7:
Hyakka the Senior Apprentice

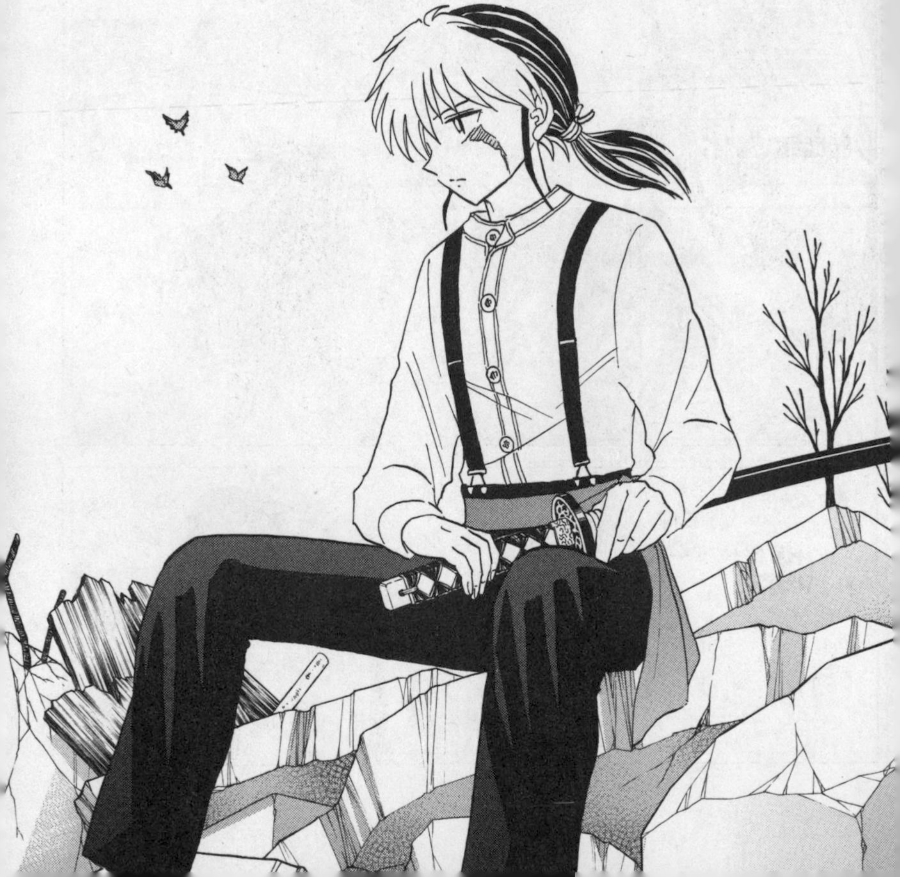

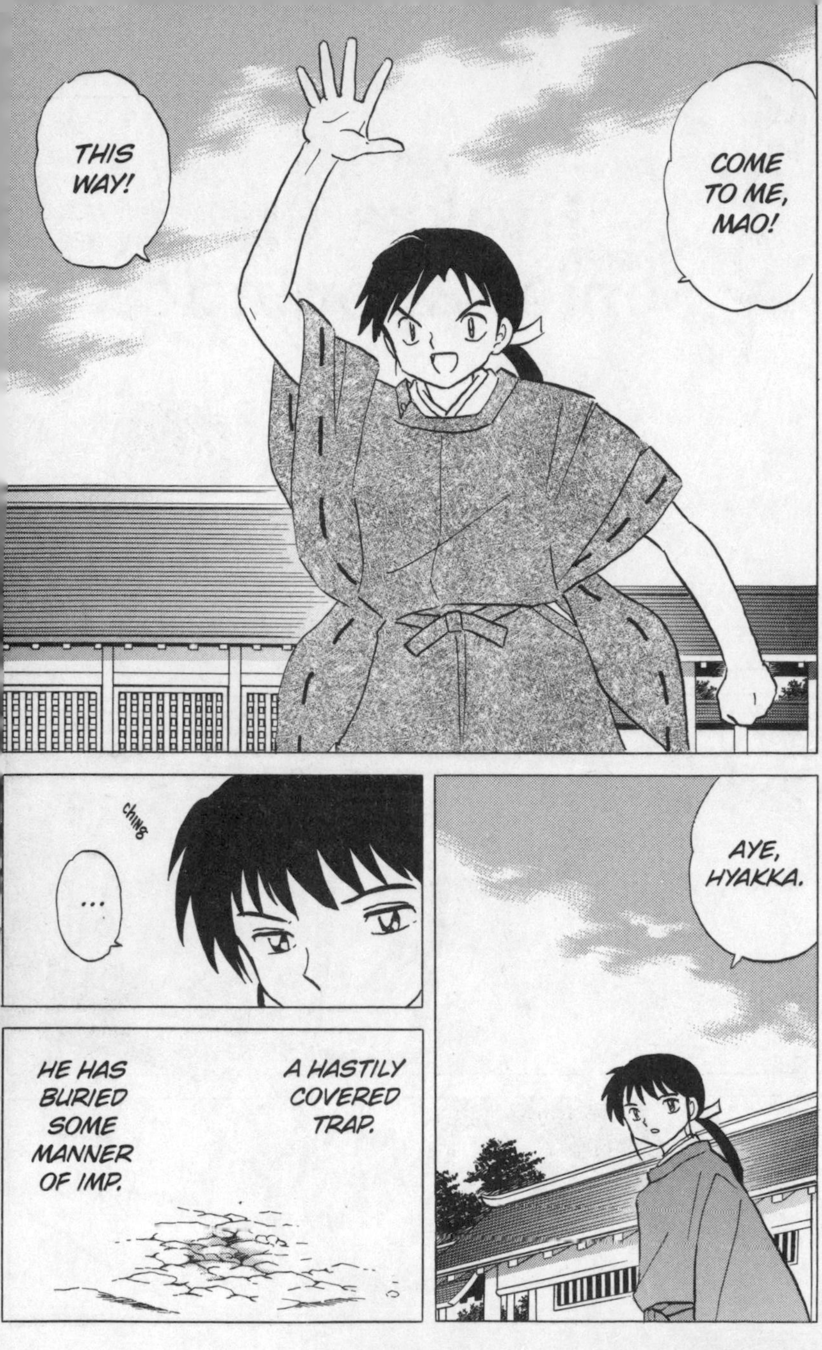
COME TO ME, MAO!
THIS WAY!
AYE, HYAKKA.
ching
...
A HASTILY COVERED TRAP.
HE HAS BURIED SOME MANNER OF IMP.

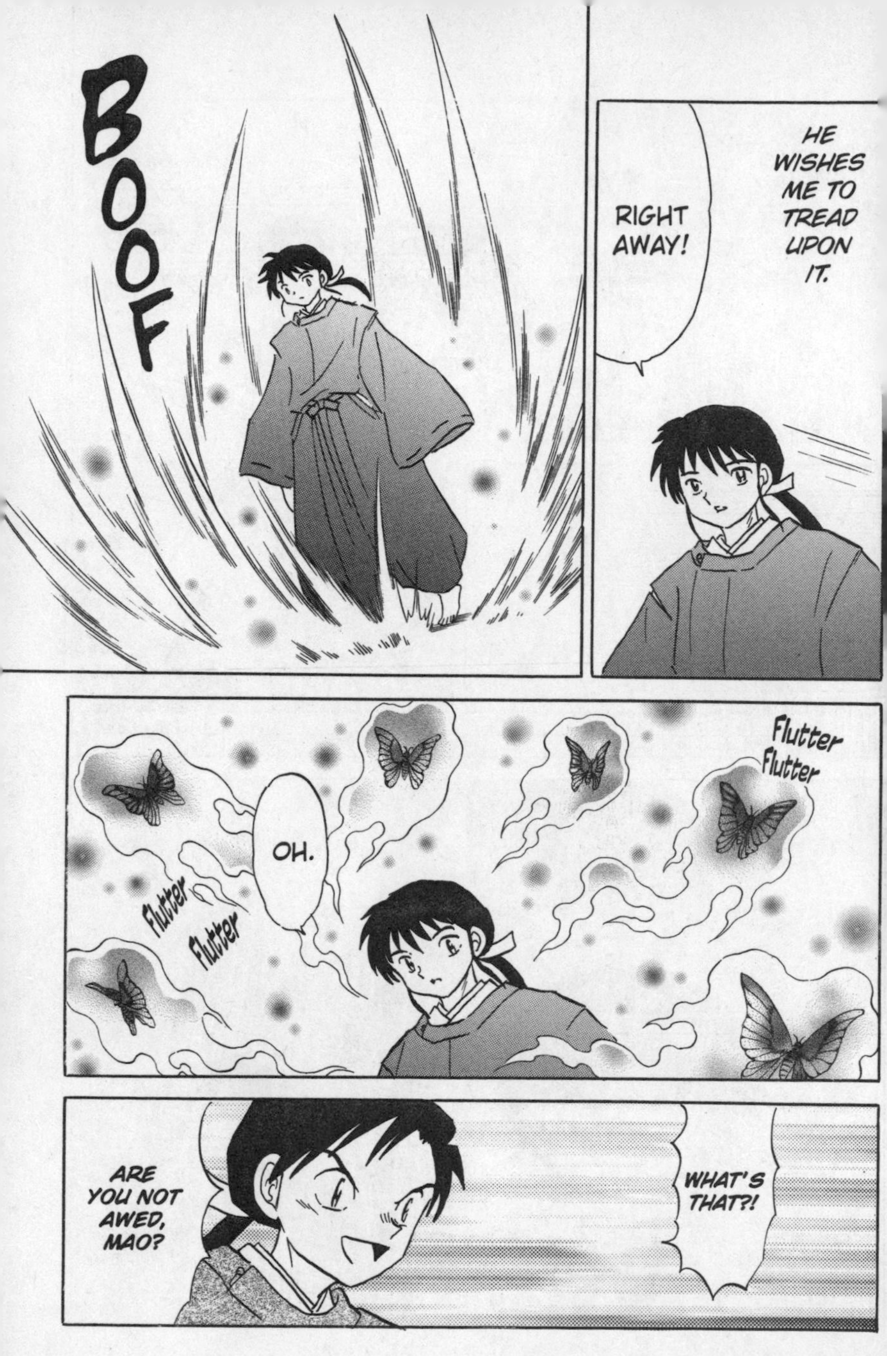
HE WISHES ME TO TREAD UPON IT.
RIGHT AWAY!
BOOF
Flutter Flutter
OH.
Flutter Flutter
WHAT'S THAT?!
ARE YOU NOT AWED, MAO?

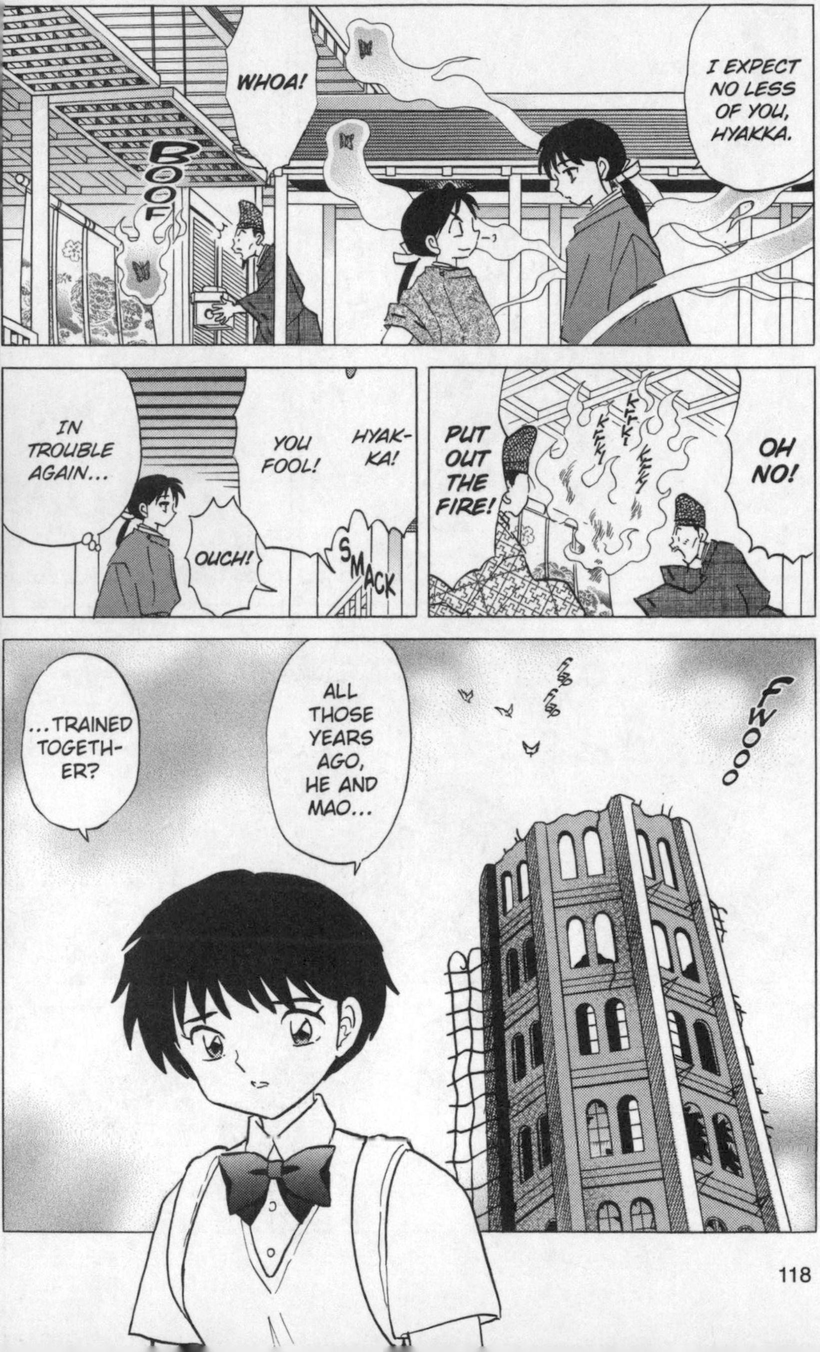
I EXPECT NO LESS OF YOU, HYAKKA.
WHOA!
BOOF
OH NO!
PUT OUT THE FIRE!
HYAK-KA!
YOU FOOL!
SMACK
OUCH!
IN TROUBLE AGAIN...
FWOOO
ALL THOSE YEARS AGO, HE AND MAO...
...TRAINED TOGETH-ER?

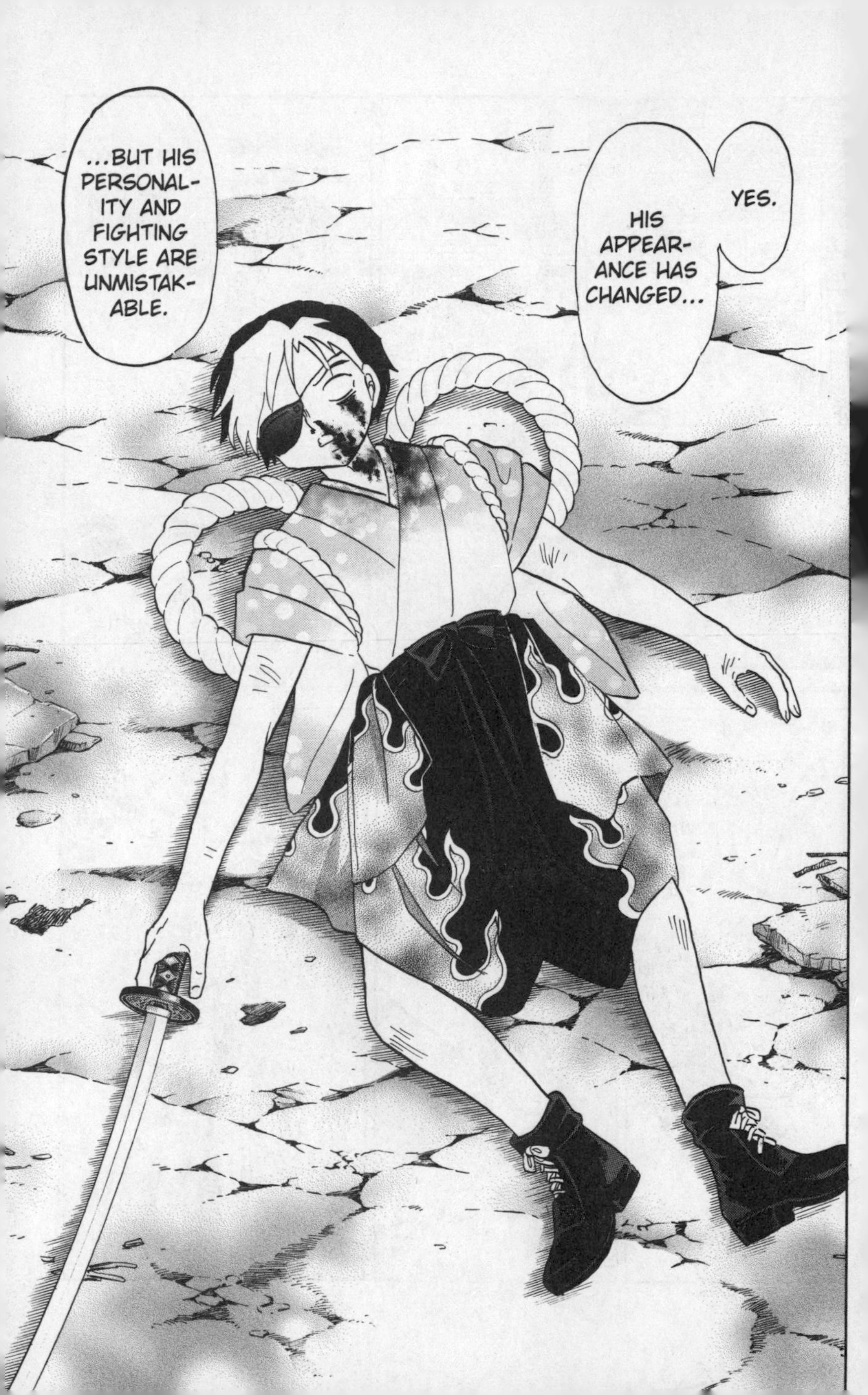
YES.
HIS APPEARANCE HAS CHANGED...
...BUT HIS PERSONALITY AND FIGHTING STYLE ARE UNMISTAKABLE.

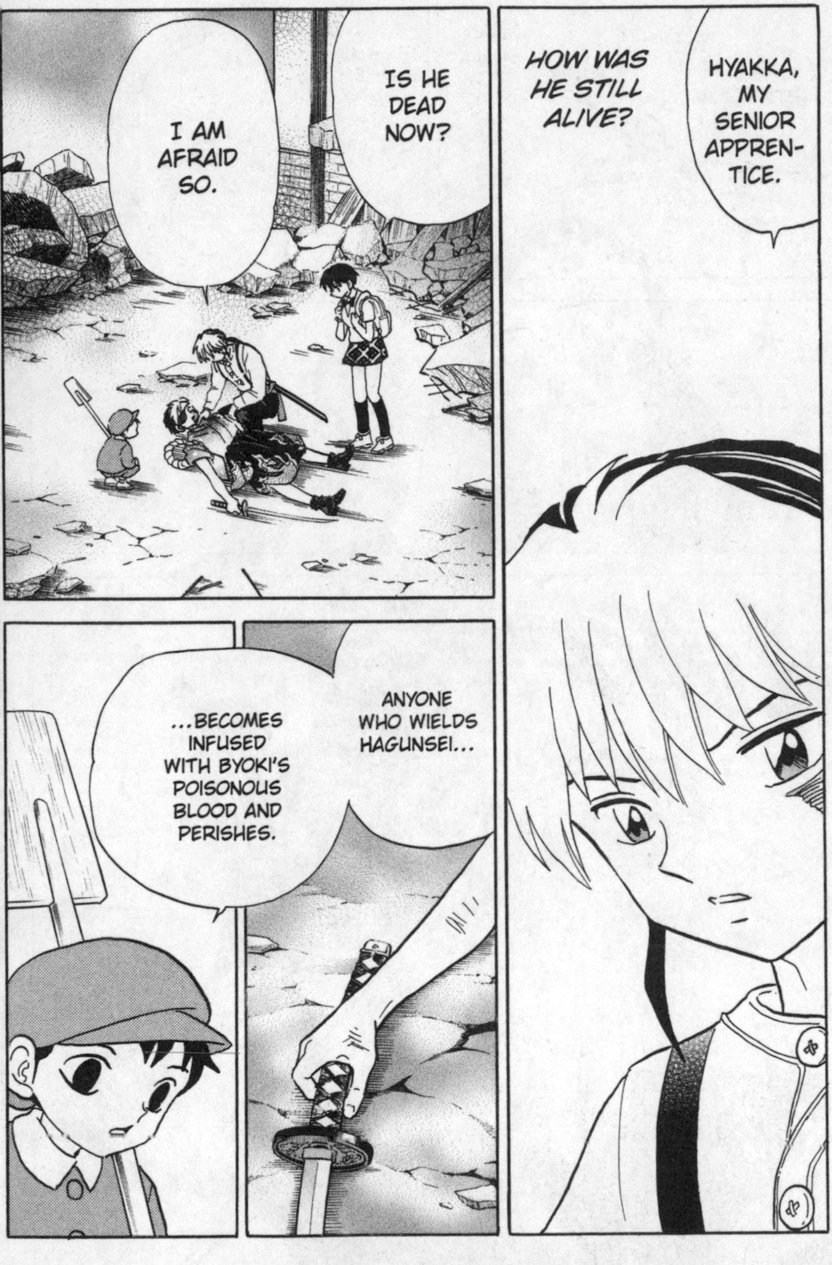
HYAKKA, MY SENIOR APPRENTICE.
HOW WAS HE STILL ALIVE?
IS HE DEAD NOW?
I AM AFRAID SO.
ANYONE WHO WIELDS HAGUNSEI...
...BECOMES INFUSED WITH BYOKI'S POISONOUS BLOOD AND PERISHES.

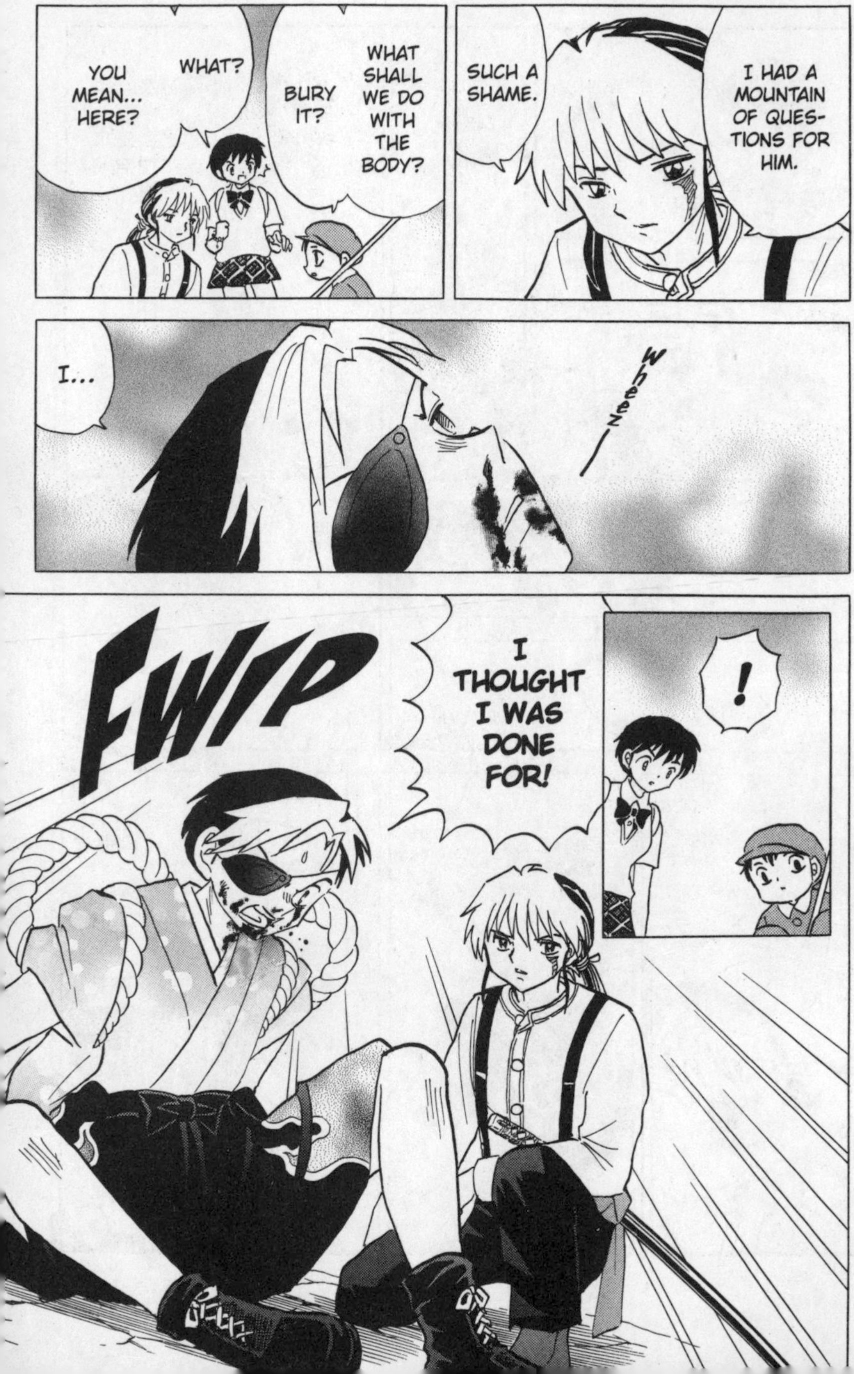
I HAD A MOUNTAIN OF QUES-TIONS FOR HIM.
SUCH A SHAME.
WHAT SHALL WE DO WITH THE BODY?
BURY IT?
WHAT?
YOU MEAN... HERE?
Wheez
I...
!
I THOUGHT I WAS DONE FOR!
FWIP

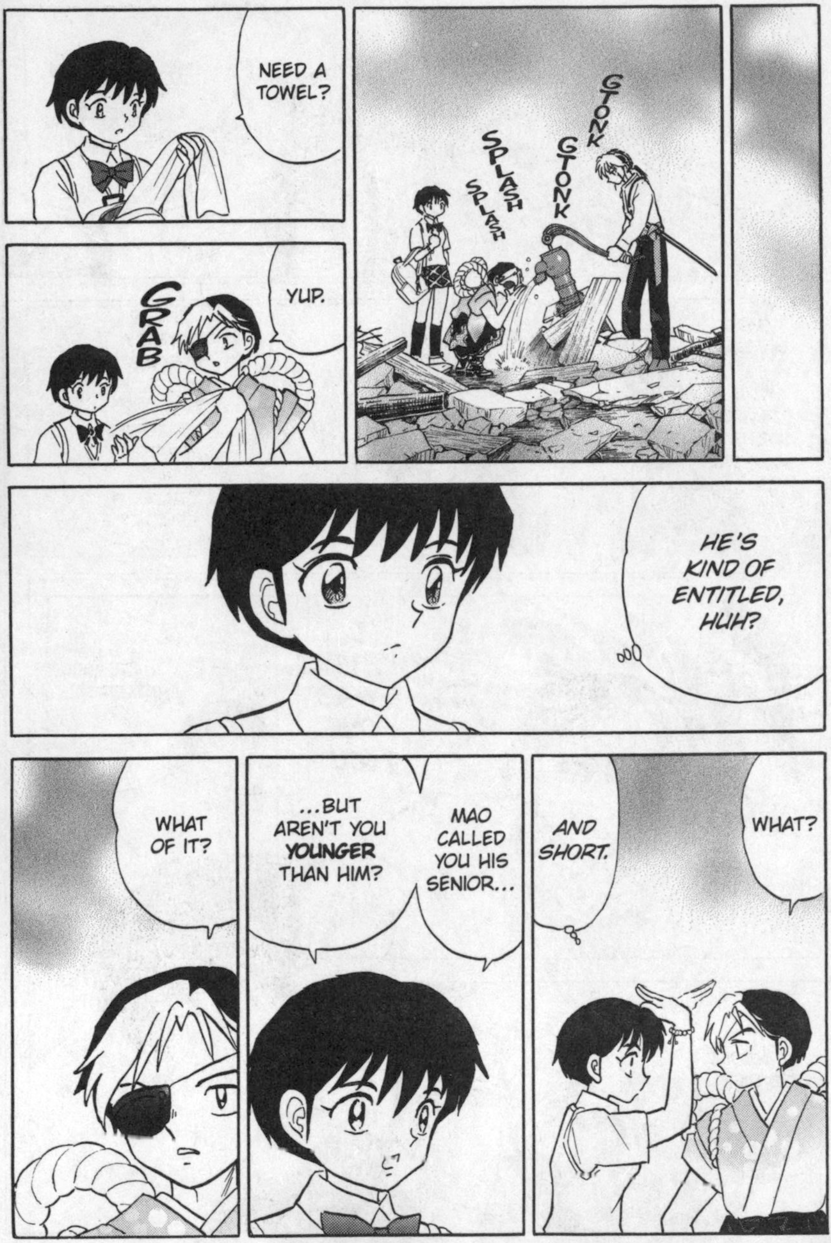
GTONK
GTONK
SPLASH
SPLASH
NEED A TOWEL?
GRAB
YUP.
HE'S KIND OF ENTITLED, HUH?
WHAT?
AND SHORT.
MAO CALLED YOU HIS SENIOR...
...BUT AREN'T YOU **YOUNGER** THAN HIM?
WHAT OF IT?

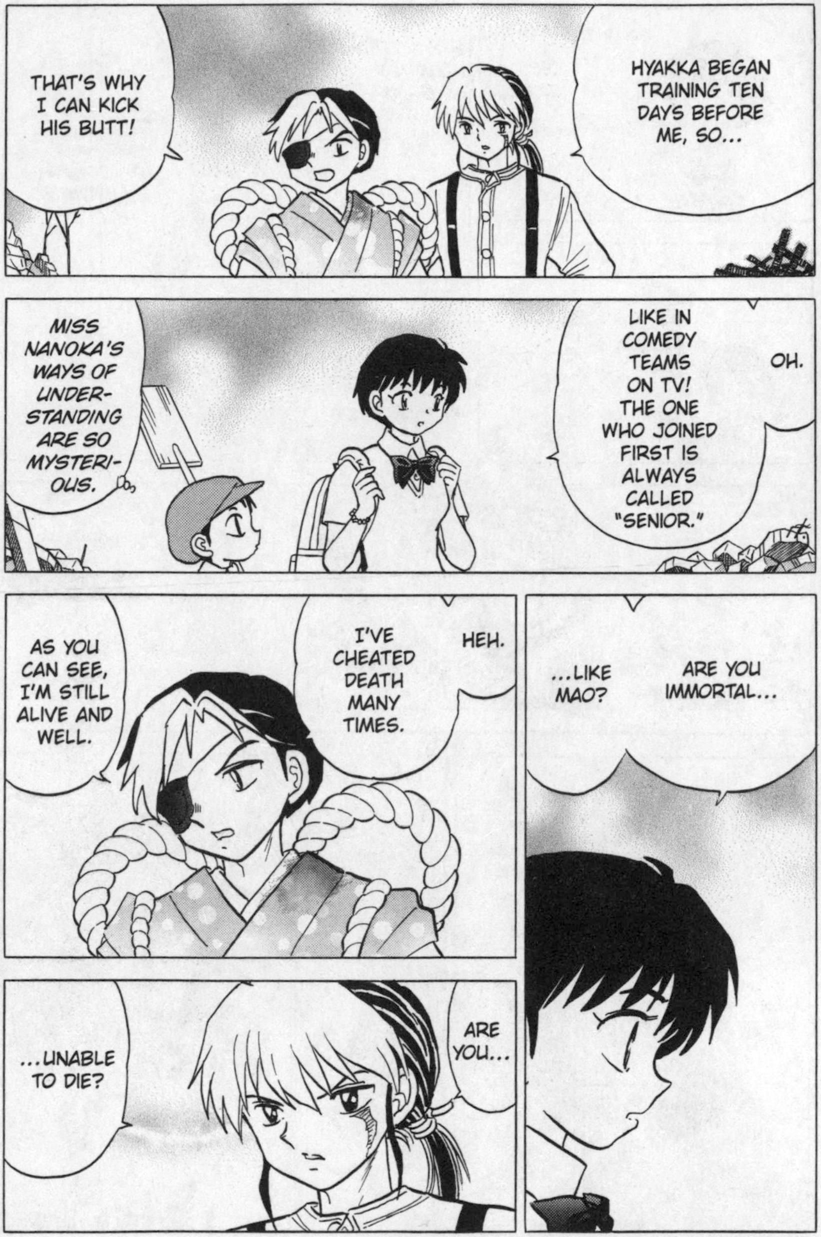
HYAKKA BEGAN TRAINING TEN DAYS BEFORE ME, SO...
THAT'S WHY I CAN KICK HIS BUTT!
OH.
LIKE IN COMEDY TEAMS ON TV! THE ONE WHO JOINED FIRST IS ALWAYS CALLED "SENIOR."
MISS NANOKA'S WAYS OF UNDER-STANDING ARE SO MYSTERI-OUS.
ARE YOU IMMORTAL...
...LIKE MAO?
HEH.
I'VE CHEATED DEATH MANY TIMES.
AS YOU CAN SEE, I'M STILL ALIVE AND WELL.
ARE YOU...
...UNABLE TO DIE?

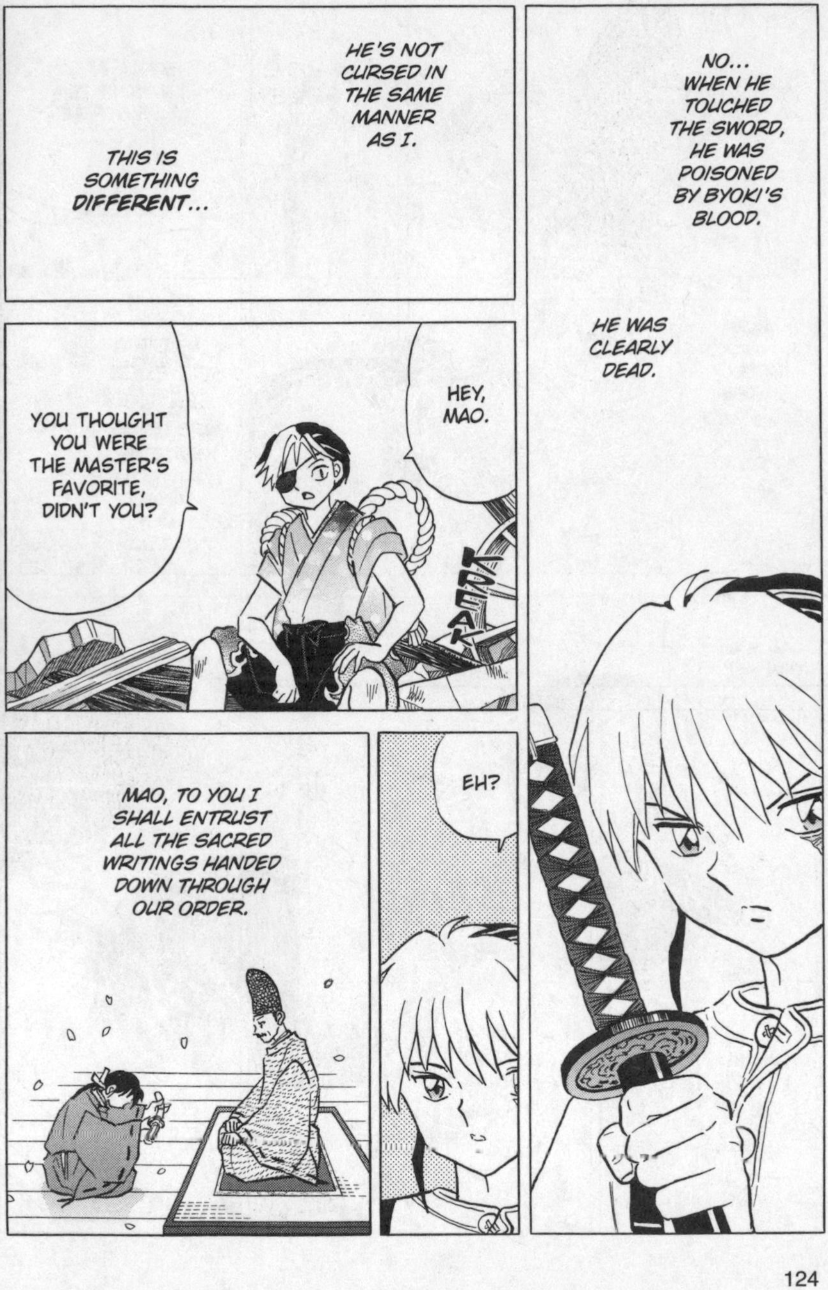
NO... WHEN HE TOUCHED THE SWORD, HE WAS POISONED BY BYOKI'S BLOOD.
HE WAS CLEARLY DEAD.
HE'S NOT CURSED IN THE SAME MANNER AS I.
THIS IS SOMETHING DIFFERENT...
HEY, MAO.
KREAK
YOU THOUGHT YOU WERE THE MASTER'S FAVORITE, DIDN'T YOU?
EH?
MAO, TO YOU I SHALL ENTRUST ALL THE SACRED WRITINGS HANDED DOWN THROUGH OUR ORDER.

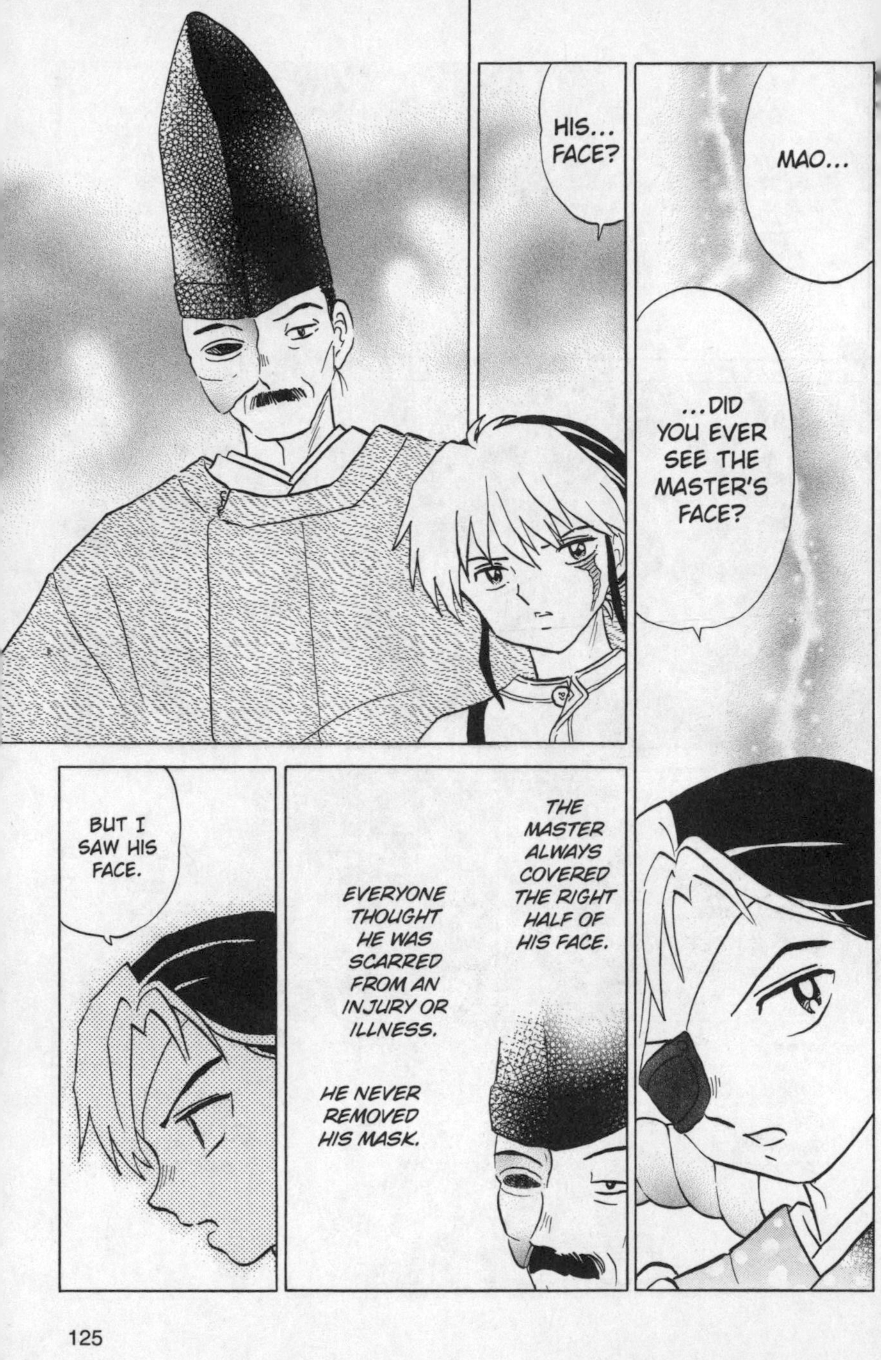
MAO...
...DID YOU EVER SEE THE MASTER'S FACE?
HIS... FACE?
THE MASTER ALWAYS COVERED THE RIGHT HALF OF HIS FACE.
EVERYONE THOUGHT HE WAS SCARRED FROM AN INJURY OR ILLNESS.
HE NEVER REMOVED HIS MASK.
BUT I SAW HIS FACE.

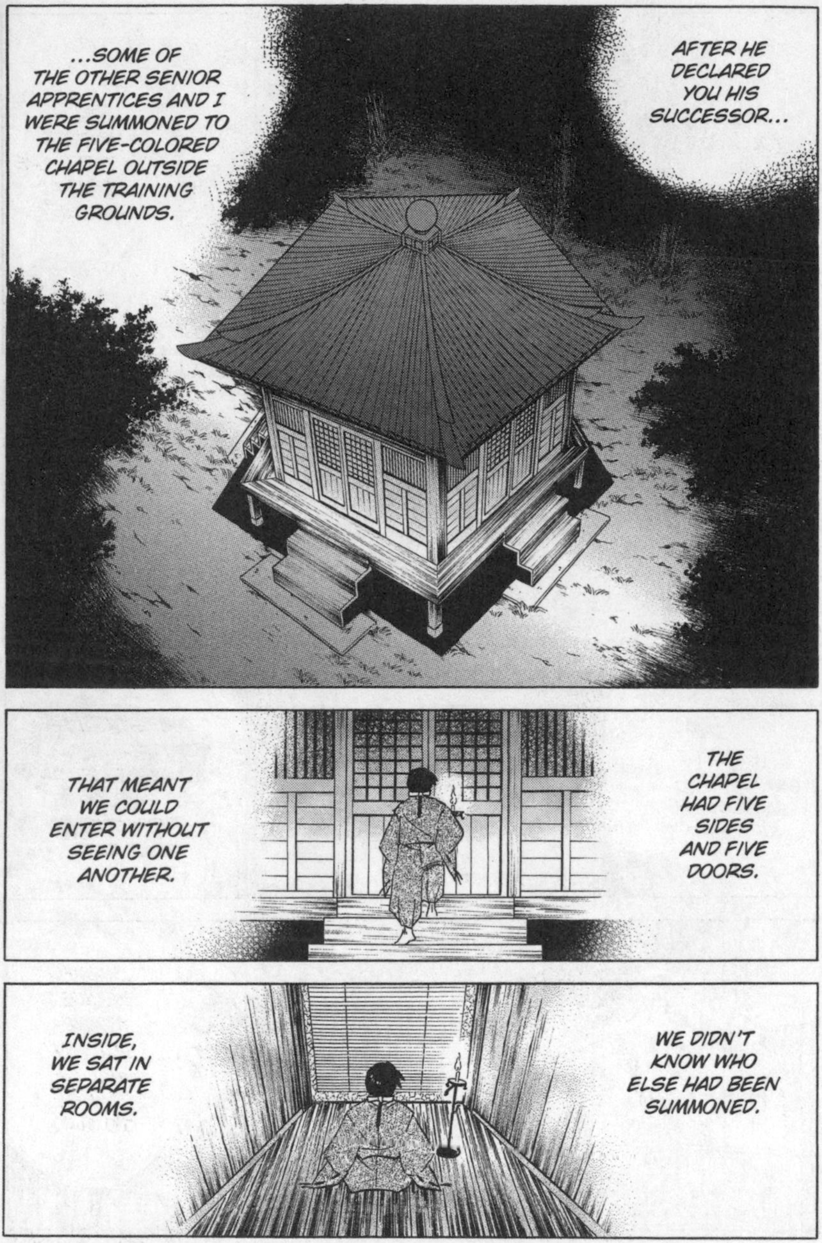
AFTER HE DECLARED YOU HIS SUCCESSOR...
...SOME OF THE OTHER SENIOR APPRENTICES AND I WERE SUMMONED TO THE FIVE-COLORED CHAPEL OUTSIDE THE TRAINING GROUNDS.
THE CHAPEL HAD FIVE SIDES AND FIVE DOORS.
THAT MEANT WE COULD ENTER WITHOUT SEEING ONE ANOTHER.
WE DIDN'T KNOW WHO ELSE HAD BEEN SUMMONED.
INSIDE, WE SAT IN SEPARATE ROOMS.

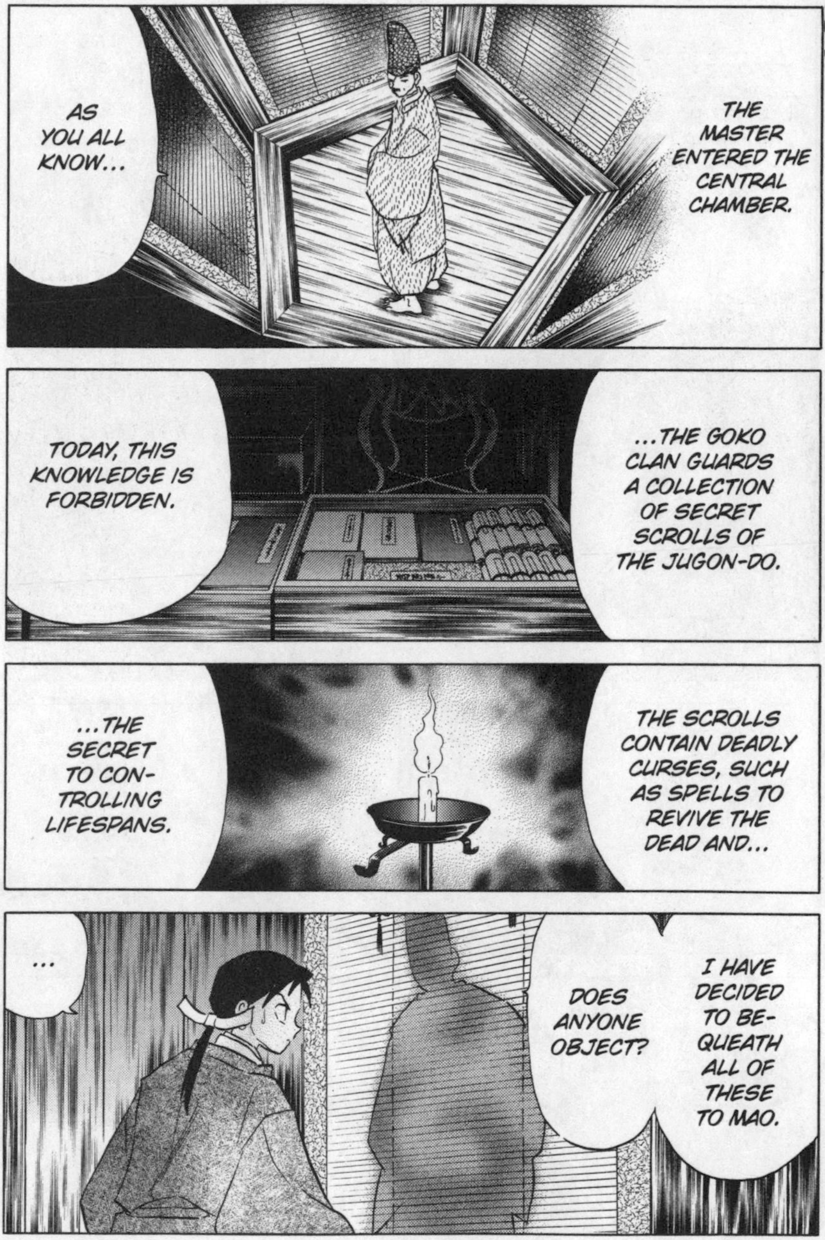
THE MASTER ENTERED THE CENTRAL CHAMBER.
AS YOU ALL KNOW...
...THE GOKO CLAN GUARDS A COLLECTION OF SECRET SCROLLS OF THE JUGON-DO.
TODAY, THIS KNOWLEDGE IS FORBIDDEN.
THE SCROLLS CONTAIN DEADLY CURSES, SUCH AS SPELLS TO REVIVE THE DEAD AND...
...THE SECRET TO CON-TROLLING LIFESPANS.
I HAVE DECIDED TO BE-QUEATH ALL OF THESE TO MAO.
DOES ANYONE OBJECT?
...

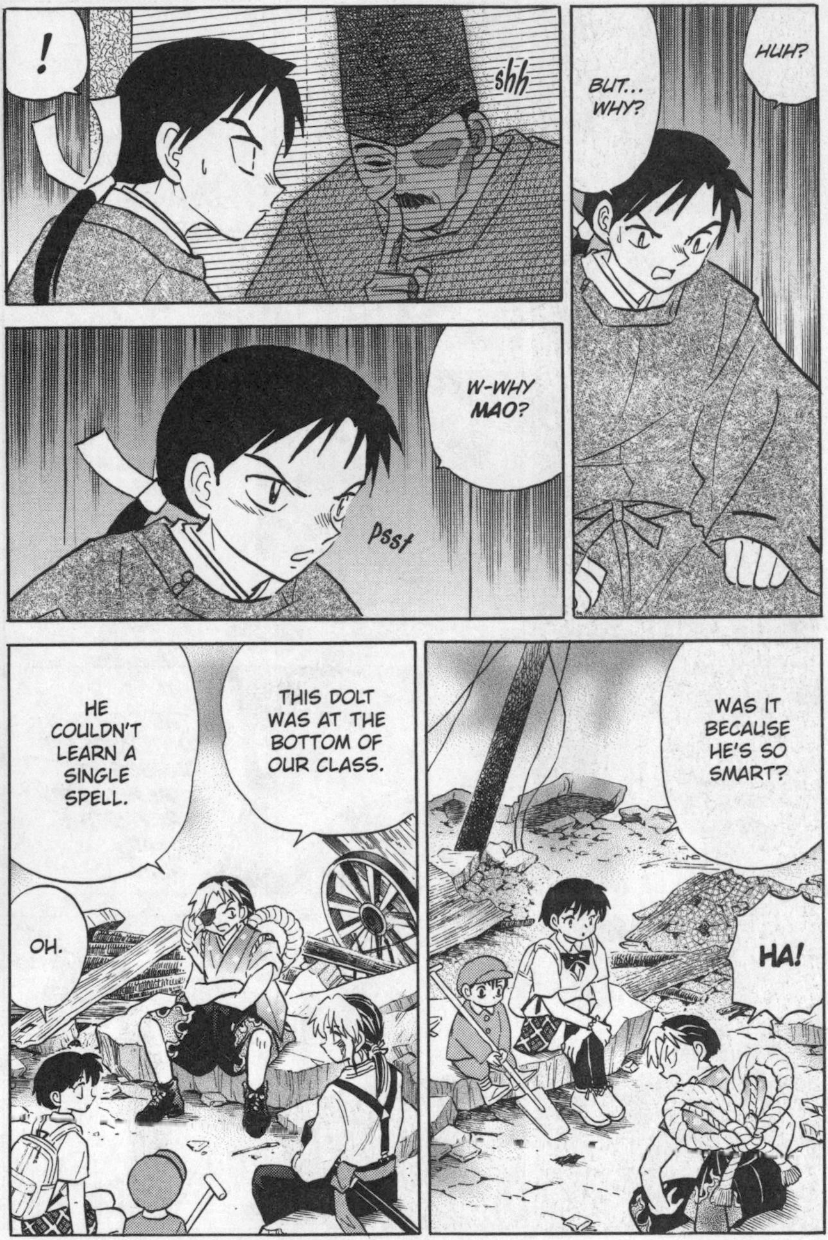
HUH?
BUT... WHY?
!
shh
W-WHY MAO?
psst
WAS IT BECAUSE HE'S SO SMART?
HA!
THIS DOLT WAS AT THE BOTTOM OF OUR CLASS.
HE COULDN'T LEARN A SINGLE SPELL.
OH.

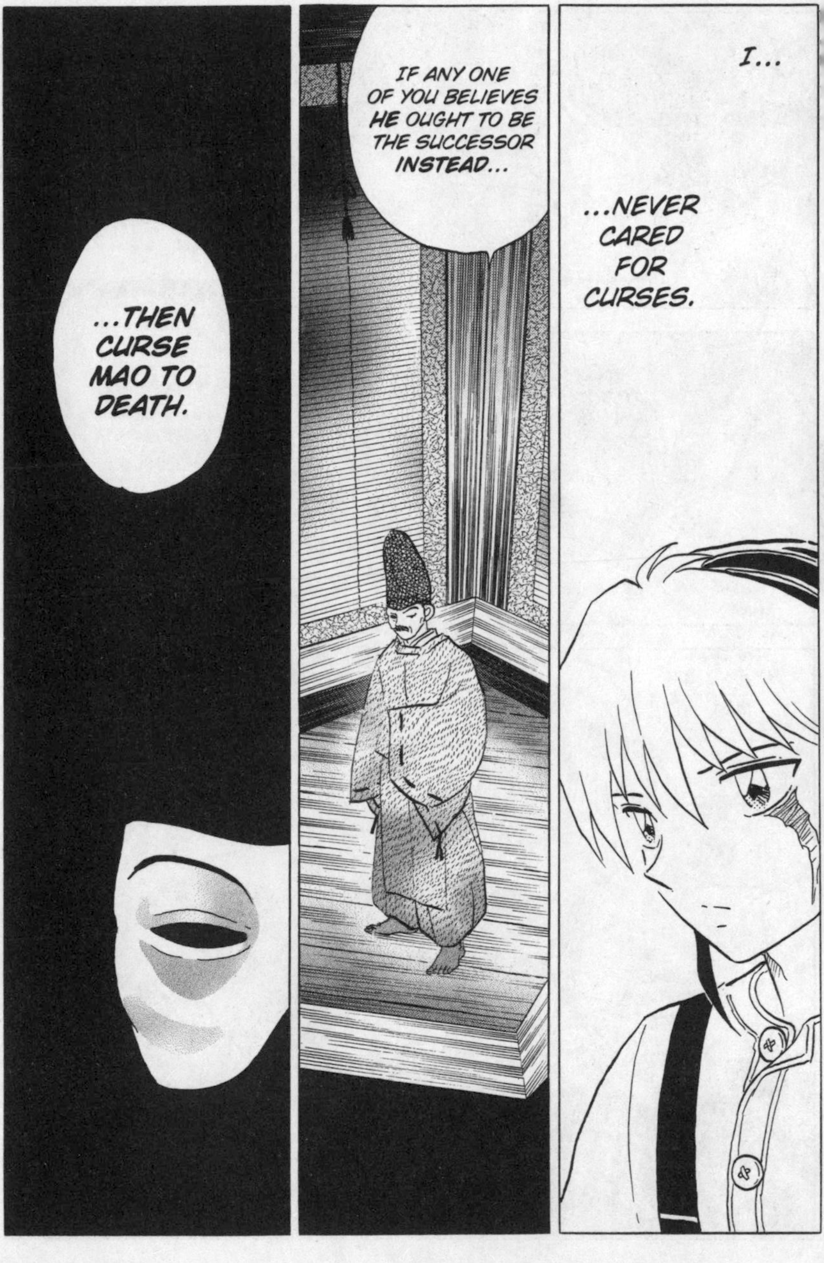
I...
...NEVER CARED FOR CURSES.
IF ANY ONE OF YOU BELIEVES HE OUGHT TO BE THE SUCCESSOR INSTEAD...
...THEN CURSE MAO TO DEATH.

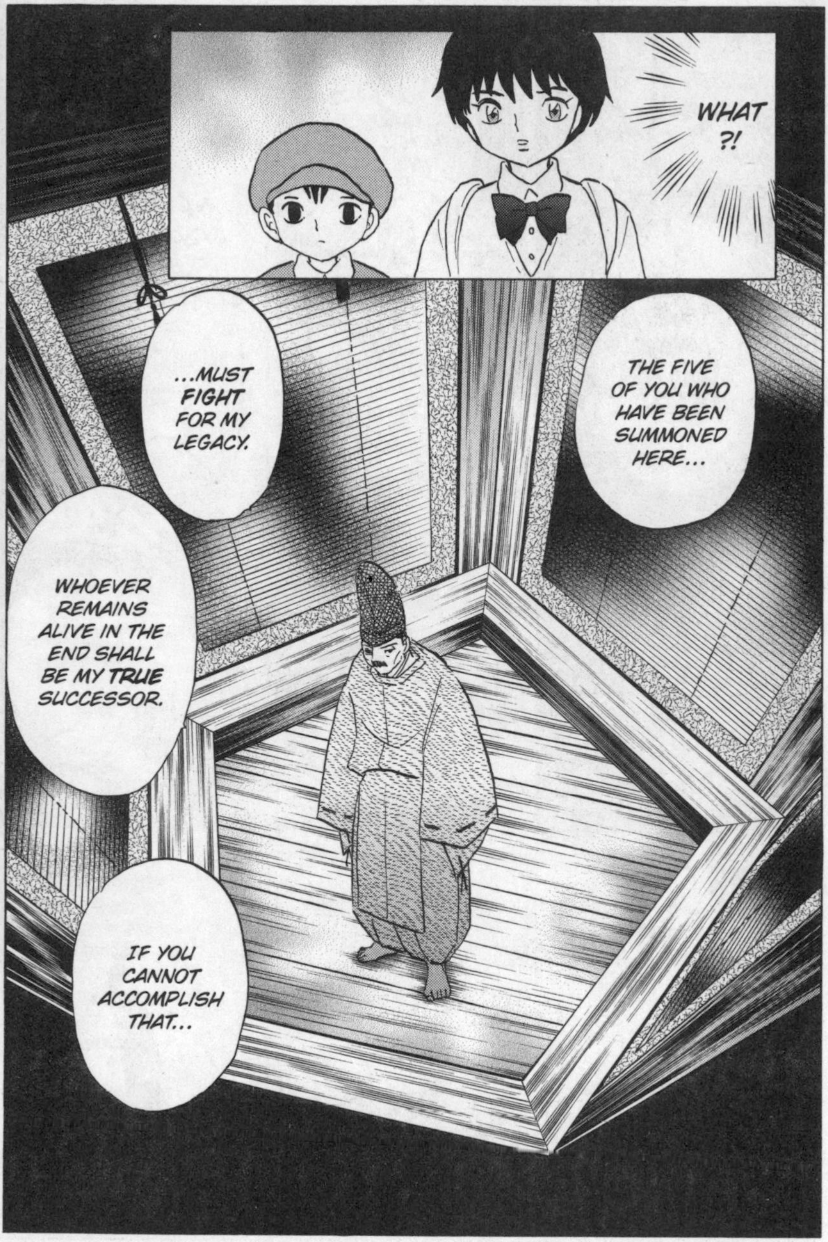
WHAT?!
THE FIVE OF YOU WHO HAVE BEEN SUMMONED HERE...
...MUST FIGHT FOR MY LEGACY.
WHOEVER REMAINS ALIVE IN THE END SHALL BE MY TRUE SUCCESSOR.
IF YOU CANNOT ACCOMPLISH THAT...

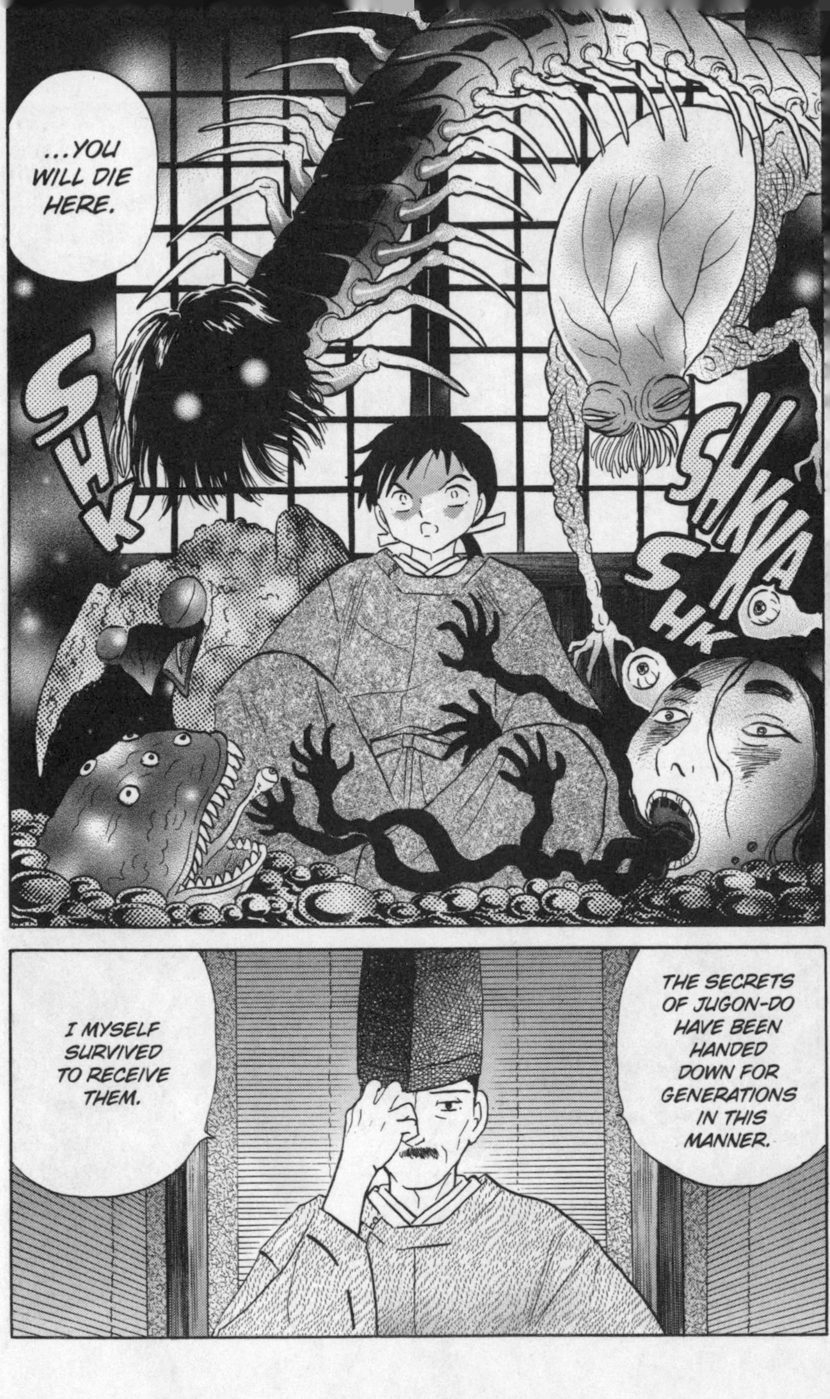
...YOU WILL DIE HERE.
SHKA
SHK
SHK
THE SECRETS OF JUGON-DO HAVE BEEN HANDED DOWN FOR GENERATIONS IN THIS MANNER.
I MYSELF SURVIVED TO RECEIVE THEM.

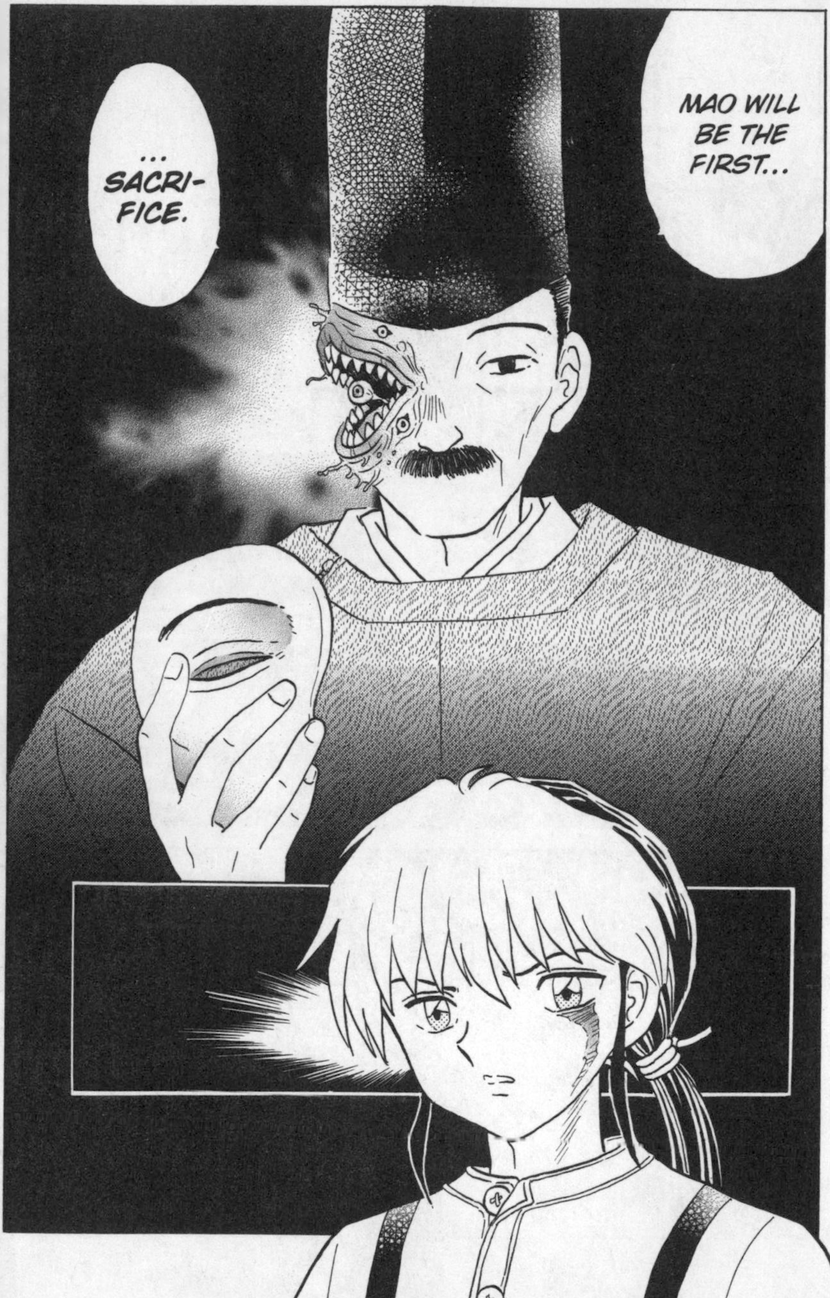
MAO WILL BE THE FIRST...
... SACRI-FICE.

Chapter 8:
Sword of Ill Omen

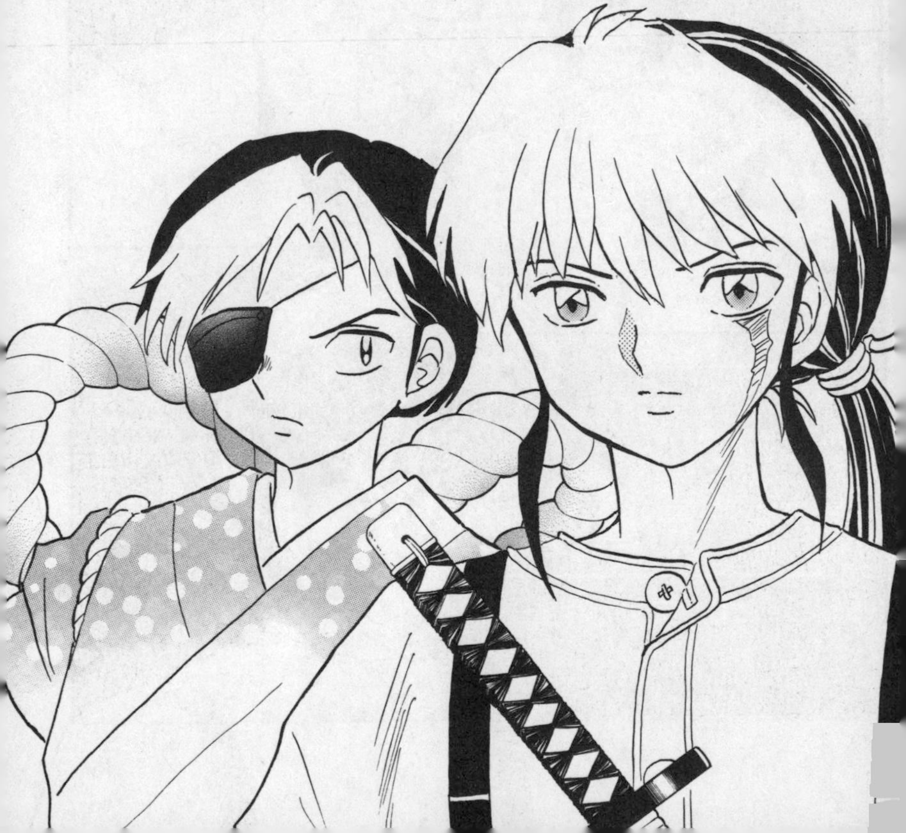

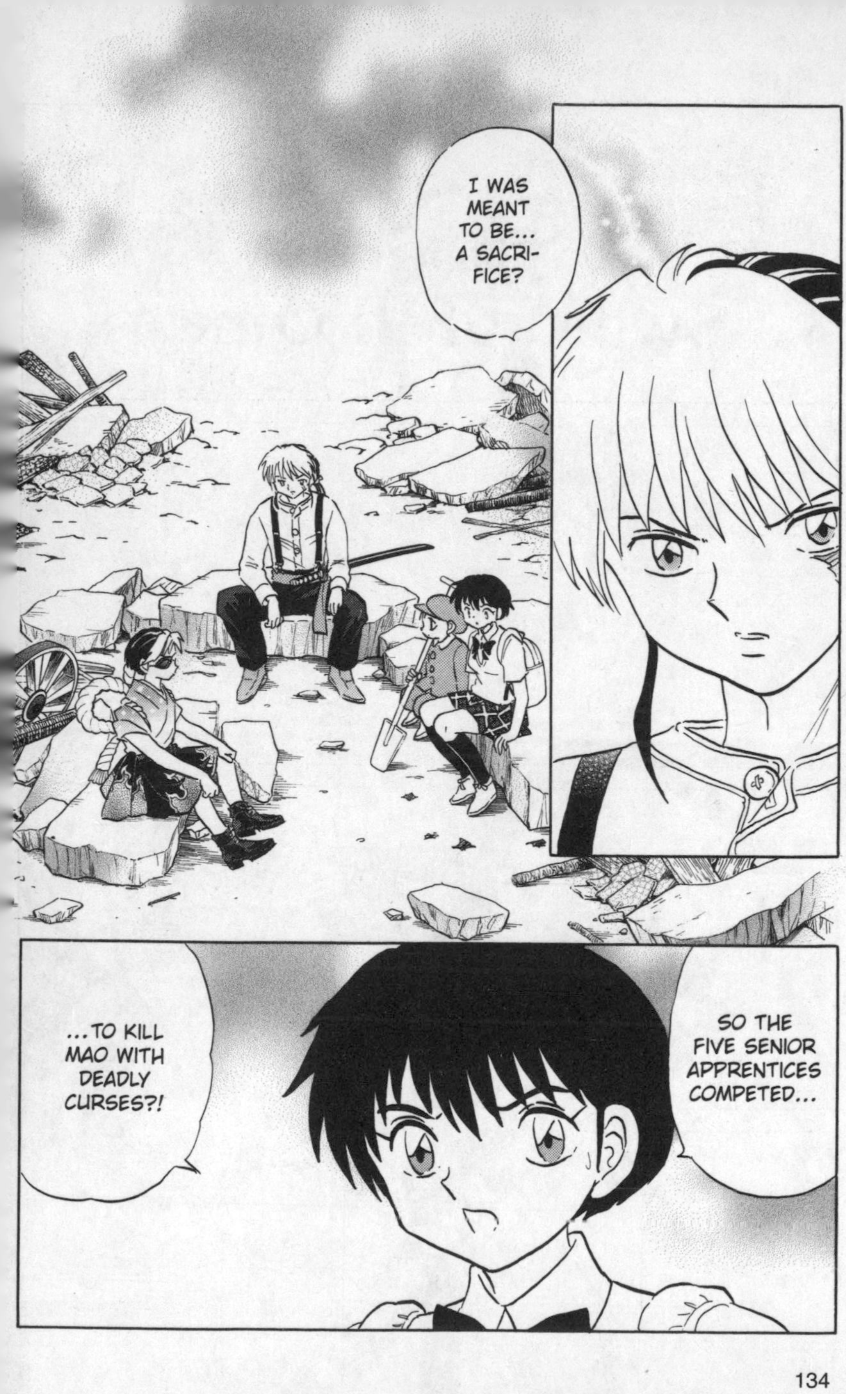
I WAS MEANT TO BE... A SACRI-FICE?
SO THE FIVE SENIOR APPRENTICES COMPETED...
...TO KILL MAO WITH DEADLY CURSES?!

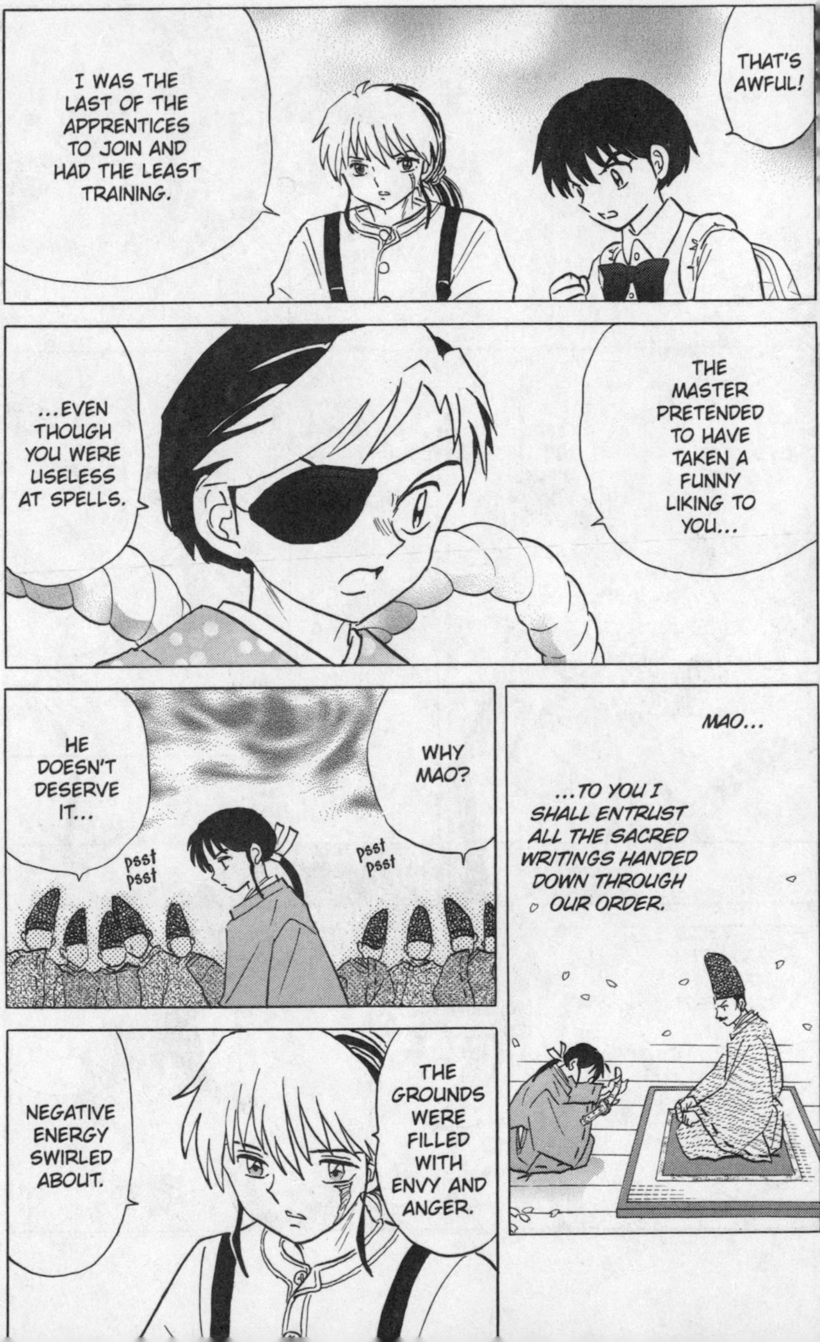
THAT'S AWFUL!
I WAS THE LAST OF THE APPRENTICES TO JOIN AND HAD THE LEAST TRAINING.
THE MASTER PRETENDED TO HAVE TAKEN A FUNNY LIKING TO YOU...
...EVEN THOUGH YOU WERE USELESS AT SPELLS.
MAO...
...TO YOU I SHALL ENTRUST ALL THE SACRED WRITINGS HANDED DOWN THROUGH OUR ORDER.
WHY MAO?
psst psst
HE DOESN'T DESERVE IT...
psst psst
THE GROUNDS WERE FILLED WITH ENVY AND ANGER.
NEGATIVE ENERGY SWIRLED ABOUT.

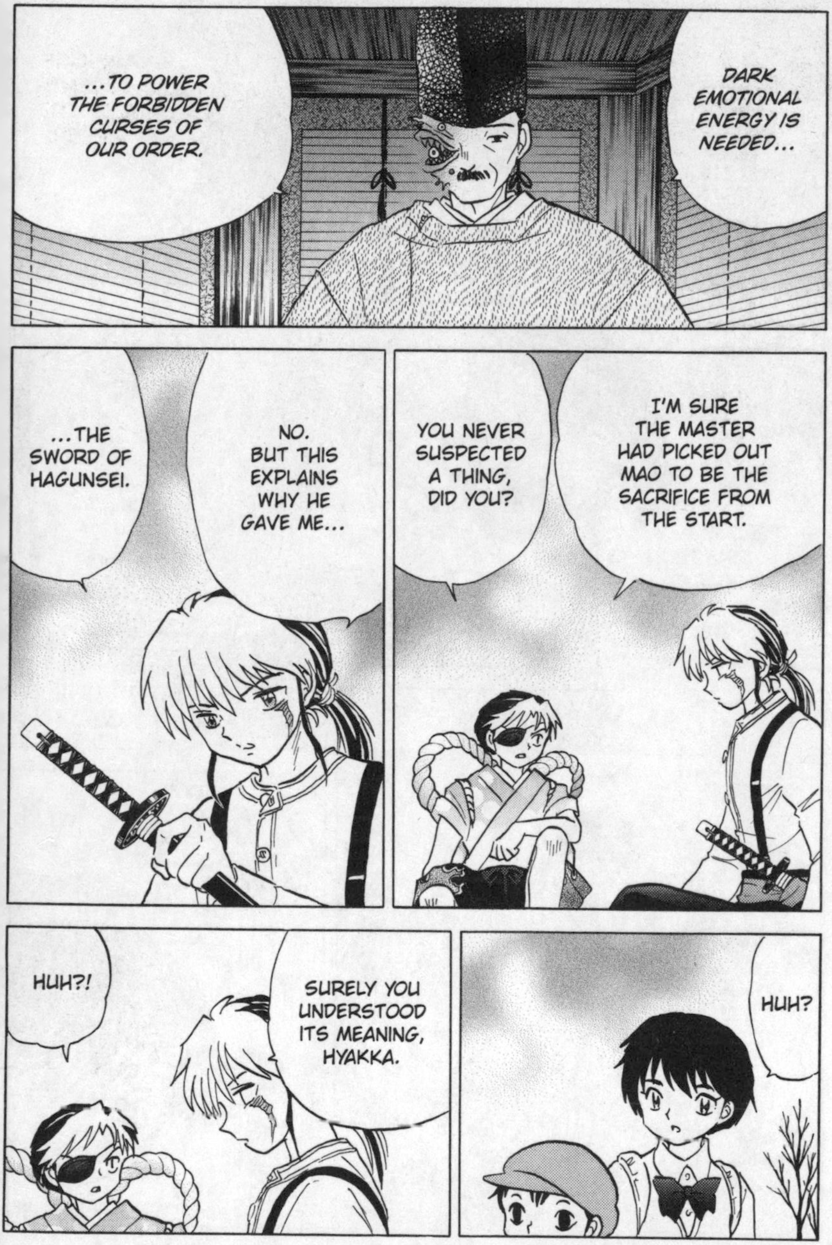
DARK EMOTIONAL ENERGY IS NEEDED...
...TO POWER THE FORBIDDEN CURSES OF OUR ORDER.
I'M SURE THE MASTER HAD PICKED OUT MAO TO BE THE SACRIFICE FROM THE START.
YOU NEVER SUSPECTED A THING, DID YOU?
NO. BUT THIS EXPLAINS WHY HE GAVE ME...
...THE SWORD OF HAGUNSEI.
HUH?
SURELY YOU UNDERSTOOD ITS MEANING, HYAKKA.
HUH?!

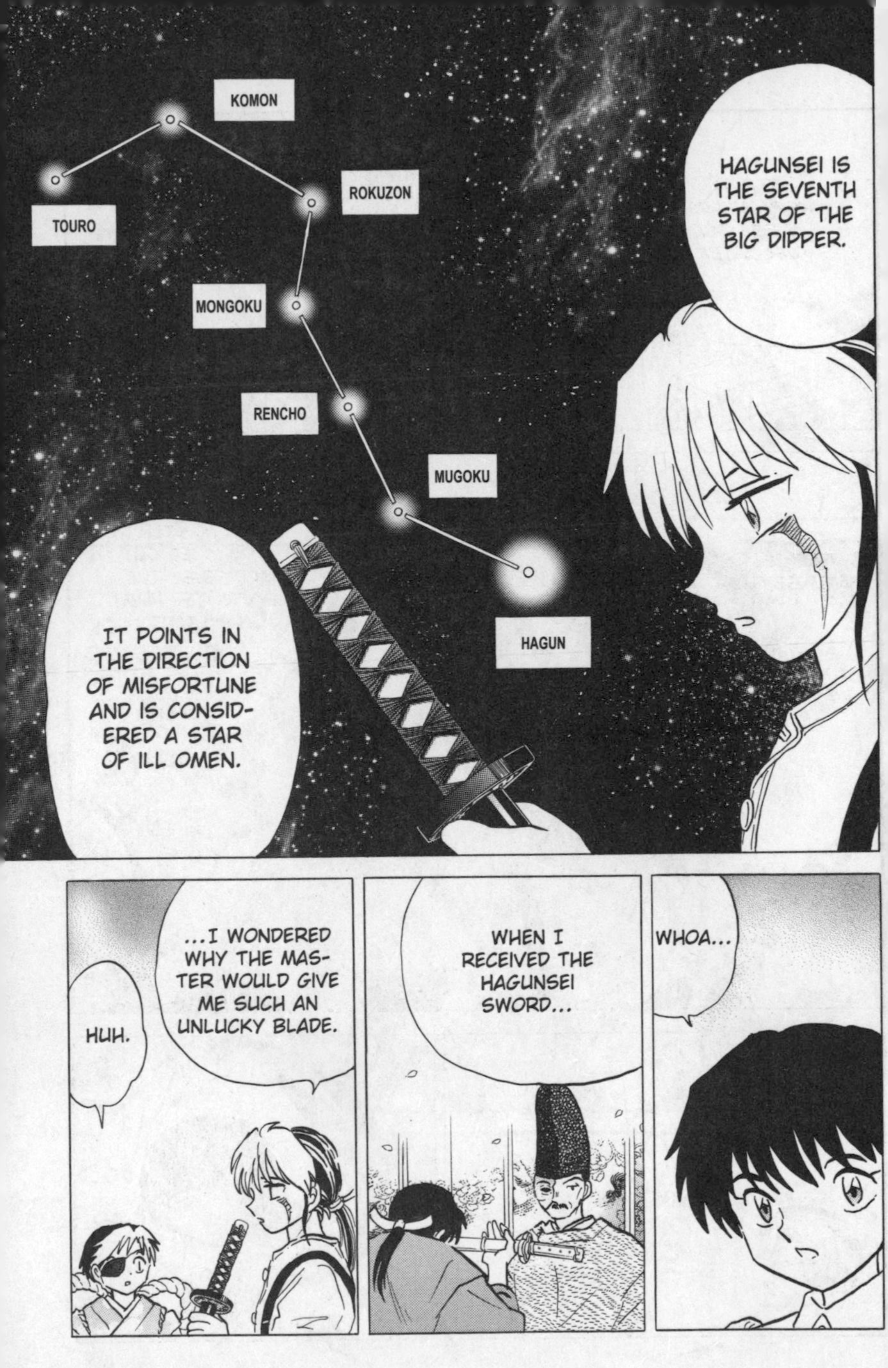
HAGUNSEI IS THE SEVENTH STAR OF THE BIG DIPPER.
KOMON
ROKUZON
TOURO
MONGOKU
RENCHO
MUGOKU
HAGUN
IT POINTS IN THE DIRECTION OF MISFORTUNE AND IS CONSIDERED A STAR OF ILL OMEN.
WHOA...
WHEN I RECEIVED THE HAGUNSEI SWORD...
...I WONDERED WHY THE MASTER WOULD GIVE ME SUCH AN UNLUCKY BLADE.
HUH.

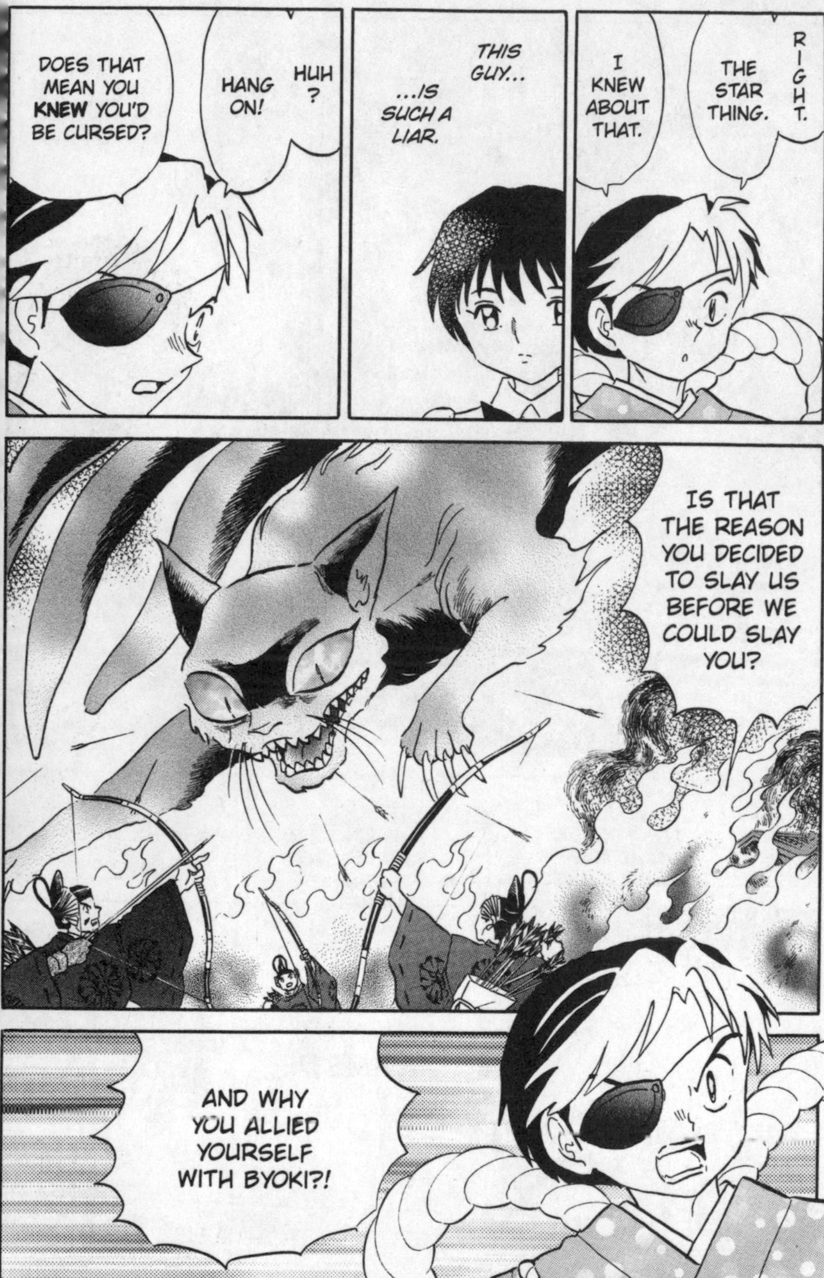
RIGHT.
THE STAR THING.
I KNEW ABOUT THAT.
THIS GUY...
...IS SUCH A LIAR.
HUH?
HANG ON!
DOES THAT MEAN YOU KNEW YOU'D BE CURSED?
IS THAT THE REASON YOU DECIDED TO SLAY US BEFORE WE COULD SLAY YOU?
AND WHY YOU ALLIED YOURSELF WITH BYOKI?!

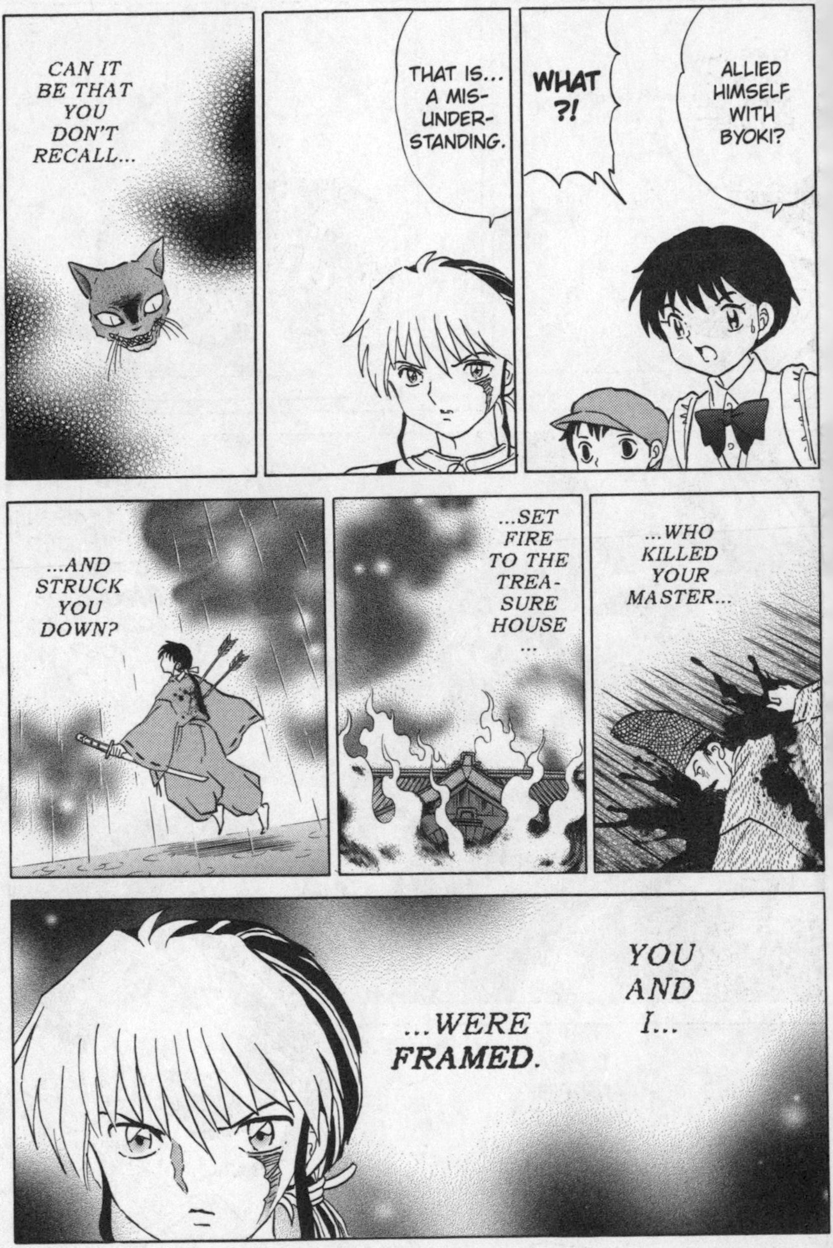
ALLIED HIMSELF WITH BYOKI?
WHAT ?!
THAT IS... A MIS-UNDER-STANDING.
CAN IT BE THAT YOU DON'T RECALL...
...WHO KILLED YOUR MASTER...
...SET FIRE TO THE TREA-SURE HOUSE ...
...AND STRUCK YOU DOWN?
YOU AND I...
...WERE FRAMED.

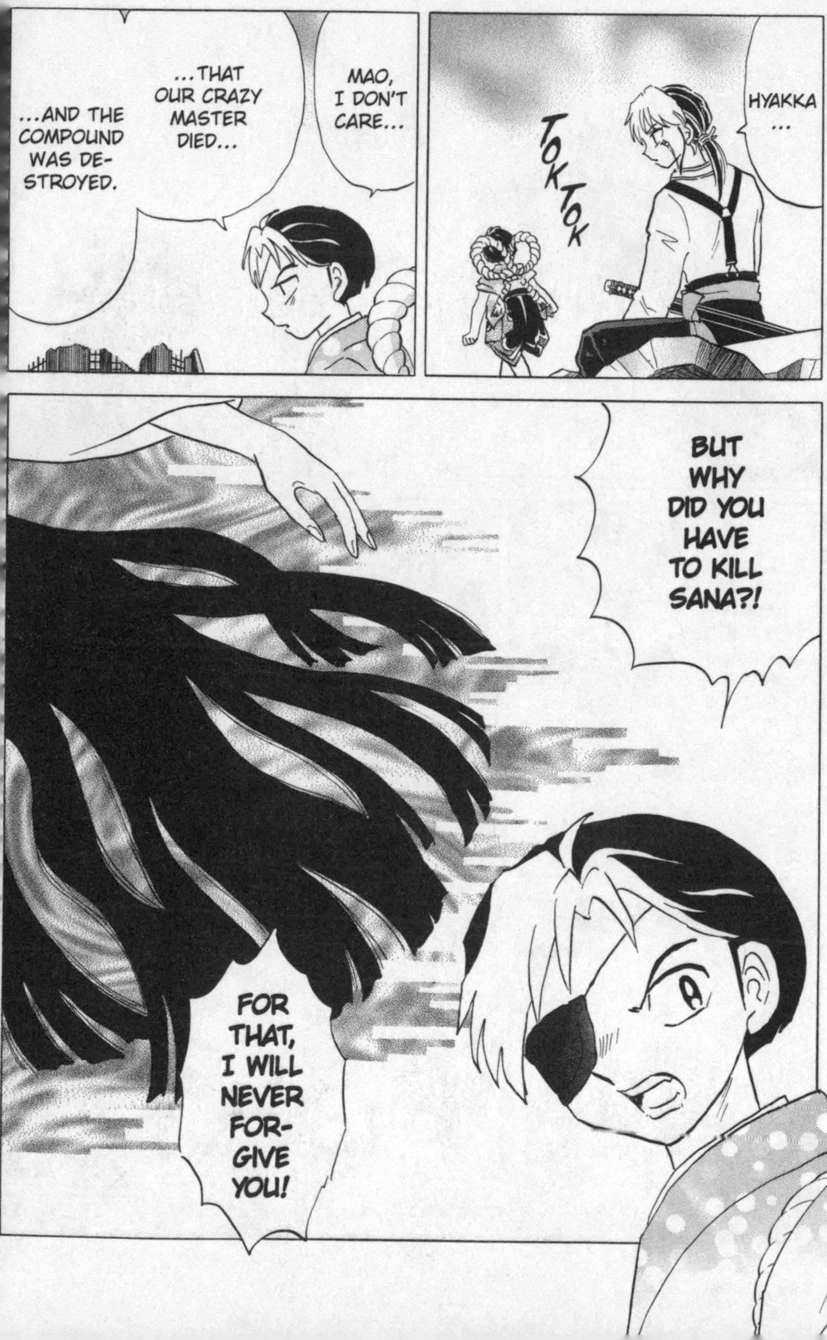
HYAKKA ...
TOK TOK
MAO, I DON'T CARE...
...THAT OUR CRAZY MASTER DIED...
...AND THE COMPOUND WAS DE-STROYED.
BUT WHY DID YOU HAVE TO KILL SANA?!
FOR THAT, I WILL NEVER FOR-GIVE YOU!

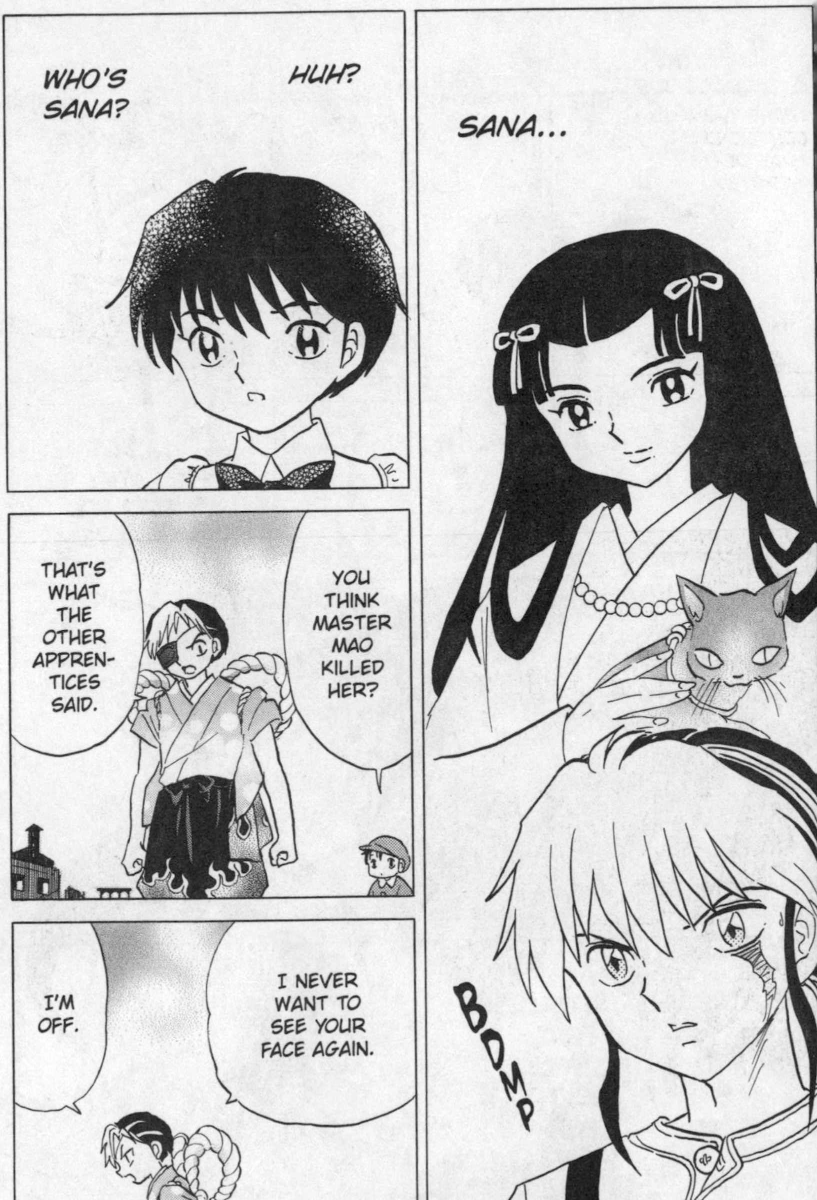
SANA...
BDMP
HUH?
WHO'S SANA?
YOU THINK MASTER MAO KILLED HER?
THAT'S WHAT THE OTHER APPREN-TICES SAID.
I NEVER WANT TO SEE YOUR FACE AGAIN.
I'M OFF.

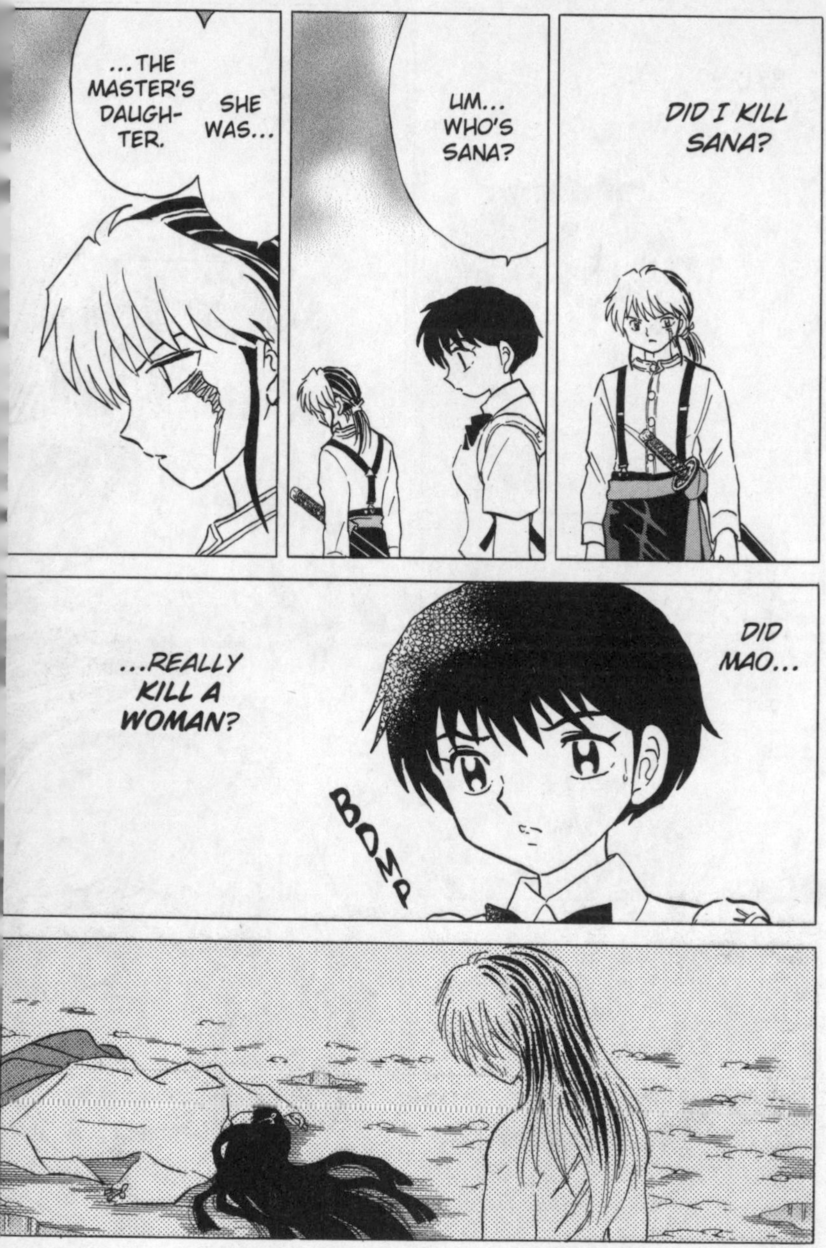
DID I KILL SANA?
UM... WHO'S SANA?
SHE WAS...
...THE MASTER'S DAUGHTER.
DID MAO...
...REALLY KILL A WOMAN?
BDMP

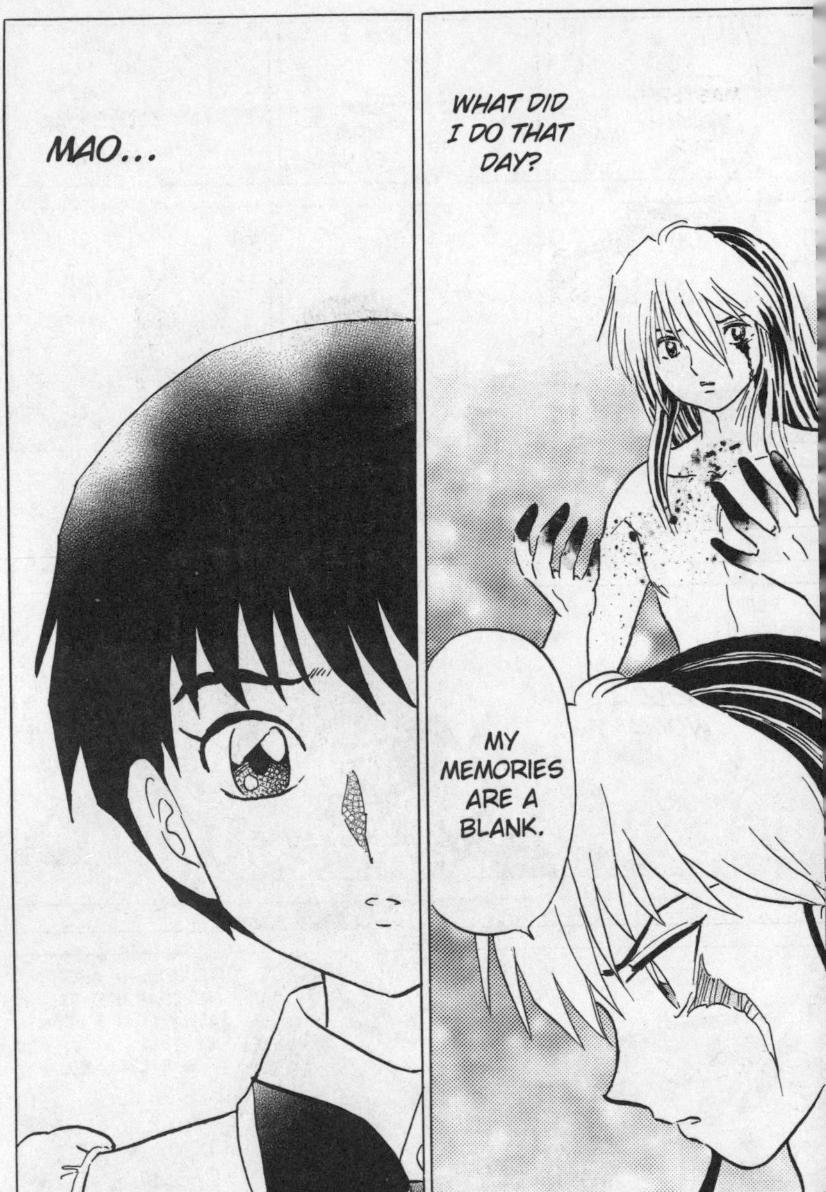
WHAT DID I DO THAT DAY?
MY MEMORIES ARE A BLANK.
MAO...

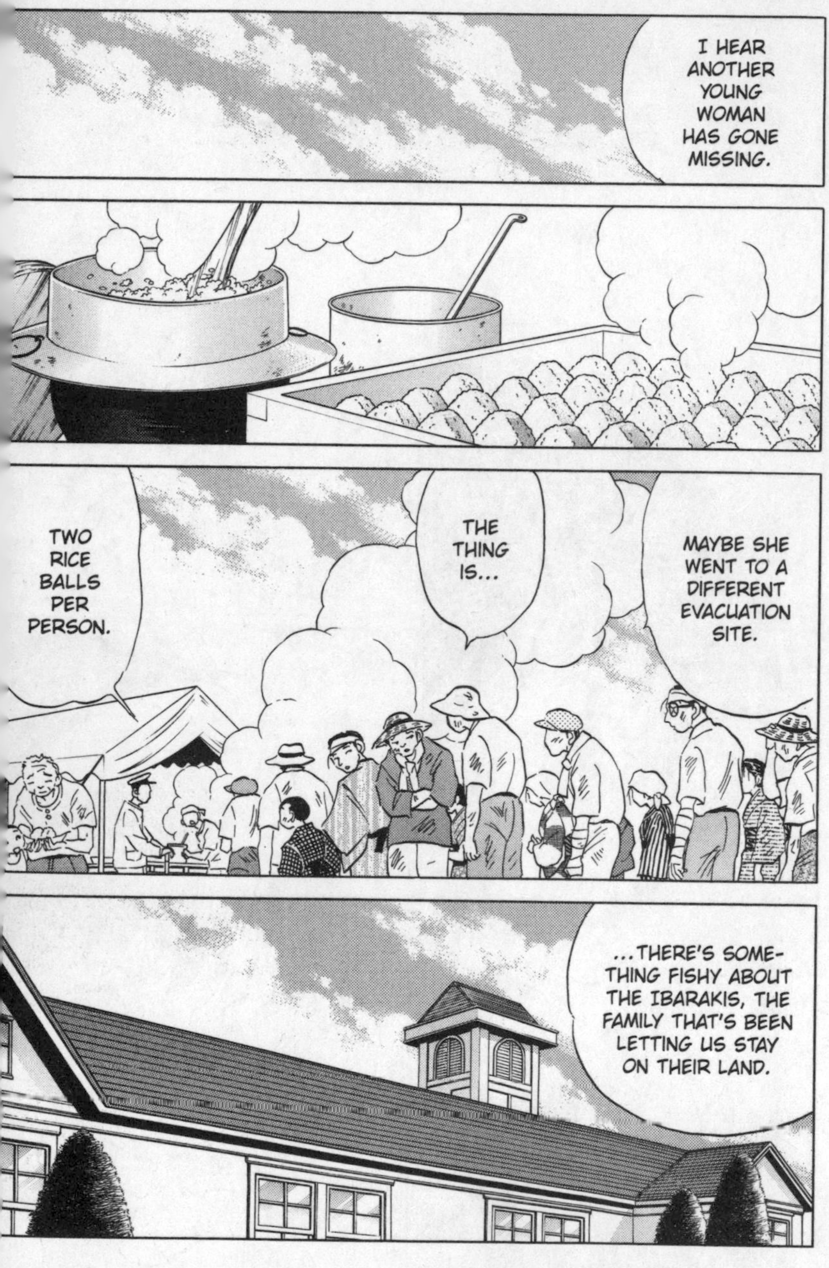
I HEAR ANOTHER YOUNG WOMAN HAS GONE MISSING.
MAYBE SHE WENT TO A DIFFERENT EVACUATION SITE.
THE THING IS...
TWO RICE BALLS PER PERSON.
...THERE'S SOME-THING FISHY ABOUT THE IBARAKIS, THE FAMILY THAT'S BEEN LETTING US STAY ON THEIR LAND.

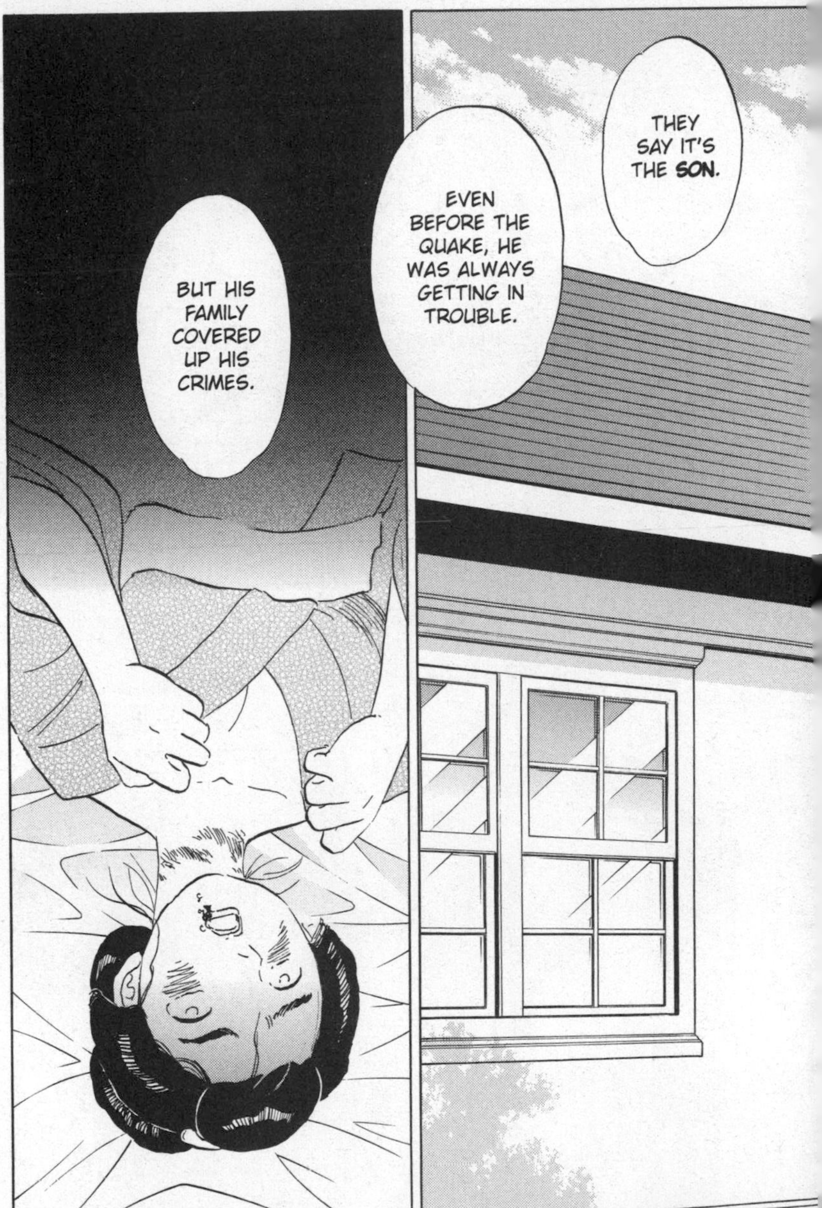
THEY SAY IT'S THE SON.
EVEN BEFORE THE QUAKE, HE WAS ALWAYS GETTING IN TROUBLE.
BUT HIS FAMILY COVERED UP HIS CRIMES.

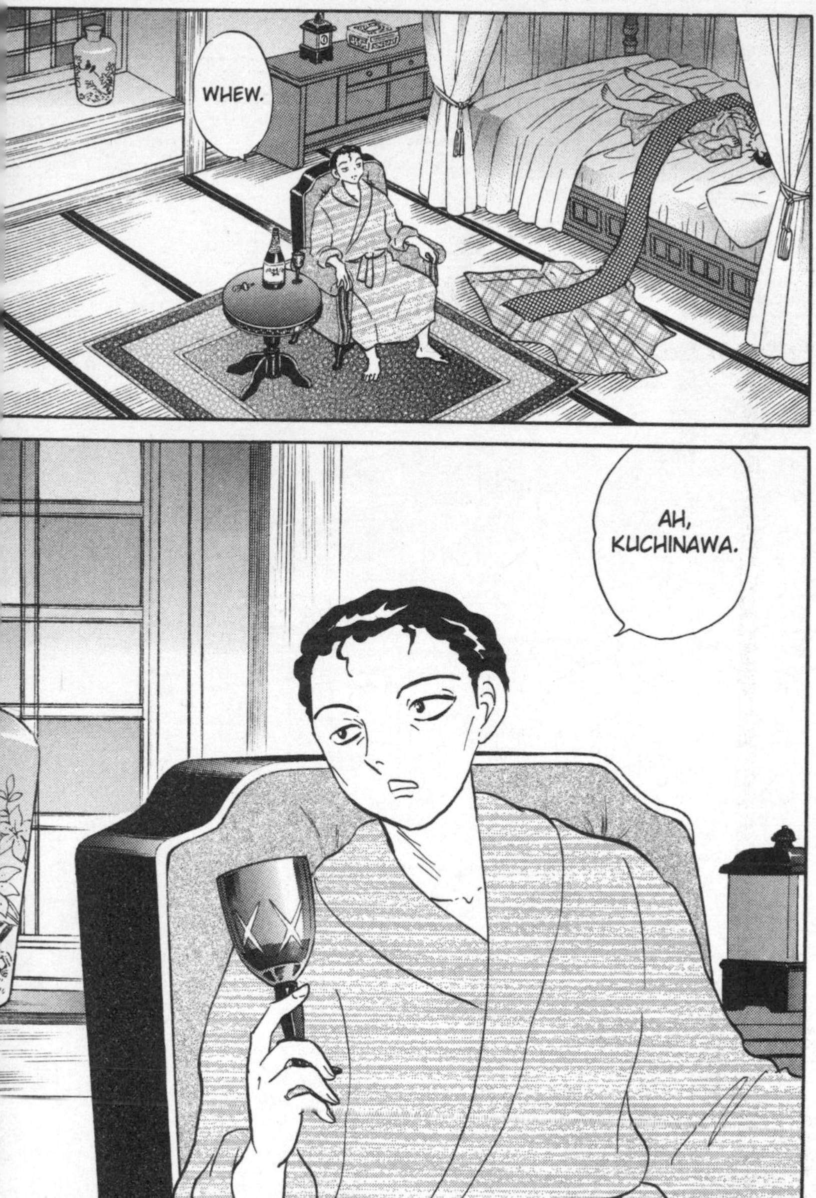
WHEW.
AH, KUCHINAWA.

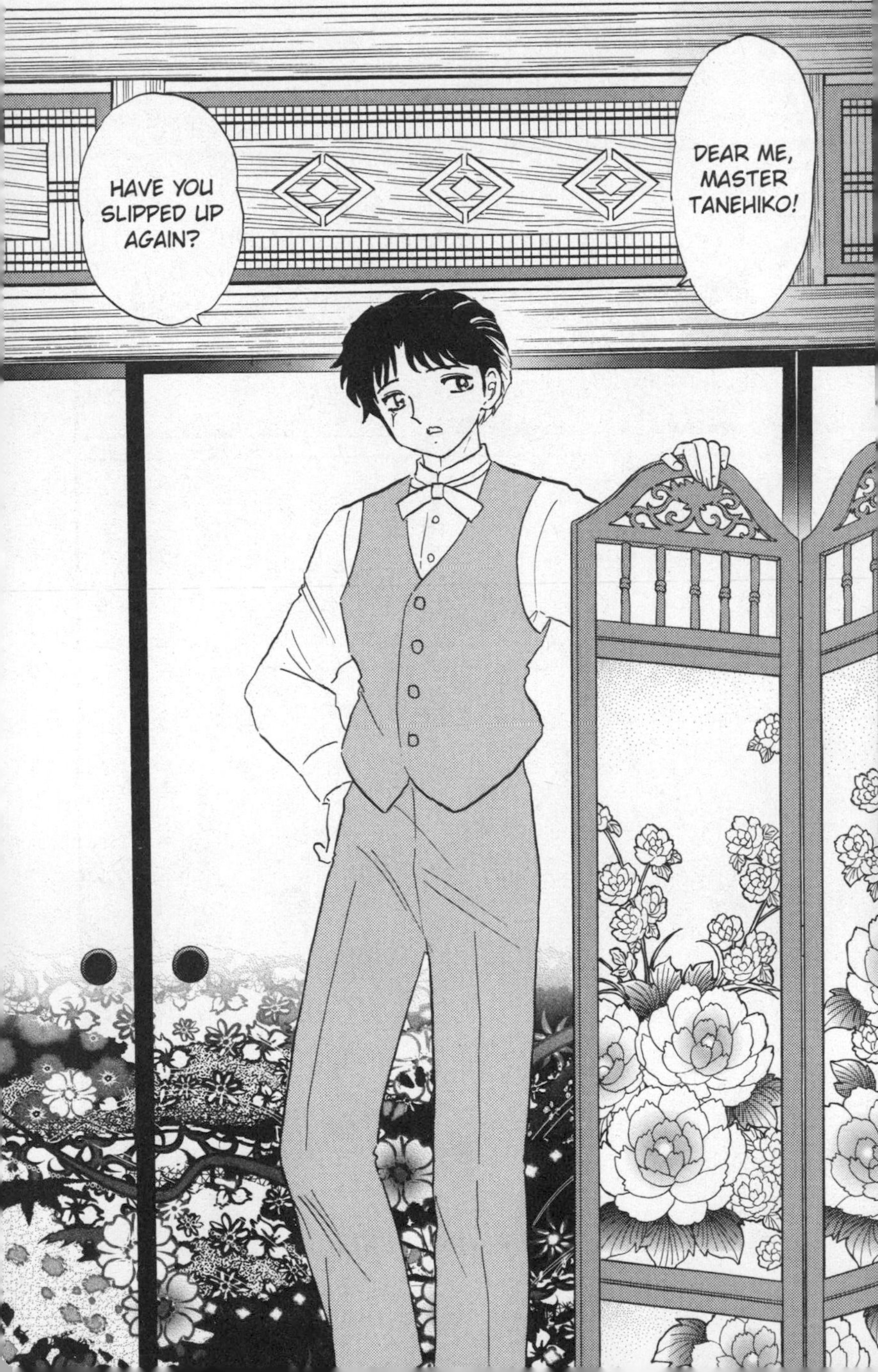
DEAR ME, MASTER TANEHIKO!
HAVE YOU SLIPPED UP AGAIN?

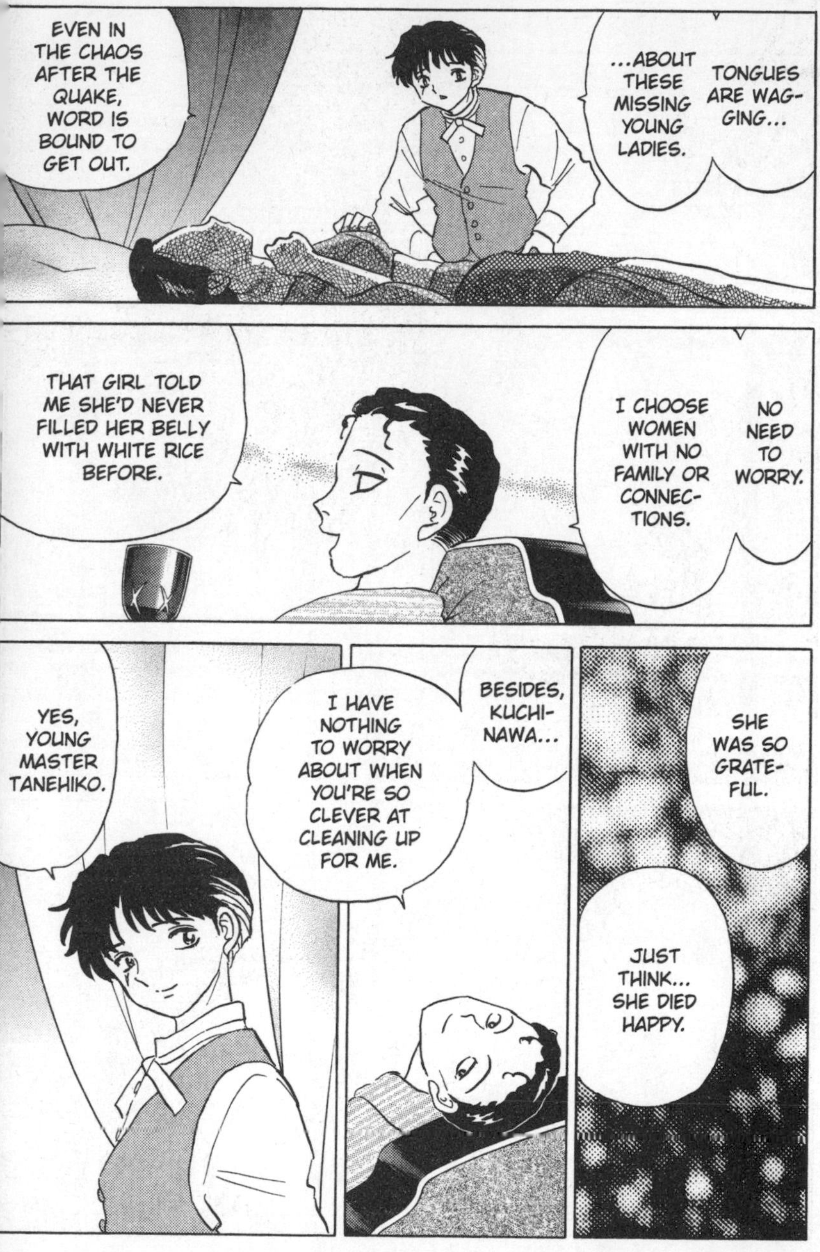
TONGUES ARE WAG-GING...
...ABOUT THESE MISSING YOUNG LADIES.
EVEN IN THE CHAOS AFTER THE QUAKE, WORD IS BOUND TO GET OUT.
NO NEED TO WORRY.
I CHOOSE WOMEN WITH NO FAMILY OR CONNEC-TIONS.
THAT GIRL TOLD ME SHE'D NEVER FILLED HER BELLY WITH WHITE RICE BEFORE.
SHE WAS SO GRATE-FUL.
JUST THINK... SHE DIED HAPPY.
BESIDES, KUCHI-NAWA...
I HAVE NOTHING TO WORRY ABOUT WHEN YOU'RE SO CLEVER AT CLEANING UP FOR ME.
YES, YOUNG MASTER TANEHIKO.

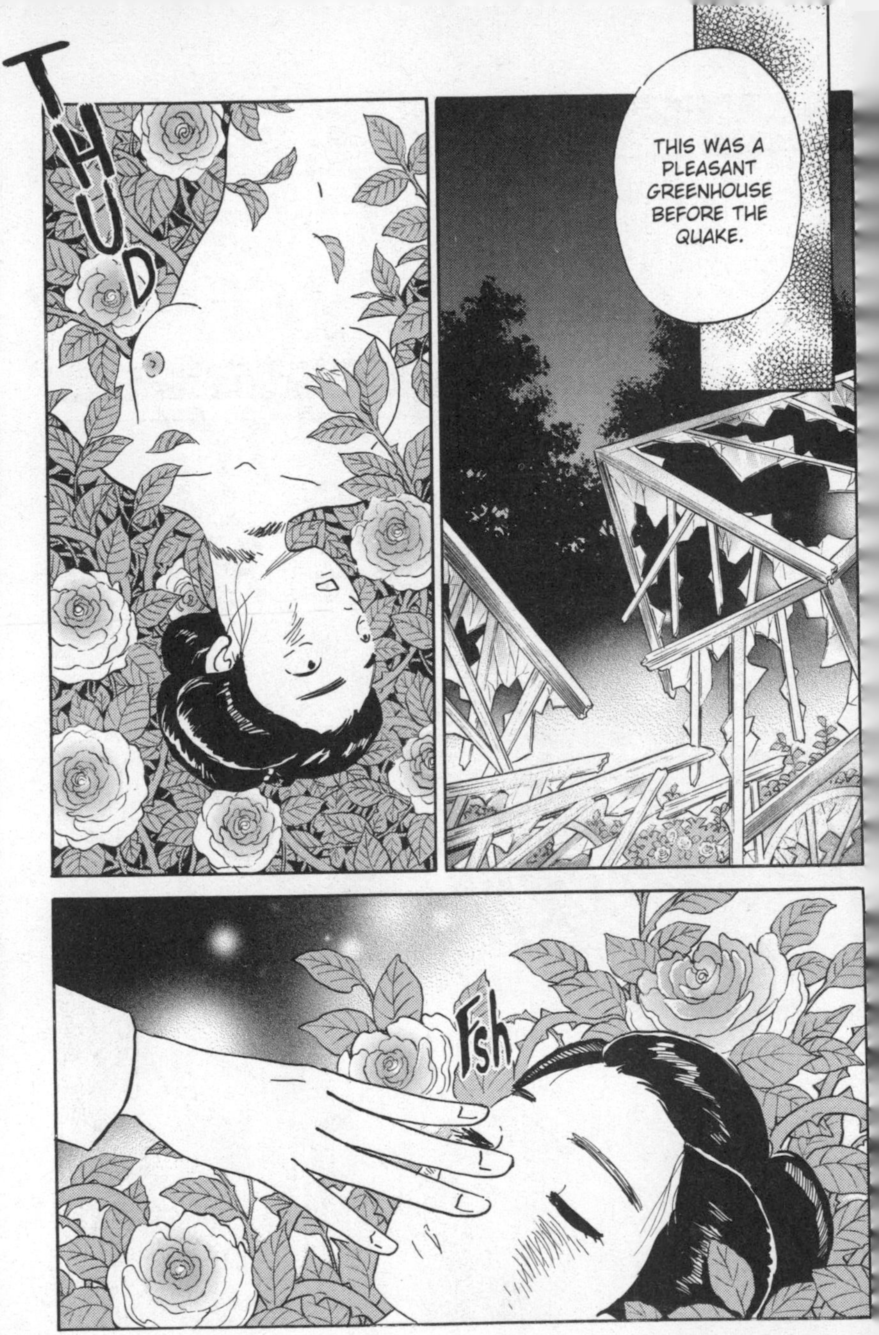
THIS WAS A PLEASANT GREENHOUSE BEFORE THE QUAKE.
THUD
Fsh

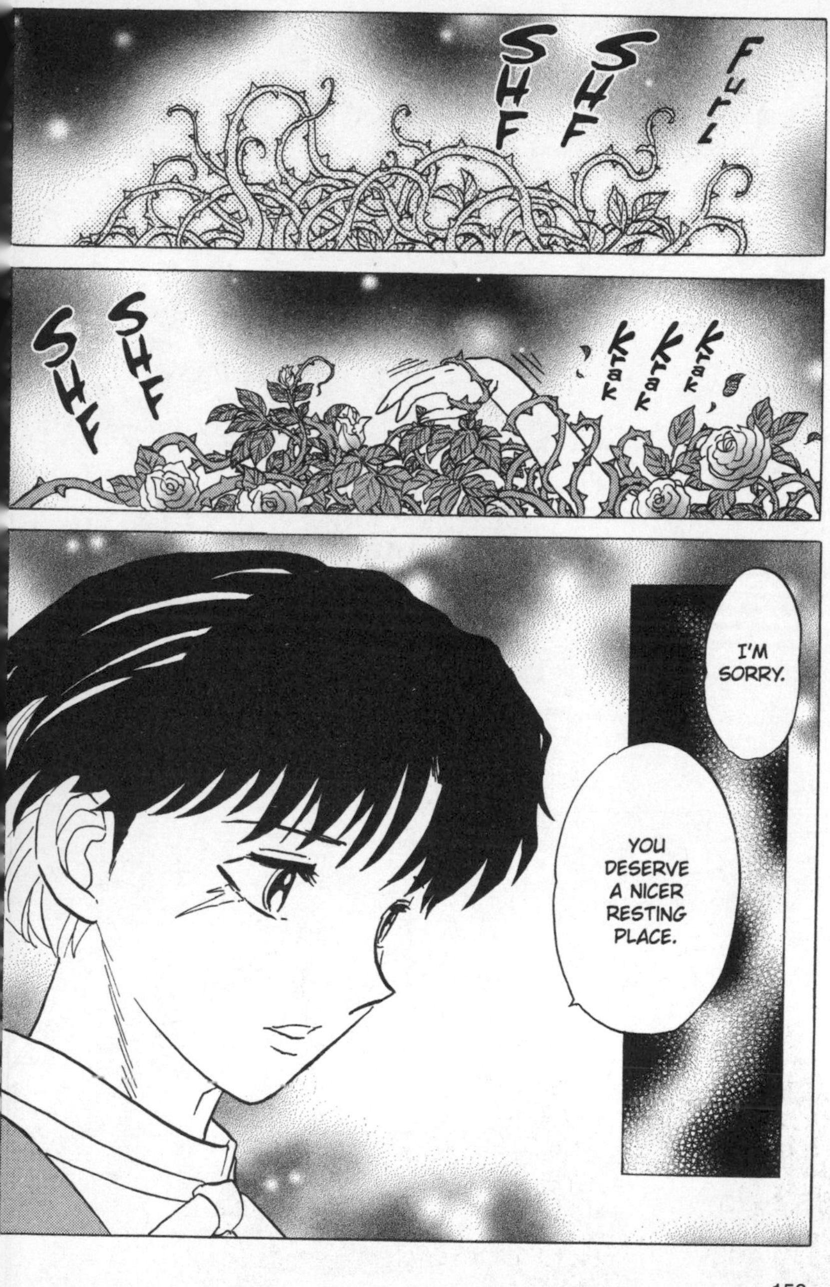
Furl
SHF
SHF
Krak
Krak
Krak
SHF
SHF
I'M SORRY.
YOU DESERVE A NICER RESTING PLACE.

Chapter 9:
Haimaru

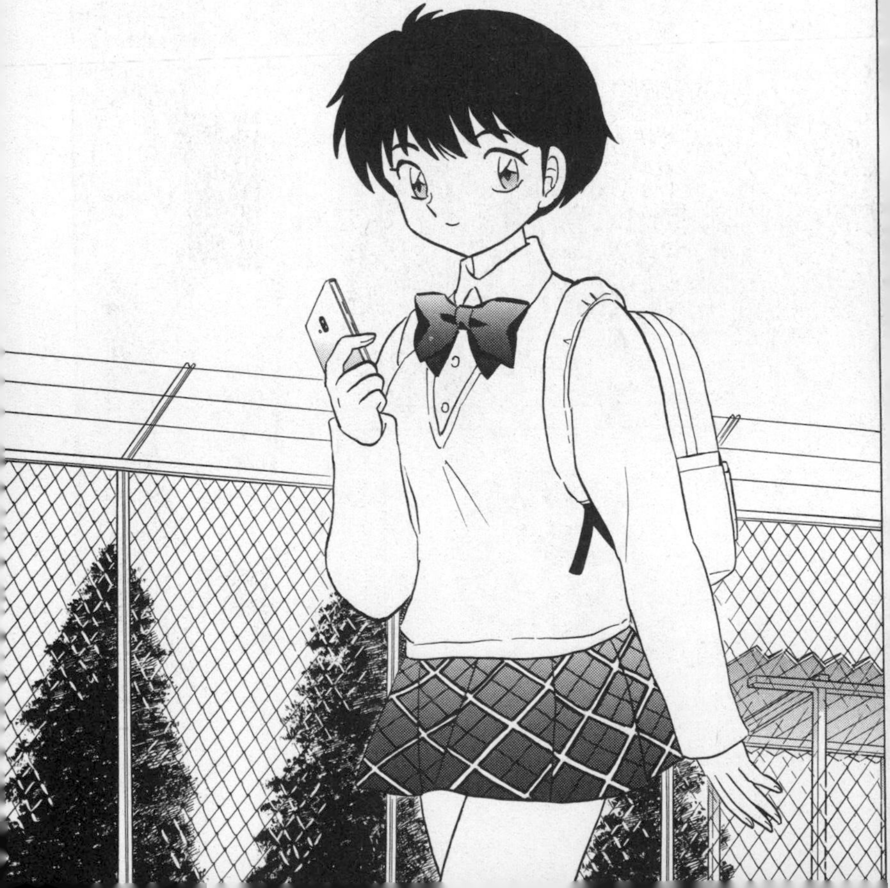

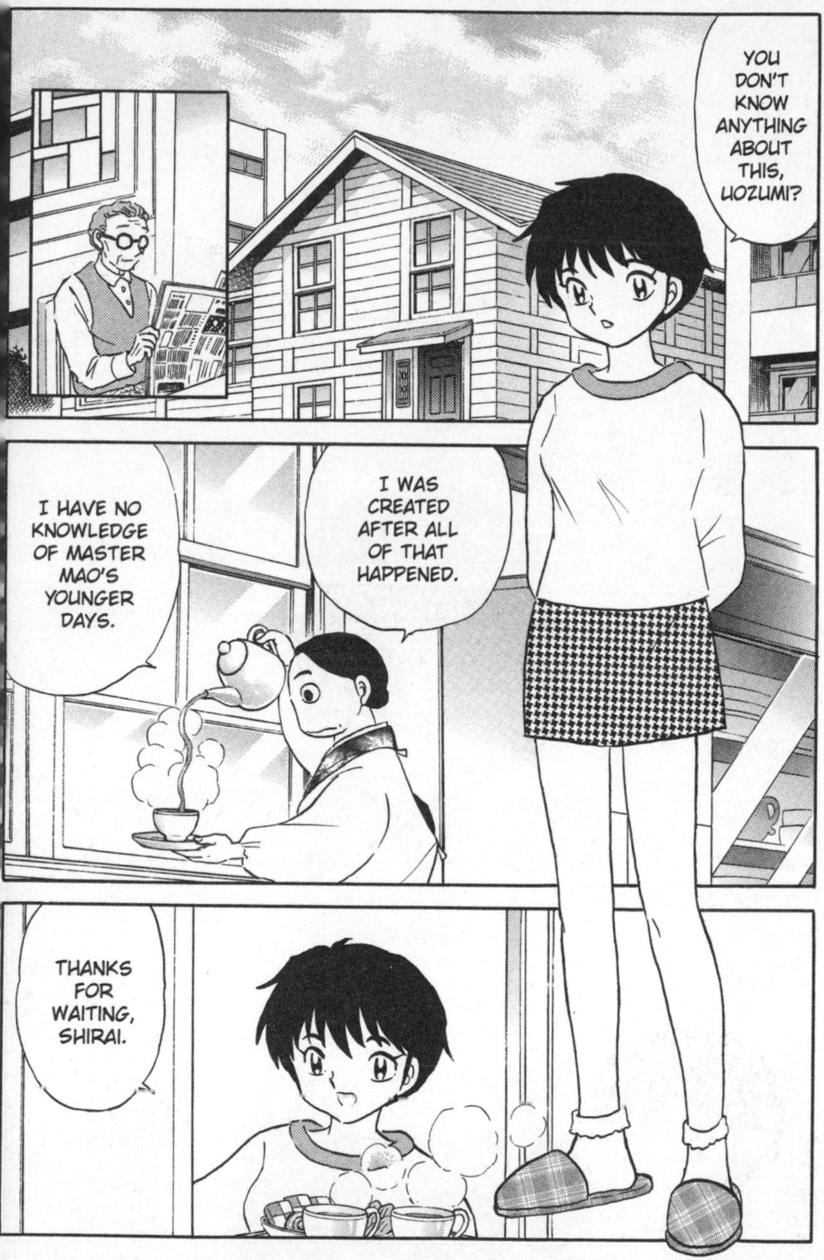
YOU DON'T KNOW ANYTHING ABOUT THIS, UOZUMI?
I WAS CREATED AFTER ALL OF THAT HAPPENED.
I HAVE NO KNOWLEDGE OF MASTER MAO'S YOUNGER DAYS.
THANKS FOR WAITING, SHIRAI.

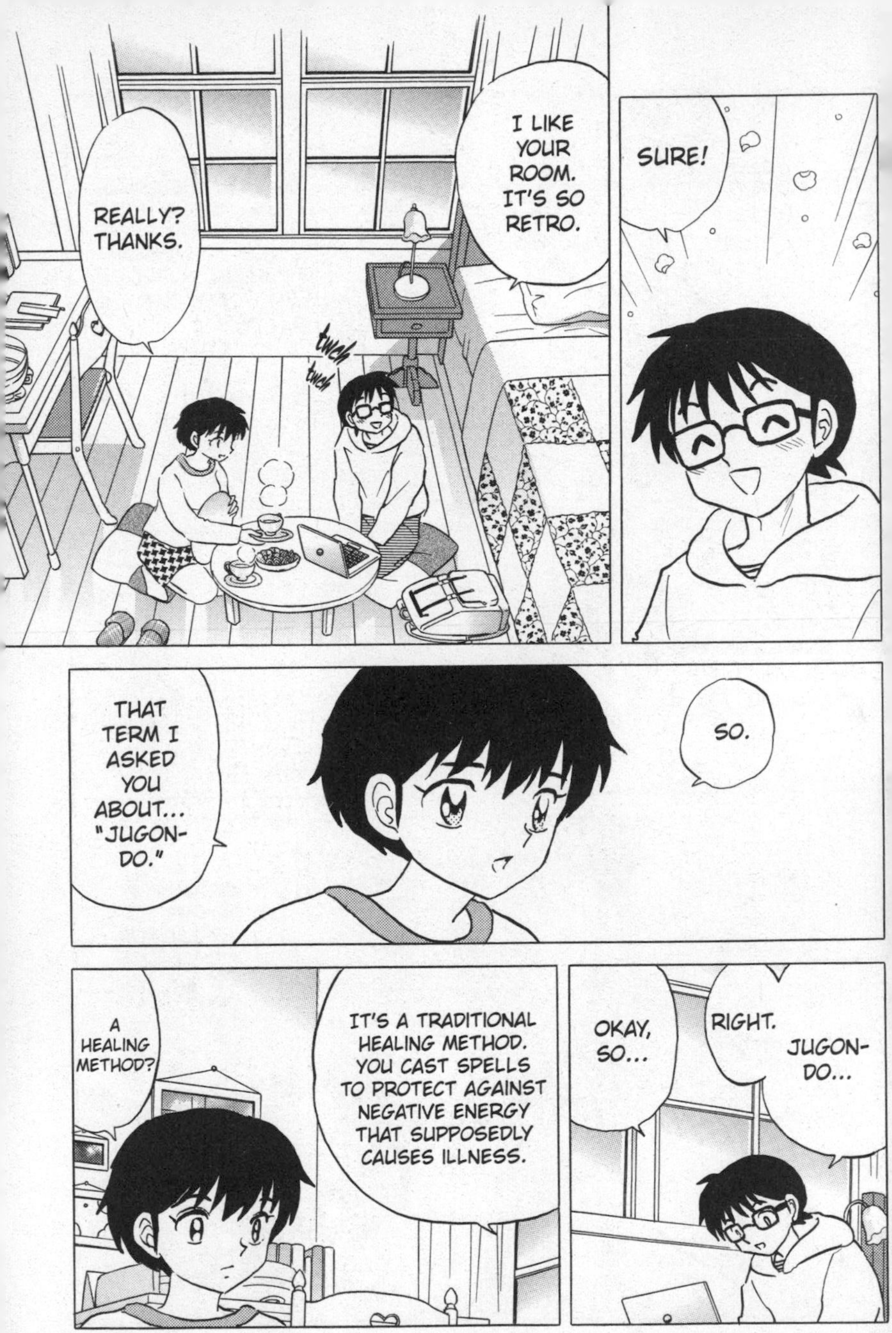
SURE!
I LIKE YOUR ROOM. IT'S SO RETRO.
REALLY? THANKS.
twch twch
SO.
THAT TERM I ASKED YOU ABOUT... "JUGON-DO."
RIGHT. JUGON-DO...
OKAY, SO...
IT'S A TRADITIONAL HEALING METHOD. YOU CAST SPELLS TO PROTECT AGAINST NEGATIVE ENERGY THAT SUPPOSEDLY CAUSES ILLNESS.
A HEALING METHOD?

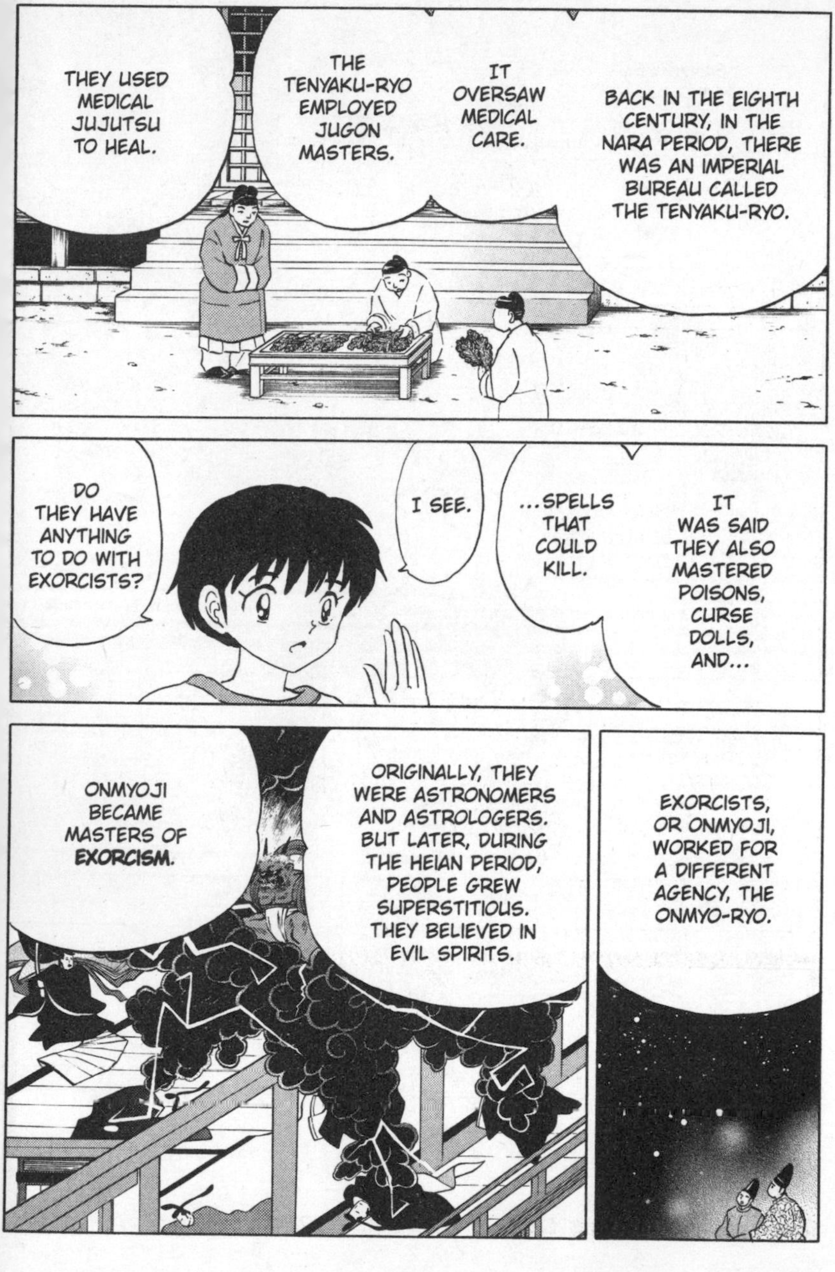
BACK IN THE EIGHTH CENTURY, IN THE NARA PERIOD, THERE WAS AN IMPERIAL BUREAU CALLED THE TENYAKU-RYO.
IT OVERSAW MEDICAL CARE.
THE TENYAKU-RYO EMPLOYED JUGON MASTERS.
THEY USED MEDICAL JUJUTSU TO HEAL.
IT WAS SAID THEY ALSO MASTERED POISONS, CURSE DOLLS, AND...
...SPELLS THAT COULD KILL.
I SEE.
DO THEY HAVE ANYTHING TO DO WITH EXORCISTS?
EXORCISTS, OR ONMYOJI, WORKED FOR A DIFFERENT AGENCY, THE ONMYO-RYO.
ORIGINALLY, THEY WERE ASTRONOMERS AND ASTROLOGERS. BUT LATER, DURING THE HEIAN PERIOD, PEOPLE GREW SUPERSTITIOUS. THEY BELIEVED IN EVIL SPIRITS.
ONMYOJI BECAME MASTERS OF **EXORCISM**.

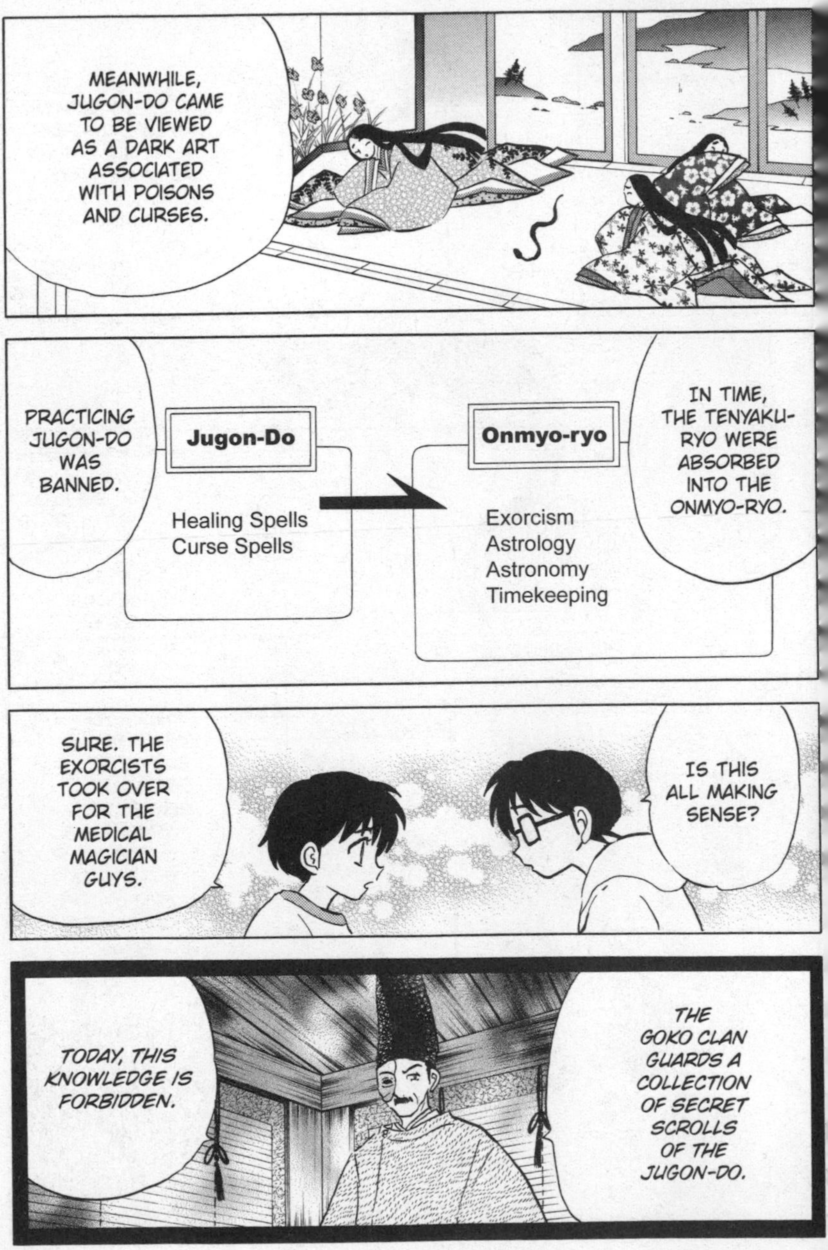
MEANWHILE, JUGON-DO CAME TO BE VIEWED AS A DARK ART ASSOCIATED WITH POISONS AND CURSES.
IN TIME, THE TENYAKU-RYO WERE ABSORBED INTO THE ONMYO-RYO.
Onmyo-ryo
Exorcism
Astrology
Astronomy
Timekeeping
Jugon-Do
Healing Spells
Curse Spells
PRACTICING JUGON-DO WAS BANNED.
IS THIS ALL MAKING SENSE?
SURE. THE EXORCISTS TOOK OVER FOR THE MEDICAL MAGICIAN GUYS.
THE GOKO CLAN GUARDS A COLLECTION OF SECRET SCROLLS OF THE JUGON-DO.
TODAY, THIS KNOWLEDGE IS FORBIDDEN.

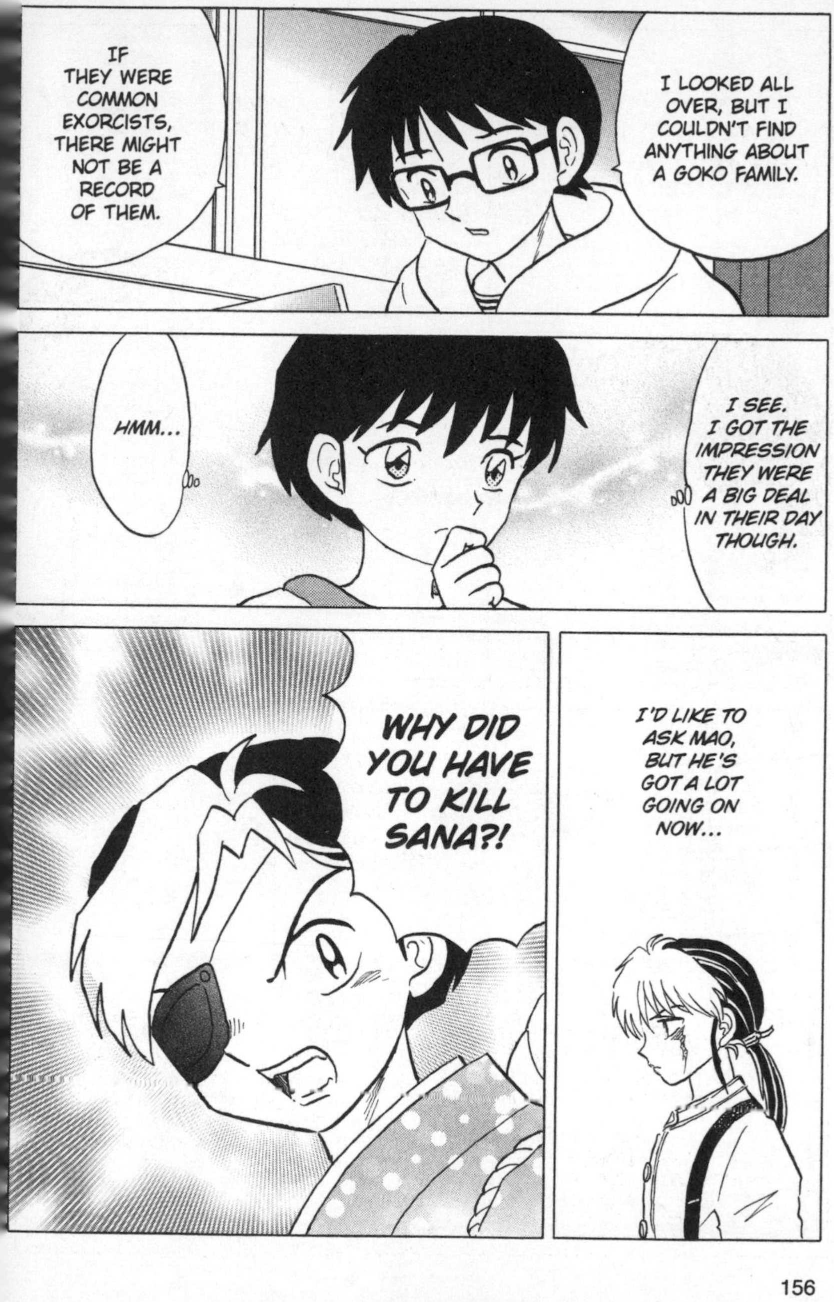
I LOOKED ALL OVER, BUT I COULDN'T FIND ANYTHING ABOUT A GOKO FAMILY.
IF THEY WERE COMMON EXORCISTS, THERE MIGHT NOT BE A RECORD OF THEM.
I SEE. I GOT THE IMPRESSION THEY WERE A BIG DEAL IN THEIR DAY THOUGH.
HMM...
I'D LIKE TO ASK MAO, BUT HE'S GOT A LOT GOING ON NOW...
WHY DID YOU HAVE TO KILL SANA?!

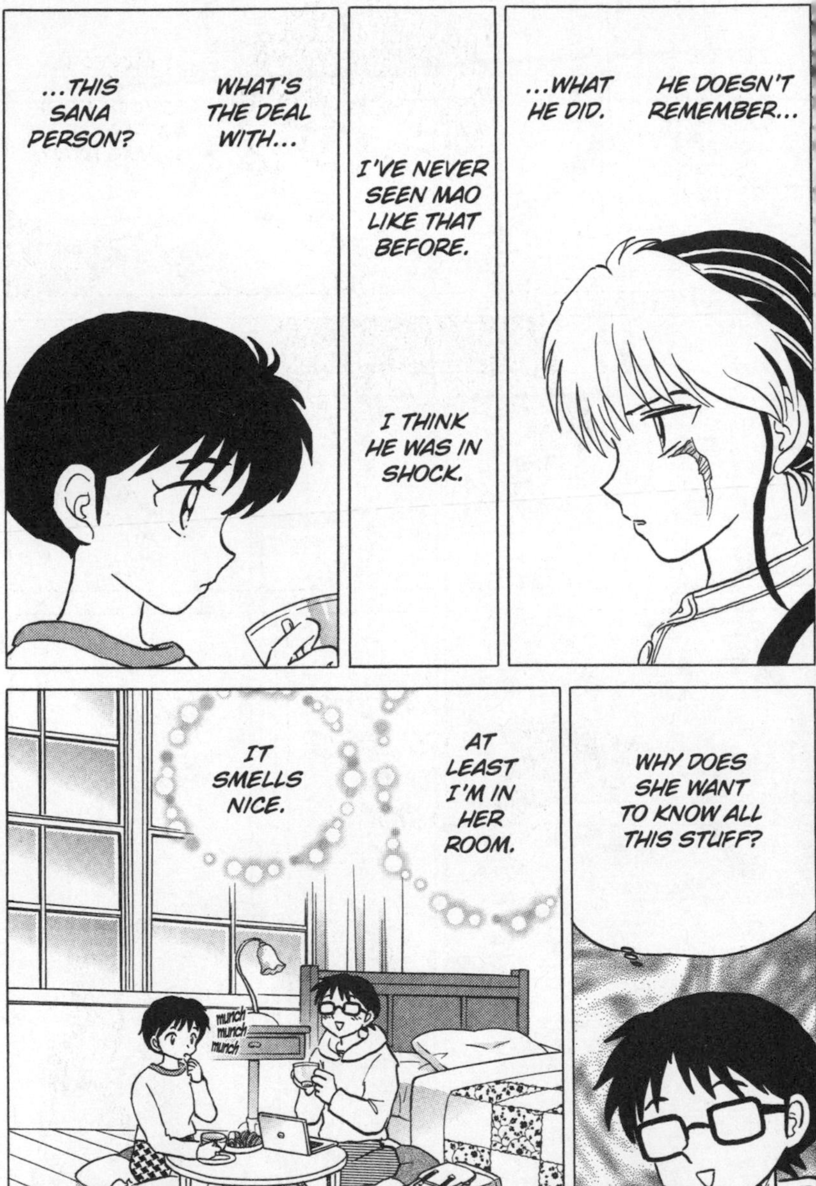
HE DOESN'T REMEMBER...
...WHAT HE DID.
I'VE NEVER SEEN MAO LIKE THAT BEFORE.
I THINK HE WAS IN SHOCK.
WHAT'S THE DEAL WITH...
...THIS SANA PERSON?
WHY DOES SHE WANT TO KNOW ALL THIS STUFF?
AT LEAST I'M IN HER ROOM.
IT SMELLS NICE.
munch munch munch

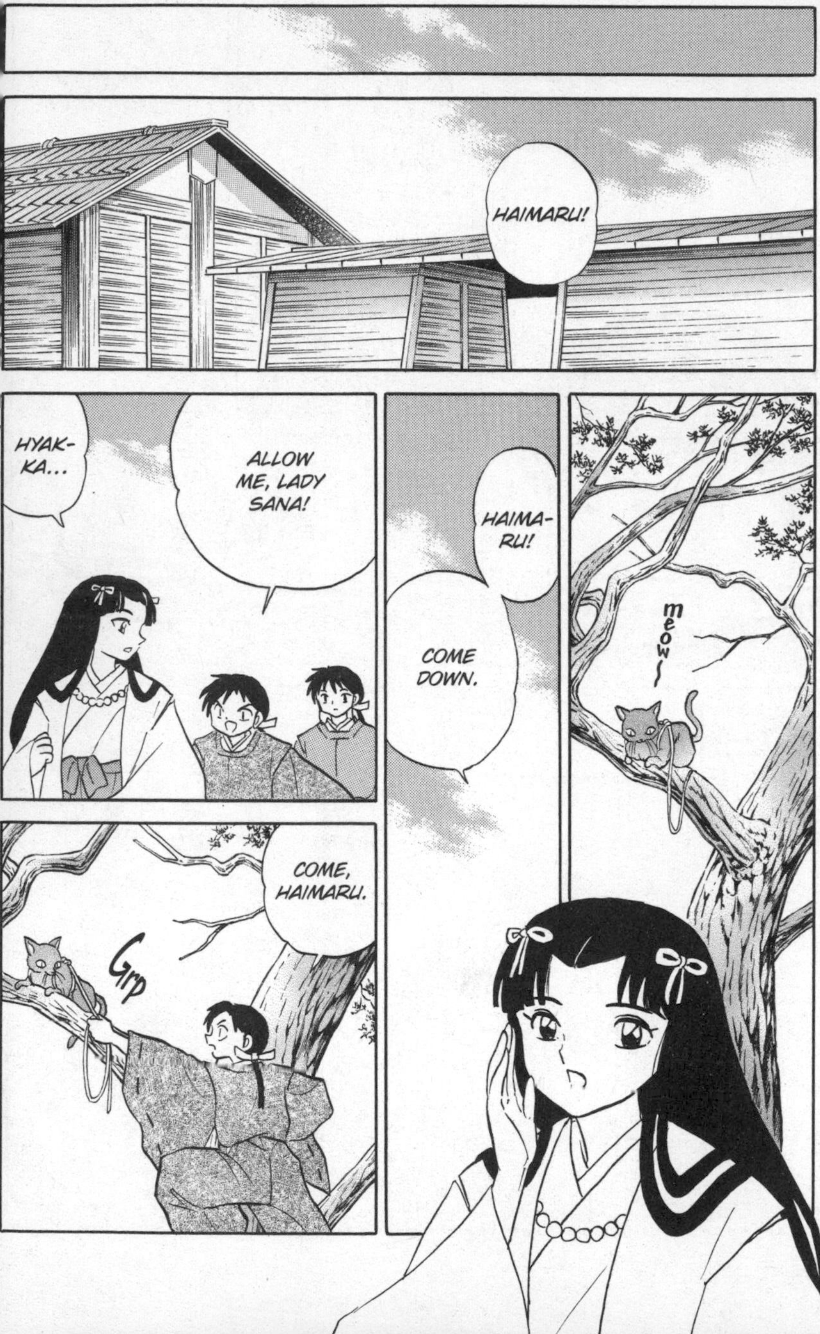
HAIMARU!
meow~
HAIMA-RU!
COME DOWN.
ALLOW ME, LADY SANA!
HYAK-KA...
COME, HAIMARU.
Grp

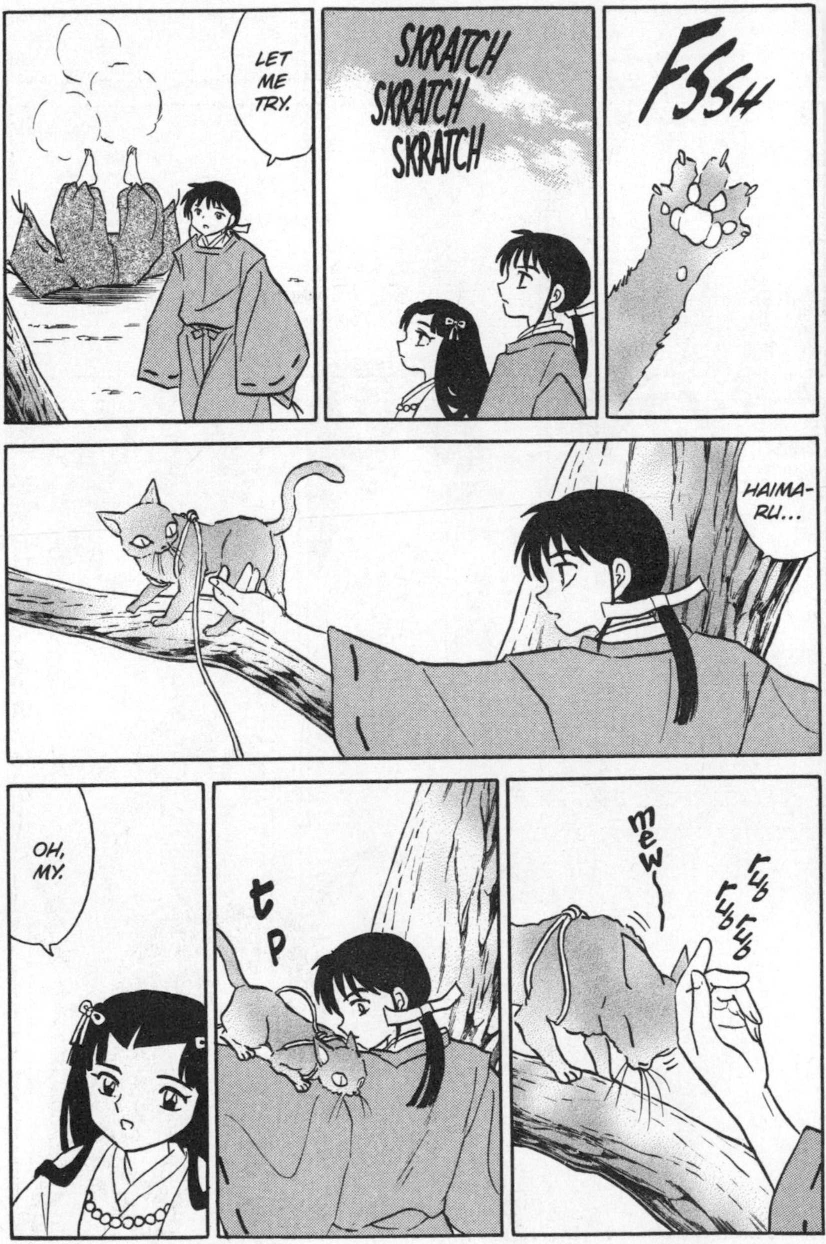
FSSH
SKRATCH SKRATCH SKRATCH
LET ME TRY.
HAIMA-RU...
mew~
rub rub rub rub
tp
OH, MY.

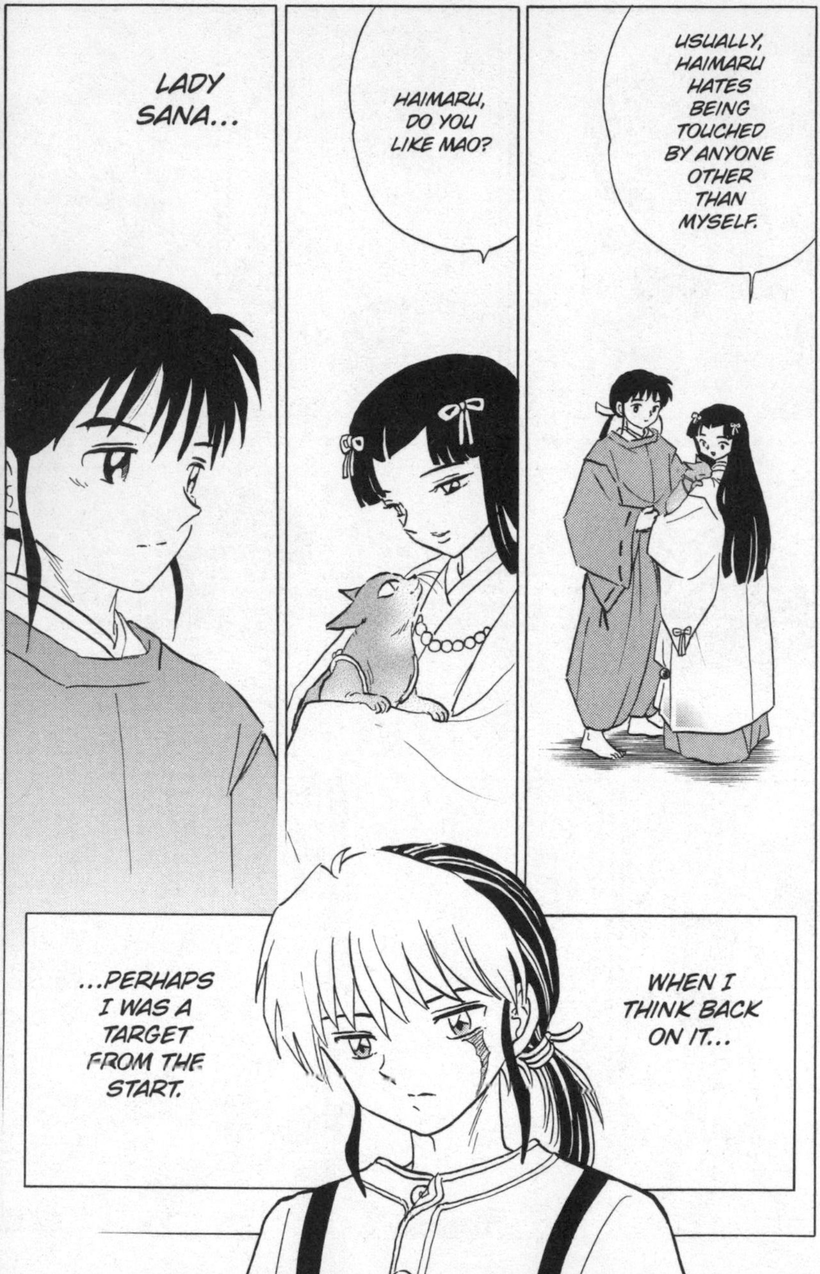
USUALLY, HAIMARU HATES BEING TOUCHED BY ANYONE OTHER THAN MYSELF.
HAIMARU, DO YOU LIKE MAO?
LADY SANA...
WHEN I THINK BACK ON IT...
...PERHAPS I WAS A TARGET FROM THE START.

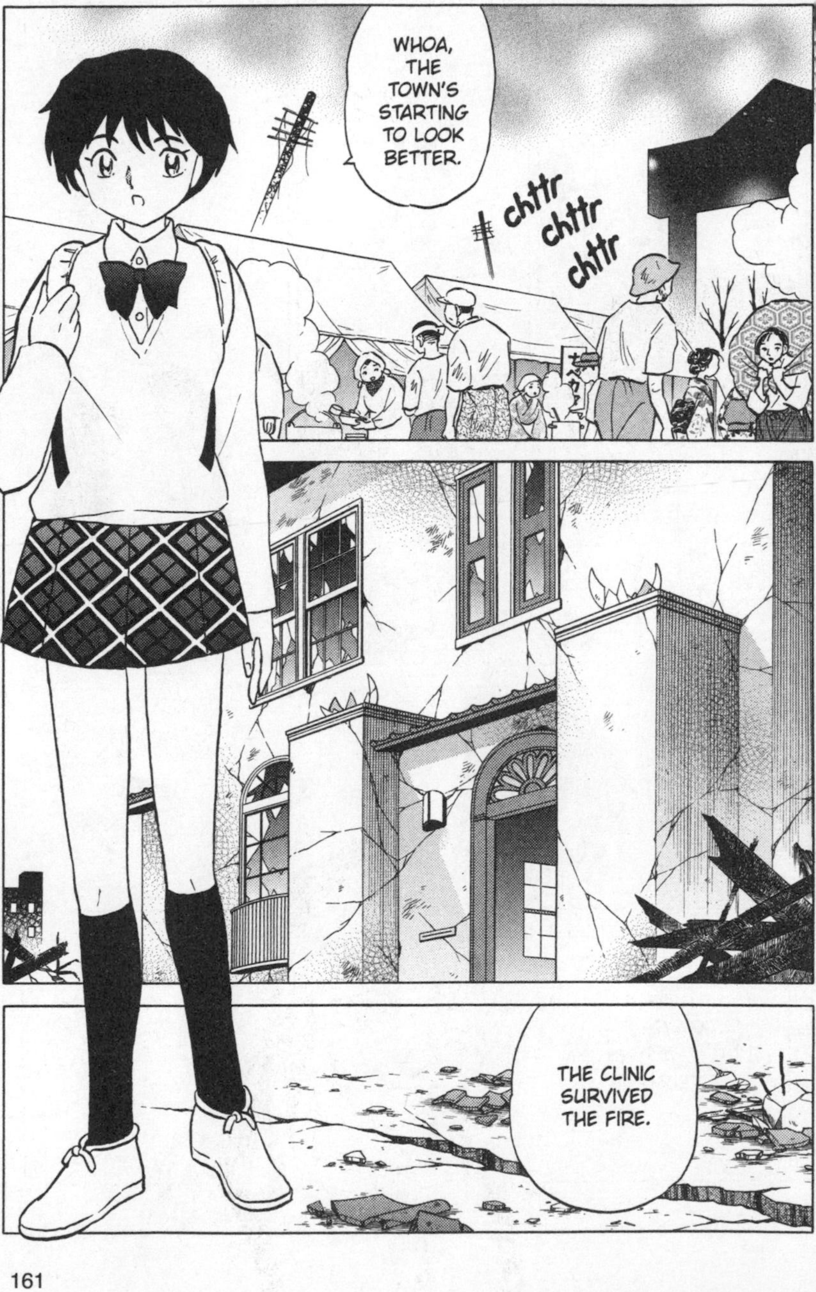
WHOA, THE TOWN'S STARTING TO LOOK BETTER.
chttr chttr chttr
THE CLINIC SURVIVED THE FIRE.

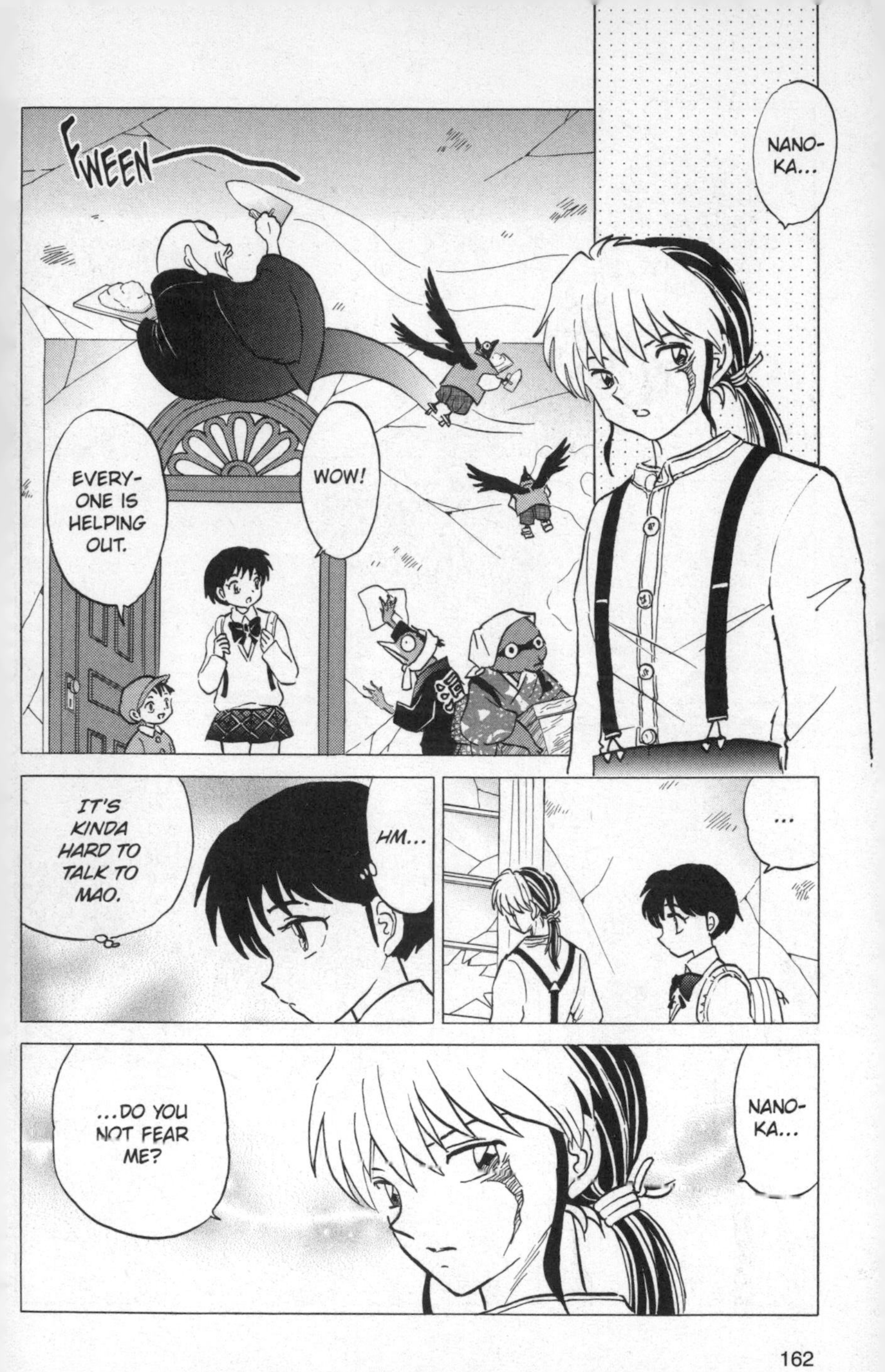
NANO-KA...
FWEEN
WOW!
EVERY-ONE IS HELPING OUT.
...
HM...
IT'S KINDA HARD TO TALK TO MAO.
NANO-KA...
...DO YOU NOT FEAR ME?

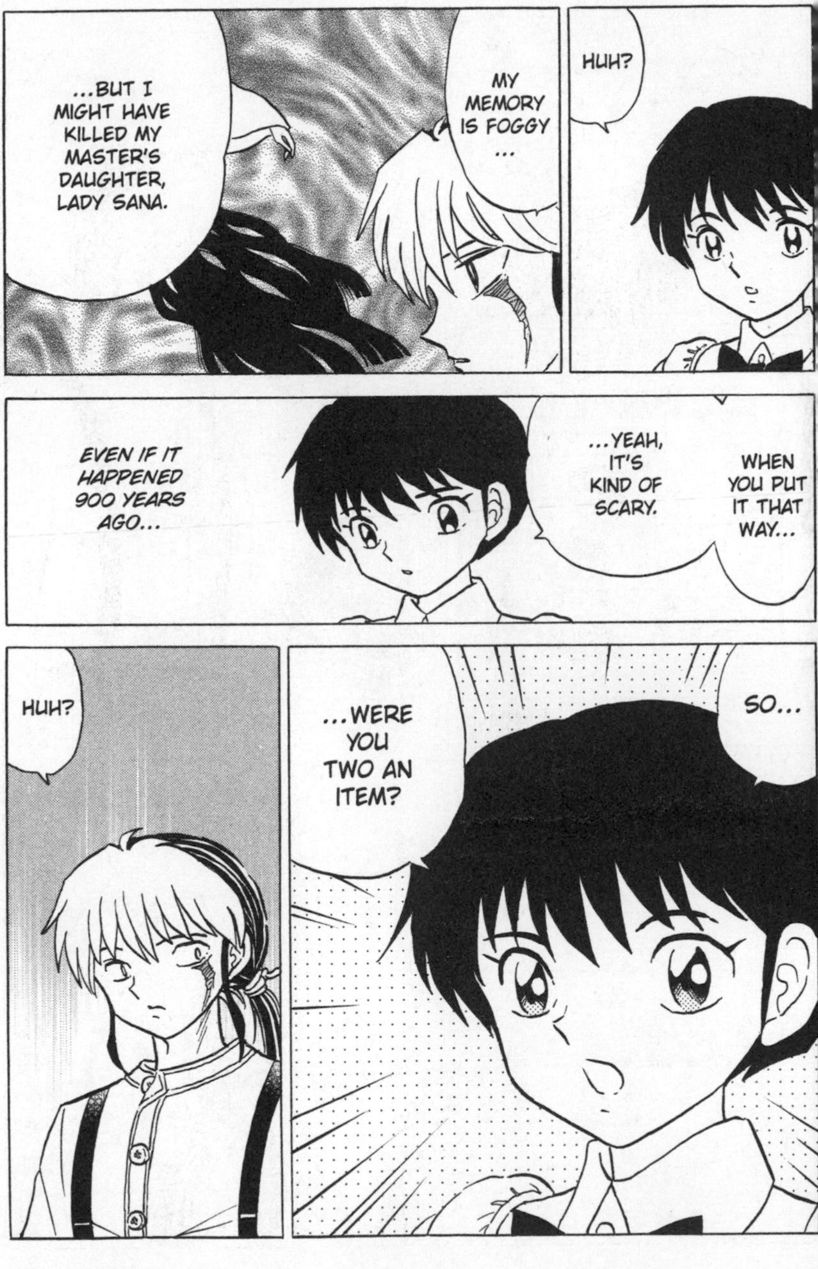
HUH?
MY MEMORY IS FOGGY ...
...BUT I MIGHT HAVE KILLED MY MASTER'S DAUGHTER, LADY SANA.
WHEN YOU PUT IT THAT WAY...
...YEAH, IT'S KIND OF SCARY.
EVEN IF IT HAPPENED 900 YEARS AGO...
SO...
...WERE YOU TWO AN ITEM?
HUH?

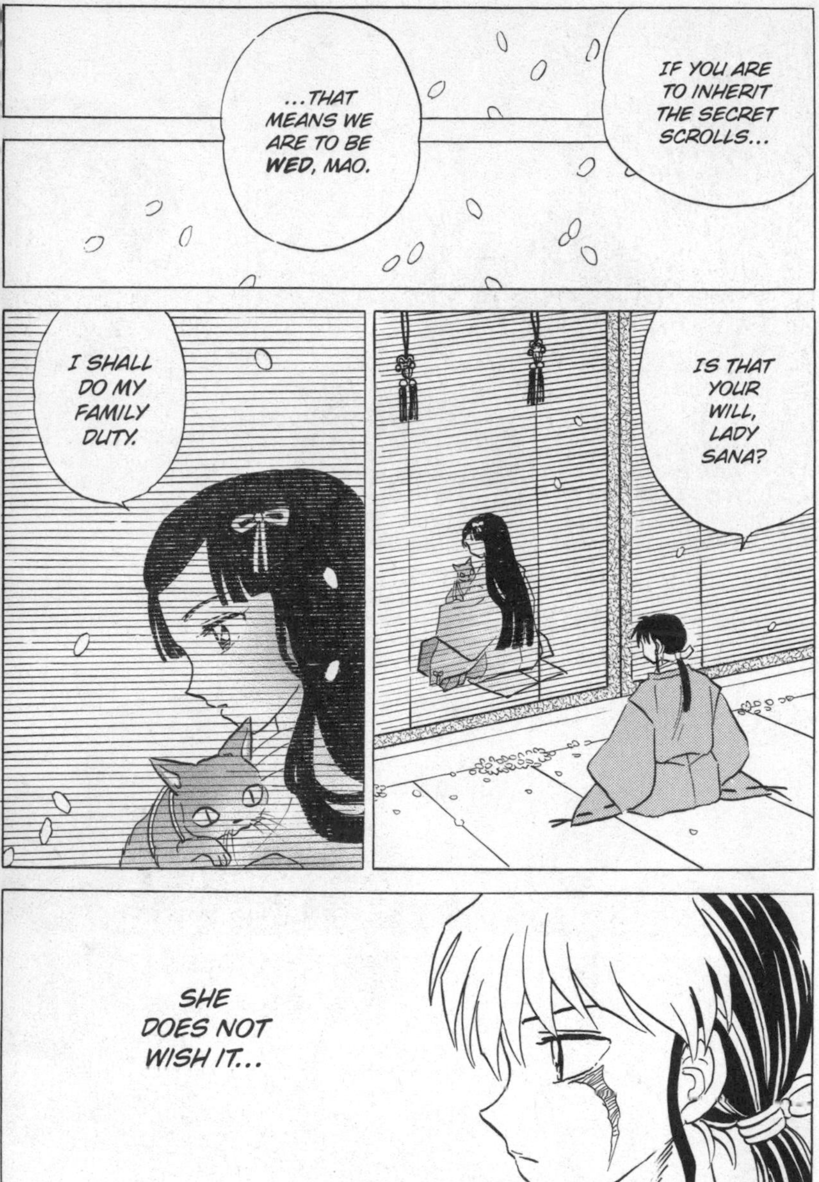
IF YOU ARE TO INHERIT THE SECRET SCROLLS...
...THAT MEANS WE ARE TO BE WED, MAO.
IS THAT YOUR WILL, LADY SANA?
I SHALL DO MY FAMILY DUTY.
SHE DOES NOT WISH IT...

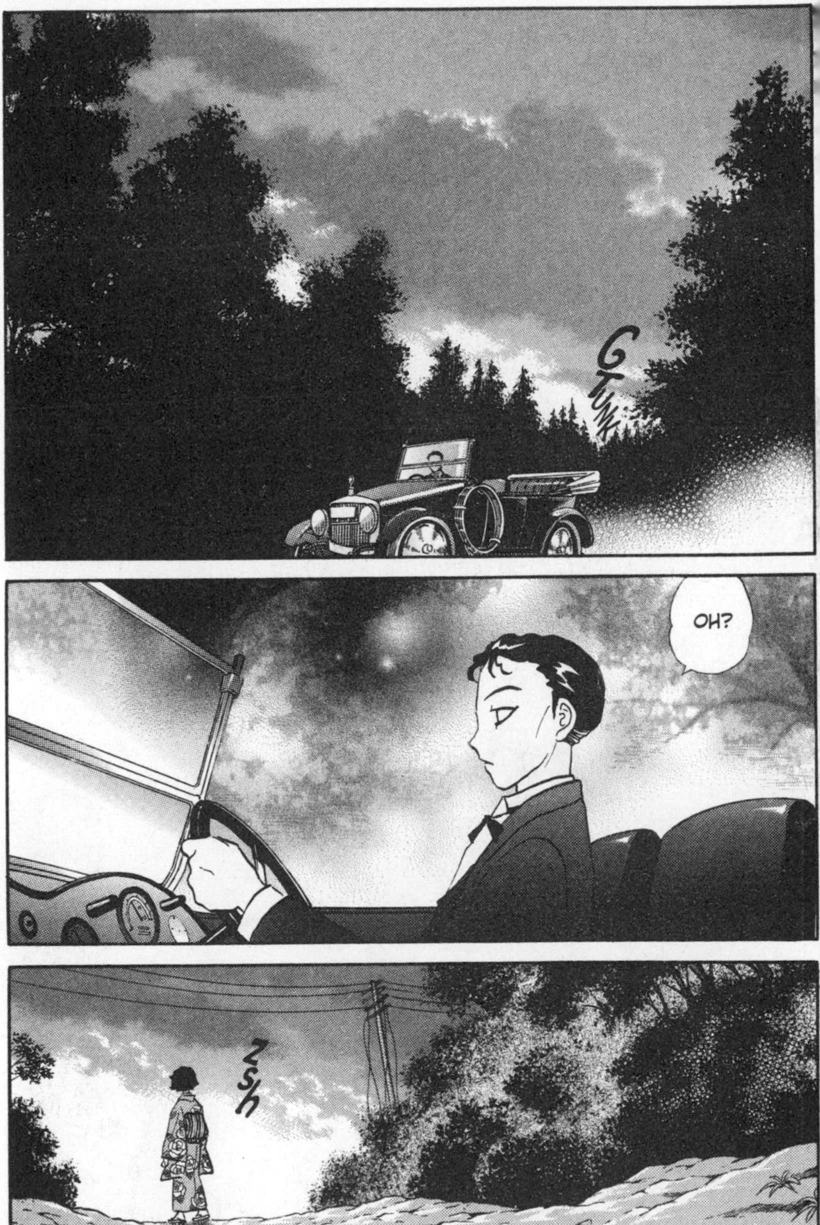
GTUNK
OH?
ZSH

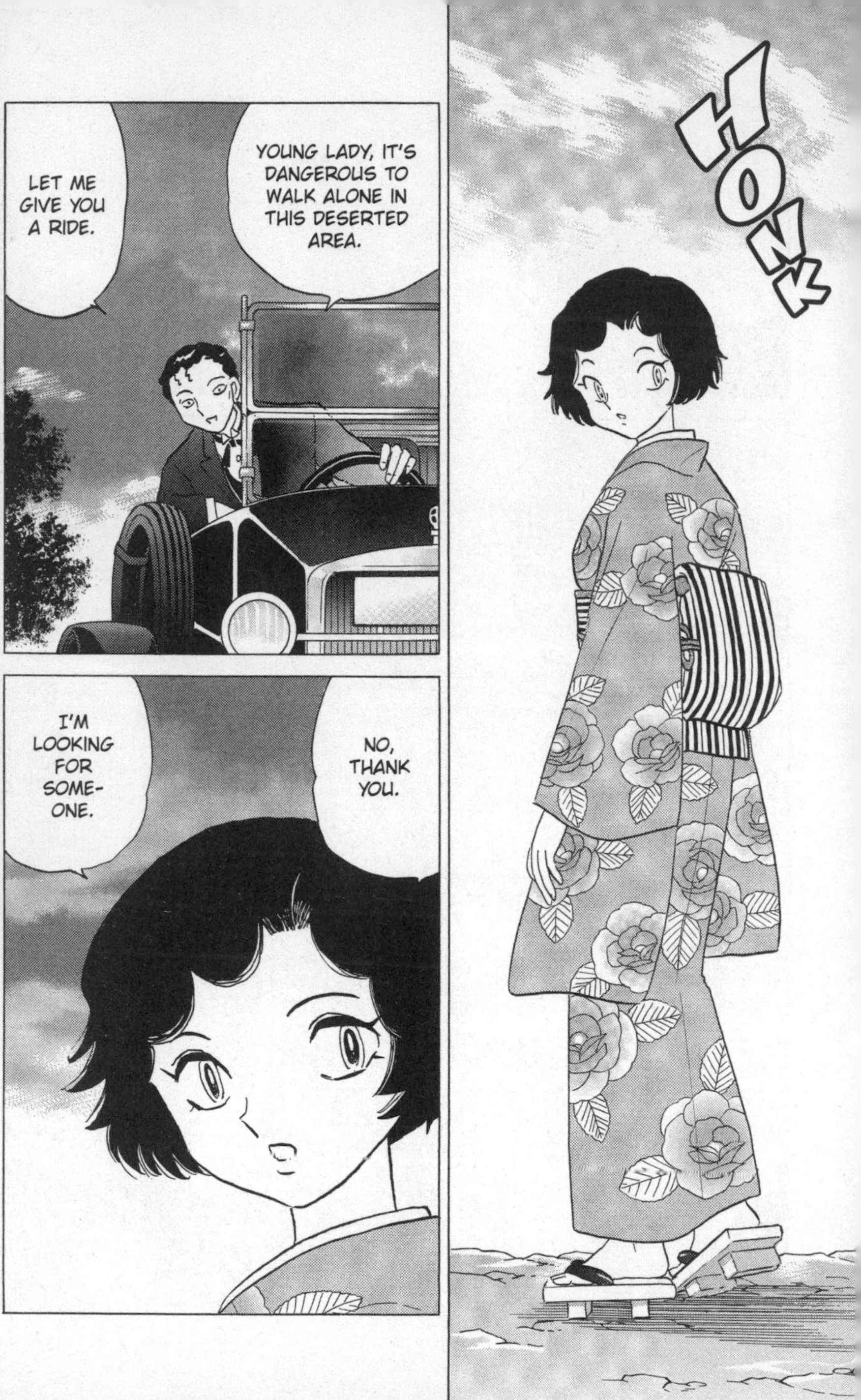
HONK
YOUNG LADY, IT'S DANGEROUS TO WALK ALONE IN THIS DESERTED AREA.
LET ME GIVE YOU A RIDE.
NO, THANK YOU.
I'M LOOKING FOR SOME-ONE.

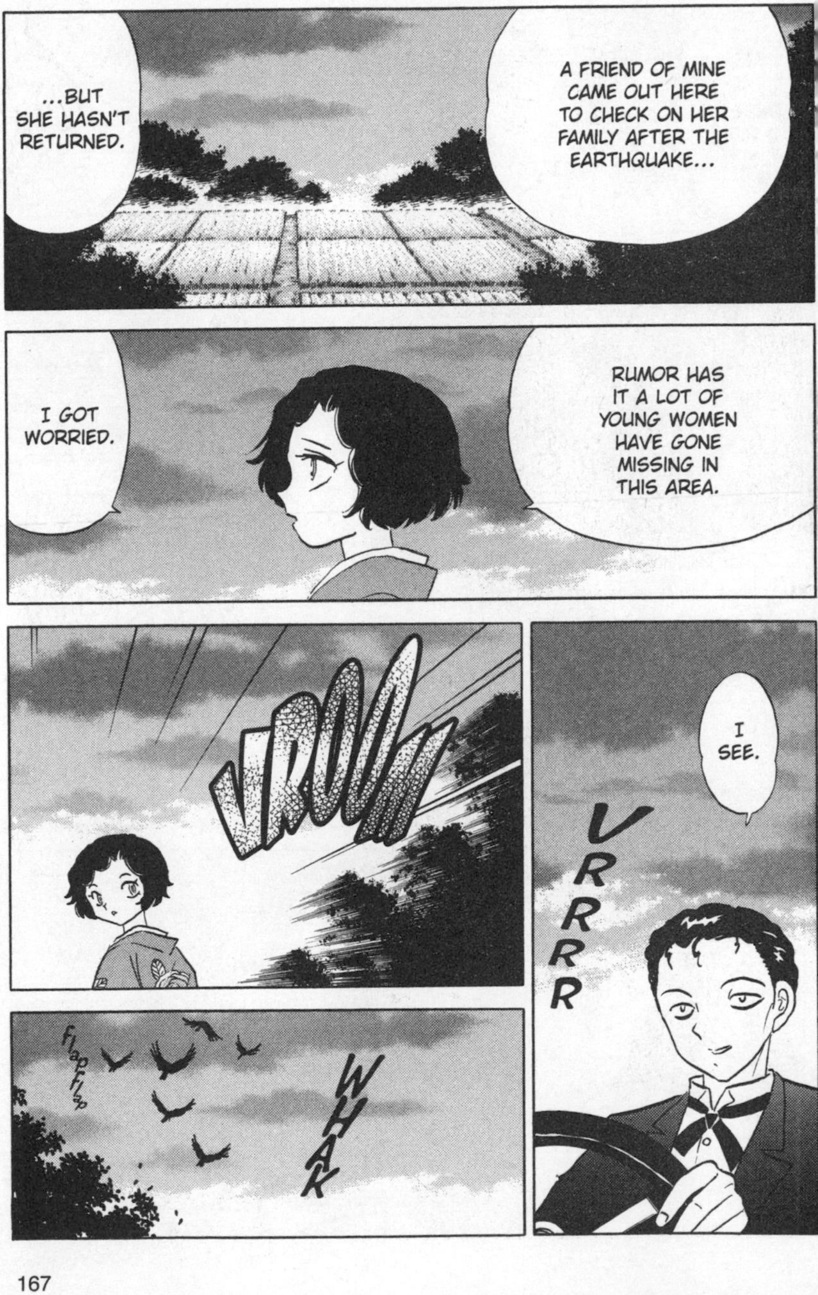
A FRIEND OF MINE CAME OUT HERE TO CHECK ON HER FAMILY AFTER THE EARTHQUAKE...
...BUT SHE HASN'T RETURNED.
RUMOR HAS IT A LOT OF YOUNG WOMEN HAVE GONE MISSING IN THIS AREA.
I GOT WORRIED.
I SEE.
VRRRR
VROOM
WHAK
flapflap

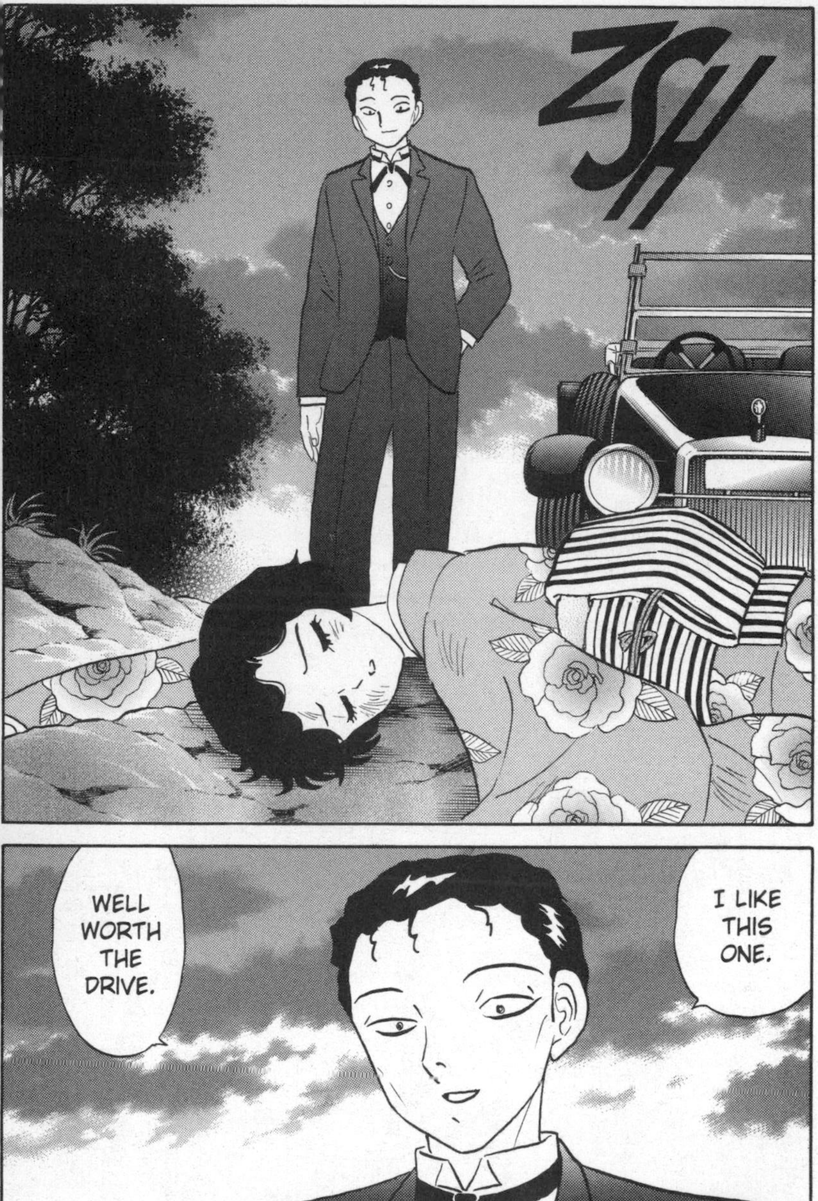
ZSH
I LIKE THIS ONE.
WELL WORTH THE DRIVE.

Chapter 10:
Kuchinawa

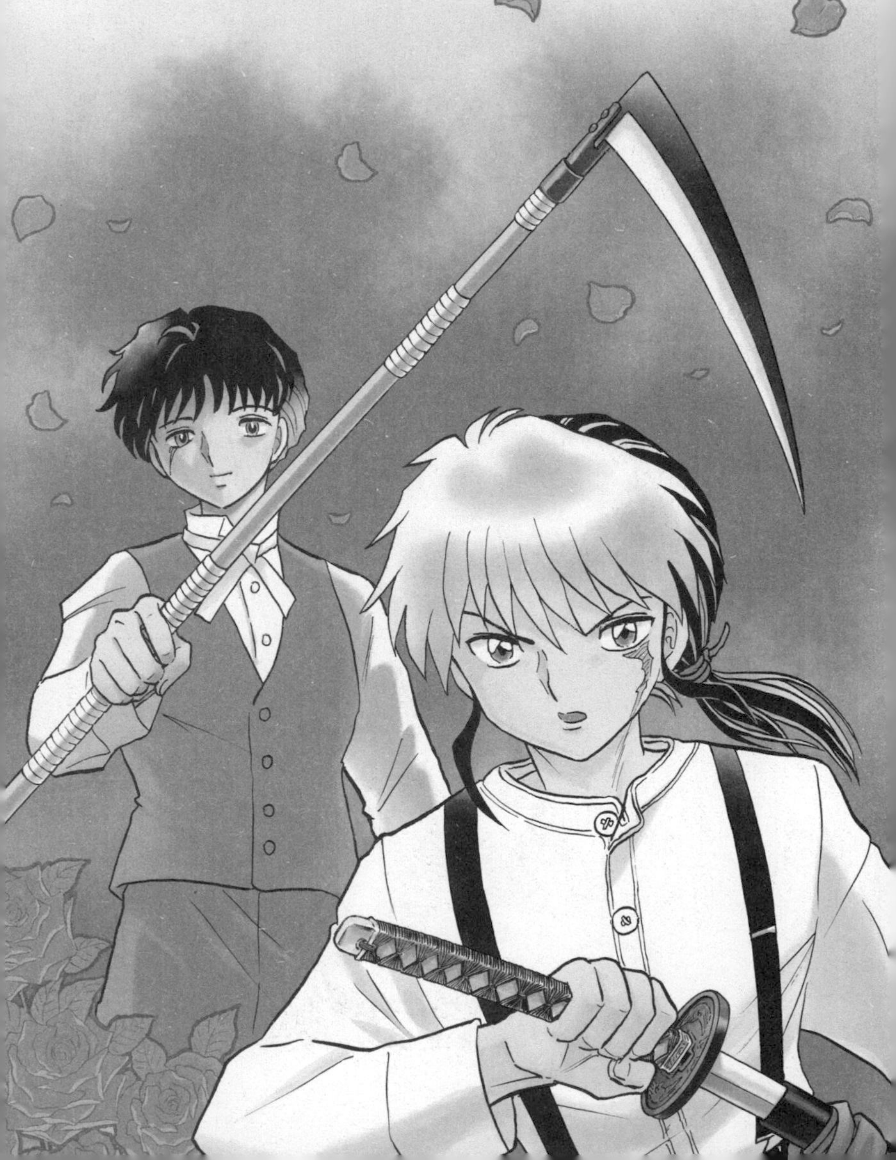

MAO

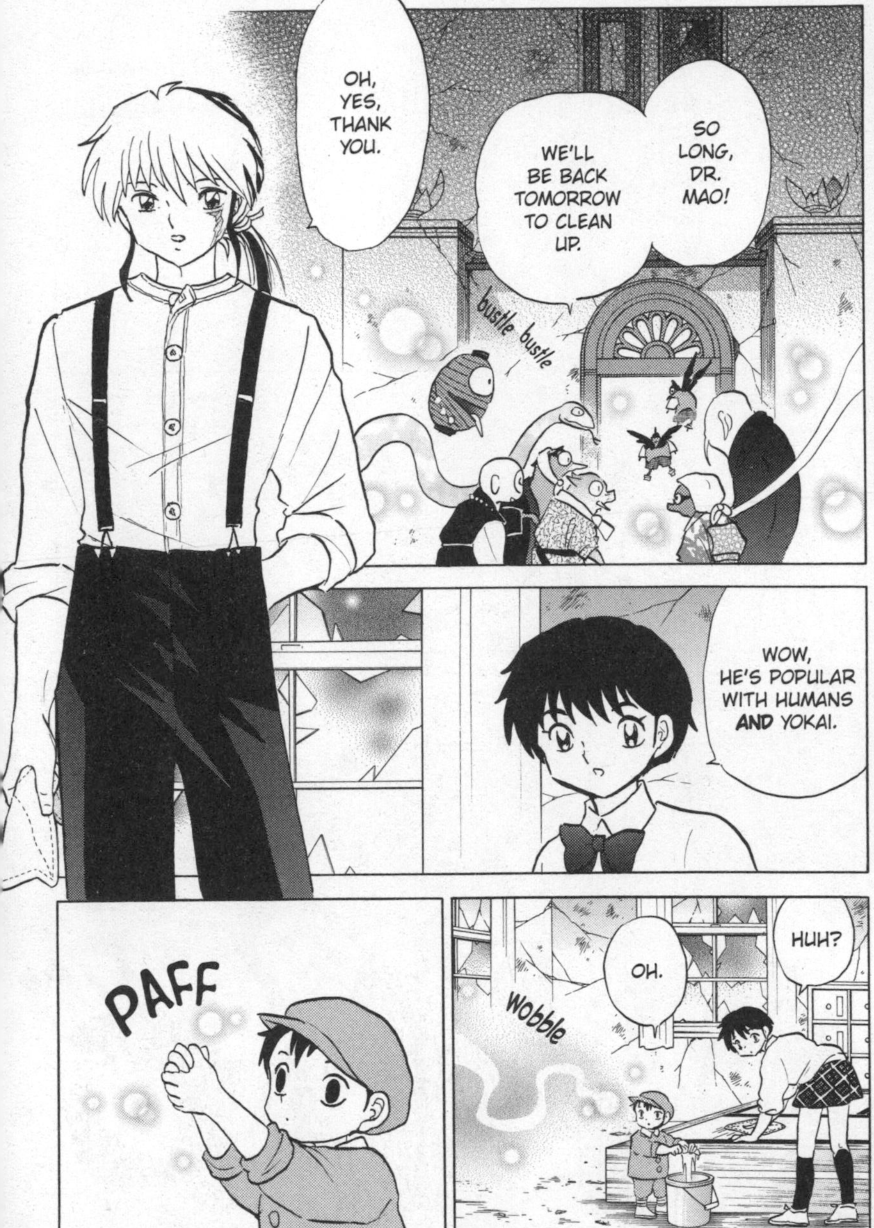
SO LONG, DR. MAO!
WE'LL BE BACK TOMORROW TO CLEAN UP.
bustle bustle
OH, YES, THANK YOU.
WOW, HE'S POPULAR WITH HUMANS AND YOKAI.
HUH?
OH.
wobble
PAFF

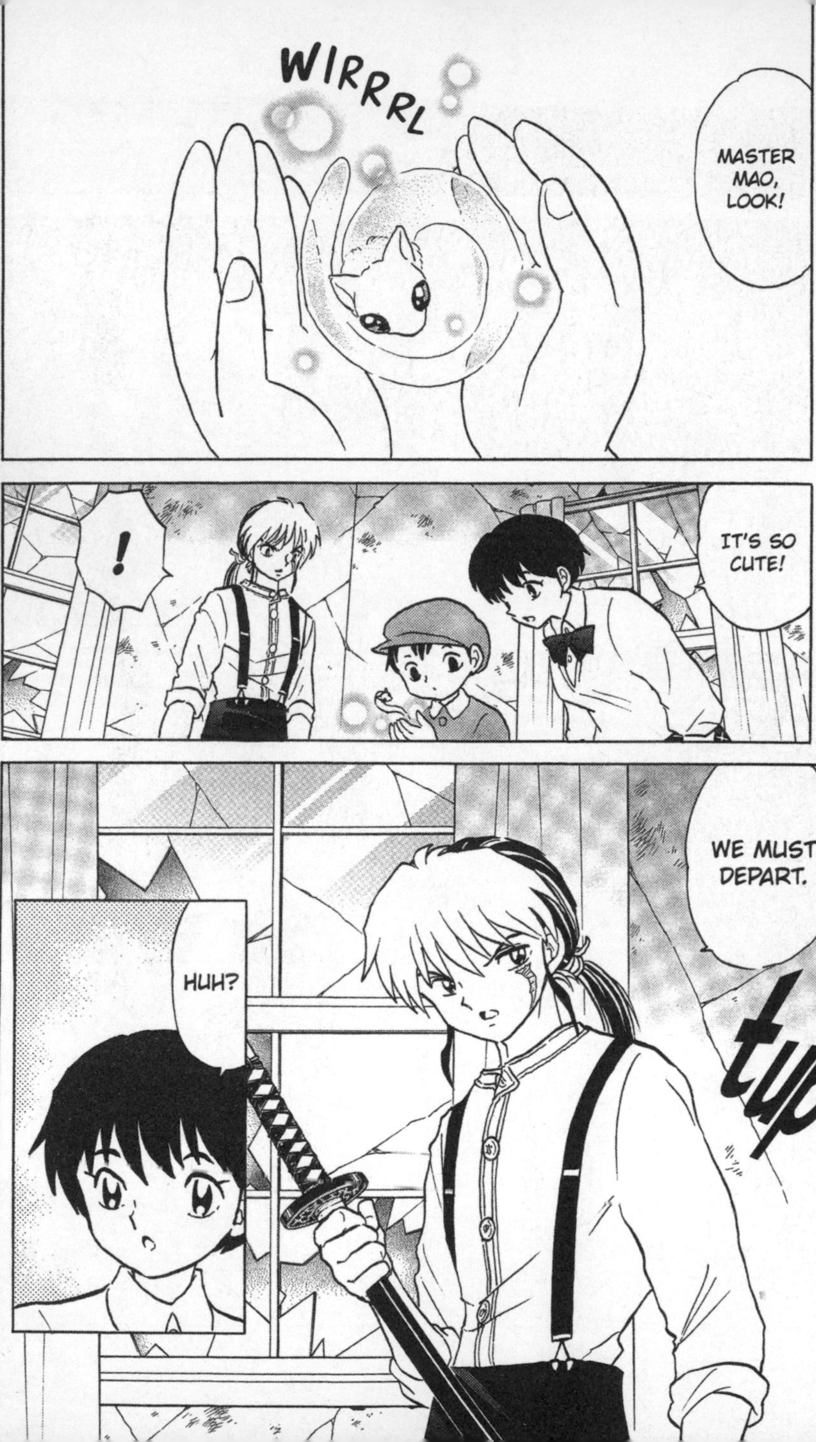
MASTER MAO, LOOK!
WIRRRL
IT'S SO CUTE!
!
WE MUST DEPART.
tup
HUH?

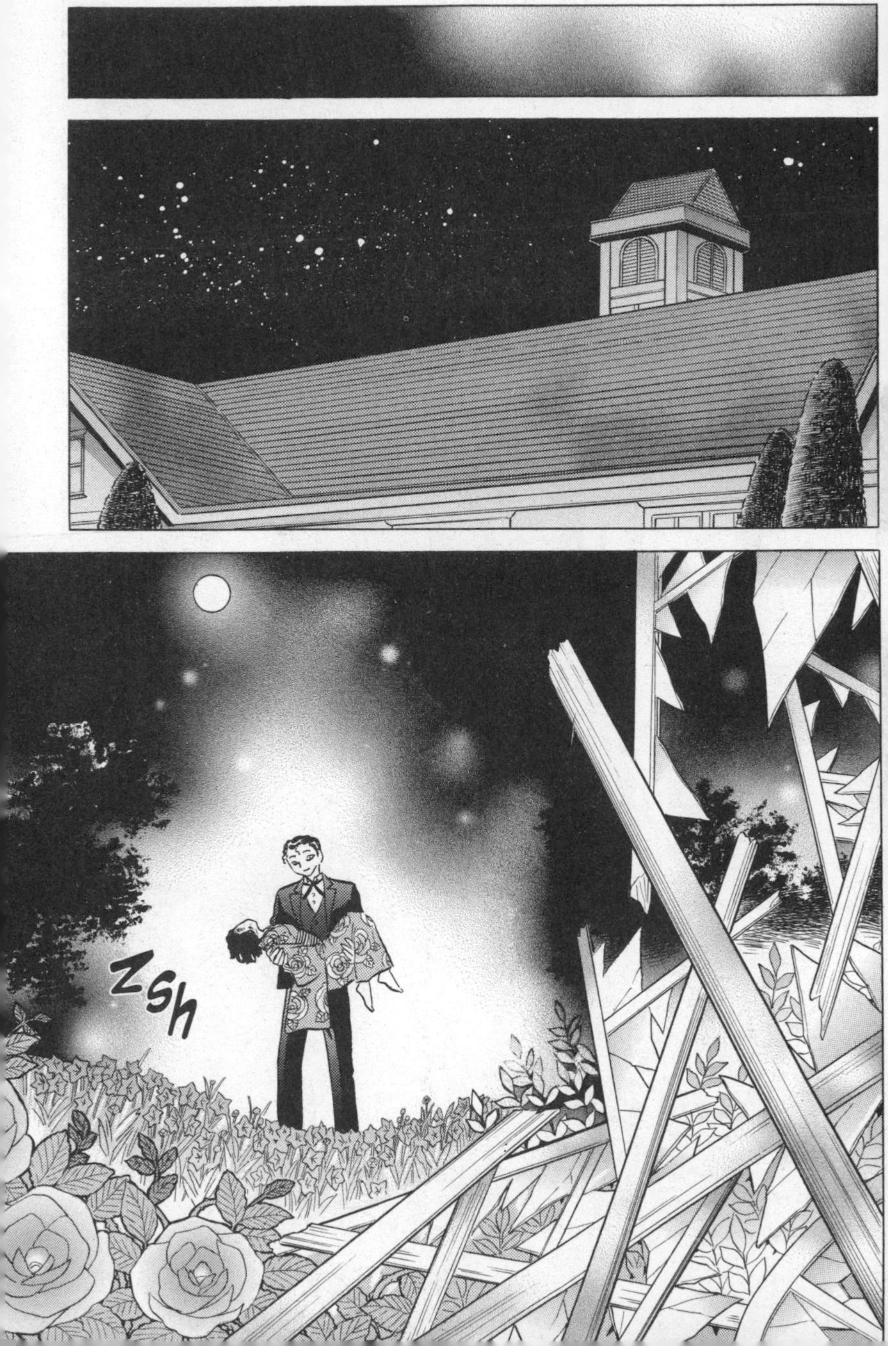
Zsh

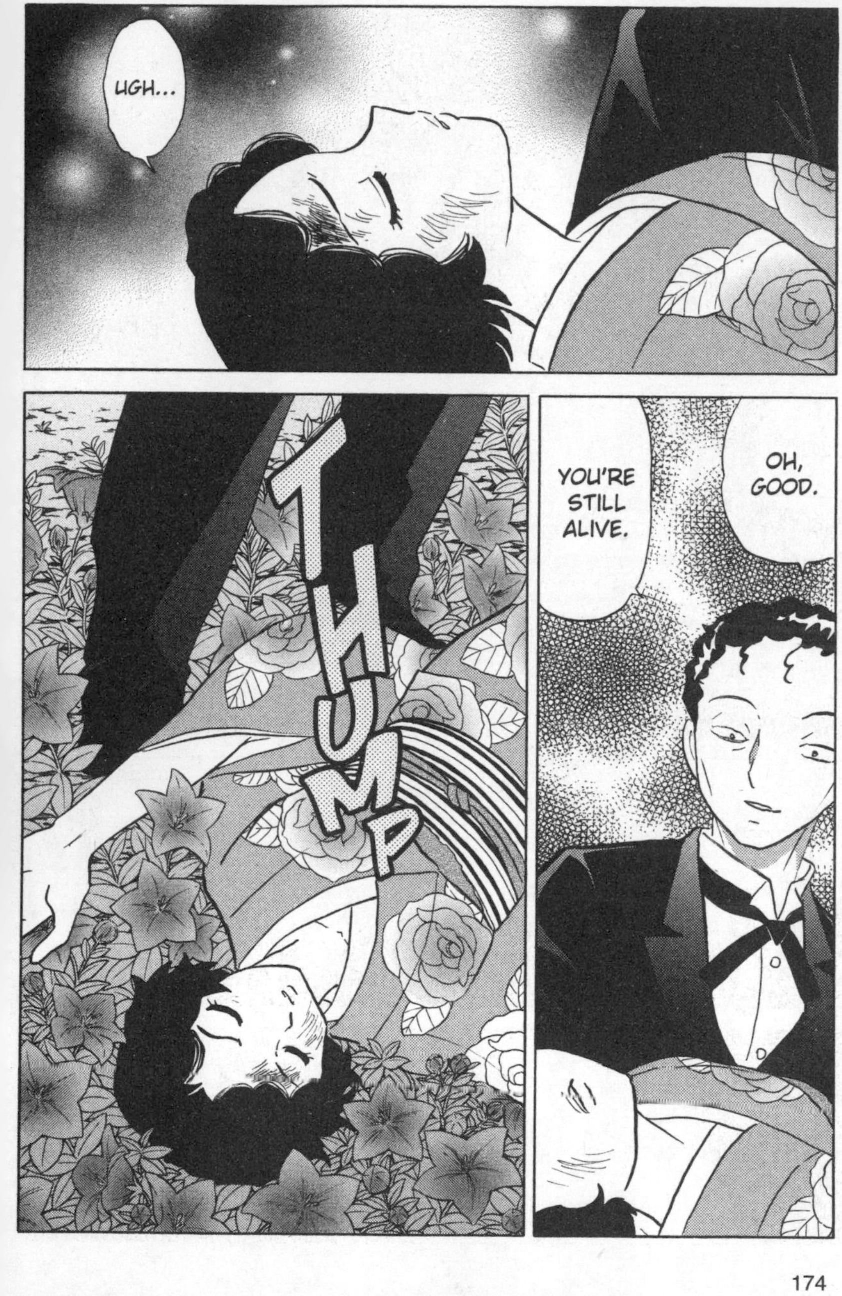
UGH...
THUMP
OH, GOOD.
YOU'RE STILL ALIVE.

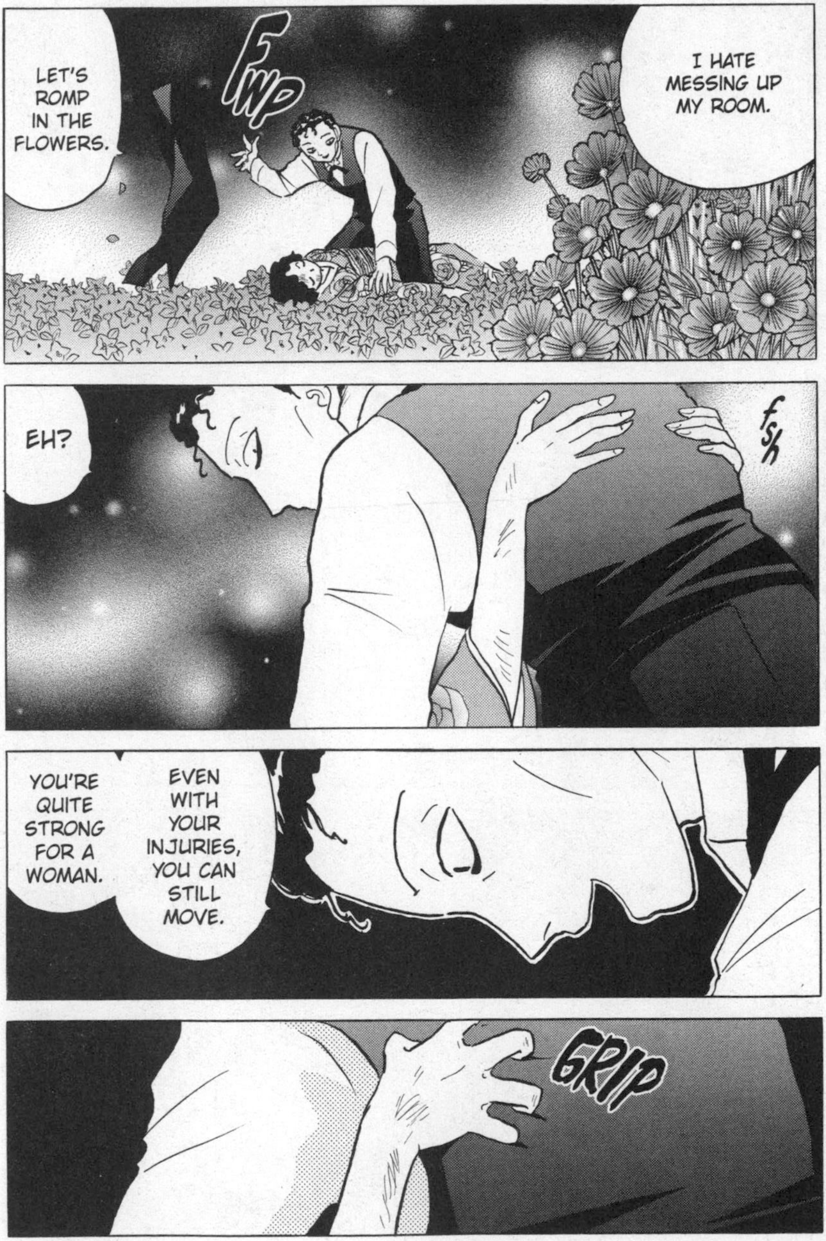
I HATE MESSING UP MY ROOM.
FWP
LET'S ROMP IN THE FLOWERS.
fsh
EH?
EVEN WITH YOUR INJURIES, YOU CAN STILL MOVE.
YOU'RE QUITE STRONG FOR A WOMAN.
GRIP

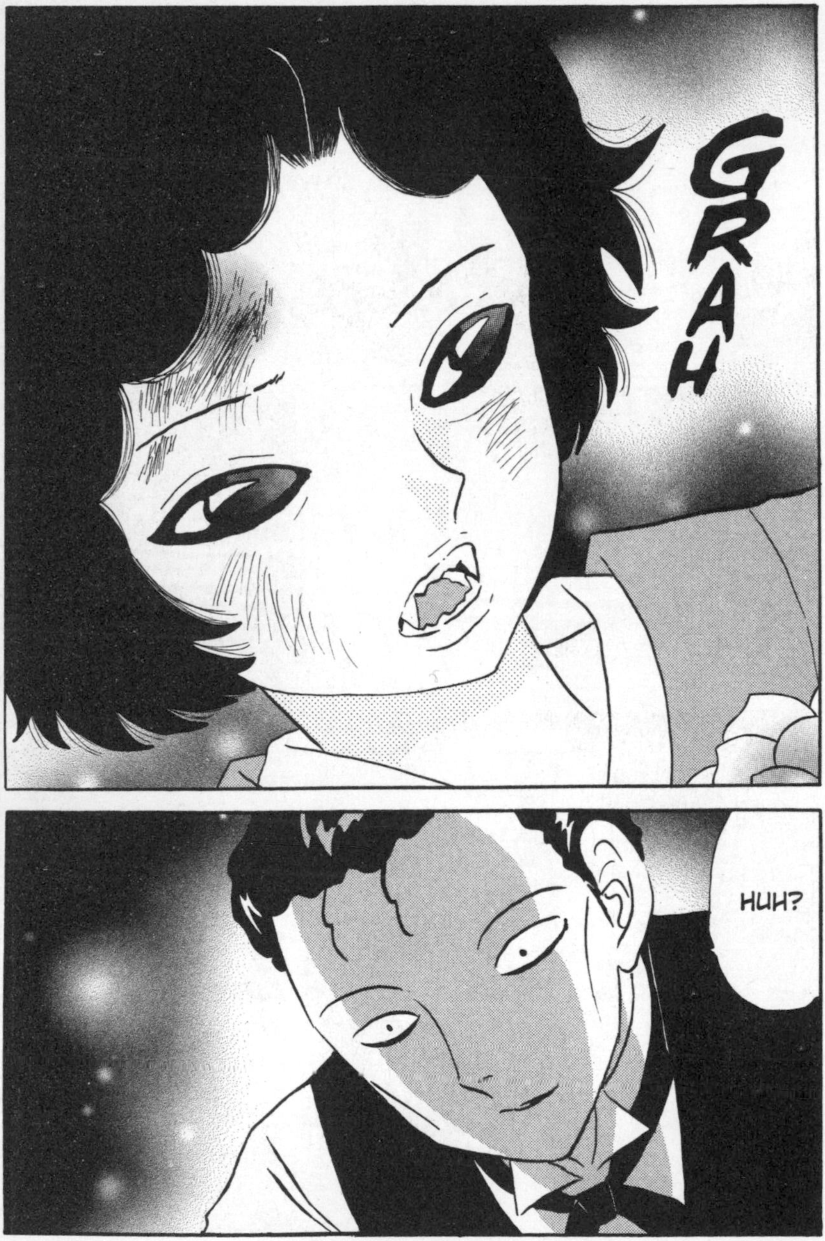
GRAH
HUH?

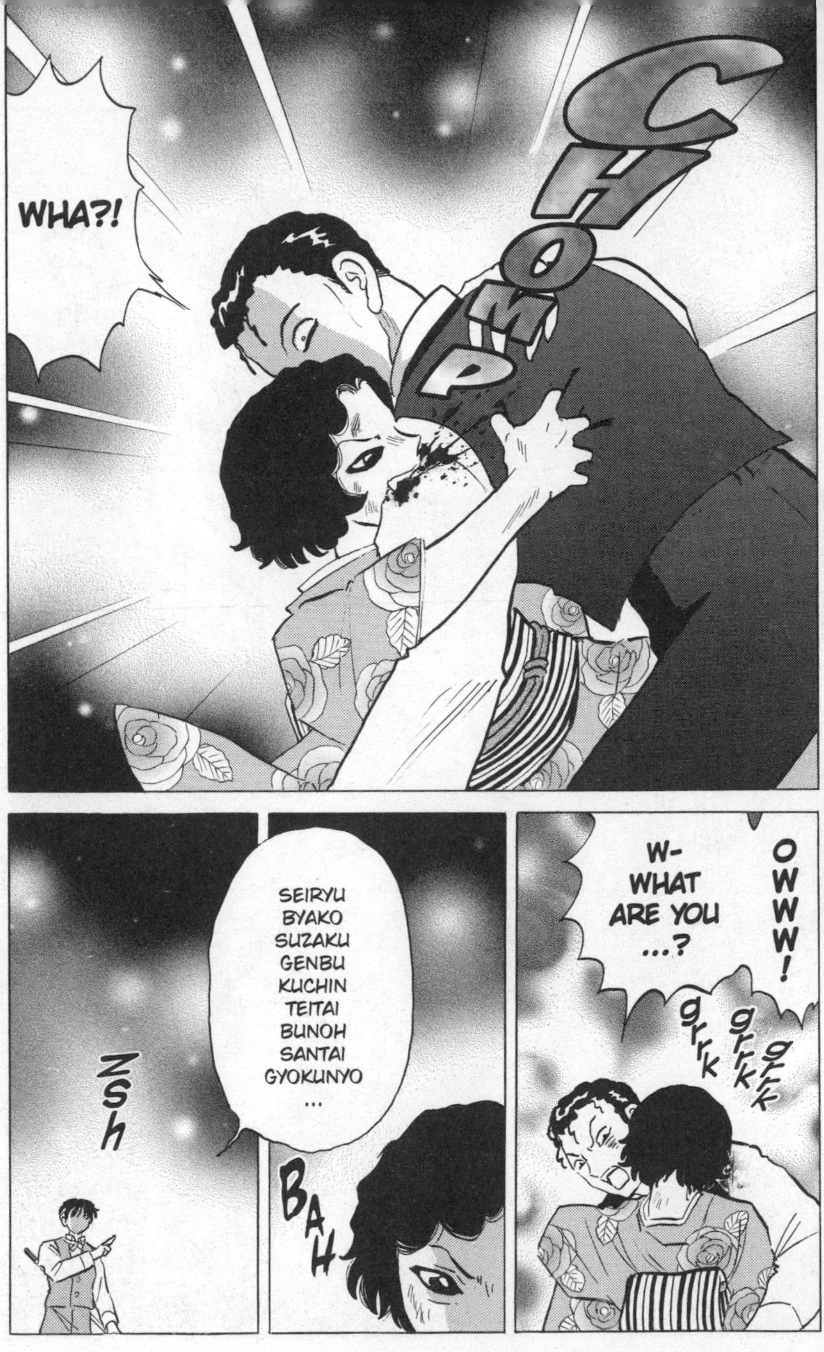
CHOMP
WHA?!
OWWW!
W-WHAT ARE YOU ...?
grrk grrk grrk
SEIRYU BYAKO SUZAKU GENBU KUCHIN TEITAI BUNOH SANTAI GYOKUNYO ...
BAH
zsh

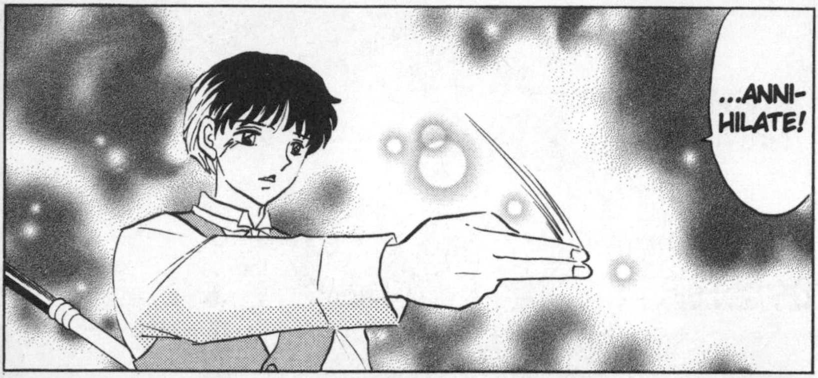
...ANNI-
HILATE!

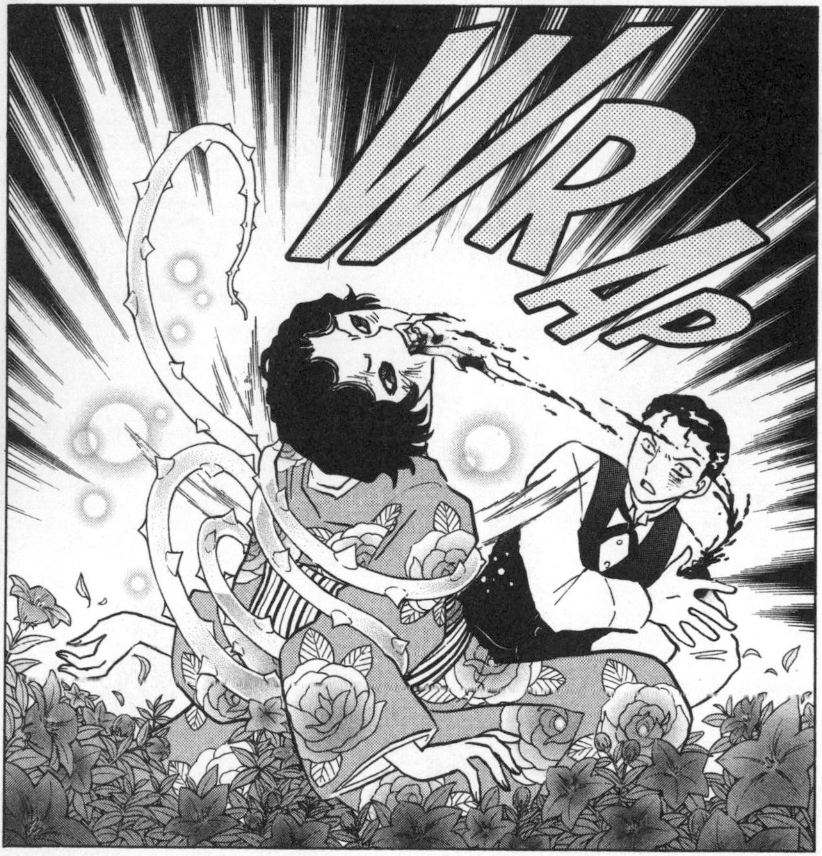
WRAP

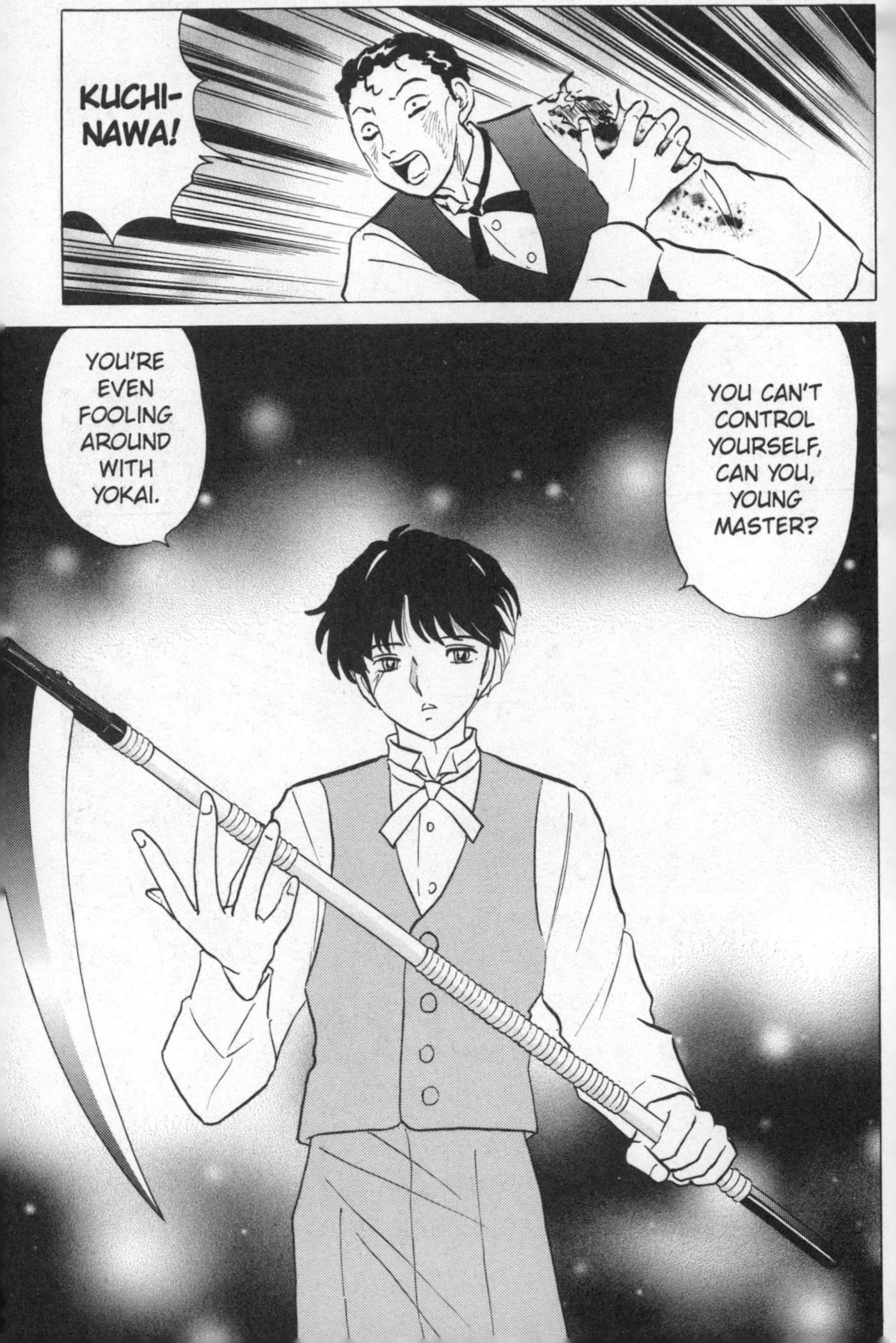
KUCHI-NAWA!
YOU CAN'T CONTROL YOURSELF, CAN YOU, YOUNG MASTER?
YOU'RE EVEN FOOLING AROUND WITH YOKAI.

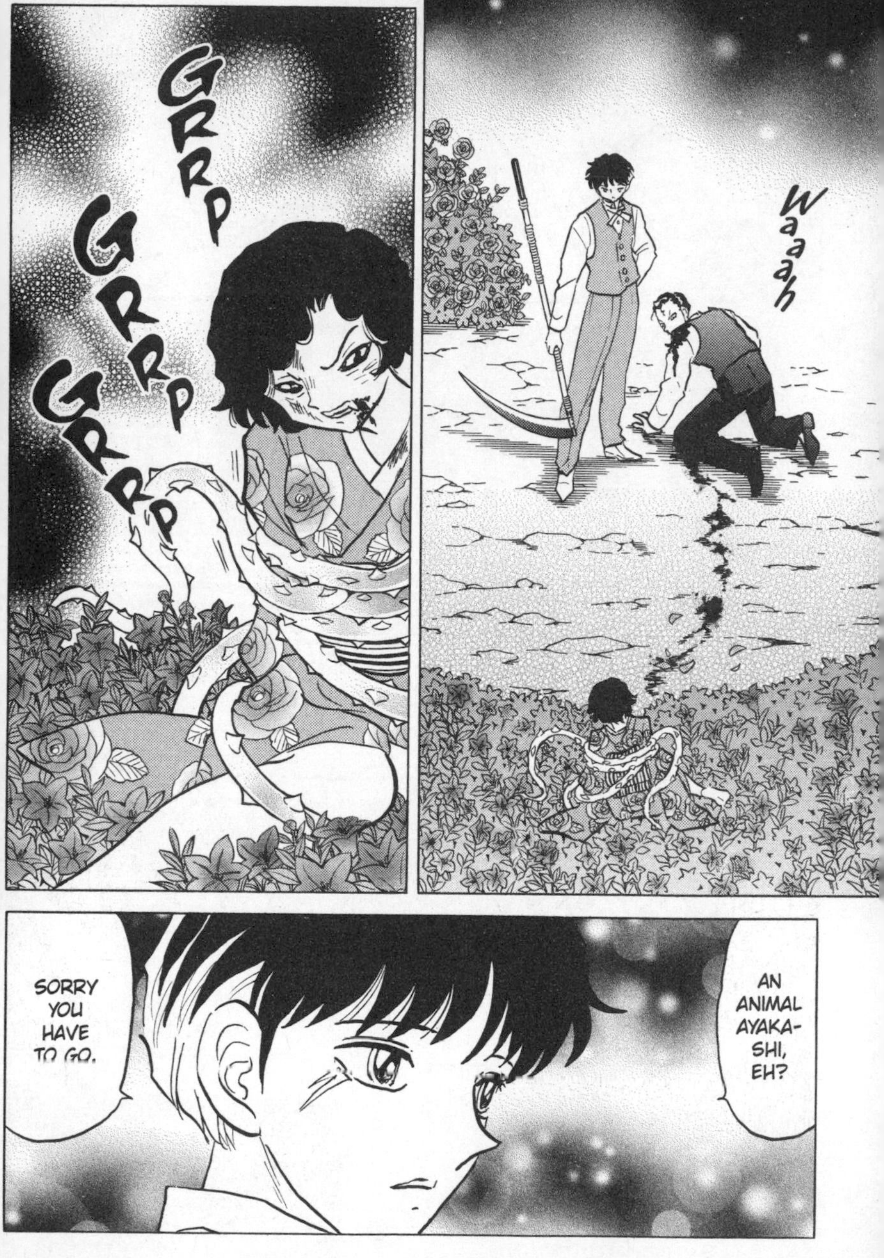
Waaah
GRRRP GRRRP GRRRP
AN ANIMAL AYAKA-SHI, EH?
SORRY YOU HAVE TO GO.

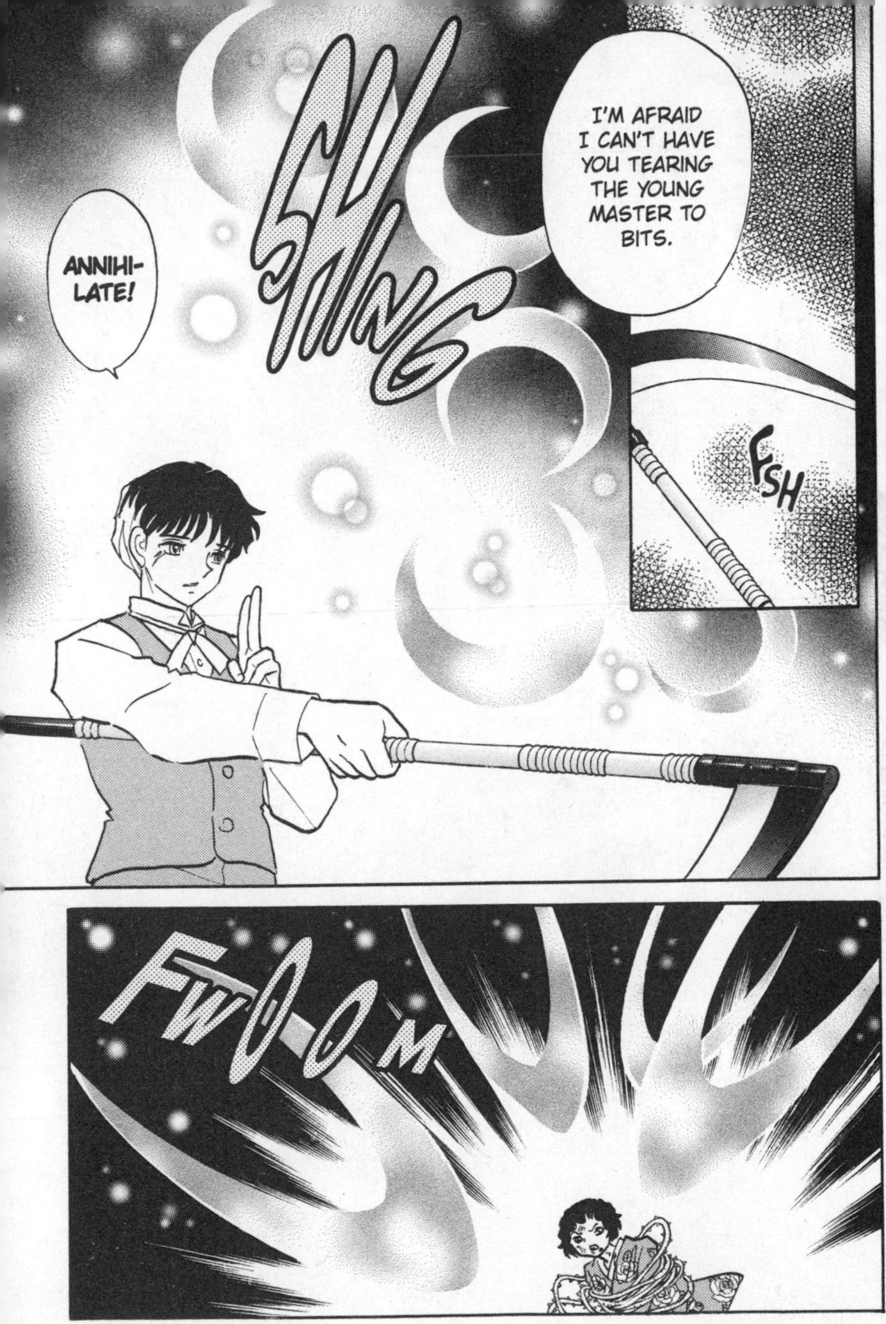
I'M AFRAID I CAN'T HAVE YOU TEARING THE YOUNG MASTER TO BITS.
FSH
SHING
ANNIHI-LATE!
FWOOM

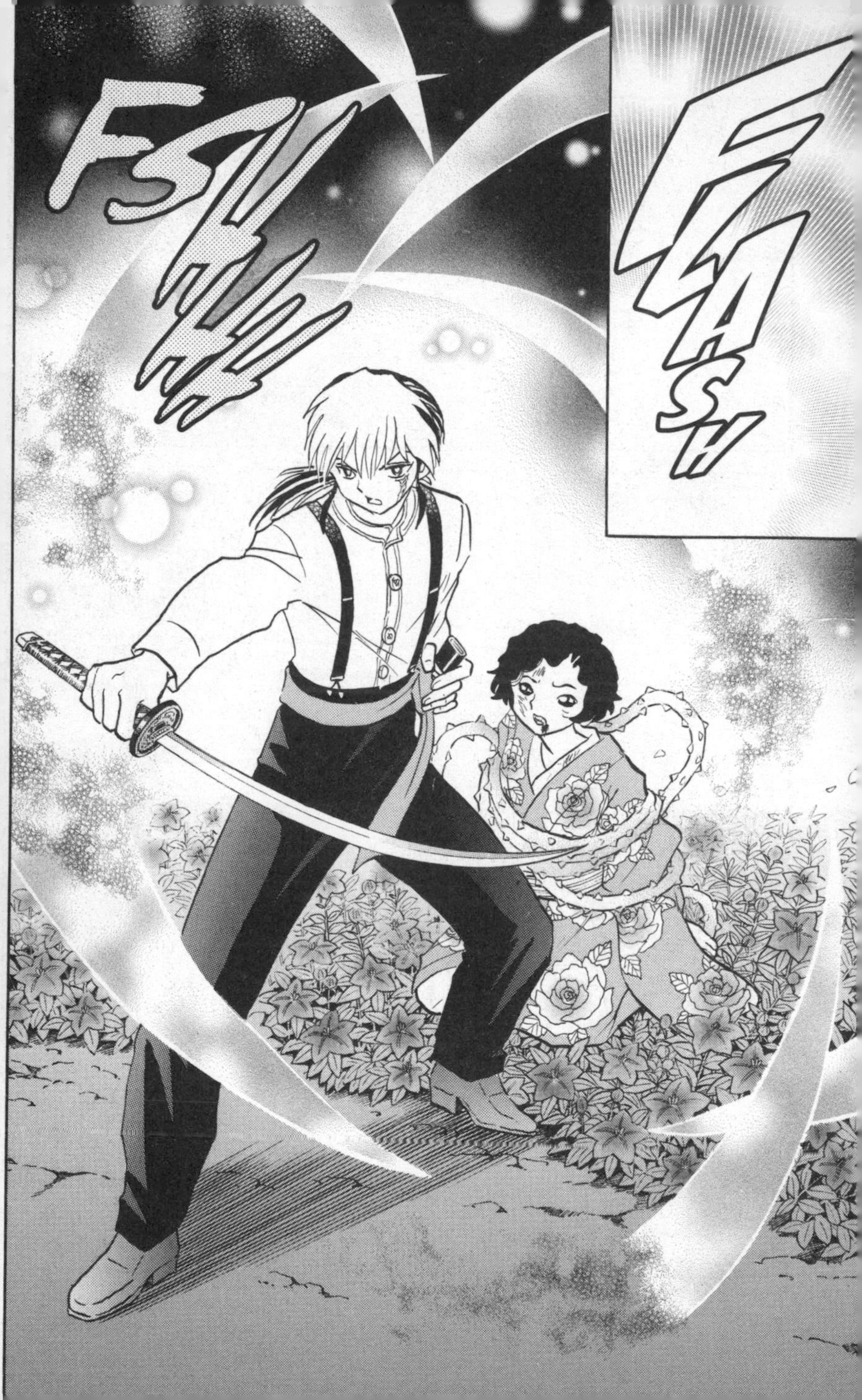
FLASH
FSHHH

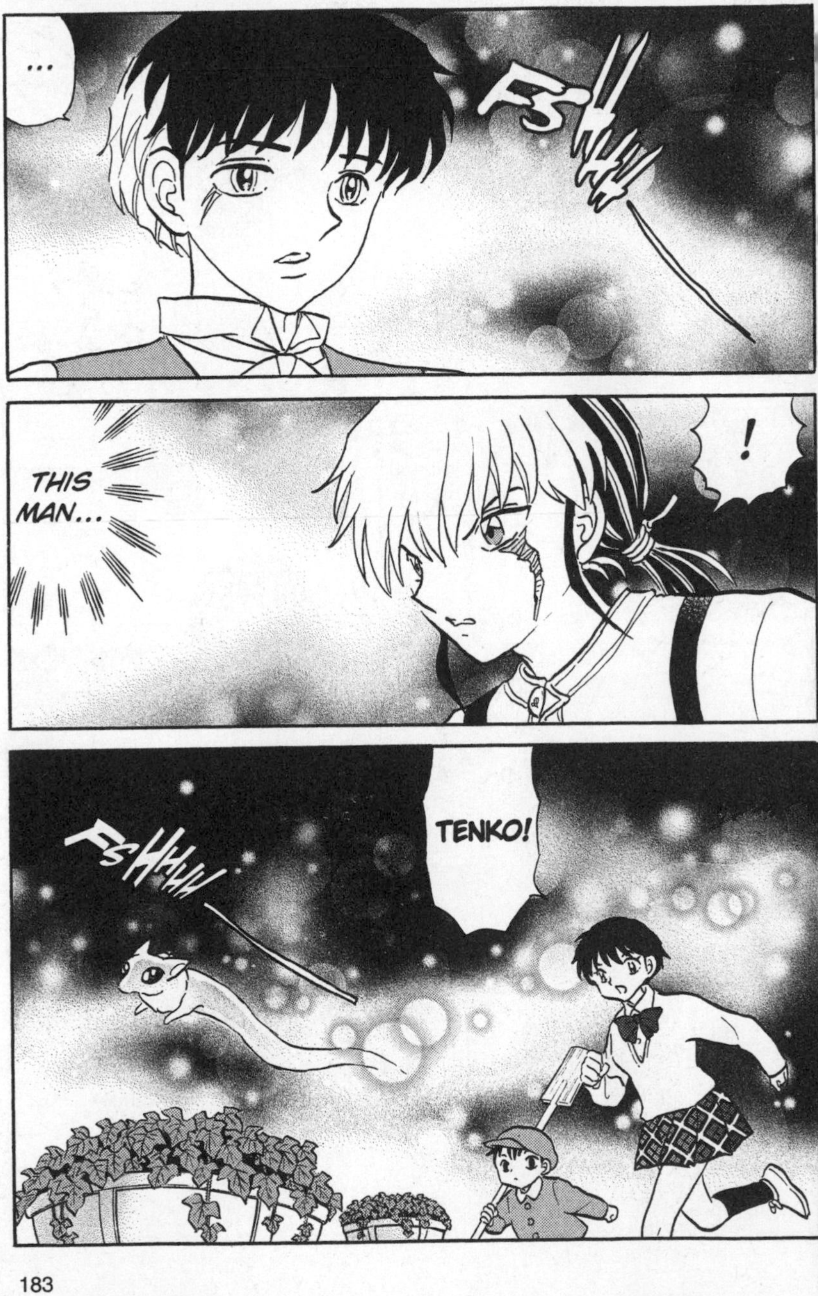
FSHHH
...
!
THIS MAN...
TENKO!
FSHHHH

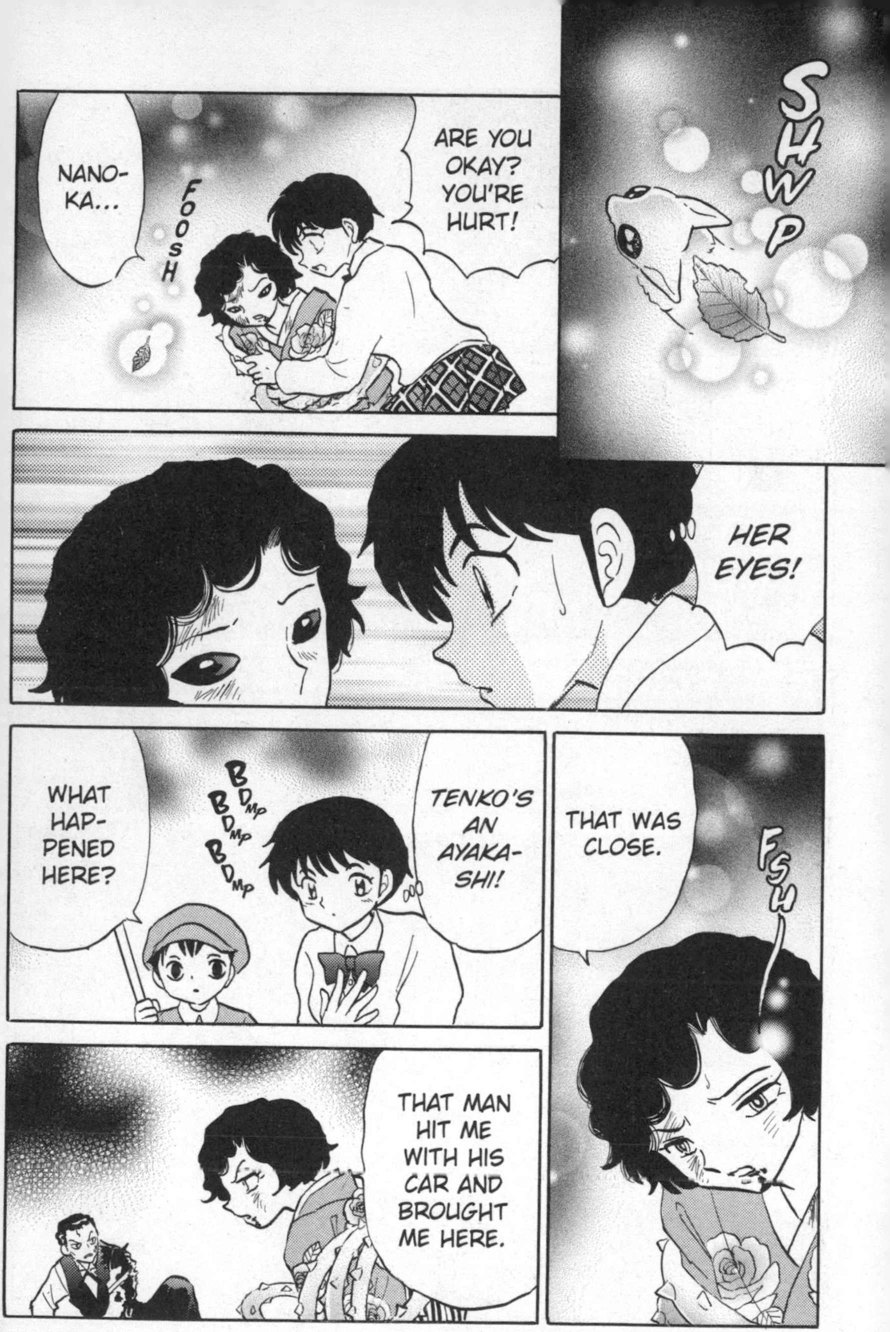
SHWP
ARE YOU OKAY? YOU'RE HURT!
FOOSH
NANO-KA...
HER EYES!
THAT WAS CLOSE.
FSH
TENKO'S AN AYAKA-SHI!
BDMP BDMP BDMP
WHAT HAP-PENED HERE?
THAT MAN HIT ME WITH HIS CAR AND BROUGHT ME HERE.

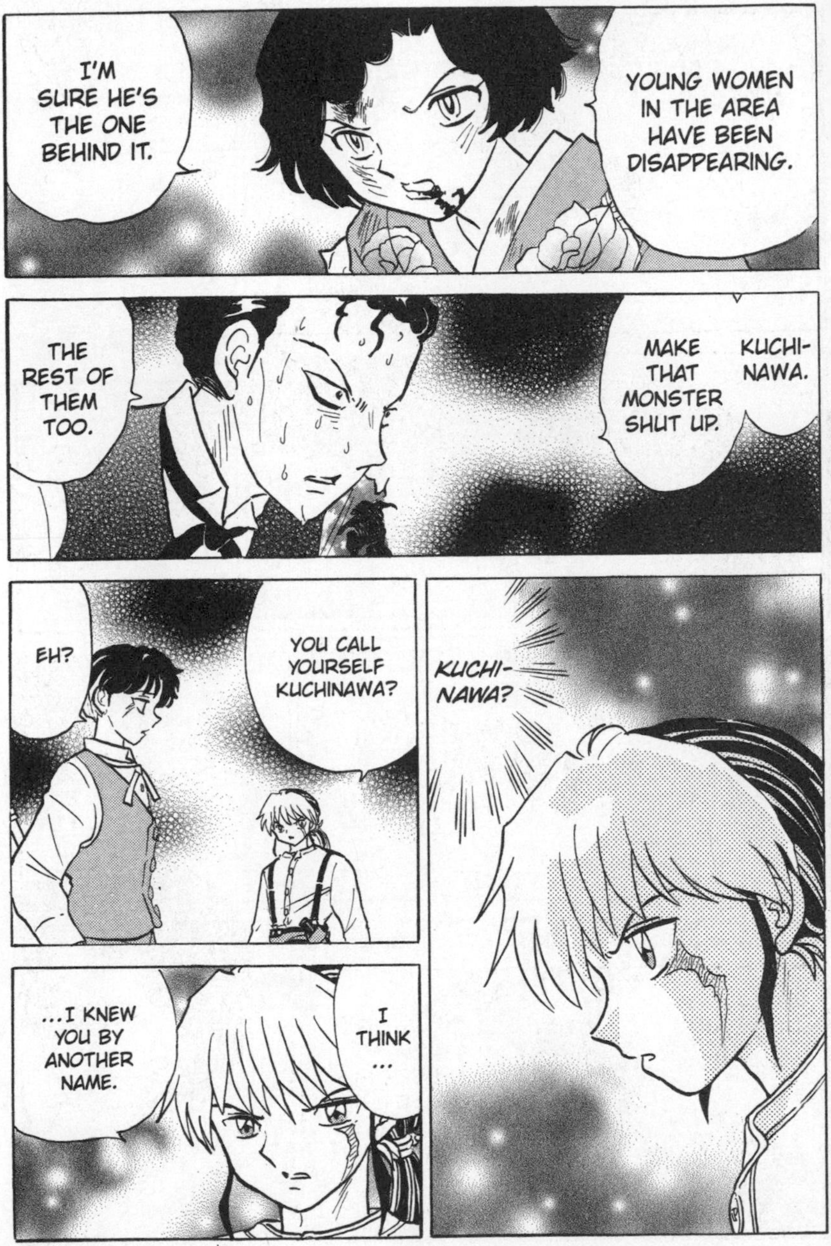
YOUNG WOMEN IN THE AREA HAVE BEEN DISAPPEARING.
I'M SURE HE'S THE ONE BEHIND IT.
MAKE THAT MONSTER SHUT UP. KUCHI-NAWA.
THE REST OF THEM TOO.
KUCHI-NAWA?
YOU CALL YOURSELF KUCHINAWA?
EH?
I THINK...
...I KNEW YOU BY ANOTHER NAME.

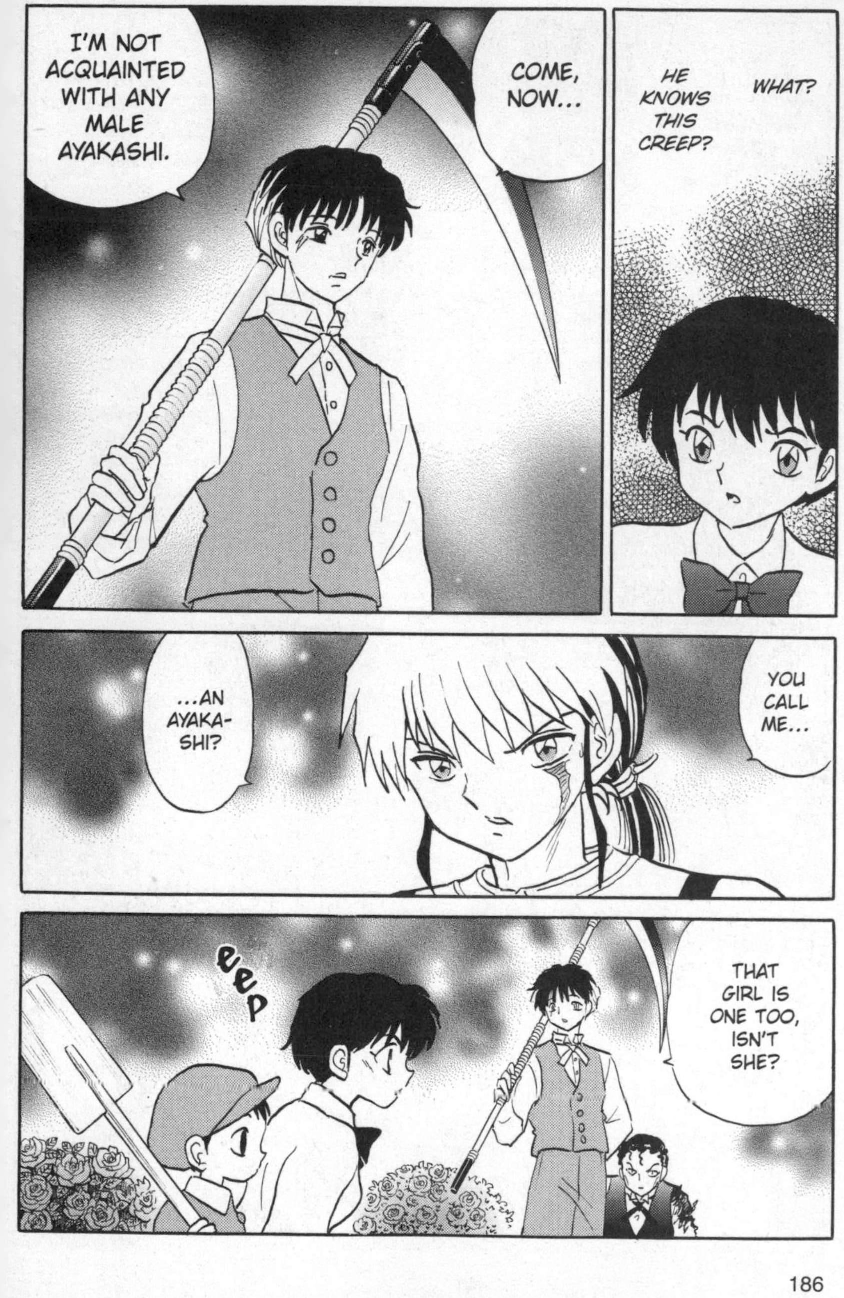
WHAT?
HE KNOWS THIS CREEP?
COME, NOW...
I'M NOT ACQUAINTED WITH ANY MALE AYAKASHI.
YOU CALL ME...
...AN AYAKA-SHI?
THAT GIRL IS ONE TOO, ISN'T SHE?
eep

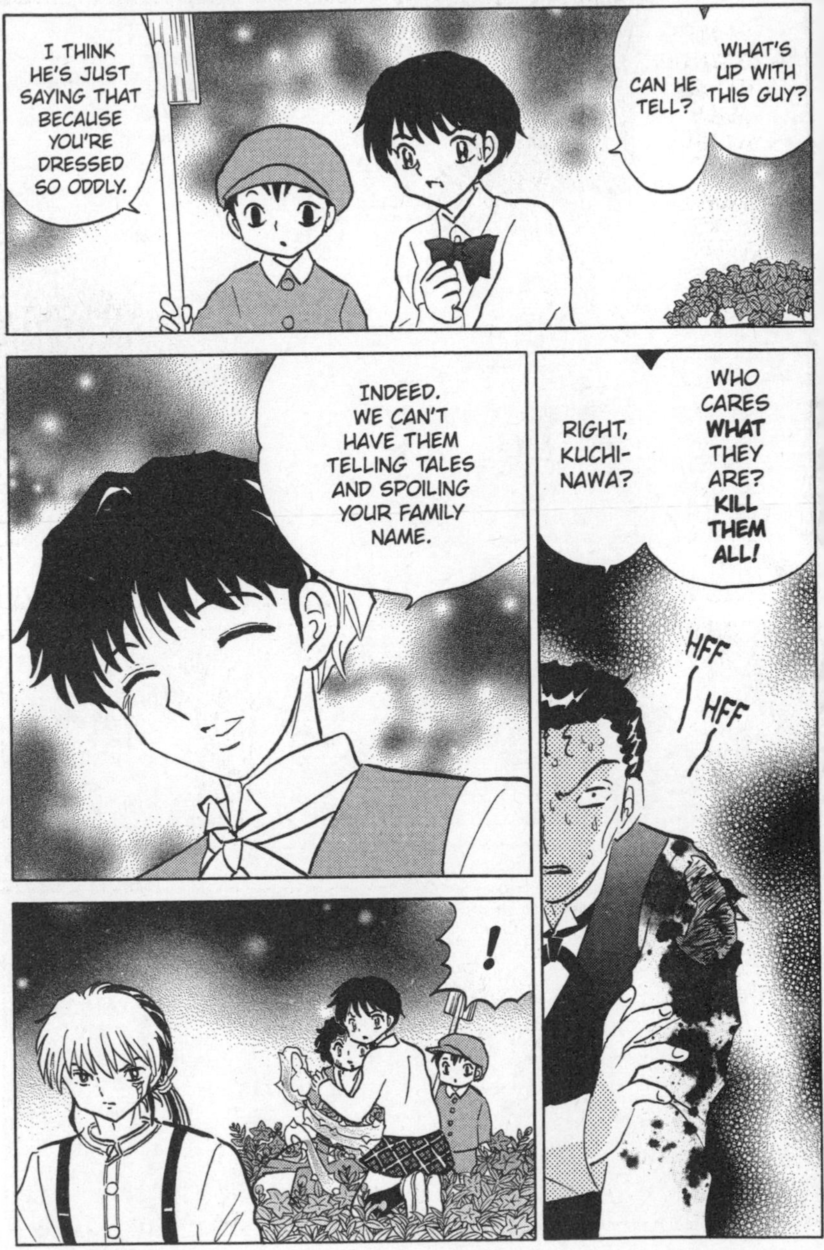
WHAT'S UP WITH THIS GUY?
CAN HE TELL?
I THINK HE'S JUST SAYING THAT BECAUSE YOU'RE DRESSED SO ODDLY.
WHO CARES **WHAT** THEY ARE? **KILL THEM ALL!**
RIGHT, KUCHINAWA?
HFF
HFF
INDEED. WE CAN'T HAVE THEM TELLING TALES AND SPOILING YOUR FAMILY NAME.
!

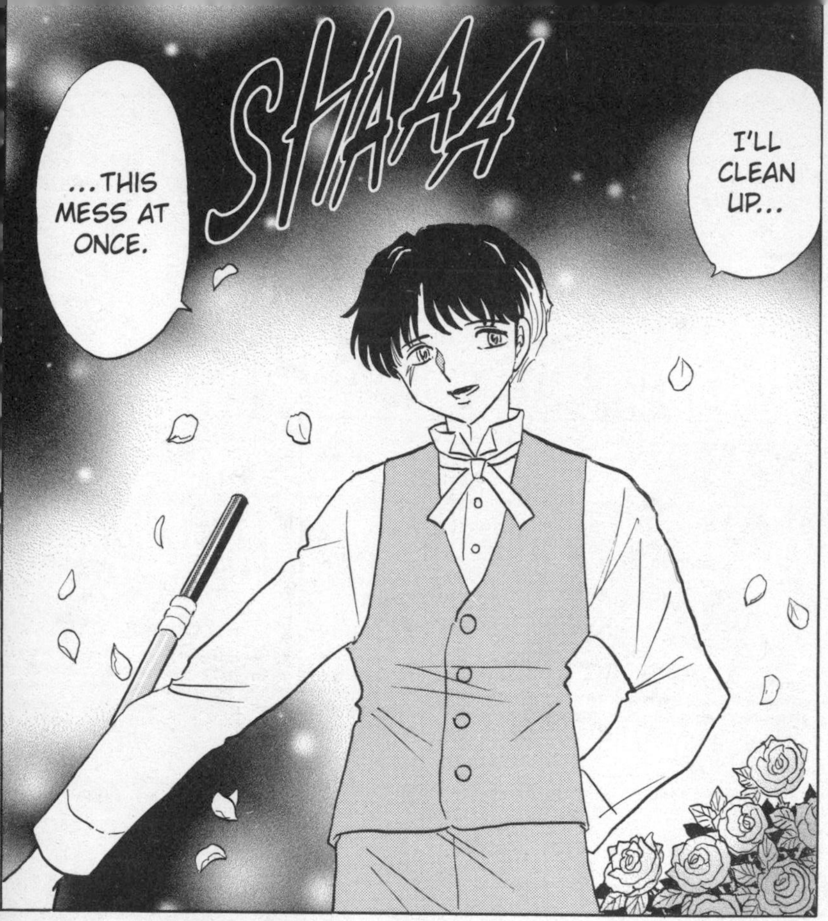
I'LL CLEAN UP...
SHAAA
...THIS MESS AT ONCE.

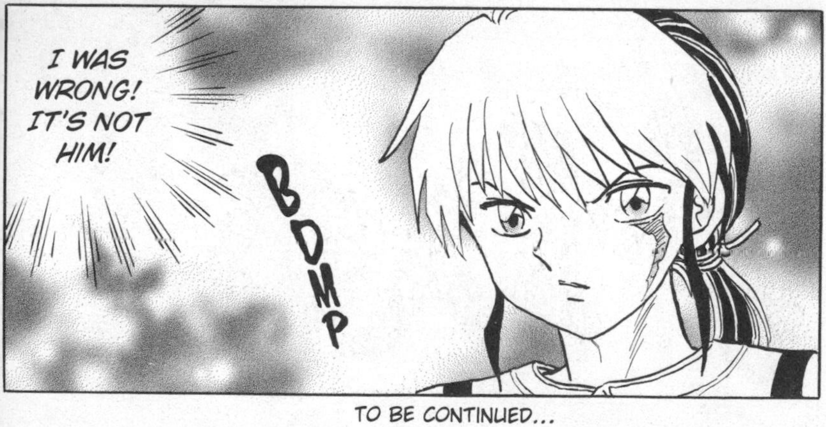
I WAS WRONG! IT'S NOT HIM!
BDMP

TO BE CONTINUED...

MAO

Rumiko Takahashi

The spotlight on Rumiko Takahashi's career began in 1978 when she won an honorable mention in Shogakukan's prestigious New Comic Artist Contest for *Those Selfish Aliens*. Later that same year, her boy-meets-alien comedy series, *Urusei Yatsura*, was serialized in *Weekly Shonen Sunday*. This phenomenally successful manga series was adapted into anime format and spawned a TV series and half a dozen theatrical-release movies, all incredibly popular in their own right. Takahashi followed up the success of her debut series with one blockbuster hit after another—*Maison Ikkoku* ran from 1980 to 1987, *Ranma ½* from 1987 to 1996, and *Inuyasha* from 1996 to 2008. Other notable works include *Mermaid Saga*, *Rumic Theater*, and *One-Pound Gospel*.

Takahashi was inducted into the Will Eisner Comic Awards Hall of Fame in 2018. She won the prestigious Shogakukan Manga Award twice in her career, once for *Urusei Yatsura* in 1981 and the second time for *Inuyasha* in 2002. A majority of the Takahashi canon has been adapted into other media such as anime, live-action TV series, and film. Takahashi's manga, as well as the other formats her work has been adapted into, have continued to delight generations of fans around the world. Distinguished by her wonderfully endearing characters, Takahashi's work adeptly incorporates a wide variety of elements such as comedy, romance, fantasy, and martial arts. While her series are difficult to pin down into one simple genre, the signature style she has created has come to be known as the "Rumic World." Rumiko Takahashi is an artist who truly represents the very best from the world of manga.

MAO
VOLUME 3
Shonen Sunday Edition

STORY AND ART BY
RUMIKO TAKAHASHI

MAO Vol. 3
by Rumiko TAKAHASHI

Original Japanese edition published by SHOGAKUKAN.
English translation rights in the United States of America, Canada, the United Kingdom, Ireland, Australia, and New Zealand arranged with SHOGAKUKAN.

Original Cover Design: Chie SATO + Bay Bridge Studio

Translation/Junko Goda
English Adaptation/Shaenon Garrity
Touch-up Art & Lettering/James Gaubatz
Cover & Interior Design/Yukiko Whitley
Editor/Annette Roman

Printed in Canada

Published by VIZ Media, LLC
P.O. Box 77010
San Francisco, CA 94107

10 9 8 7 6 5 4 3 2 1
First printing, January 2022

ratings.viz.com RATED T+ OLDER TEEN

PARENTAL ADVISORY
MAO is rated T+ for Older Teen and is recommended for ages 16 and up. This volume contains fantasy violence.

viz.com

shonensunday.com

Coming Next Volume

Mao continues to confront former fellow apprentices who should have died of old age long ago. What is the connection between them and cat demon Byoki? After a major battle, Nanoka returns to the present upset that Mao doesn't seem to care about her. But there's no time for matters of the heart because a dangerous nemesis has entered her reality with her! Then, when someone steals the source of Mao's life, can Nanoka save him from a *natural* death...?

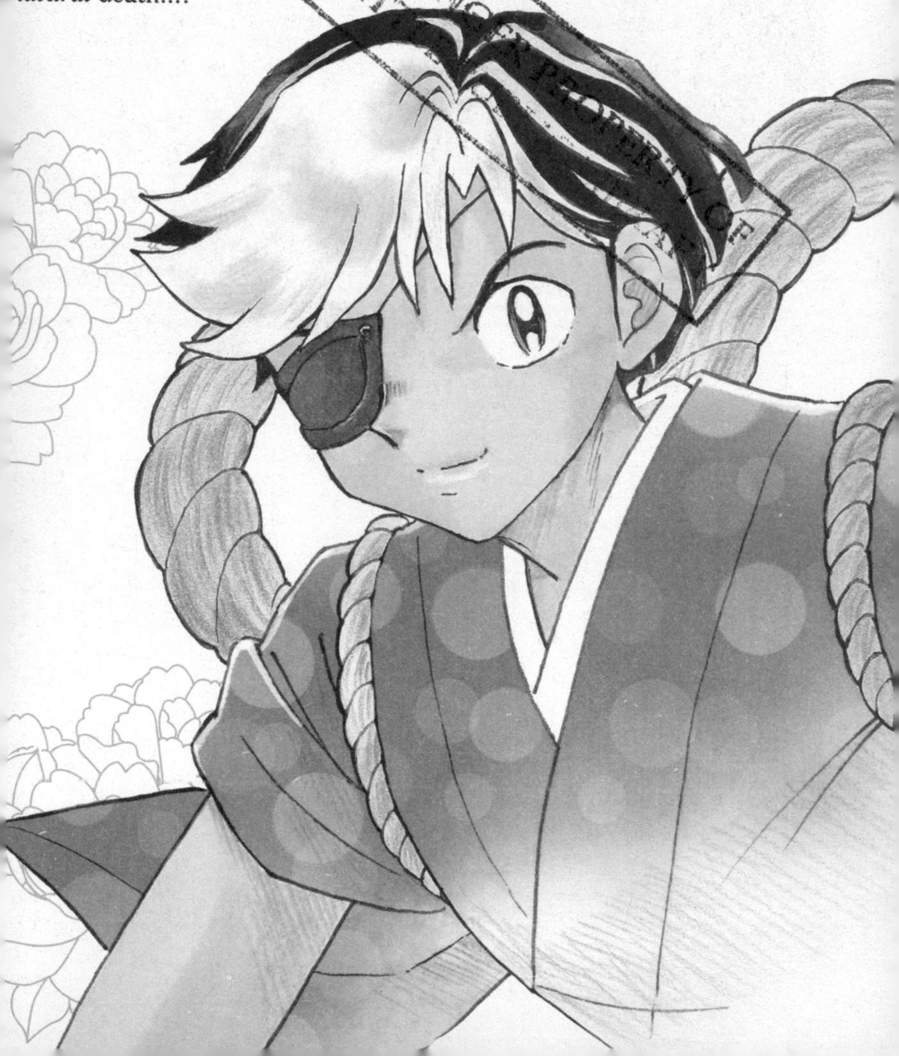